Pumpkin Scissors

Imperial Army State Section III

by
Ryotaro Iwanaga

Translated and adapted by
Ikoi Hiroe

Lettered by
North Market Street Graphics

DEL
REY

Ballantine Books • New York

Pumpkin Scissors volume 2 is a work of fiction. Names, characters, places, and incidents are the products of the author's imagination or are used fictitiously. Any resemblance to actual events, locales, or persons, living or dead, is entirely coincidental.

A Del Rey Manga/Kodansha Trade Paperback Original

Published in the United States by Del Rey Books, an imprint of The Random House Publishing Group, a division of Random House, Inc., New York.

Publication rights arranged through Kodansha Ltd.

First published in Japan in 2004 by Kodansha Ltd., Tokyo

ISBN 978-0-345-50141-7

Printed in the United States of America

www.delreymanga.com

1 3 5 7 9 8 6 4 3 2

Translator/adapter: Ikoi Hiroe
Lettering: NMSG

Contents

**You must get to know
your teammates
first before getting
suspicious!**

Honorifics Explained

Throughout the Del Rey Manga books, you will find Japanese honorifics left intact in the translations. For those not familiar with how the Japanese use honorifics and, more important, how they differ from American honorifics, we present this brief overview.

Politeness has always been a critical facet of Japanese culture. Ever since the feudal era, when Japan was a highly stratified society, use of honorifics—which can be defined as polite speech that indicates relationship or status—has played an essential role in the Japanese language. When addressing someone in Japanese, an honorific usually takes the form of a suffix attached to one's name (example: "Asuna-san"), is used as a title at the end of one's name, or appears in place of the name itself (example: "Negi-sensei," or simply "Sensei!").

Honorifics can be expressions of respect or endearment. In the context of manga and anime, honorifics give insight into the nature of the relationship between characters. Many English translations leave out these important honorifics and therefore distort the feel of the original Japanese. Because Japanese honorifics contain nuances that English honorifics lack, it is our policy at Del Rey not to translate them. Here, instead, is a guide to some of the honorifics you may encounter in Del Rey Manga.

-san: This is the most common honorific and is equivalent to Mr., Miss, Ms., or Mrs. It is the all-purpose honorific and can be used in any situation where politeness is required.

-sama: This is one level higher than "-san." It is used to confer great respect.

-dono: This comes from the word "tono," which means "lord." It is an even higher level than "-sama" and confers utmost respect.

-kun: This suffix is used at the end of boys' names to express familiarity or endearment. It is also sometimes used by men among friends, or when addressing someone younger or of a lower station.

-chan: This is used to express endearment, mostly toward girls. It is also used for little boys, pets, and even among lovers. It gives a sense of childish cuteness.

Bozu: This is an informal way to refer to a boy, similar to the English terms "kid" and "squirt."

Sempai/Senpai: This title suggests that the addressee is one's senior in a group or organization. It is most often used in a school setting, where underclassmen refer to their upperclassmen as "sempai." It can also be used in the workplace, such as when a newer employee addresses an employee who has seniority in the company.

Kohai: This is the opposite of "sempai" and is used toward underclassmen in school or newcomers in the workplace. It connotes that the addressee is of a lower station.

Sensei: Literally meaning "one who has come before," this title is used for teachers, doctors, or masters of any profession or art.

-[blank]: This is usually forgotten in these lists, but it is perhaps the most significant difference between Japanese and English. The lack of honorific means that the speaker has permission to address the person in a very intimate way. Usually, only family, spouses, or very close friends have this kind of permission. Known as *yobisute*, it can be gratifying when someone who has earned the intimacy starts to call one by one's name without an honorific. But when that intimacy hasn't been earned, it can be very insulting.

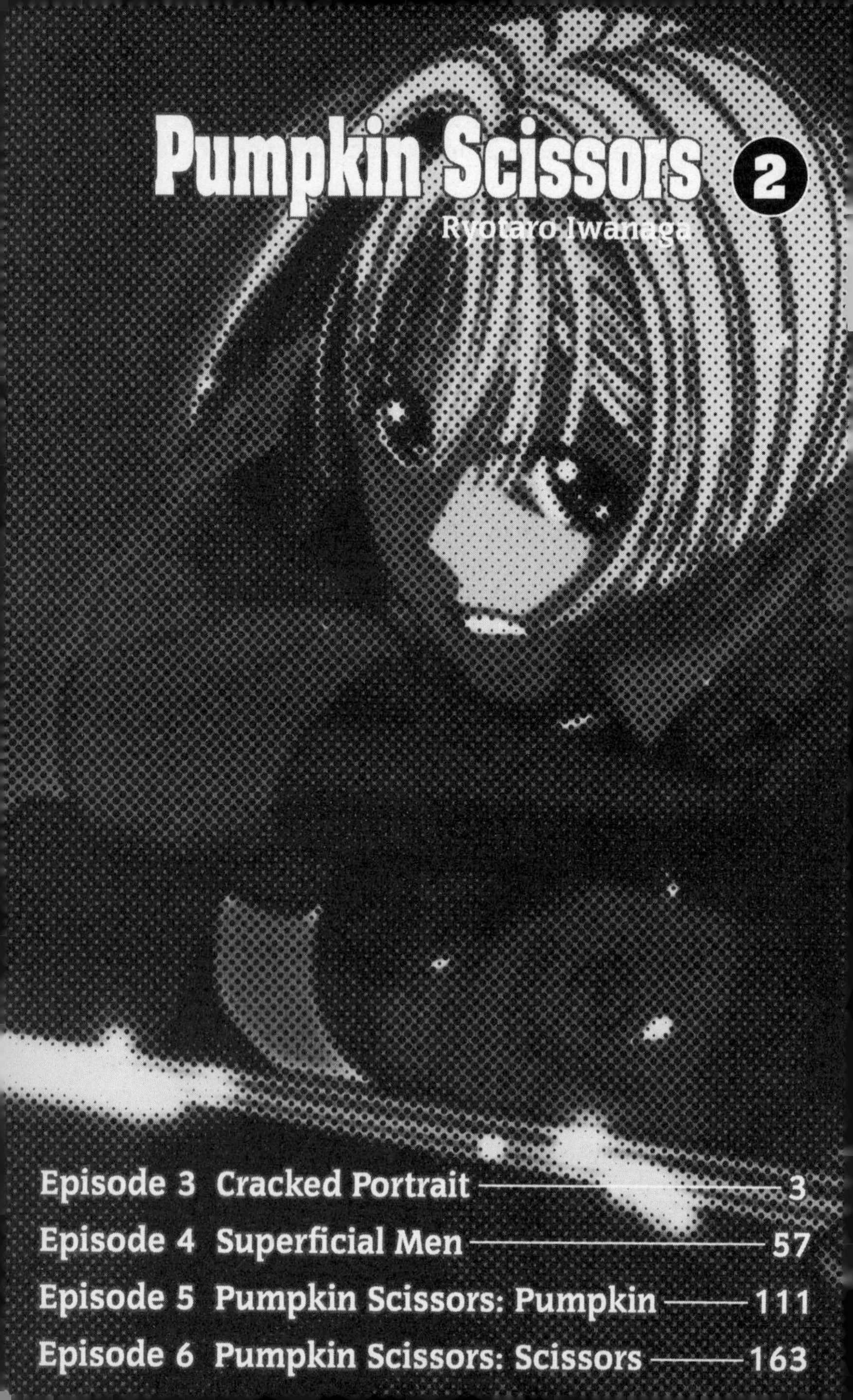

Pumpkin Scissors 2

Ryotaro Iwanaga

About This Story

The bloody war between the Empire and the Republic of Frost left a deep wound throughout the Empire.

Three years have passed since the cease-fire, now known as the Thin Ice Treaty. The Empire is still plagued with starvation and disease while gangs of former soldiers terrorize the populace. The Empire is now fighting another battle to repair the destruction from the war. Imperial Army State Section III was established as a "propaganda" tool to placate the masses. However, the members of Imperial Army State Section III, known as "Pumpkin Scissors," are committed to cutting through the thick skin of corruption and crime to bring justice to the people...

Lieutenant Alice Malvin

Born into nobility, she's a straightforward and kind soul. The second lieutenant for Pumpkin Scissors, she works hard to advance the cause of reconstruction and war relief for the people.

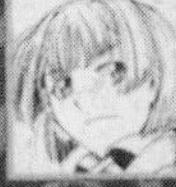

Corporal Oland

A towering giant, he was a scarred veteran who re-enlisted into Section III. During the war, he was one of the Invisible Nine unit members.

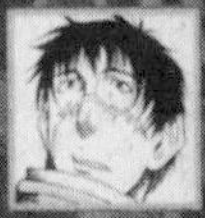

Warrant Officer Oreldo

An officer in Pumpkin Scissors, aka Stockade Houdini. He comes across as a mellow, lighthearted guy, but he also seems to have a serious side.

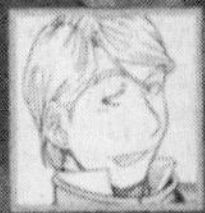

Warrant Officer Machs

He seems to be the most sensible of all the Pumpkin Scissors members. Yet, he's friends with Oreldo, so there may be more than meets the eye...

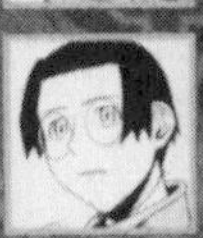

Captain Hunks

The leader of Section III, his razor-sharp mind is hidden underneath his leisurely, low-key exterior.

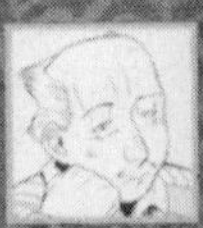

Sergeant Major Stecchin

A clumsy young girl, she's the paper-pusher for Section III. She doesn't resemble a soldier, nor does she consider herself to be one.

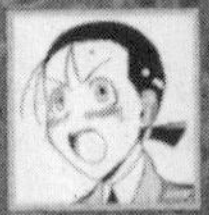

Mercury

Section III Courier Private First Class Messenger Dog. He's a lovable male with a goofy face. He hasn't been seen recently...

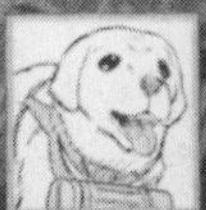

Major Connery

The leader of Section I, the elite unit in charge of national security. He appears to have more authority and responsibilities that exceed his official position...

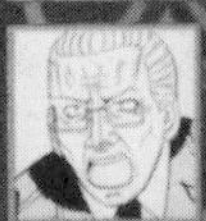

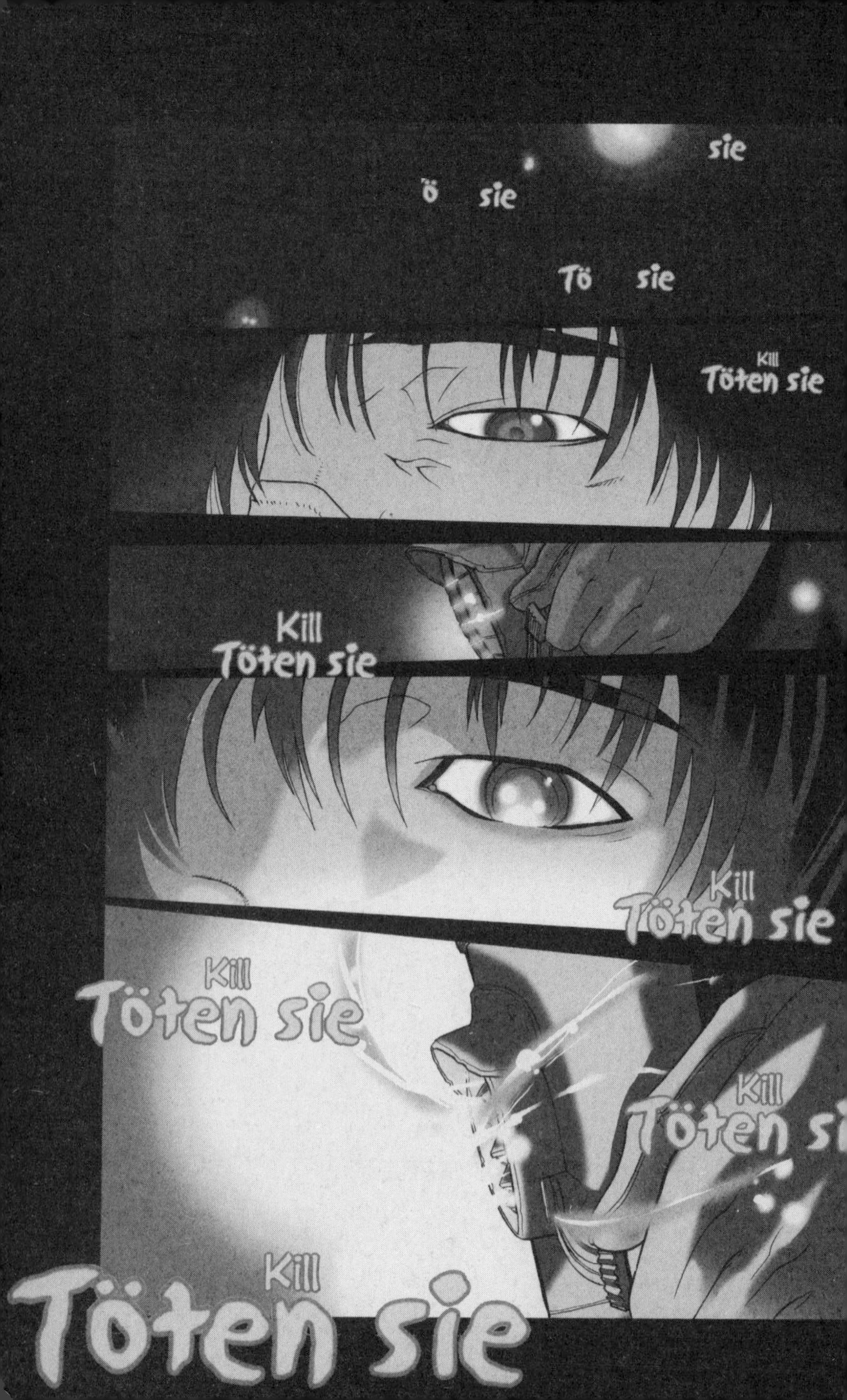
sie
ö sie
Tö sie
Kill
Töten sie
Kill
Töten sie
Kill
Töten sie
Kill
Töten sie
Kill
Töten si
Kill
Töten sie

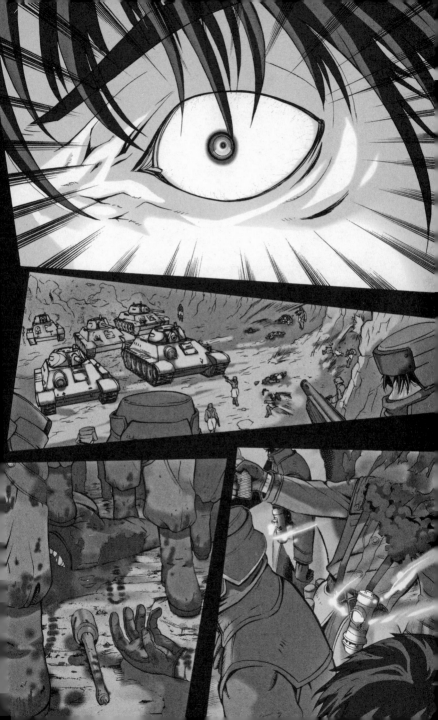

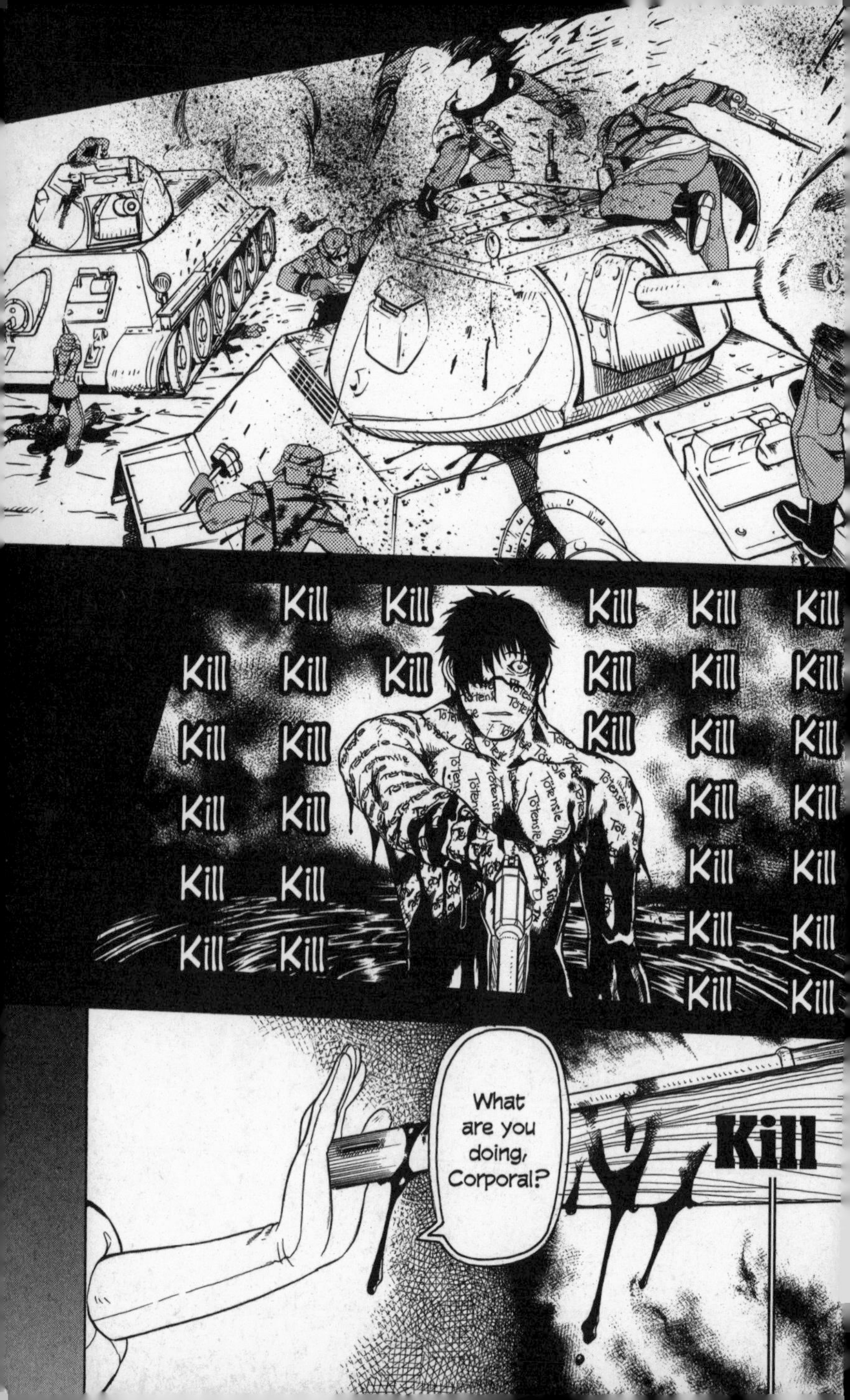
Kill Kill Kill Kill Kill
Kill Kill Kill Kill Kill Kill
Kill Kill Kill Kill Kill
Kill Kill Kill Kill
Kill Kill Kill Kill
Kill Kill Kill Kill
Kill Kill
Kill
What are you doing, Corporal?

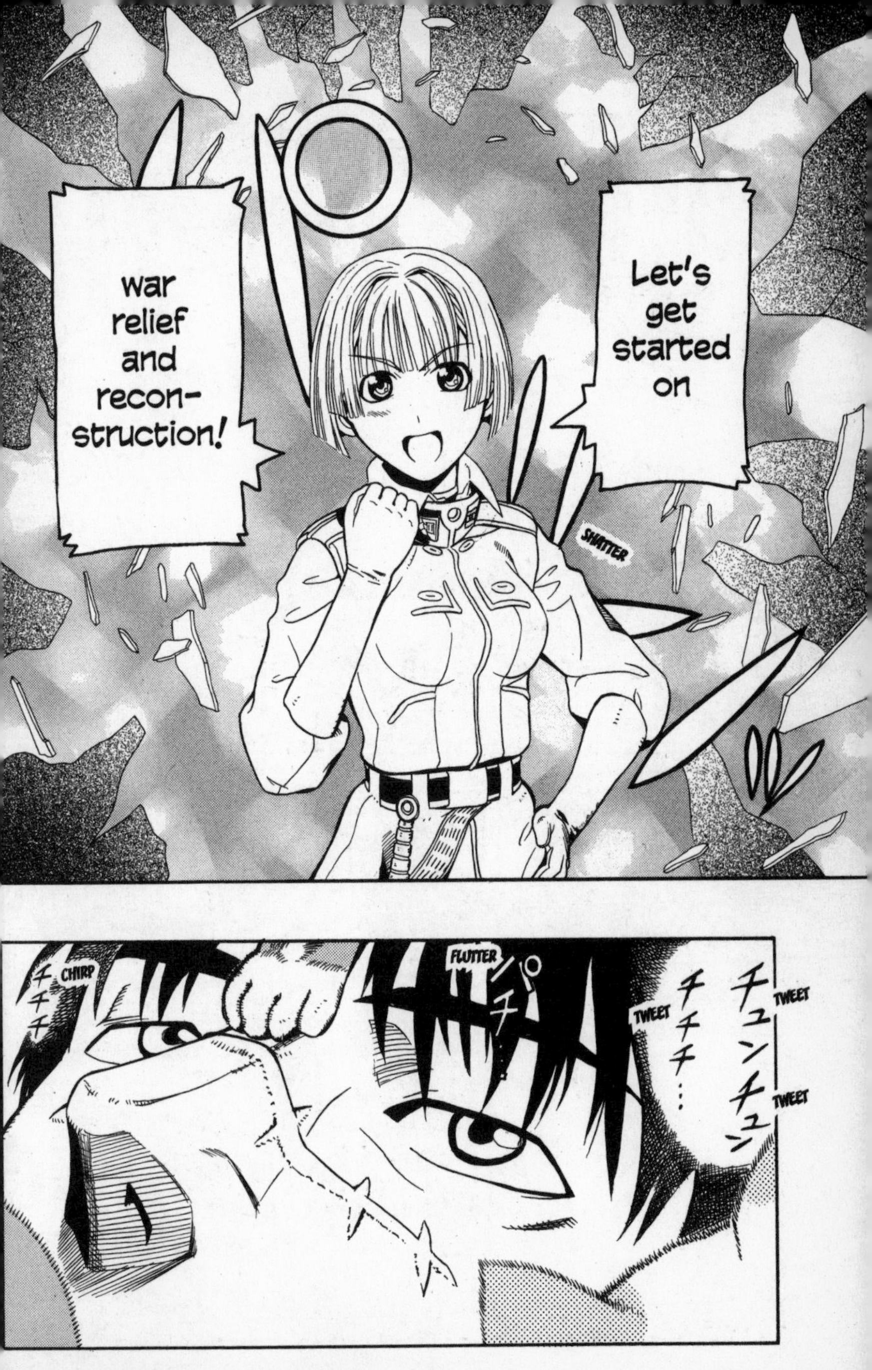
Let's get started on
war relief and recon-struction!
SHATTER
チュンチュン
TWEET
TWEET
チチチ…
TWEET
パチ
FLUTTER
チチチ
CHIRP

† **Episode 3** **Cracked Portrait**

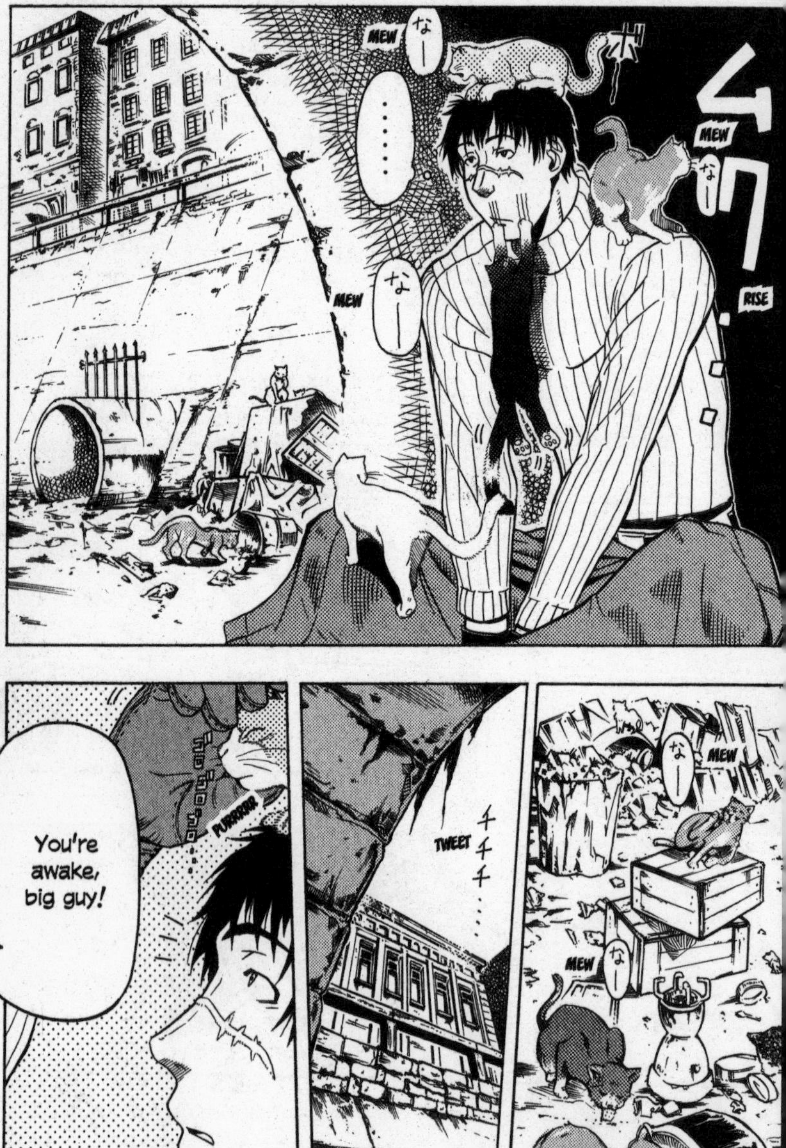
ムク
RISE
なー
MEW
なー
MEW
・・・・
なー
MEW
なー
MEW
なー
MEW
チチチ・・・・
TWEET
PURRRRR
You're awake, big guy!

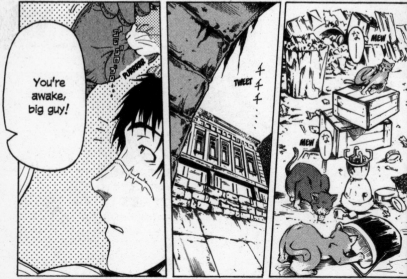

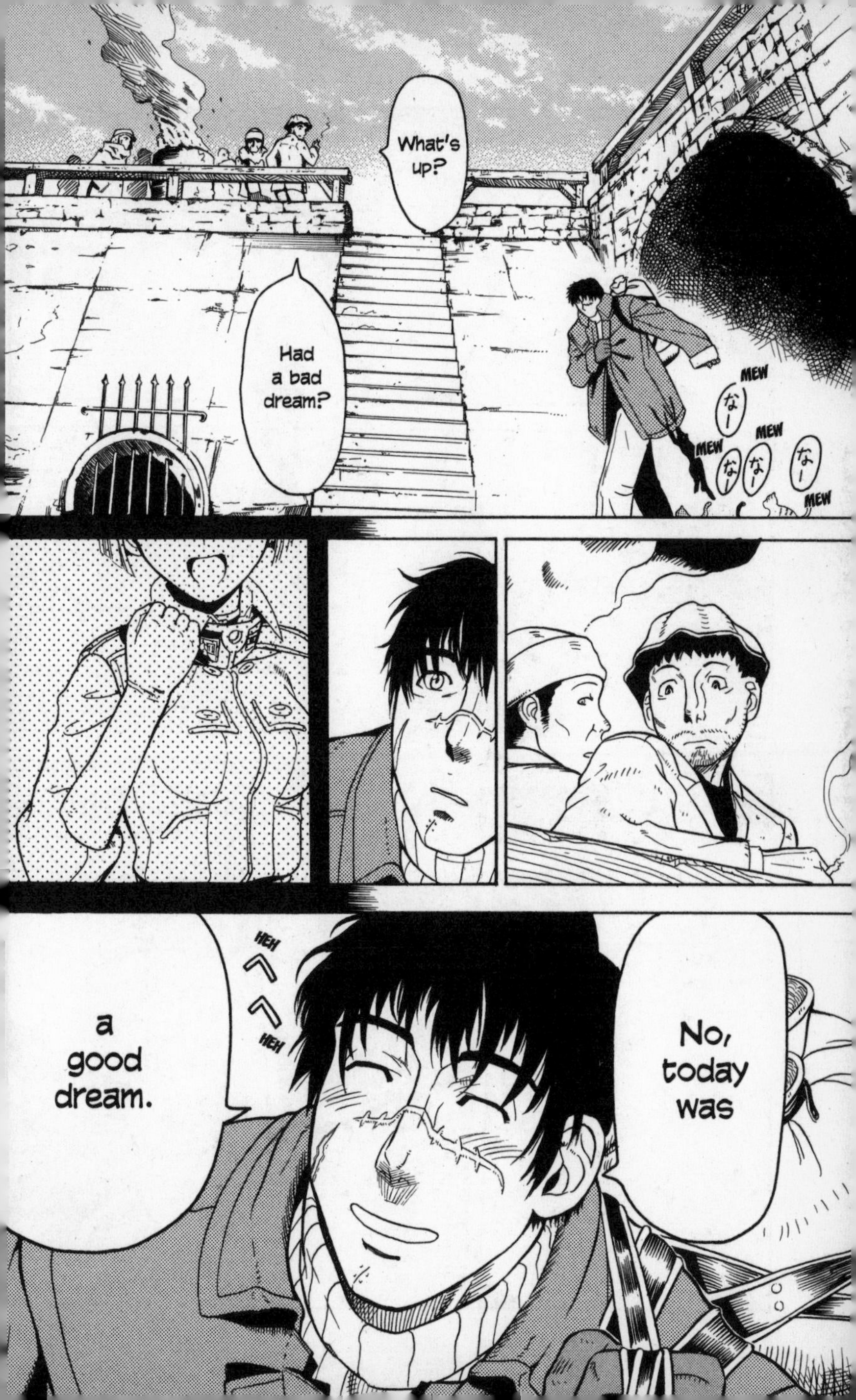
What's up?
Had a bad dream?
MEW なー
MEW なー
MEW なー
MEW なー
No, today was
HEH へへ HEH
a good dream.

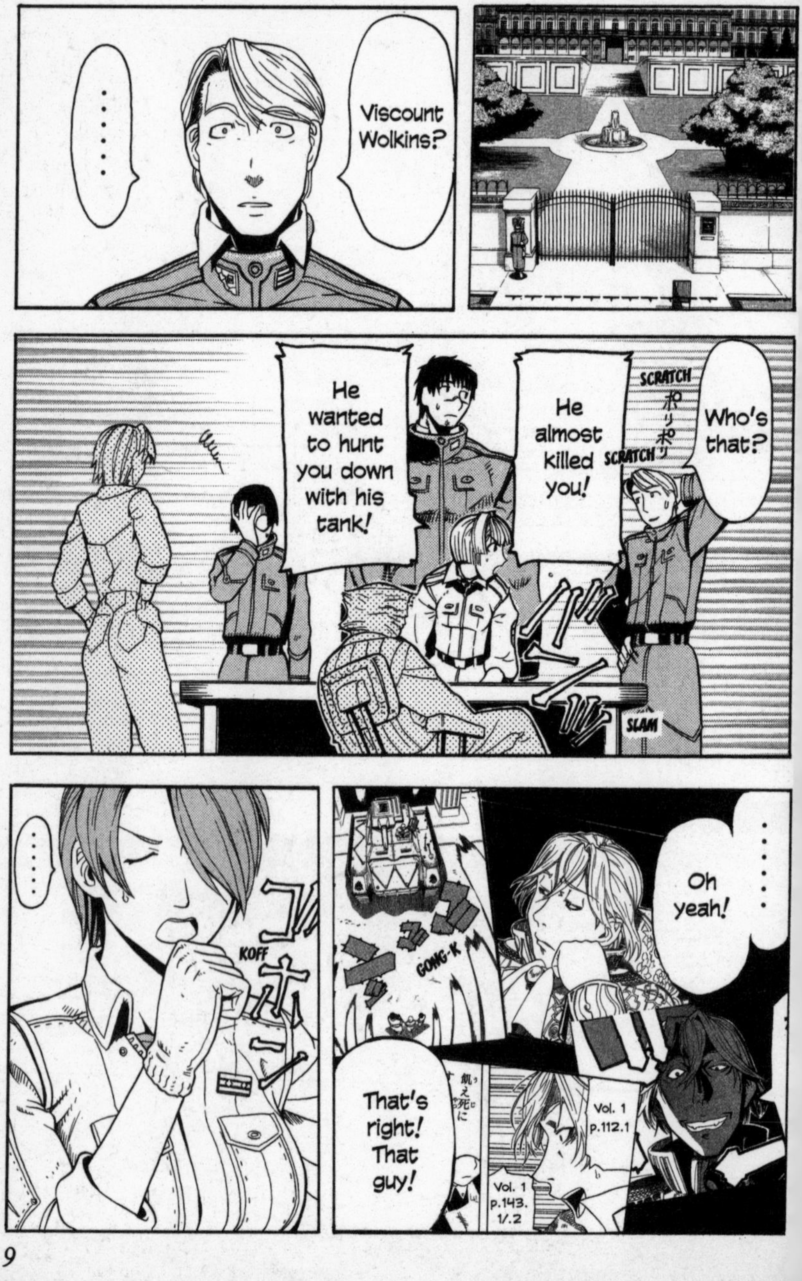

Viscount Wolkins?
......
Who's that?
SCRATCH
ポリポリ
SCRATCH
He almost killed you!
He wanted to hunt you down with his tank!
SLAM
......
Oh yeah!
GONG-K
Vol. 1 p.112.1
That's right! That guy!
Vol. 1 p.143. 1/.2
......
KOFF

The viscount isn't the problem...

It's his tank.

Technology Research and Development Manager
First Lieutenant Webner

The cannon's automatic loading system...

That isn't something a lil' viscount in the countryside could have access to.

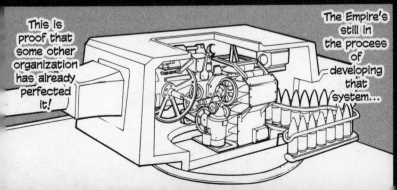

The Empire's still in the process of developing that system...

This is proof that some other organization has already perfected it!

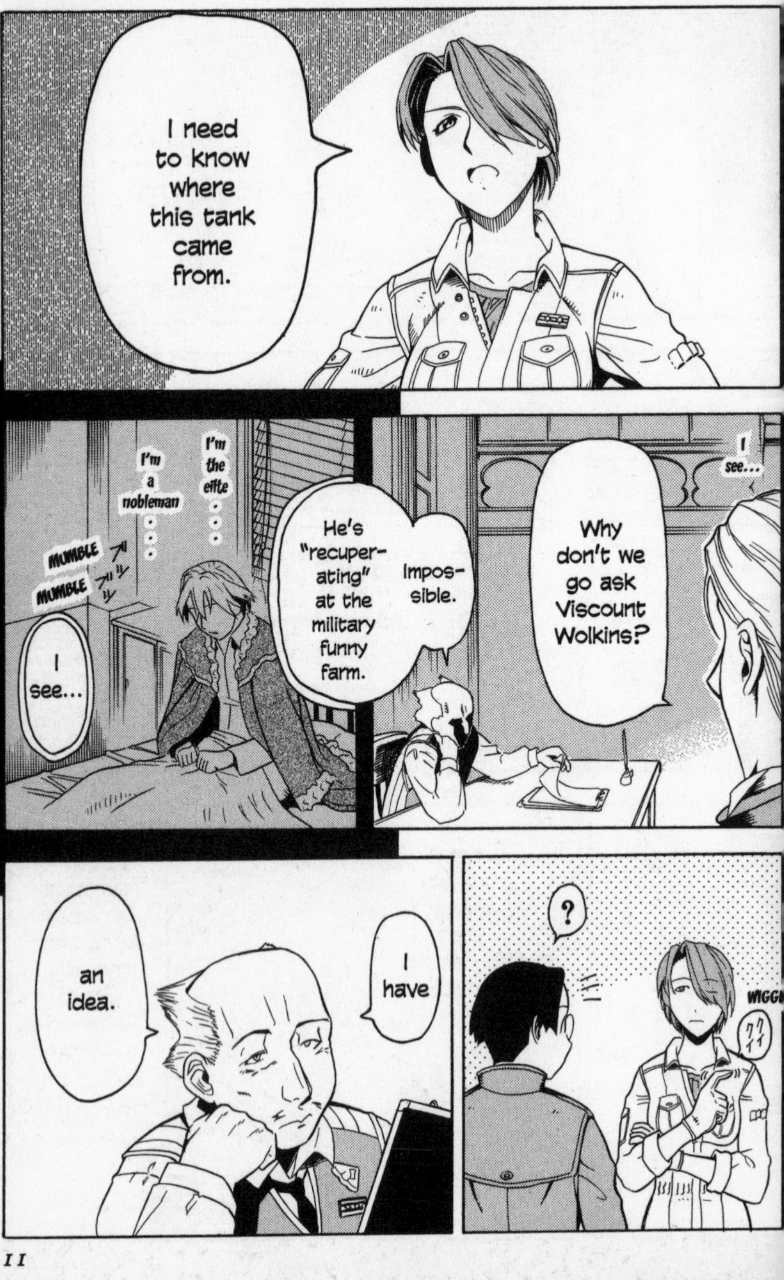

I need to know where this tank came from.
I see...
Why don't we go ask Viscount Wolkins?
Impossible.
He's "recuperating" at the military funny farm.
I'm the eilte...
I'm a nobleman...
MUMBLE MUMBLE
I see...
?
I have
an idea.

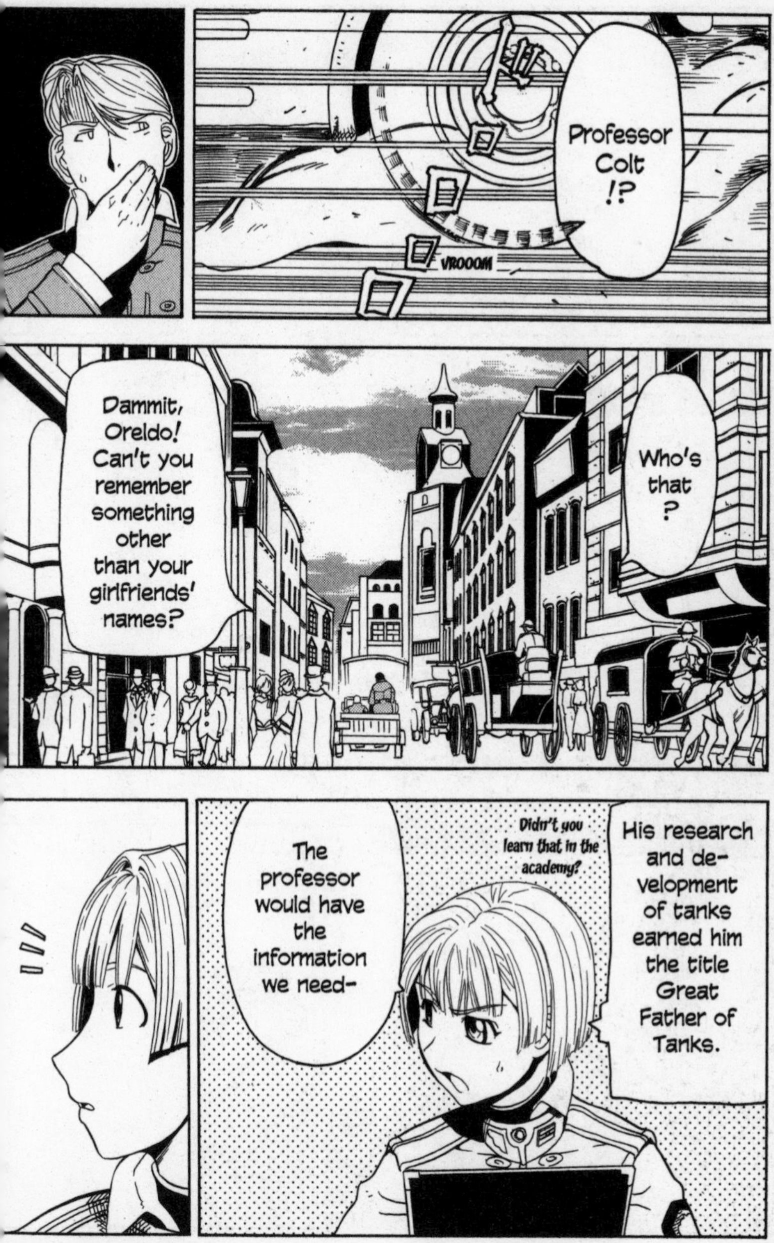
Professor Colt !?
VROOOM
Who's that?
Dammit, Oreldo! Can't you remember something other than your girlfriends' names?
His research and development of tanks earned him the title Great Father of Tanks.
Didn't you learn that in the academy?
The professor would have the information we need-

Machs, what's wrong?

TWIST

Oh, nothing.

What?

. . . . . .

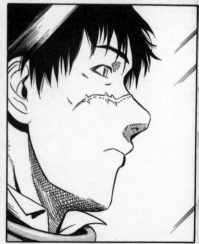

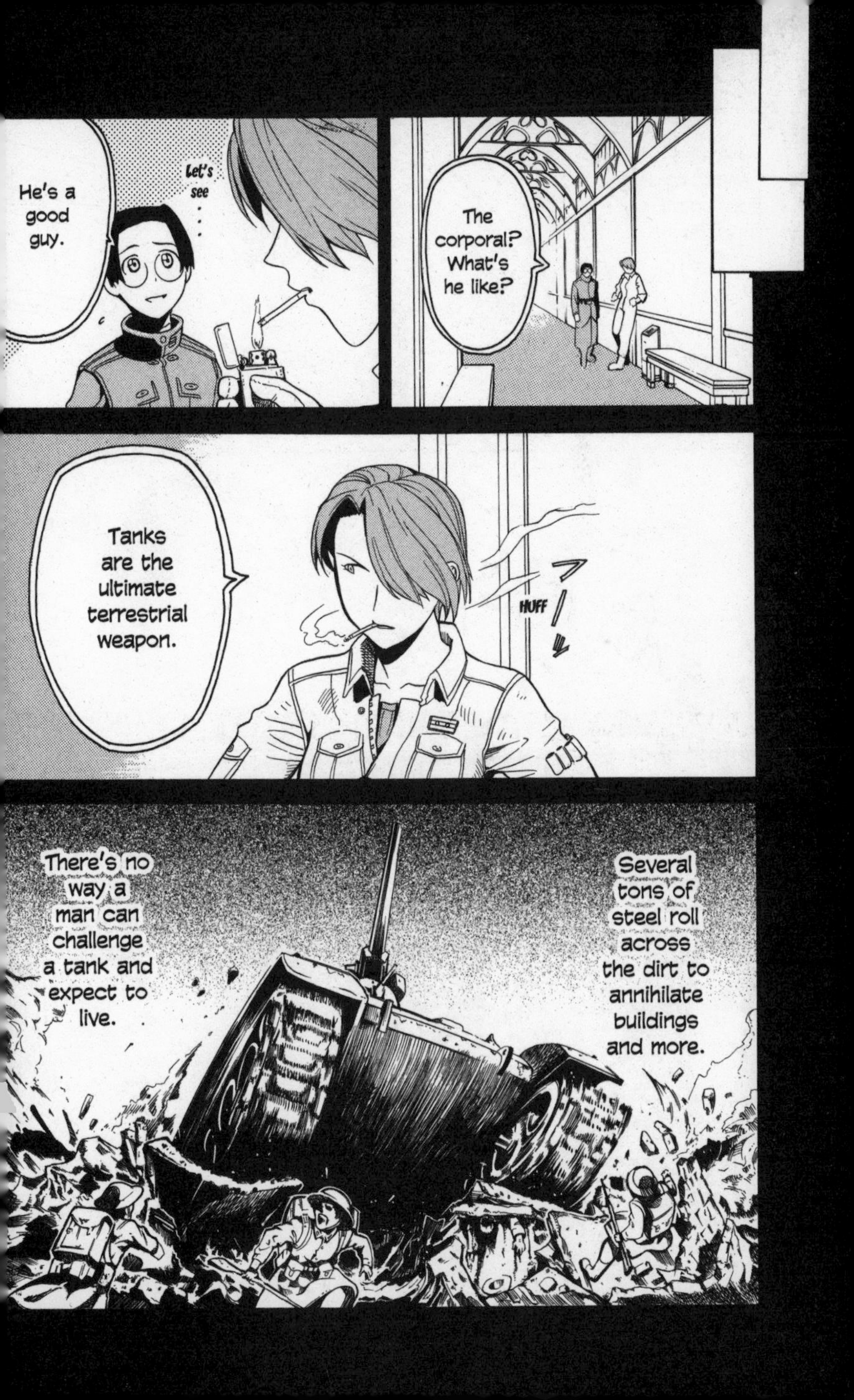

The corporal? What's he like?
Let's see . . .
He's a good guy.
Tanks are the ultimate terrestrial weapon.
HUFF
Several tons of steel roll across the dirt to annihilate buildings and more.
There's no way a man can challenge a tank and expect to live.

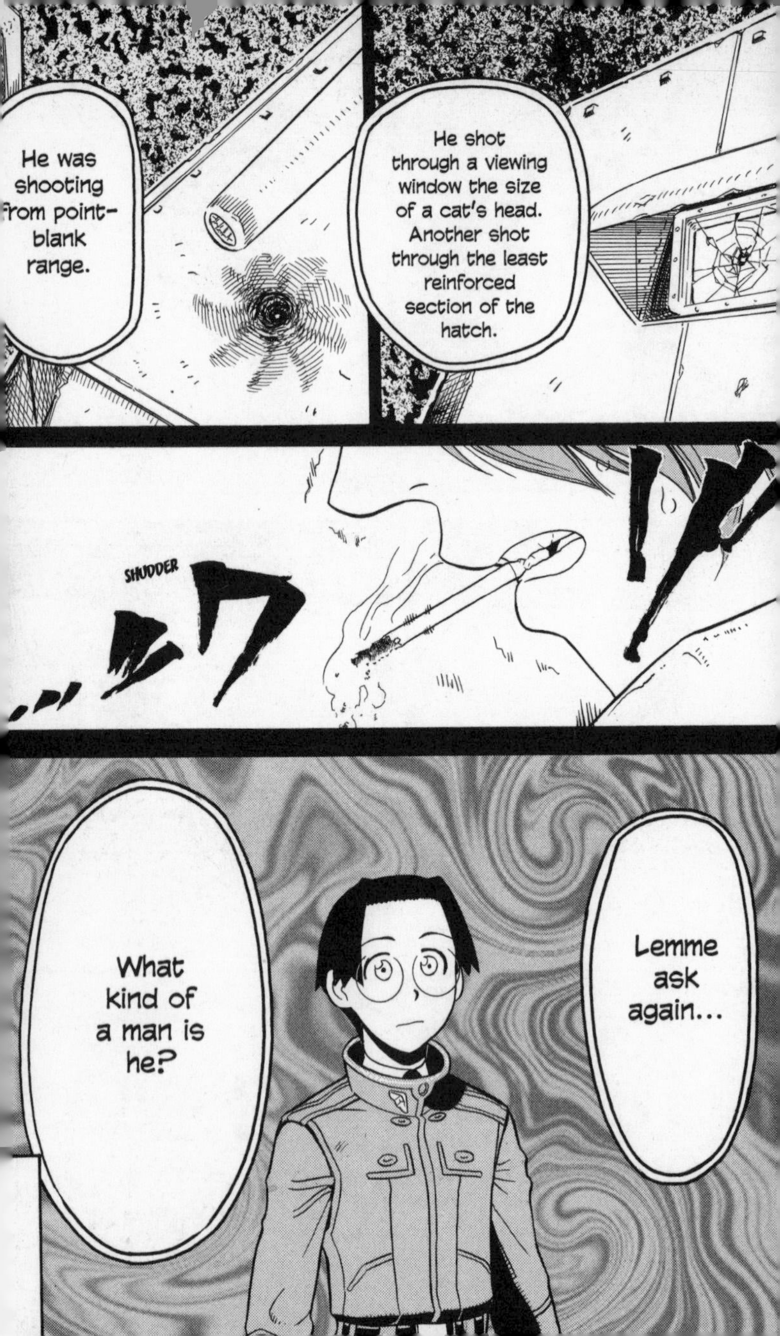
He shot through a viewing window the size of a cat's head. Another shot through the least reinforced section of the hatch.
He was shooting from point-blank range.
SHUDDER
Lemme ask again...
What kind of a man is he?

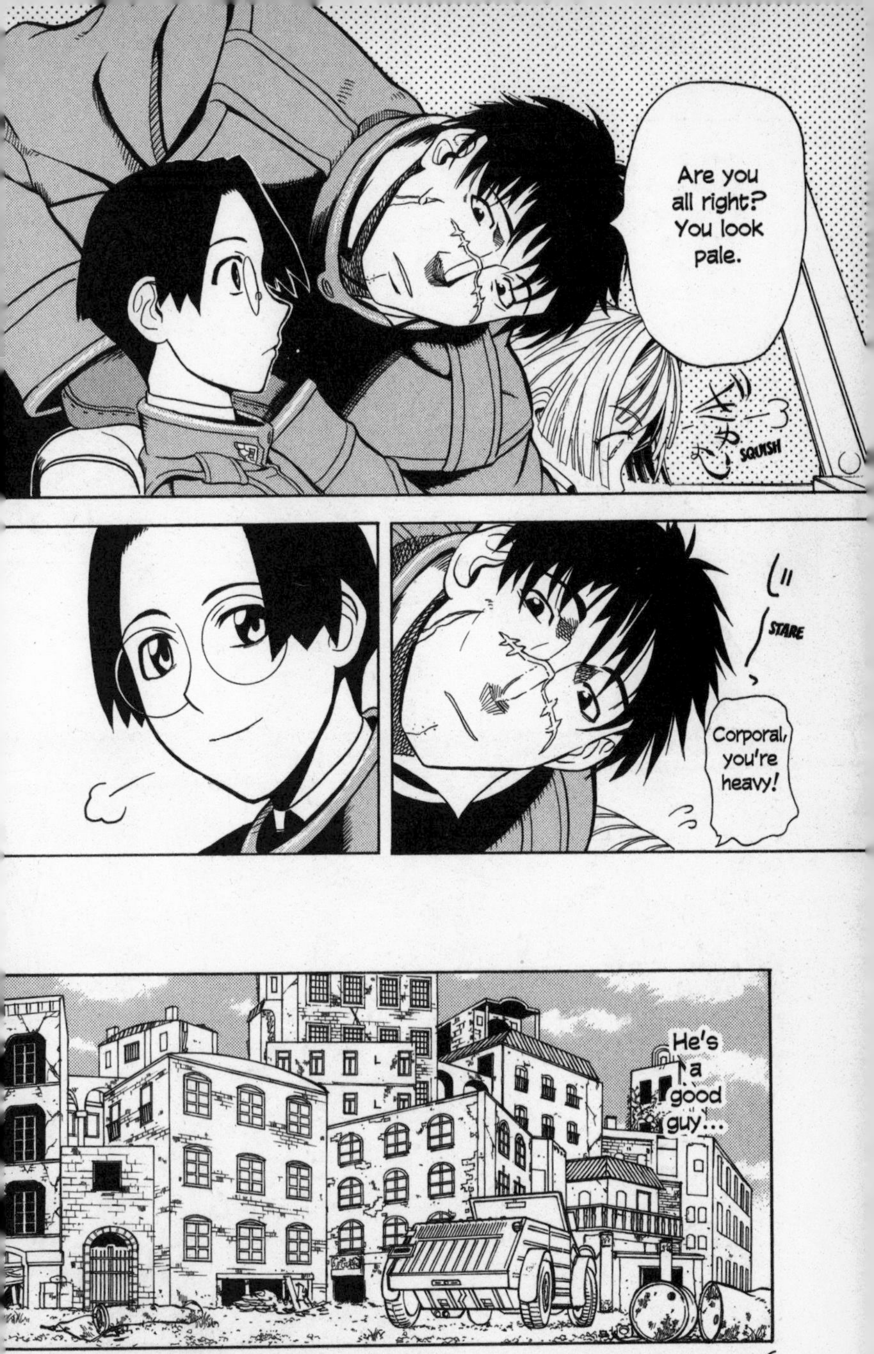
Are you all right? You look pale.
SQUISH
STARE
Corporal, you're heavy!
He's a good guy...

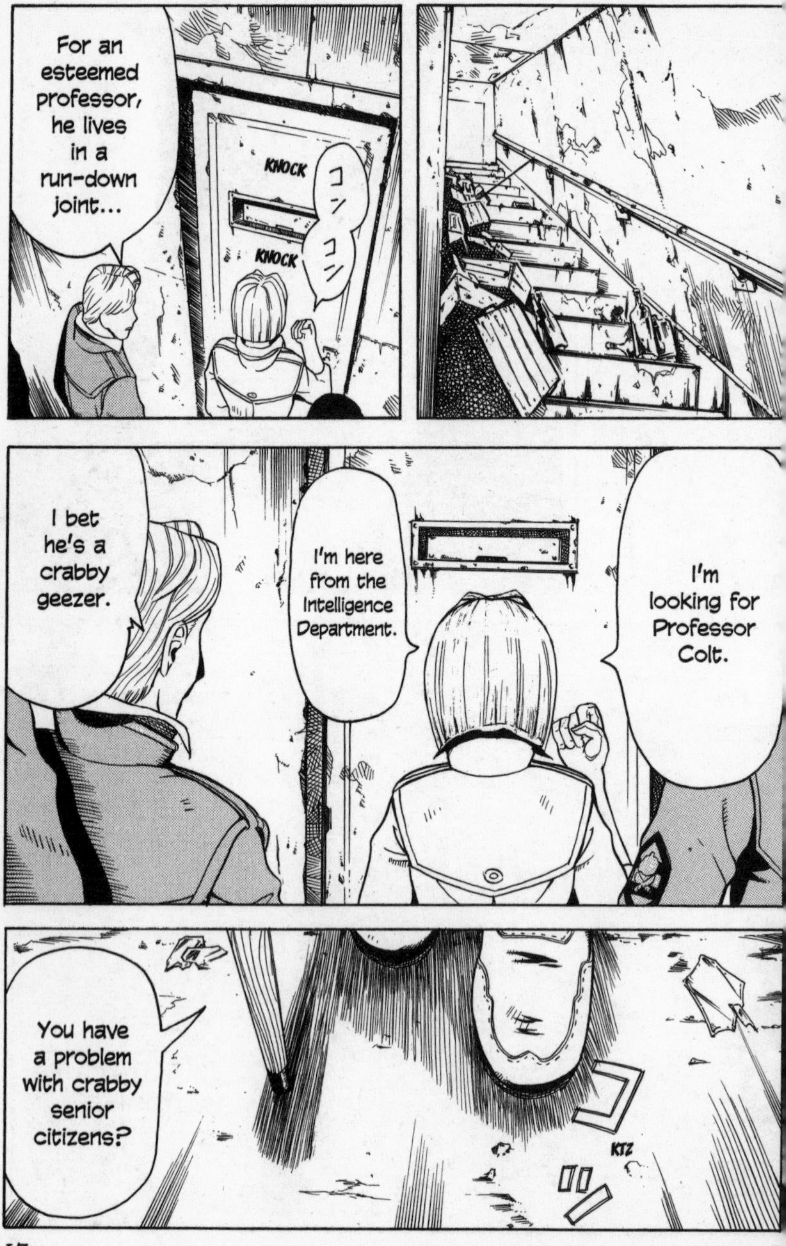
For an esteemed professor, he lives in a run-down joint...
KNOCK
コン
KNOCK
コン
I'm looking for Professor Colt.
I'm here from the Intelligence Department.
I bet he's a crabby geezer.
You have a problem with crabby senior citizens?
KTZ

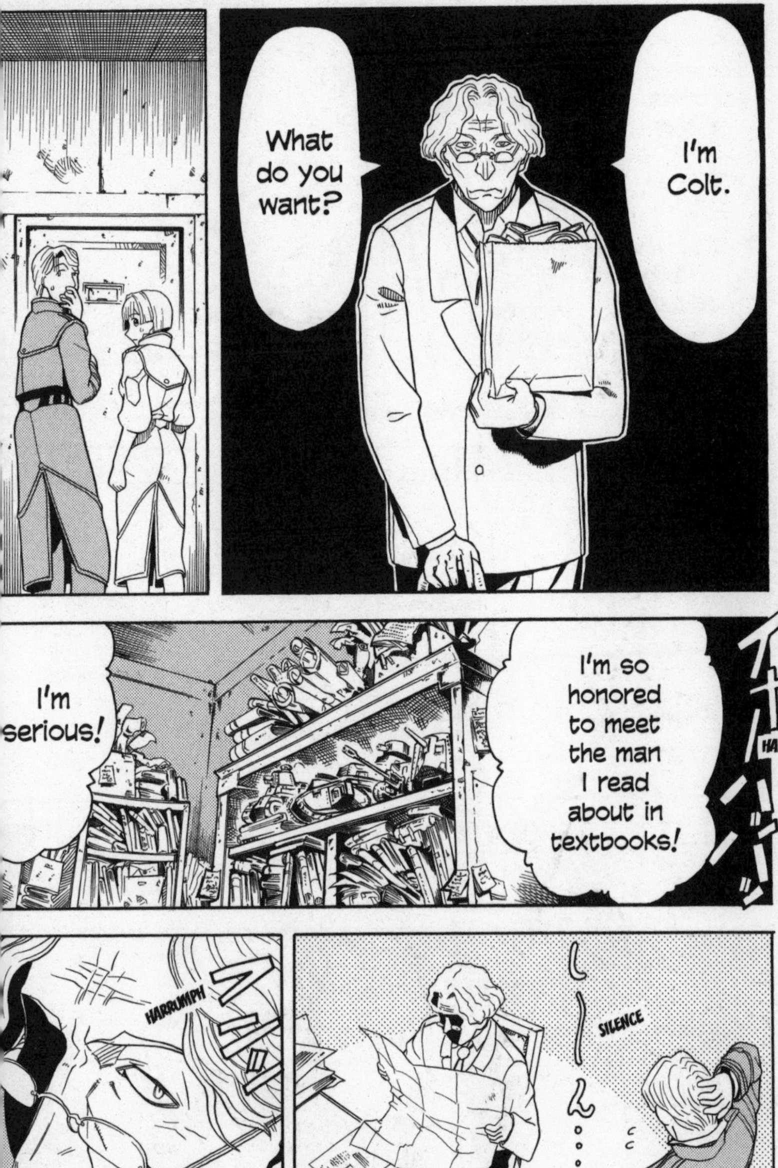
I'm Colt.
What do you want?
I'm so honored to meet the man I read about in textbooks!
HAHAHA
I'm serious!
しーん…
SILENCE
HARRUMPH

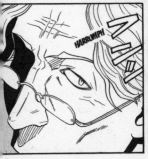

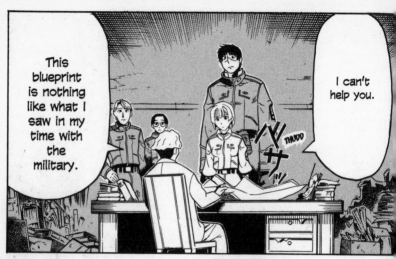

I can't help you.
THUDD
This blueprint is nothing like what I saw in my time with the military.
I never saw this at the Technological Conference for Allied Western Nations, either.
This system is technologically advanced compared to what any nation has at the moment.
I see...
Where's the analysis?
Excuse me?
Have you looked into this tank in detail?

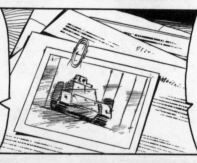

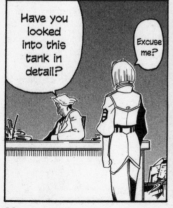

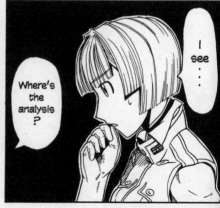

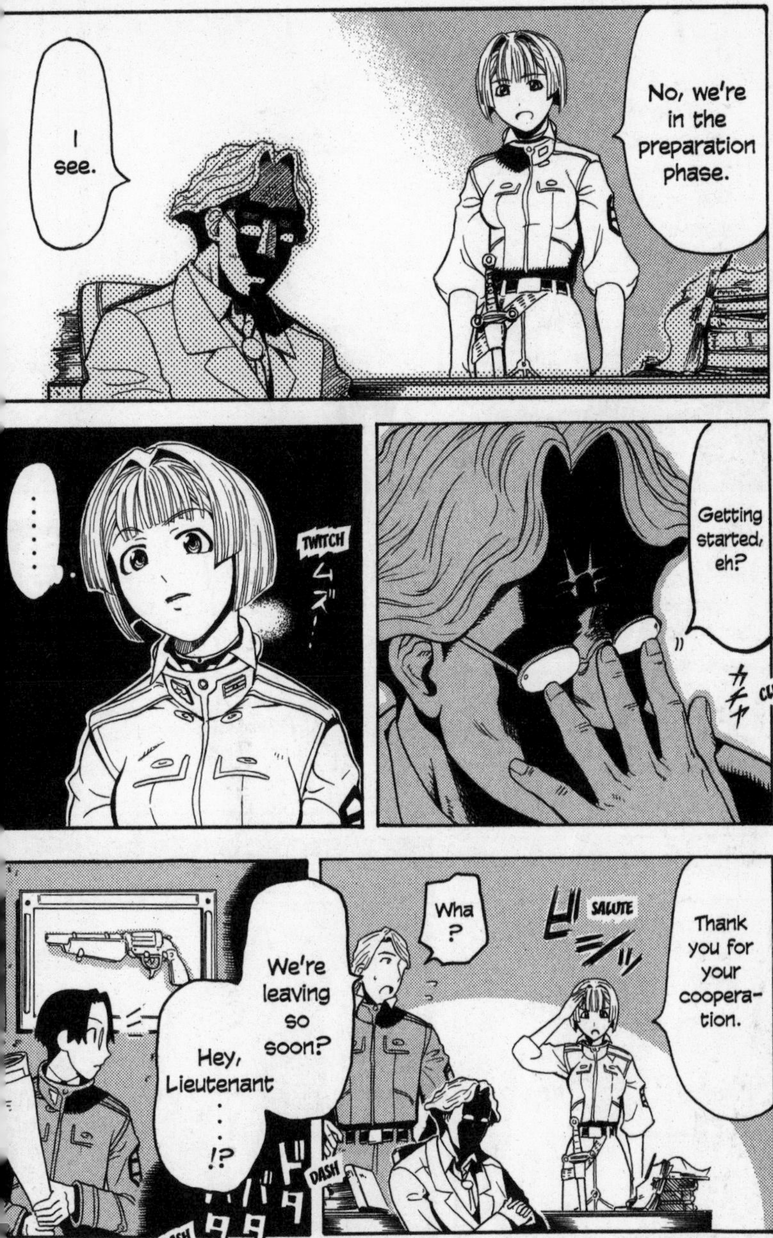
No, we're in the preparation phase.
I see.
Getting started, eh?
CLICK
......
TWITCH
Thank you for your coopera-tion.
SALUTE
Wha?
We're leaving so soon?
Hey, Lieutenant ...!?
DASH
DASH
DASH

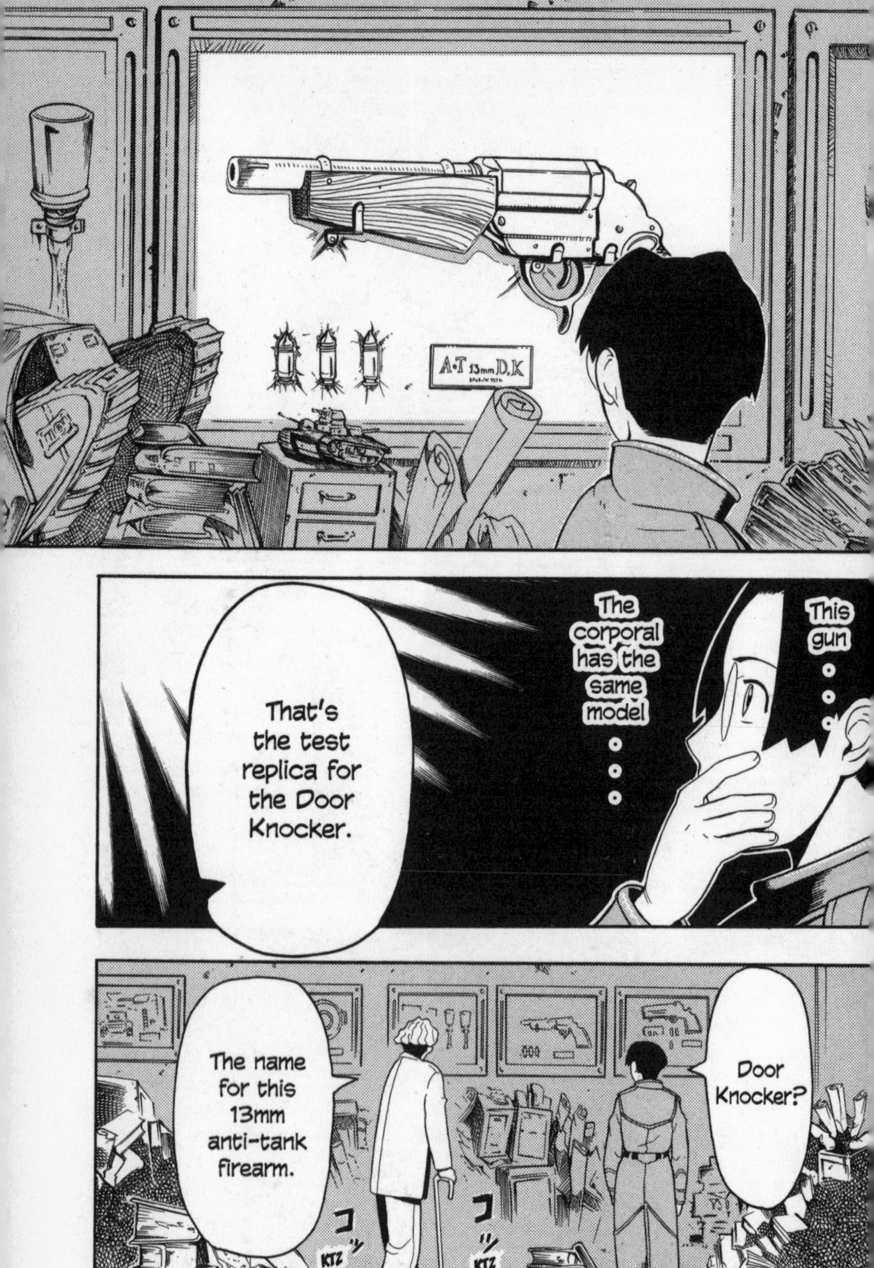
A·T 13mm D.K
This gun...
The corporal has the same model...
That's the test replica for the Door Knocker.
Door Knocker?
The name for this 13mm anti-tank firearm.
KTZ
KTZ

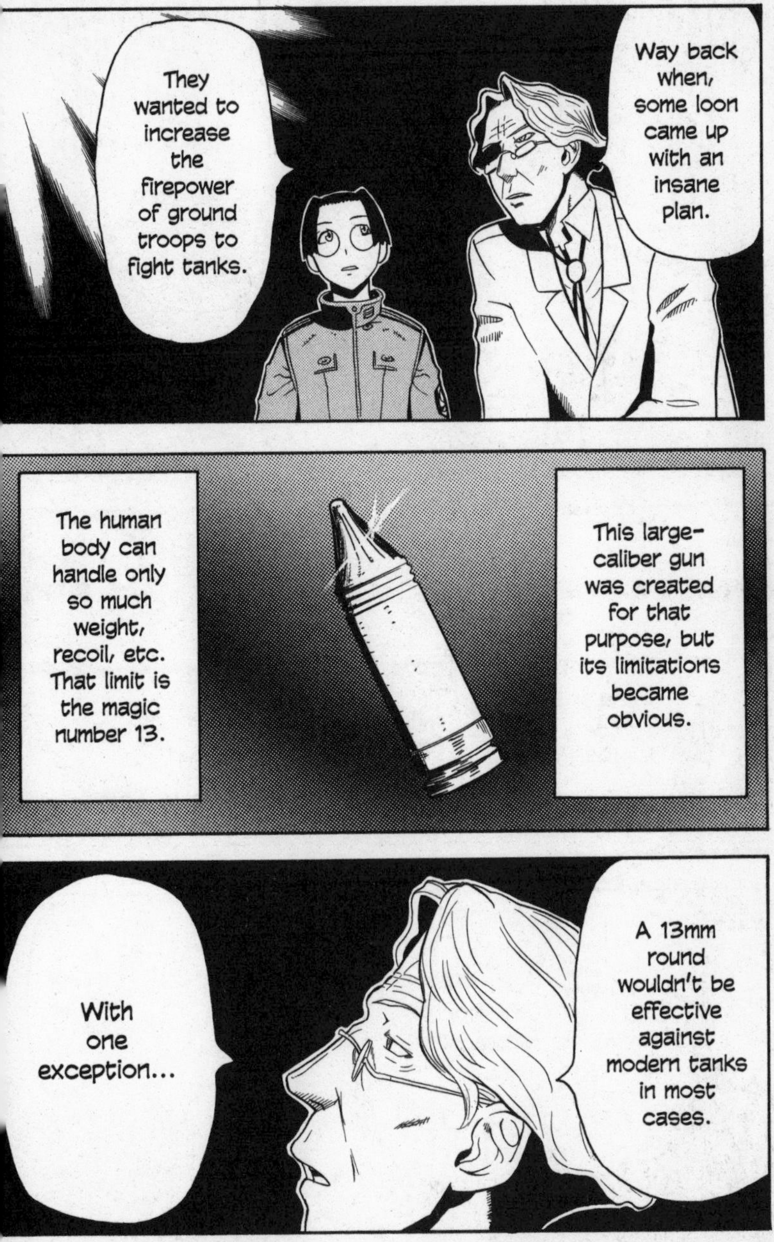
Way back when, some loon came up with an insane plan.
They wanted to increase the firepower of ground troops to fight tanks.
This large-caliber gun was created for that purpose, but its limitations became obvious.
The human body can handle only so much weight, recoil, etc. That limit is the magic number 13.
A 13mm round wouldn't be effective against modern tanks in most cases.
With one exception...

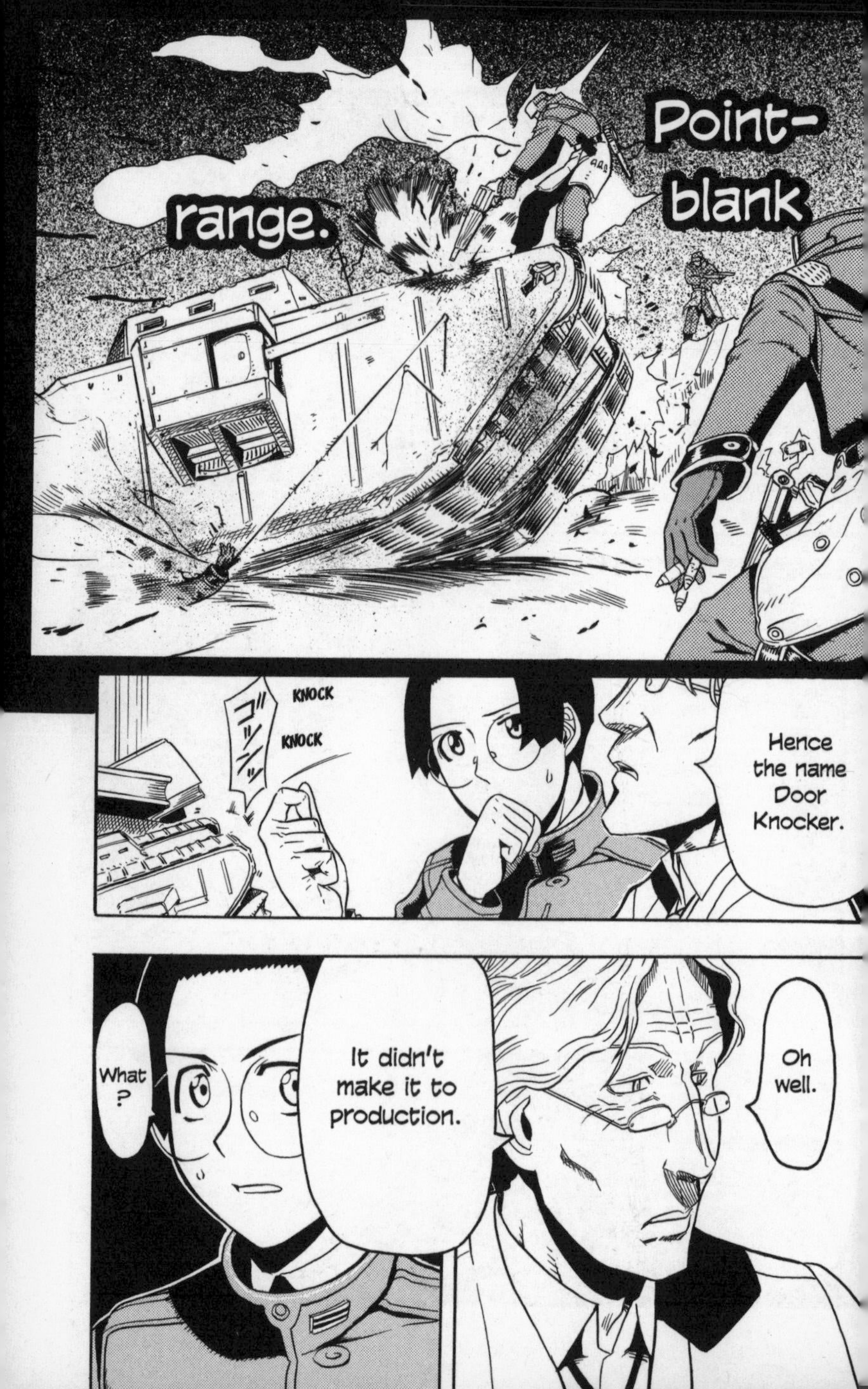
Point-blank
range.
Hence the name Door Knocker.
KNOCK
KNOCK
Oh well.
It didn't make it to production.
What?

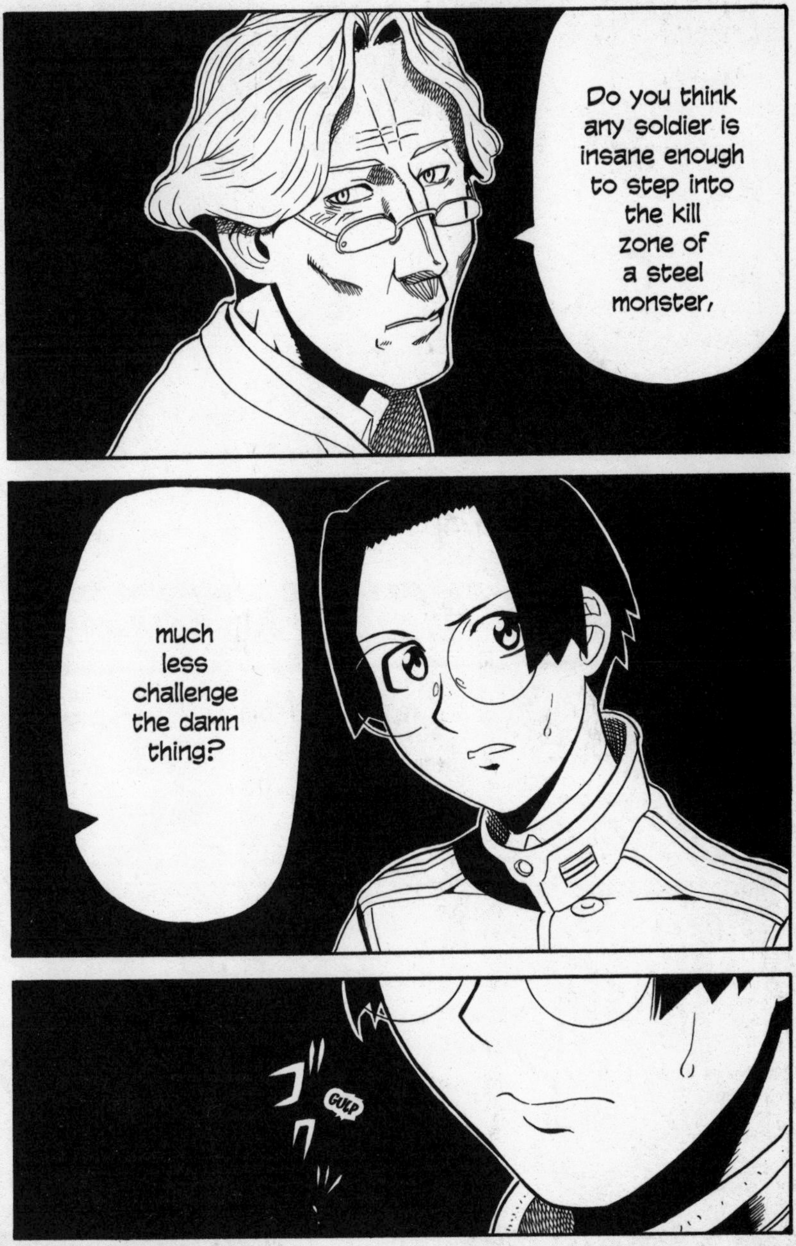
Do you think any soldier is insane enough to step into the kill zone of a steel monster,
much less challenge the damn thing?
GULP

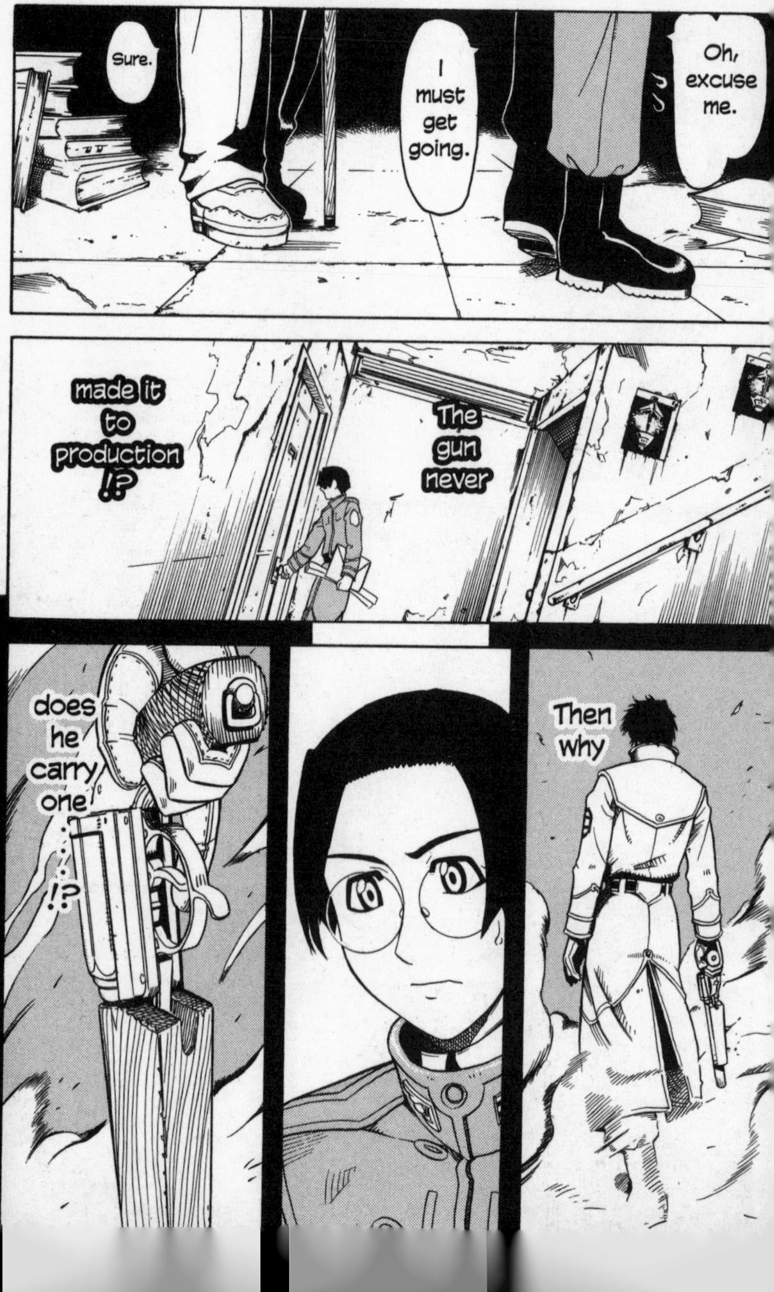
Oh, excuse me.
I must get going.
Sure.
The gun never
made it to production !?
Then why
does he carry one ......!?

SLAM

KANCE

Uh... I'm sorry!

You're lagging, Machs!

His former unit was 901ATT......

Corporal Randel Oland

Who is he ...!?

Wait a minute...!?

Huh? "901?"

26

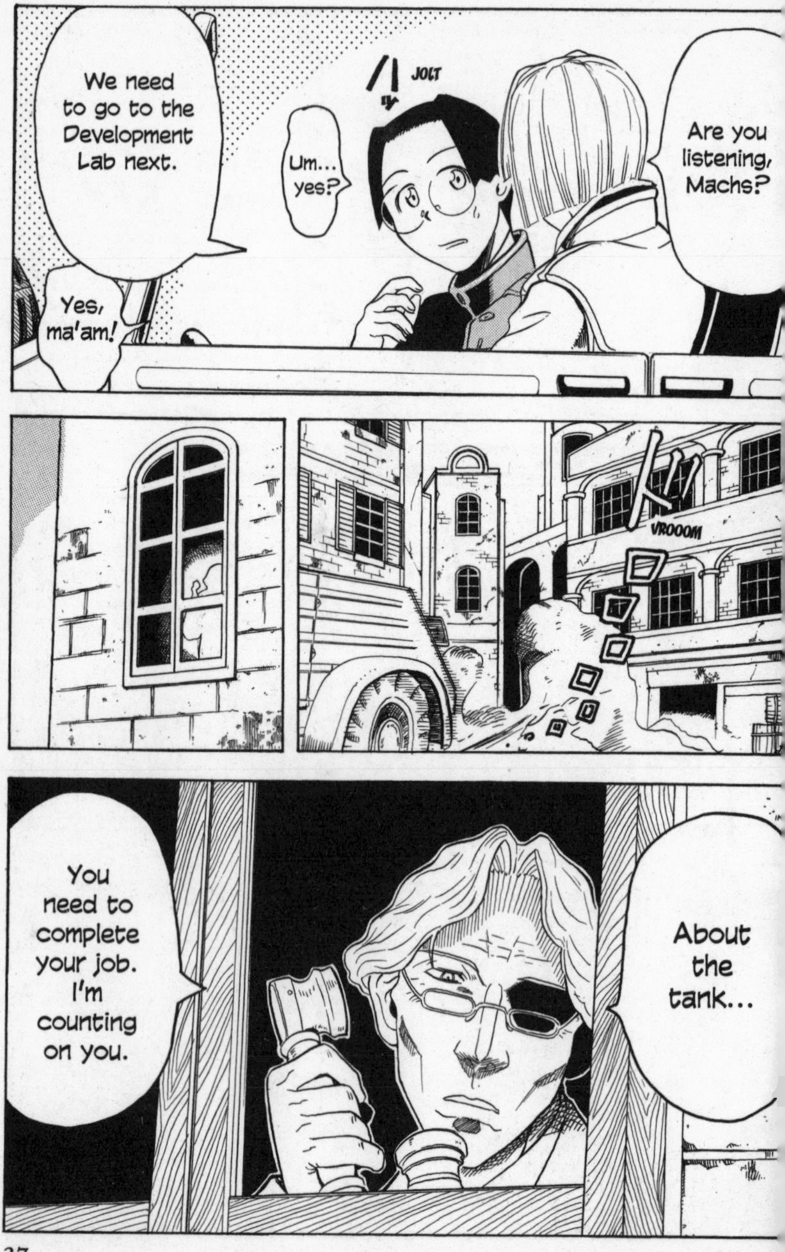
Are you listening, Machs?
JOLT
Um... yes?
We need to go to the Development Lab next.
Yes, ma'am!
VROOOM
About the tank...
You need to complete your job. I'm counting on you.

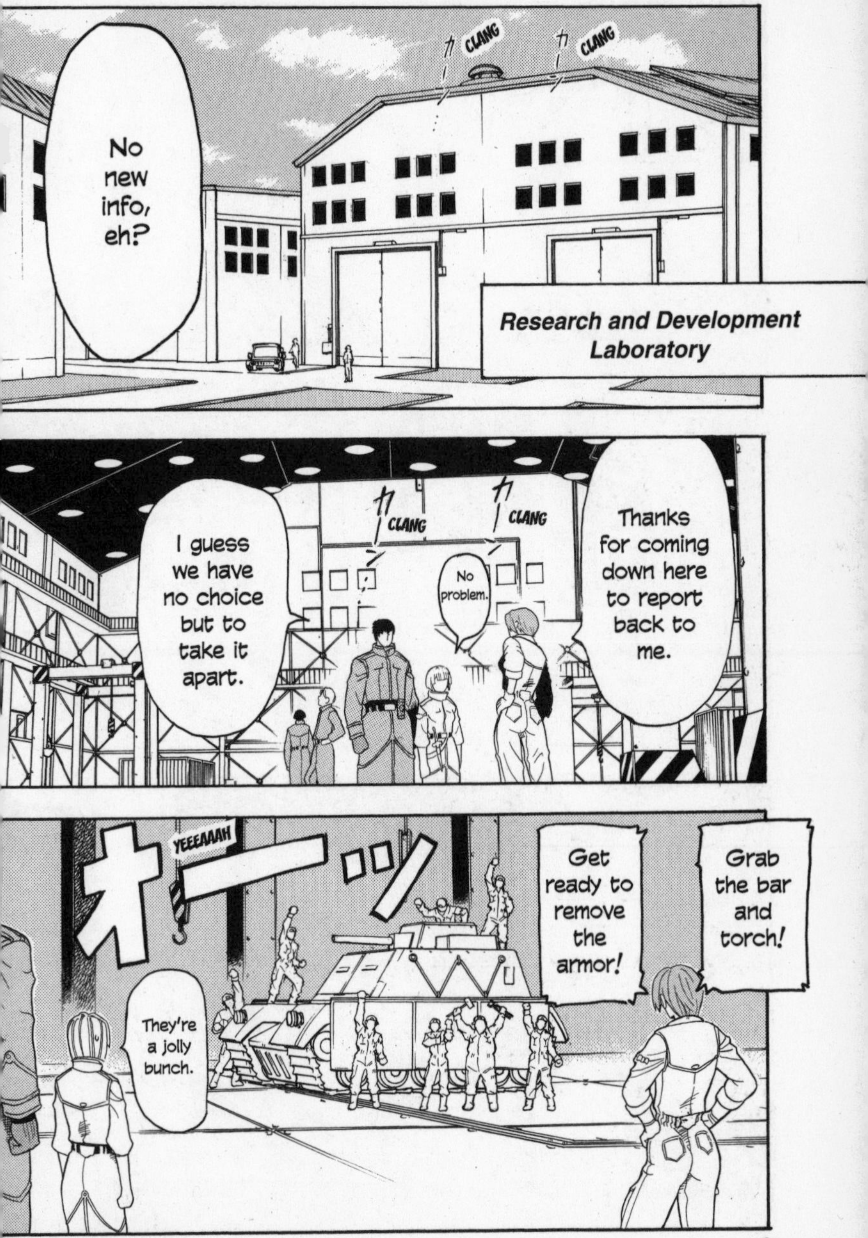
CLANG
CLANG
Research and Development Laboratory
No new info, eh?
CLANG
CLANG
Thanks for coming down here to report back to me.
No problem.
I guess we have no choice but to take it apart.
Grab the bar and torch!
Get ready to remove the armor!
YEEEAAAH
They're a jolly bunch.

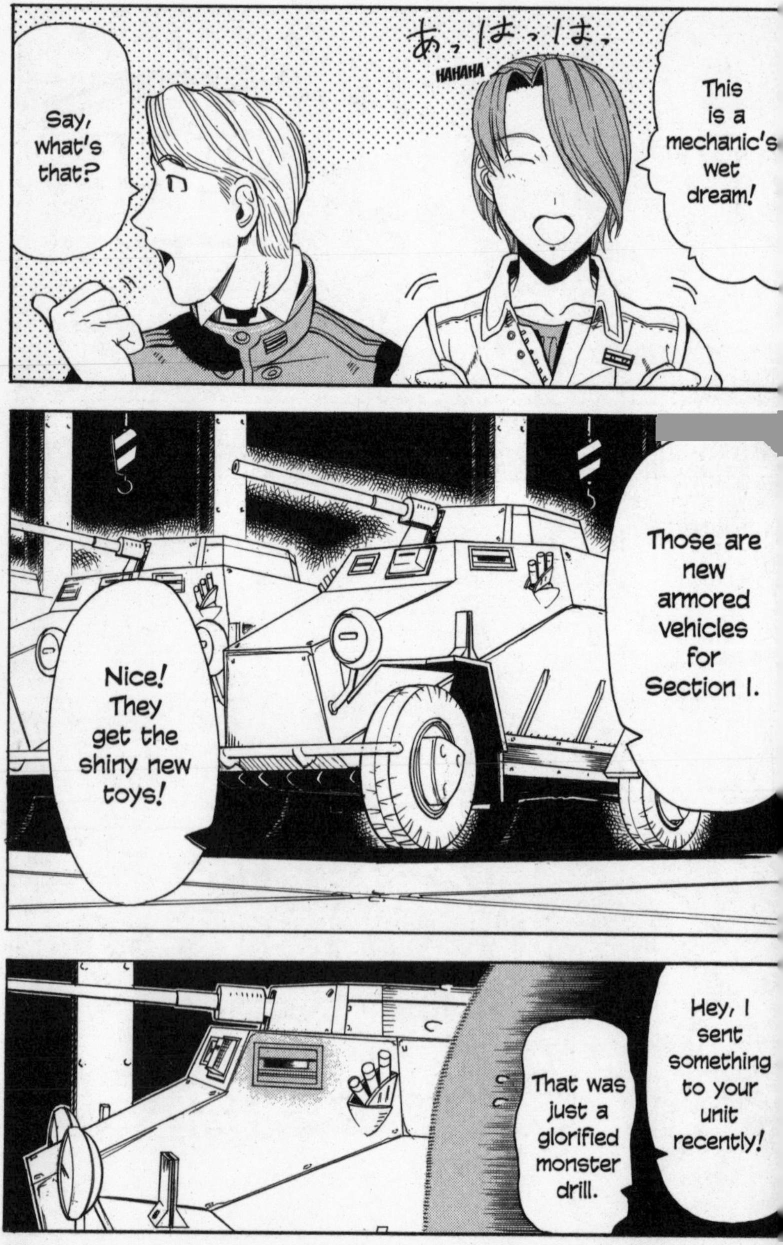
This is a mechanic's wet dream!
あっはっは。
HAHAHA
Say, what's that?
Those are new armored vehicles for Section 1.
Nice! They get the shiny new toys!
Hey, I sent something to your unit recently!
That was just a glorified monster drill.

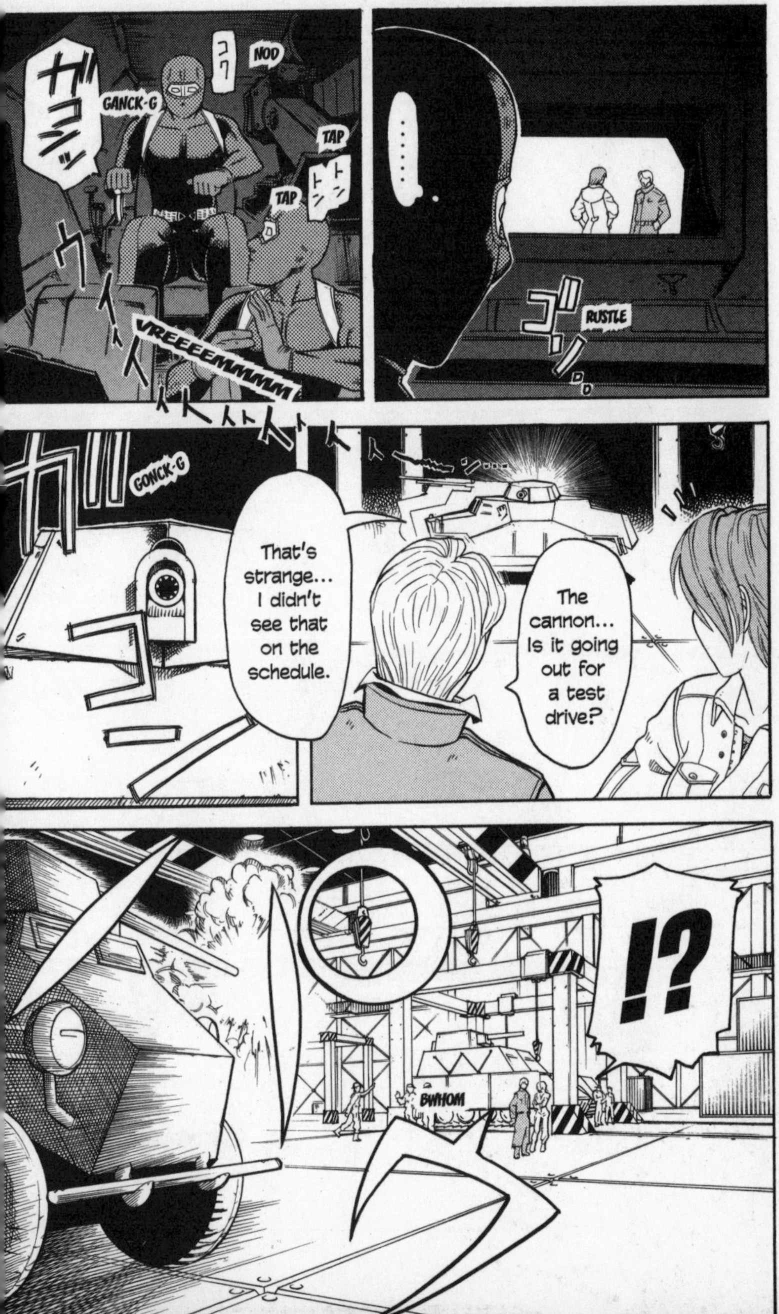

......
RUSTLE
NOD
コク
GANCK-G
TAP
TAP
VREEEEMMMMM
The cannon... Is it going out for a test drive?
That's strange... I didn't see that on the schedule.
GONCK-G
!?
BWHOM

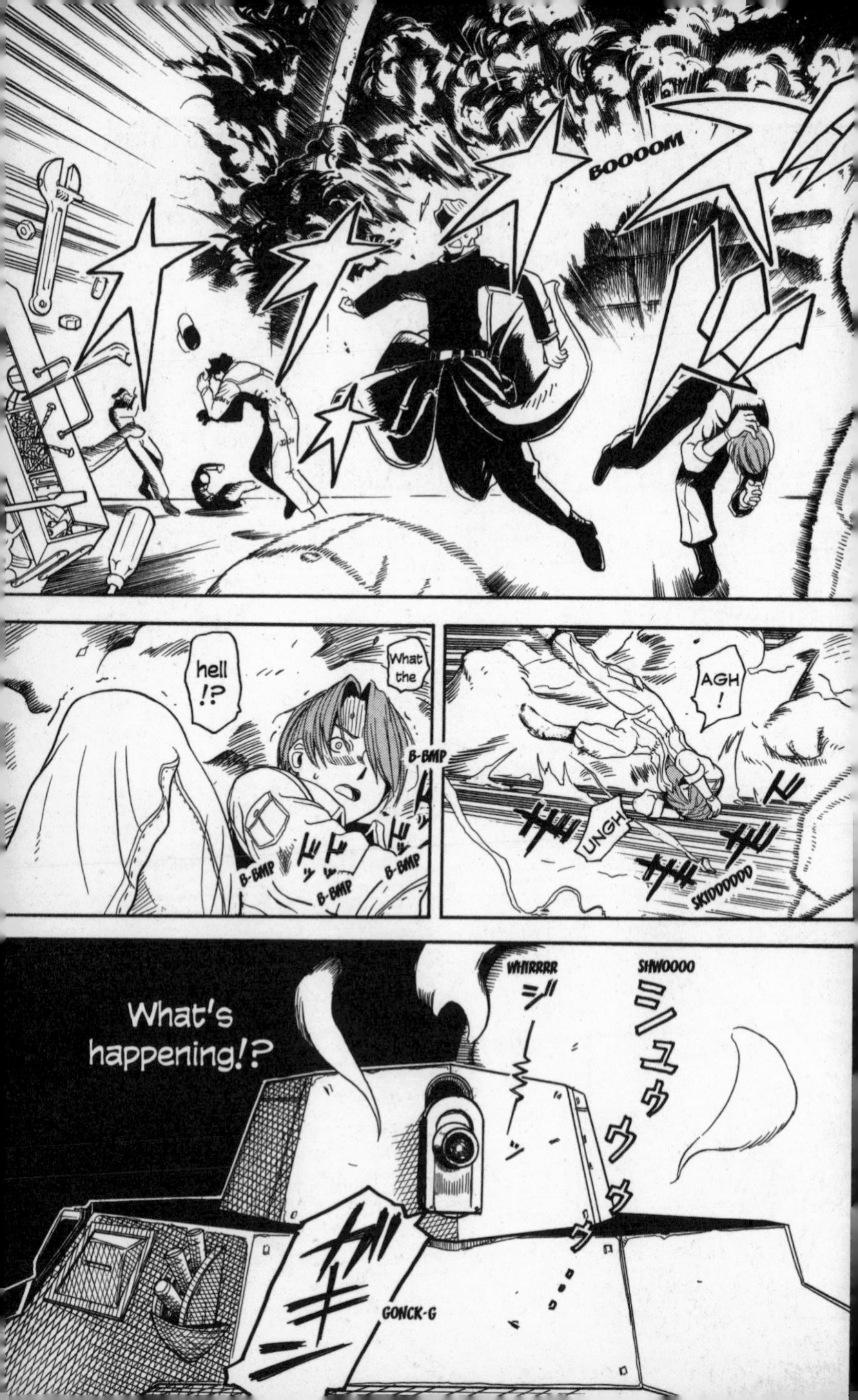
BOOOOM
AGH!
UNGH
SKIDDDDDD
What the
hell!?
B-BMP
B-BMP
B-BMP
B-BMP
SHWOOO
WHIRRRR
What's happening!?
GONCK-G

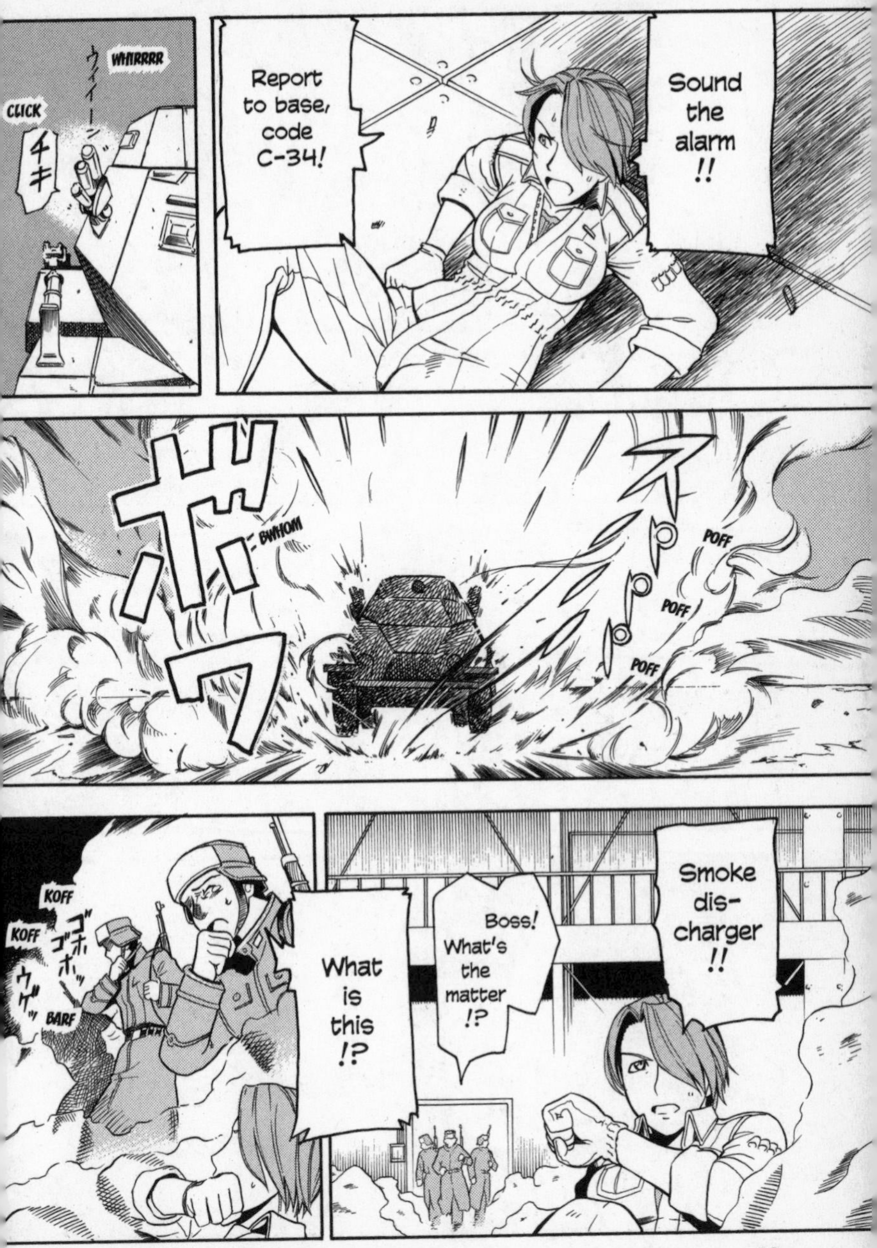
Sound the alarm!!
Report to base, code C-34!
WHIRRRR
CLICK
BWHOM
POFF
POFF
POFF
Smoke dis-charger!!
Boss! What's the matter!?
What is this!?
KOFF
KOFF
BARF

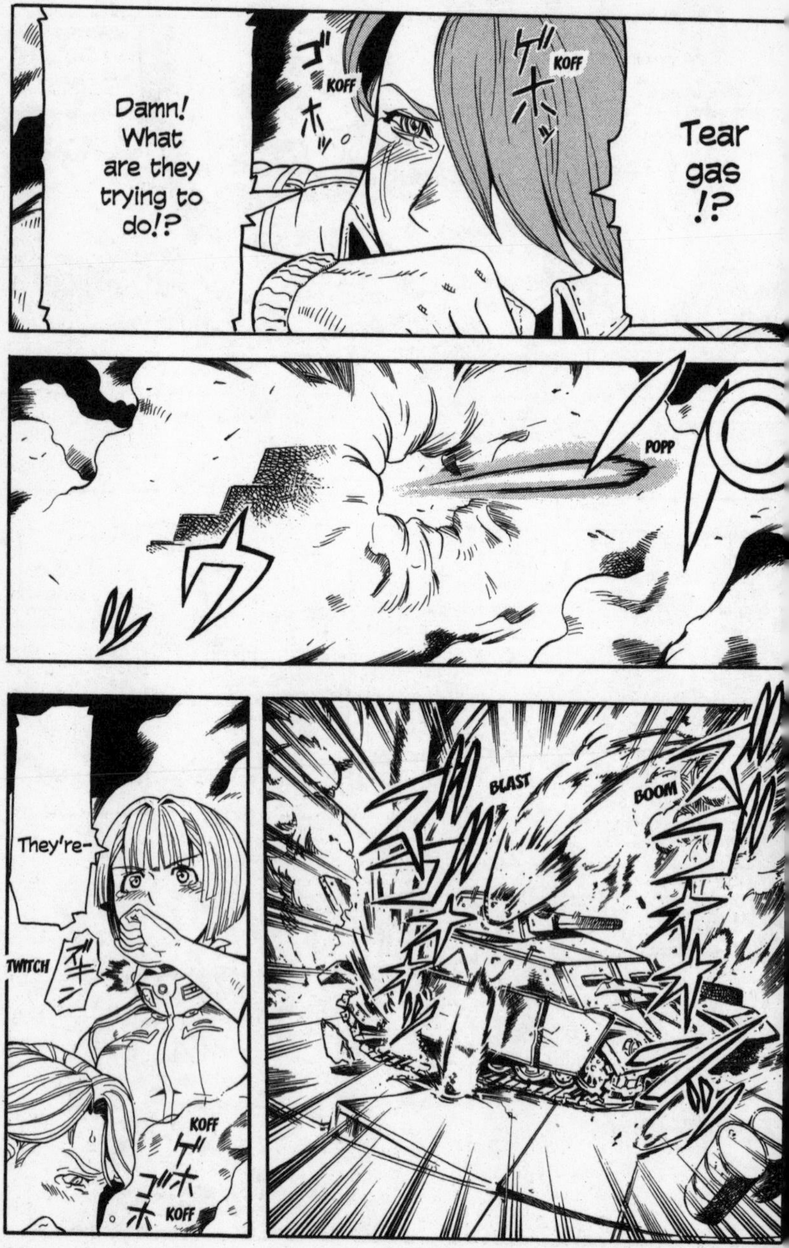
Tear gas!?
ゲホッ
KOFF
ゴホッ
KOFF
Damn! What are they trying to do!?
POPP
BOOM
BLAST
They're-
TWITCH
KOFF
KOFF

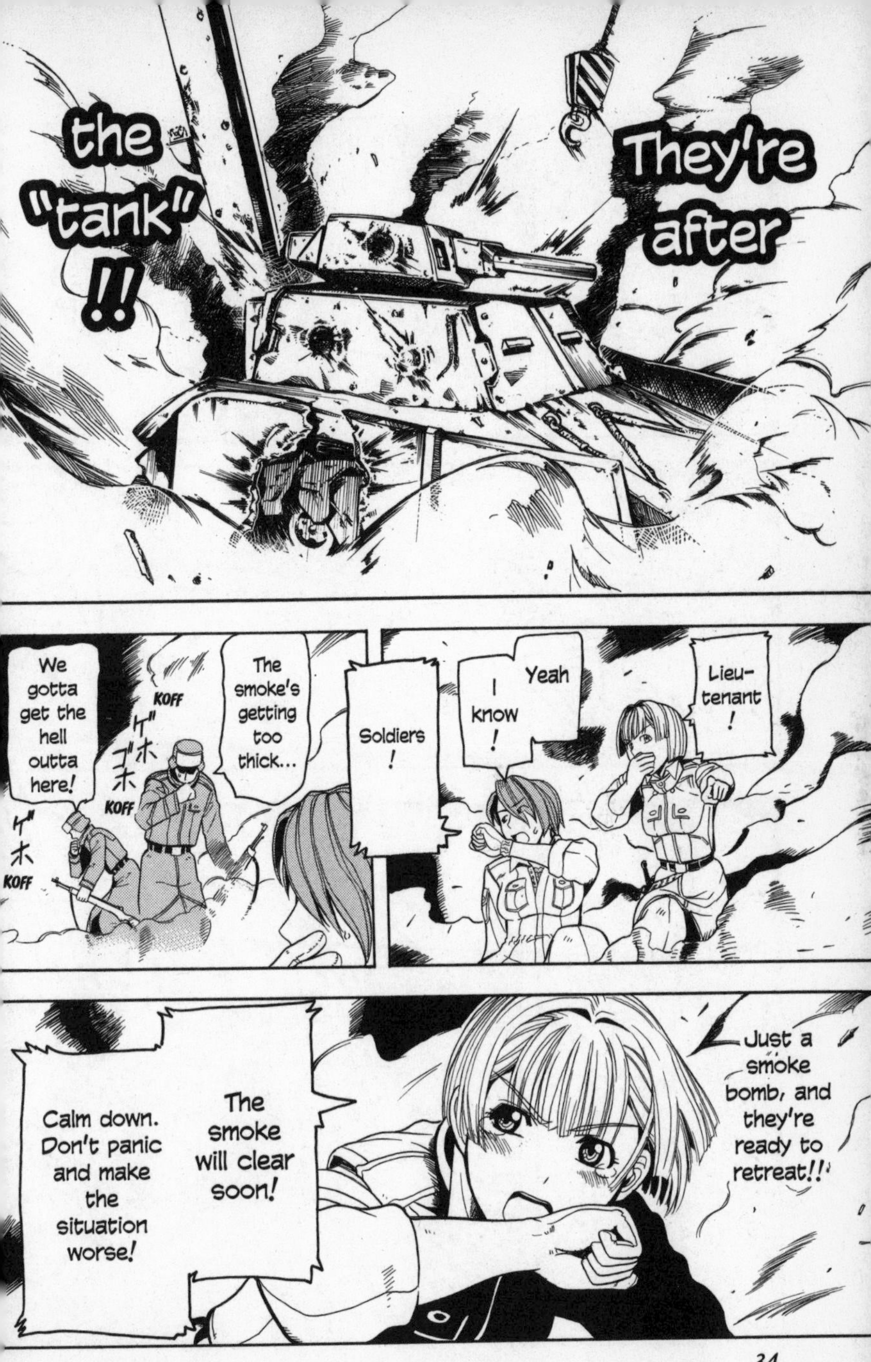
They're after
the "tank"!!
Lieutenant!
Yeah I know!
Soldiers!
The smoke's getting too thick...
KOFF
ゲホゴホ
KOFF
We gotta get the hell outta here!
ゲホ
KOFF
Just a smoke bomb, and they're ready to retreat!!
The smoke will clear soon!
Calm down. Don't panic and make the situation worse!

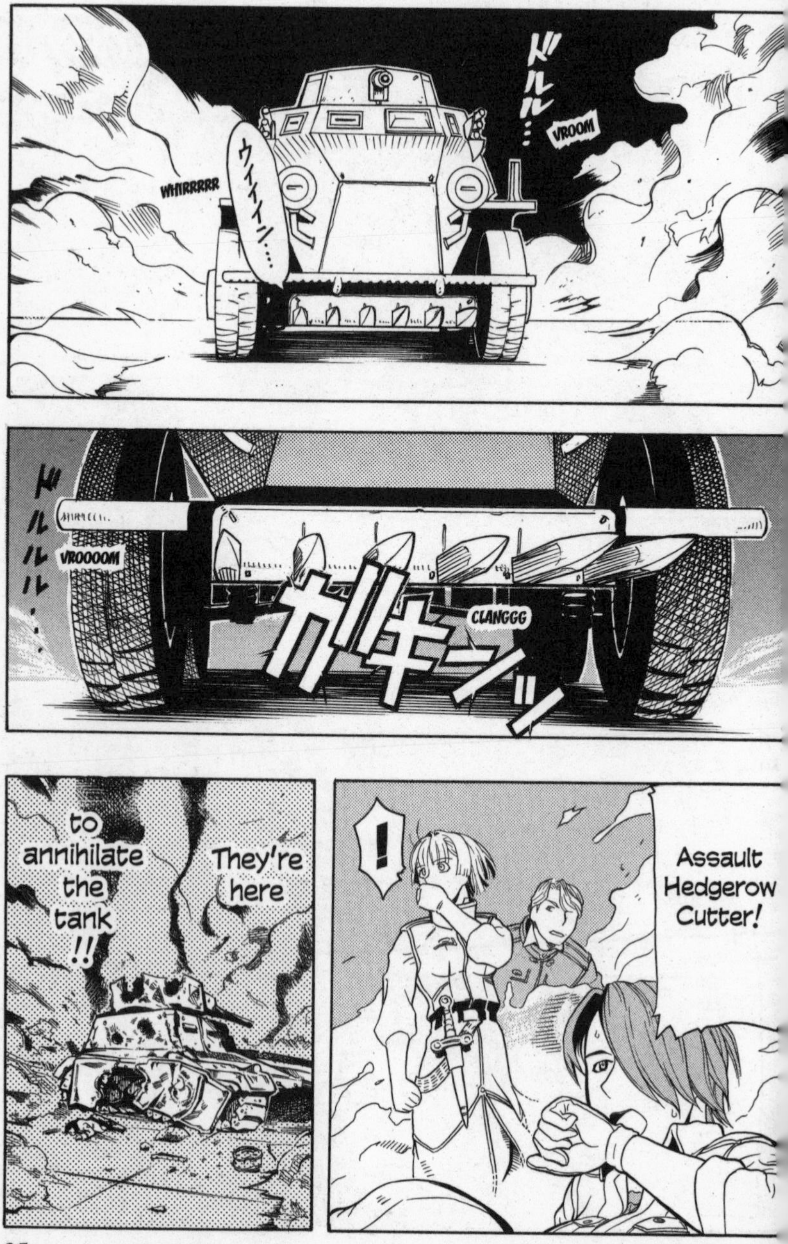
ドルル…
VROOM
ウィイイン…
WHIRRRRR
ガキーンッ
CLANGGG
ドルルル…
VROOOOM
!
Assault Hedgerow Cutter!
They're here
to annihilate the tank!!

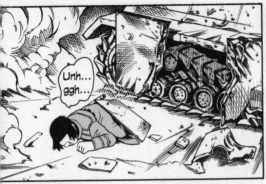

Unh...
ggh...

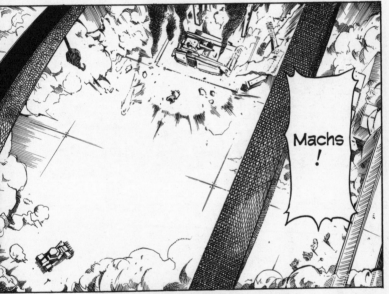

Machs
!

!!

RISE

Uh...

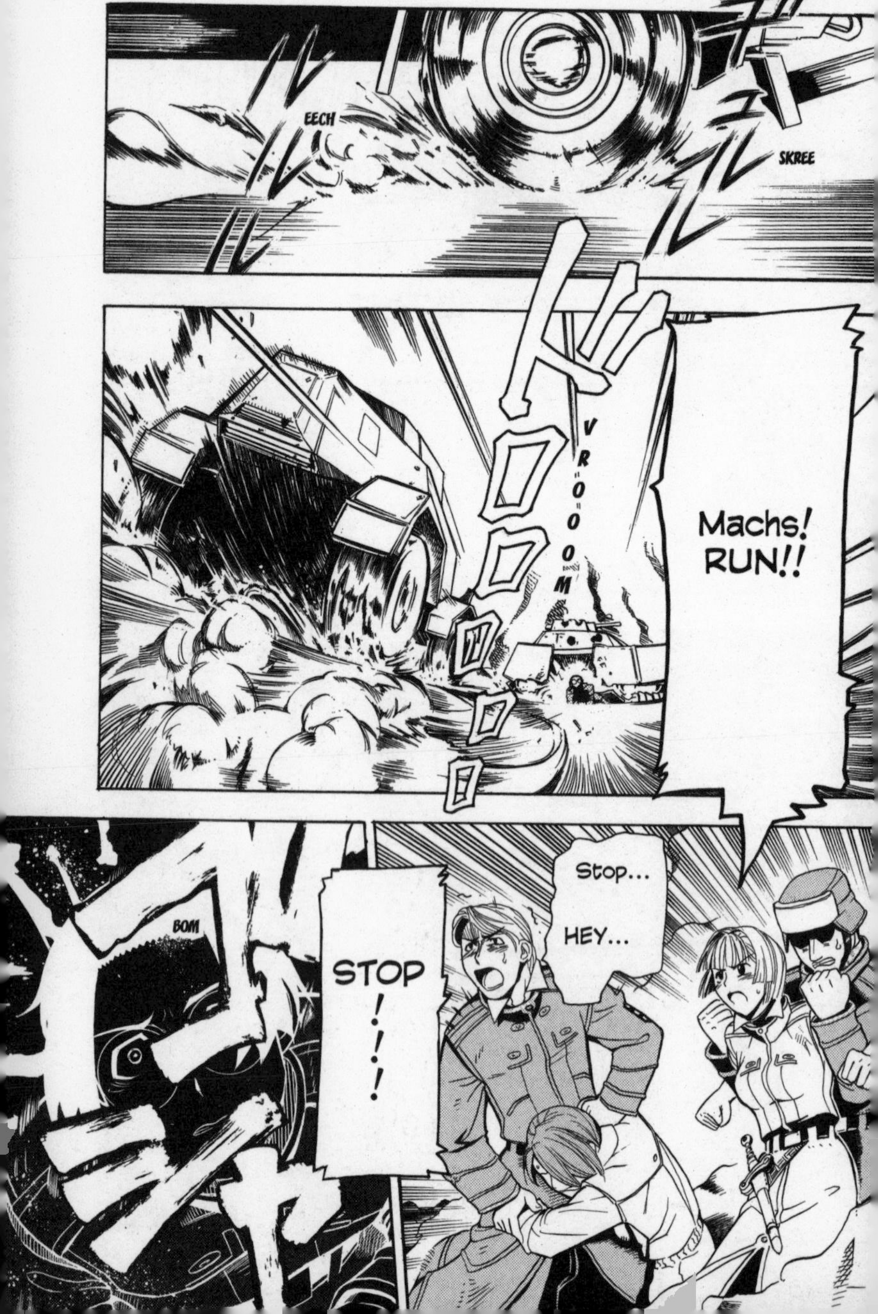
SKREE
EECH
VROOOOM
Machs! RUN!!
Stop...
HEY...
STOP!!!
BOM

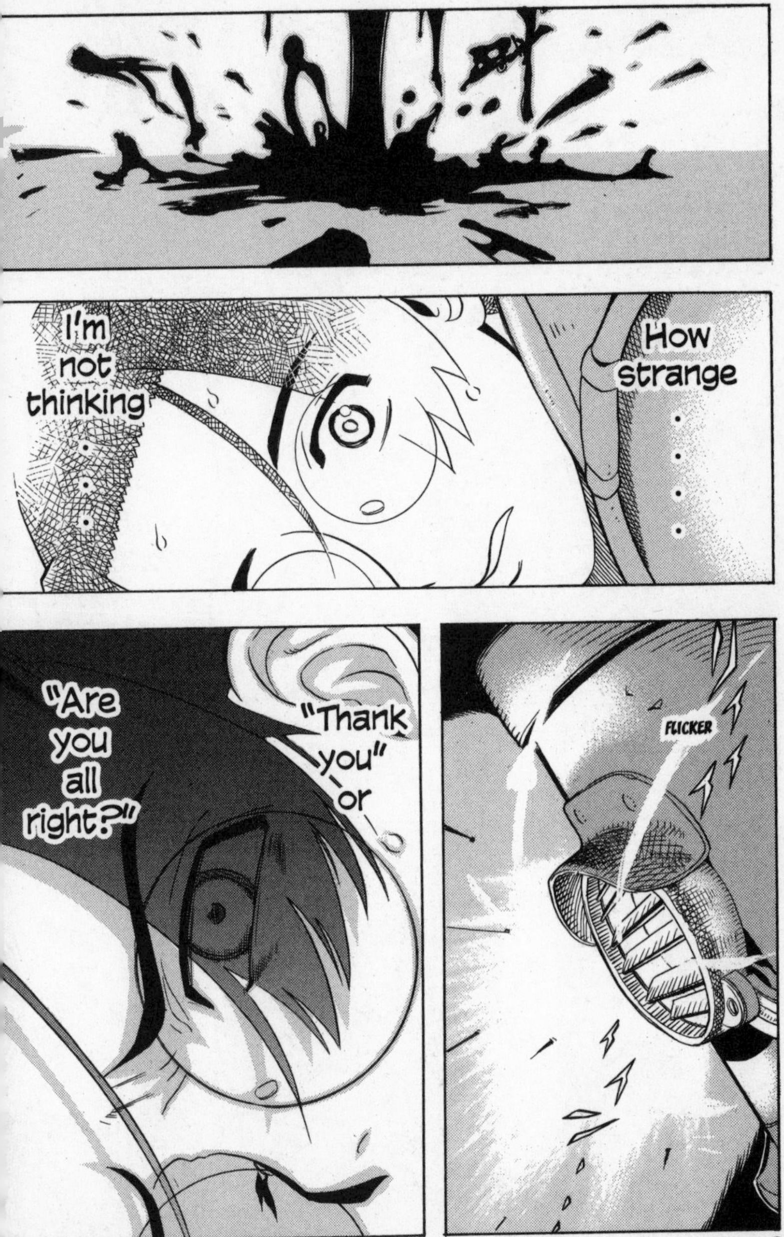
How strange....
I'm not thinking...
FLICKER
"Thank you" or
"Are you all right?"

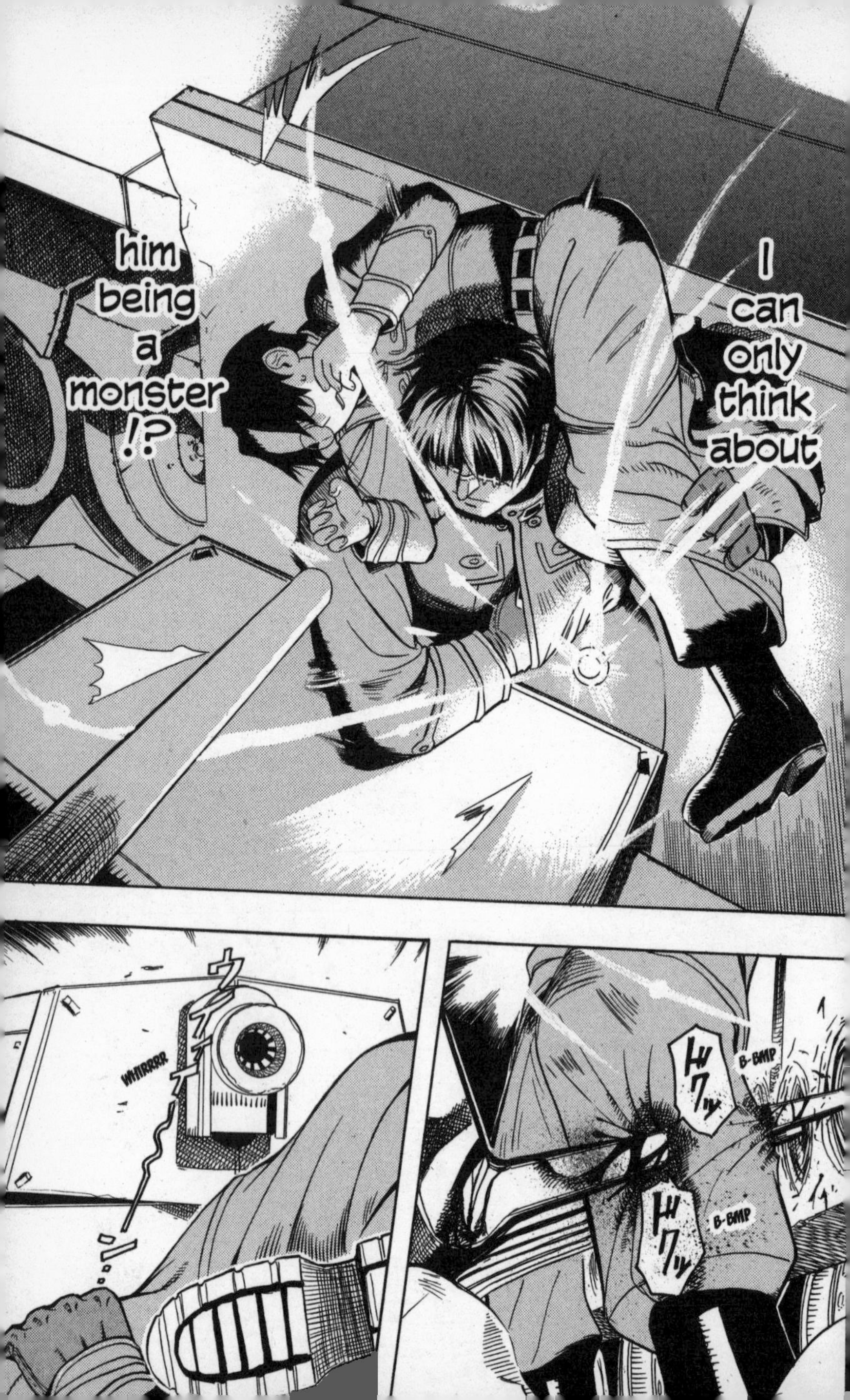
I can only think about
him being a monster!?
ドクッ
B-BMP
ドクッ
B-BMP
WHIRRRR

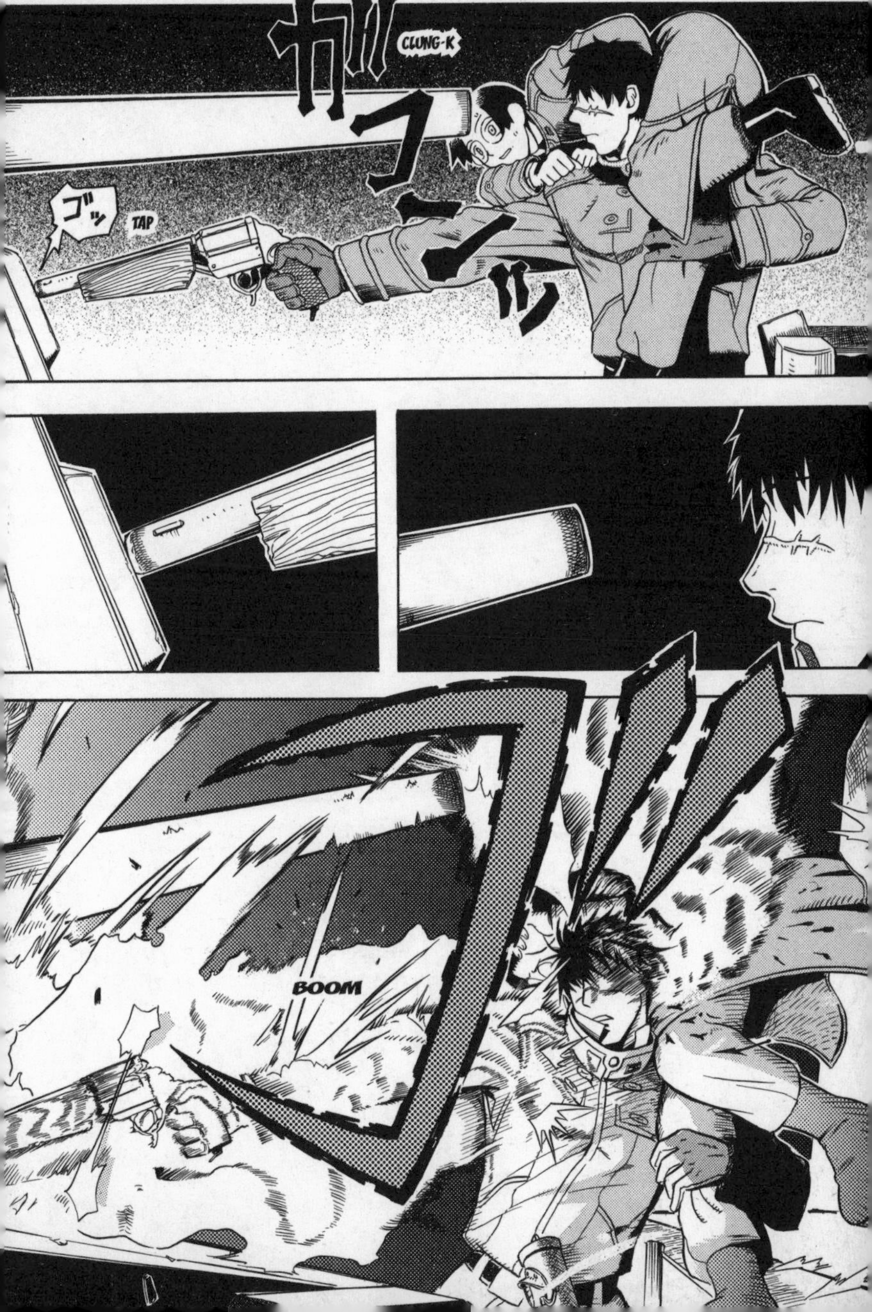
CLUNG-K
ゴッ
TAP
BOOM

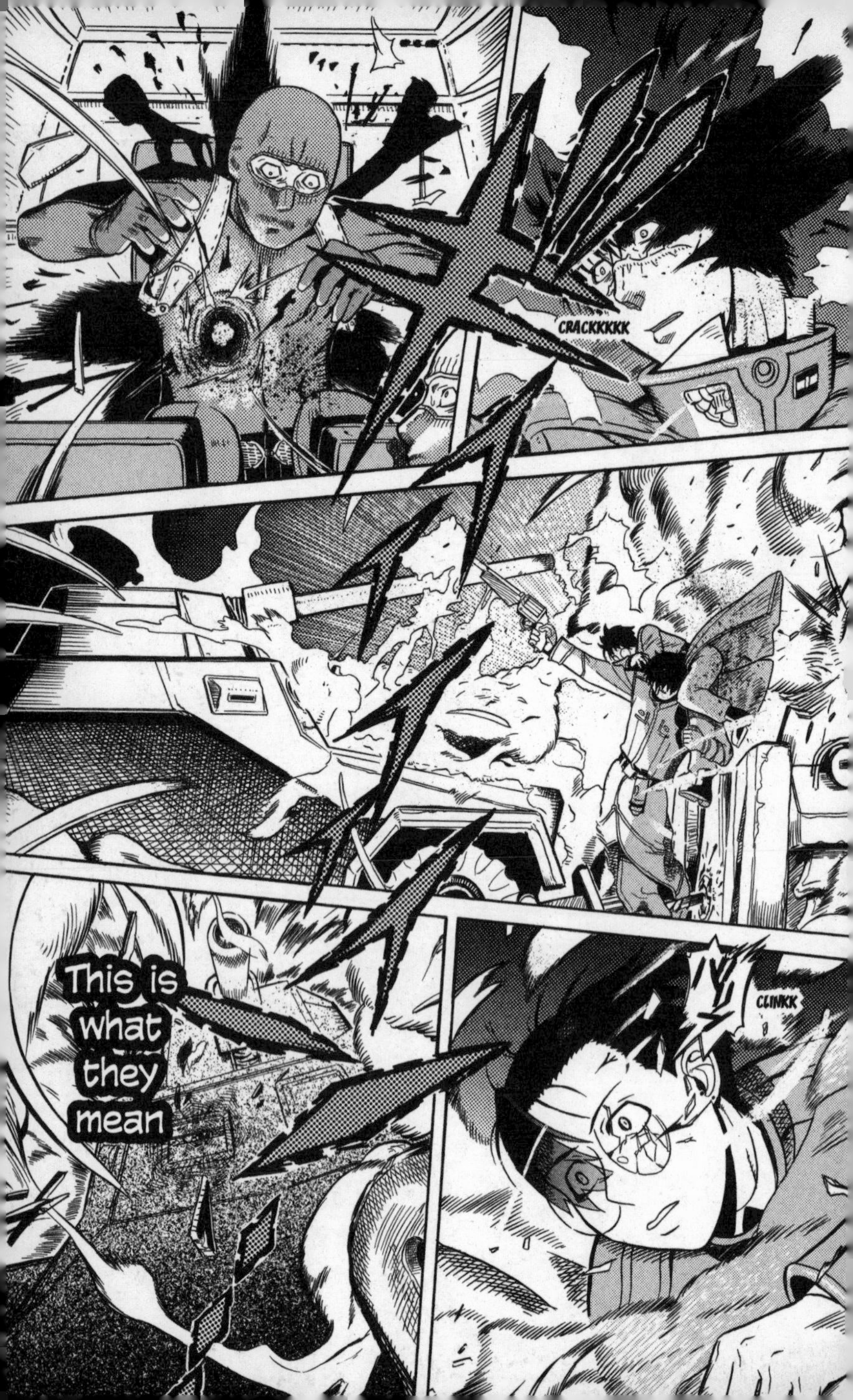
CRACKKKKK
CLINKK
This is what they mean

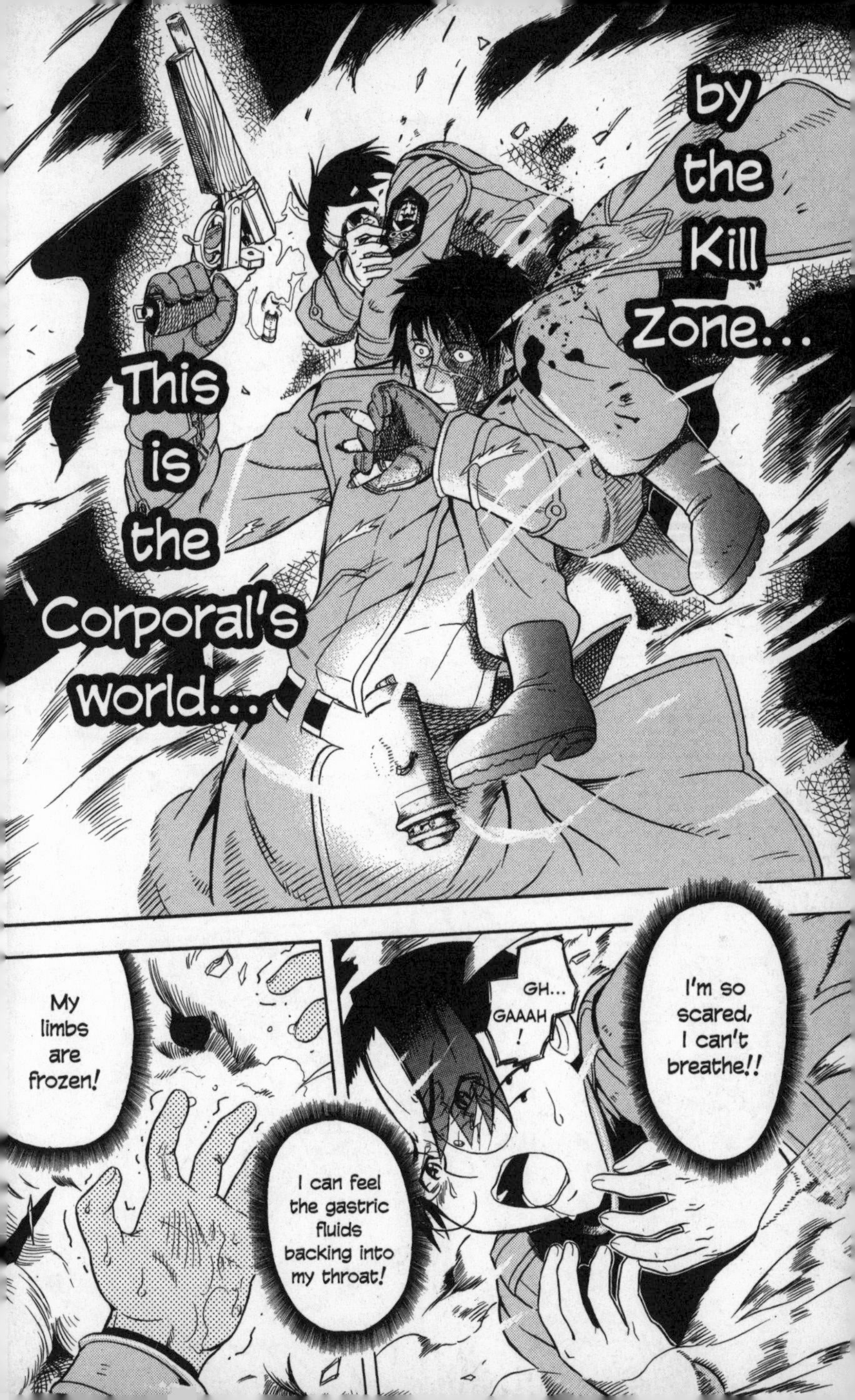
by the Kill Zone...
This is the Corporal's world...
I'm so scared, I can't breathe!!
GH... GAAAH!
I can feel the gastric fluids backing into my throat!
My limbs are frozen!

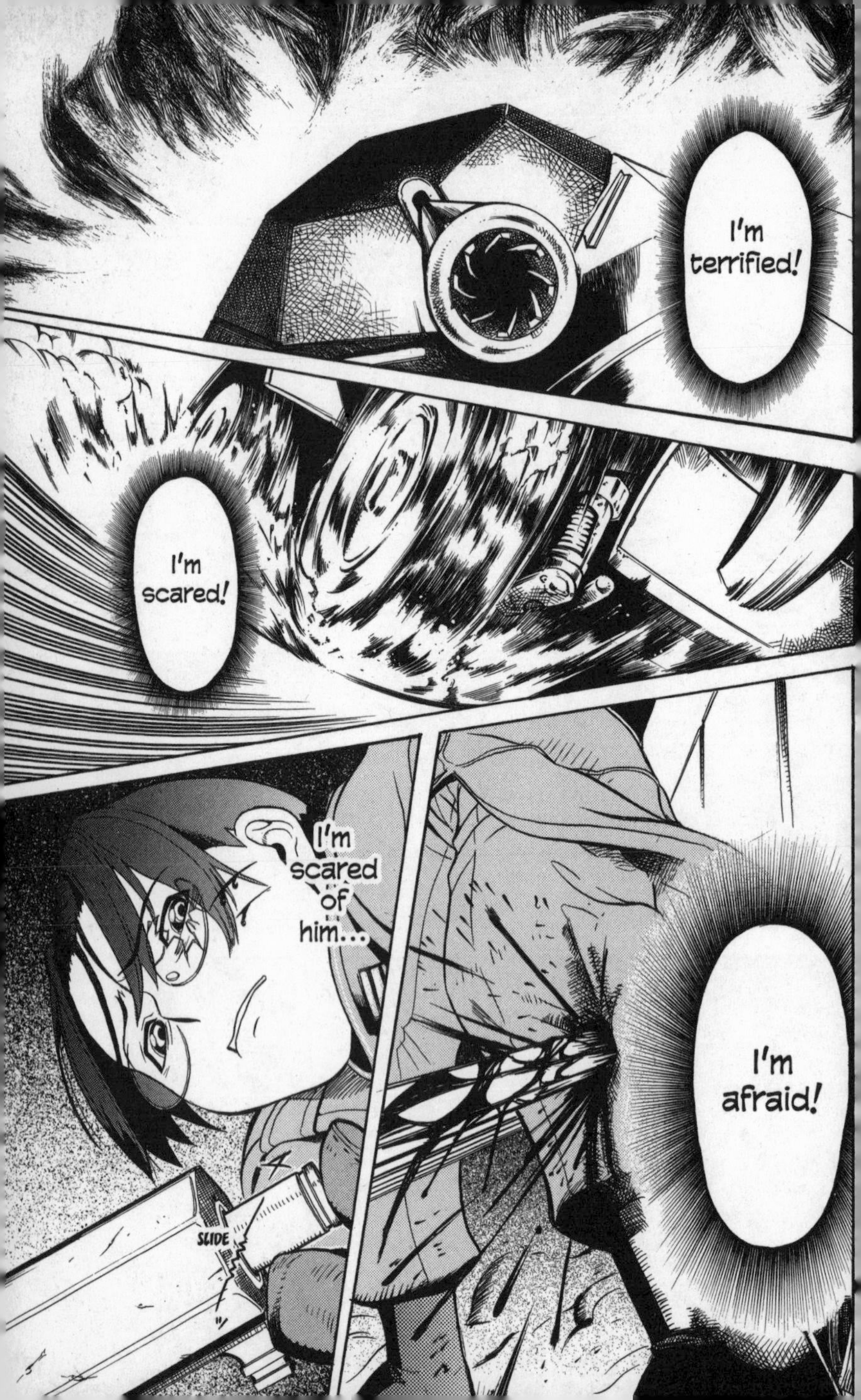
I'm terrified!
I'm scared!
I'm afraid!
I'm scared of him...
SLIDE

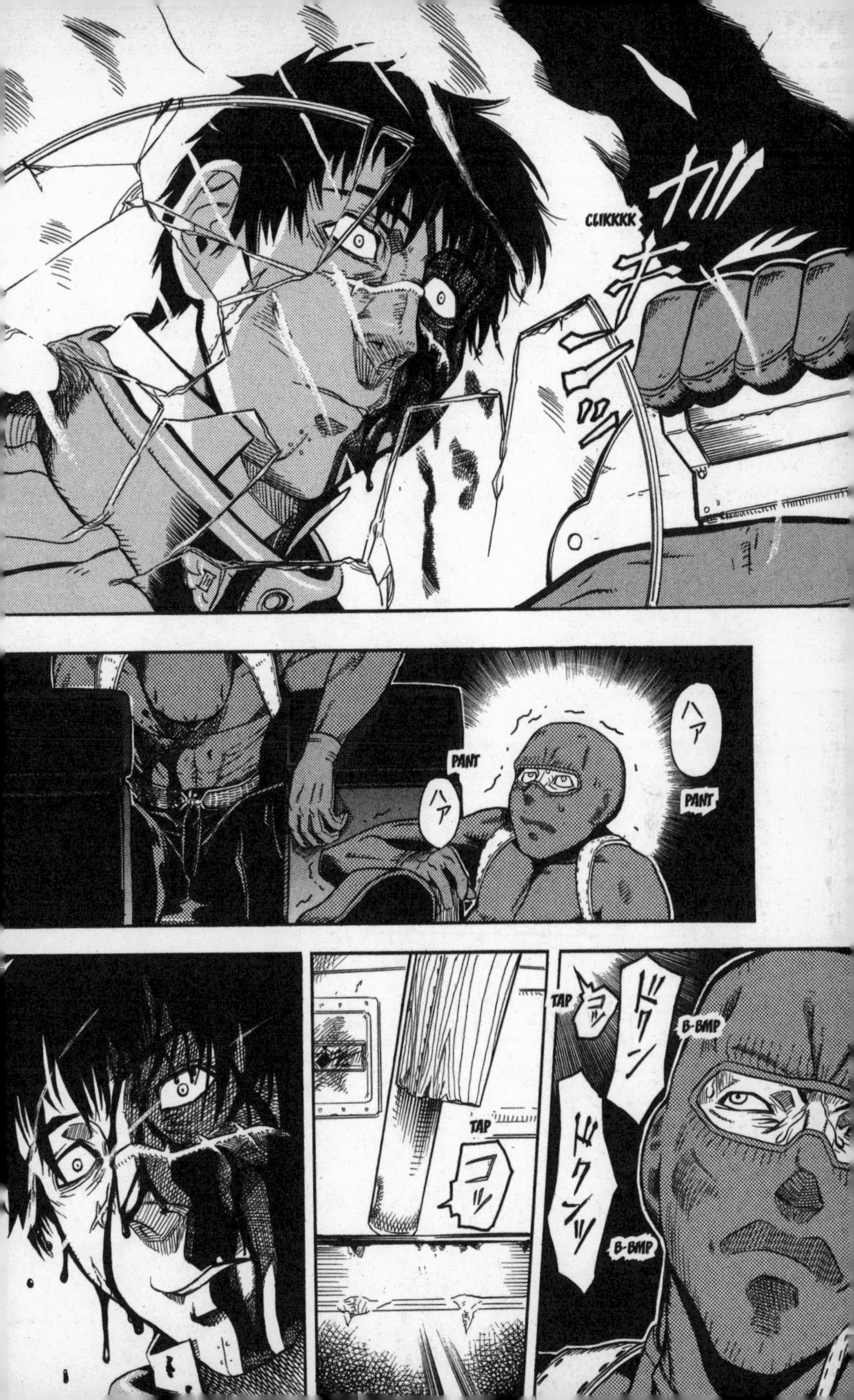
CLIKKK
ハア
PANT
ハア
PANT
TAP
コッ
ドクン
B-BMP
ドクンッ
B-BMP
TAP
コッ

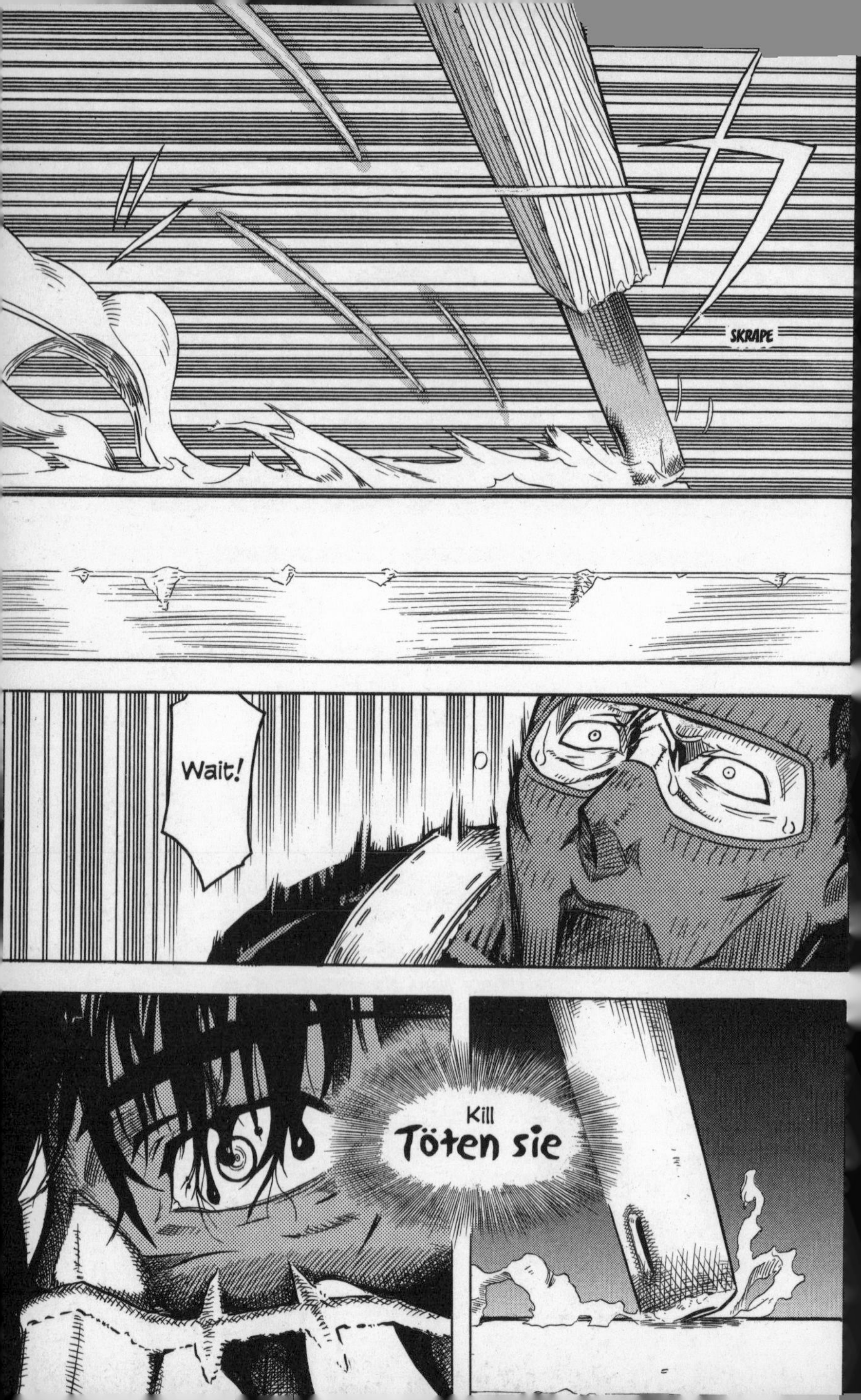
SKRAPE
Wait!
Kill
Töten sie

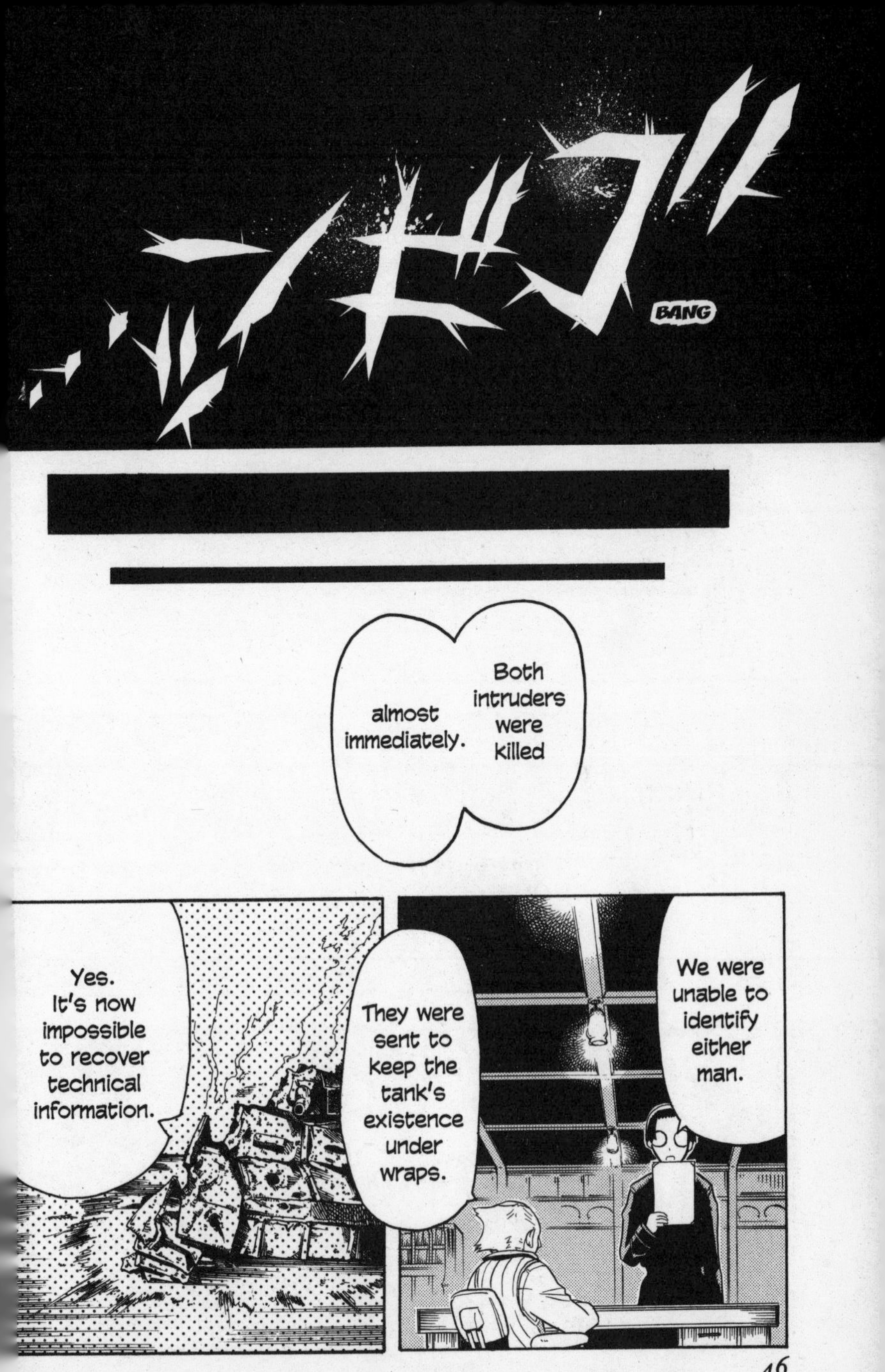
BANG
Both intruders were killed almost immediately.
We were unable to identify either man.
They were sent to keep the tank's existence under wraps.
Yes. It's now impossible to recover technical information.

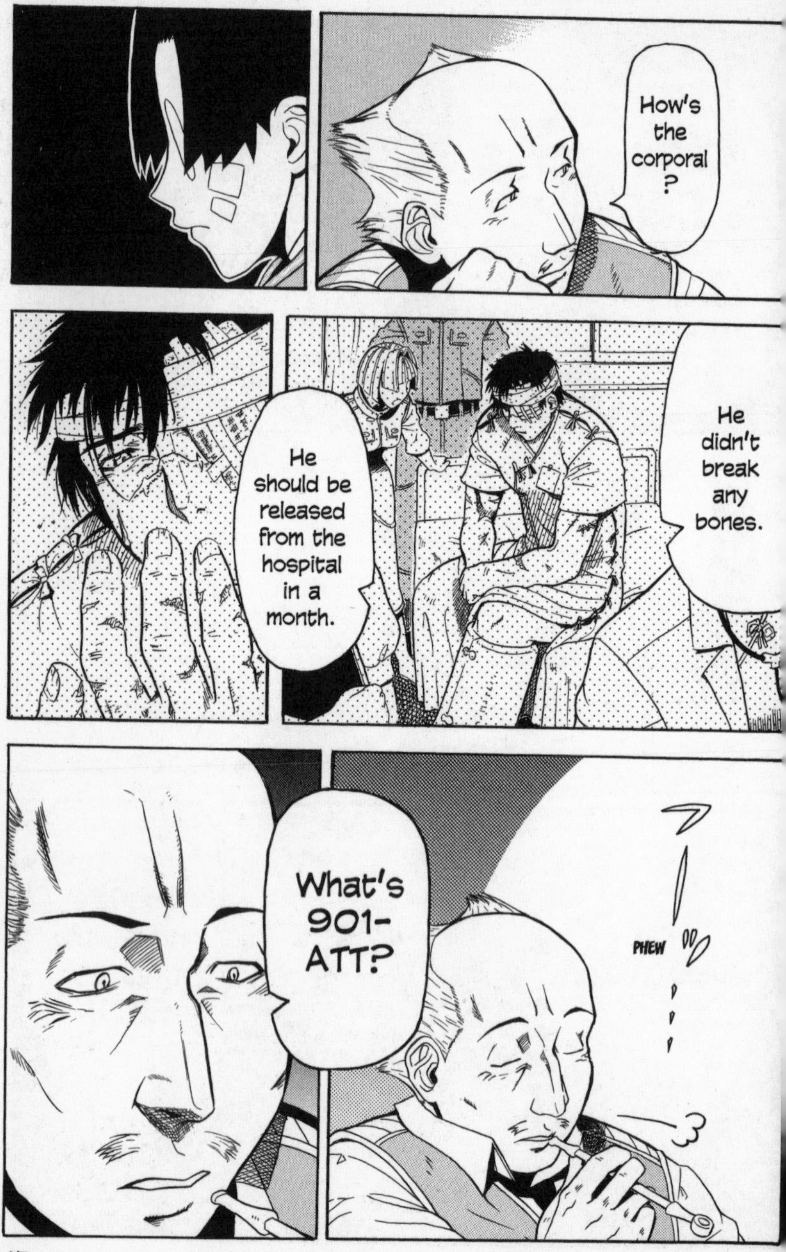
How's the corporal?
He didn't break any bones.
He should be released from the hospital in a month.
What's 901-ATT?
PHEW

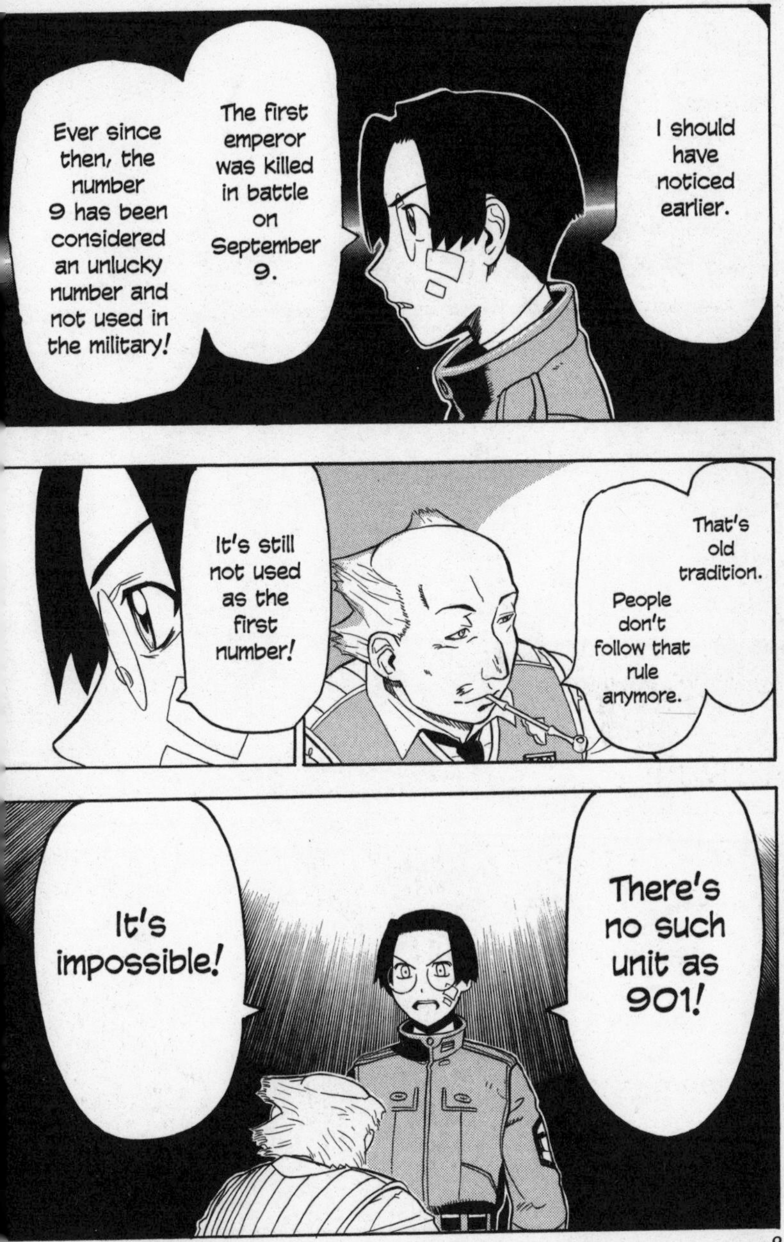
I should have noticed earlier.
The first emperor was killed in battle on September 9.
Ever since then, the number 9 has been considered an unlucky number and not used in the military!
That's old tradition.
People don't follow that rule anymore.
It's still not used as the first number!
There's no such unit as 901!
It's impossible!

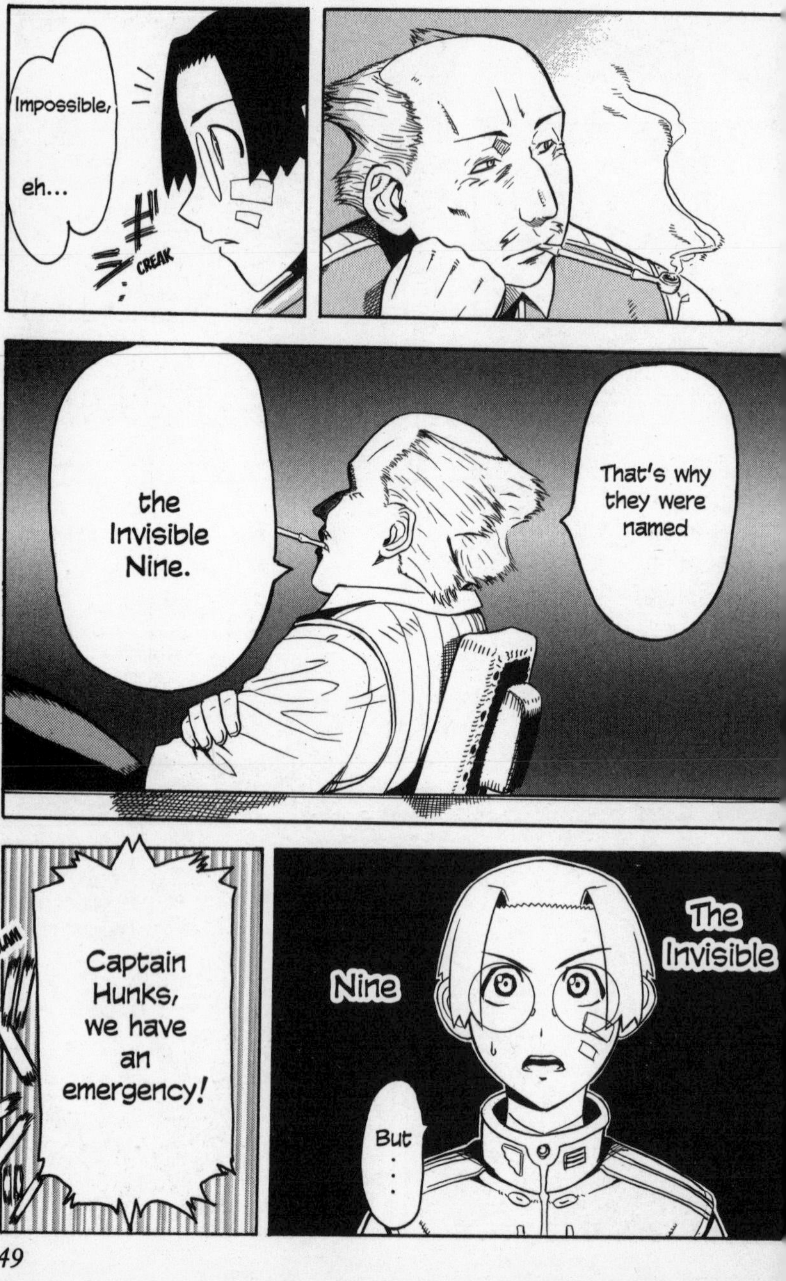
Impossible, eh...
CREAK
That's why they were named
the Invisible Nine.
The Invisible Nine
But...
SLAM
Captain Hunks, we have an emergency!

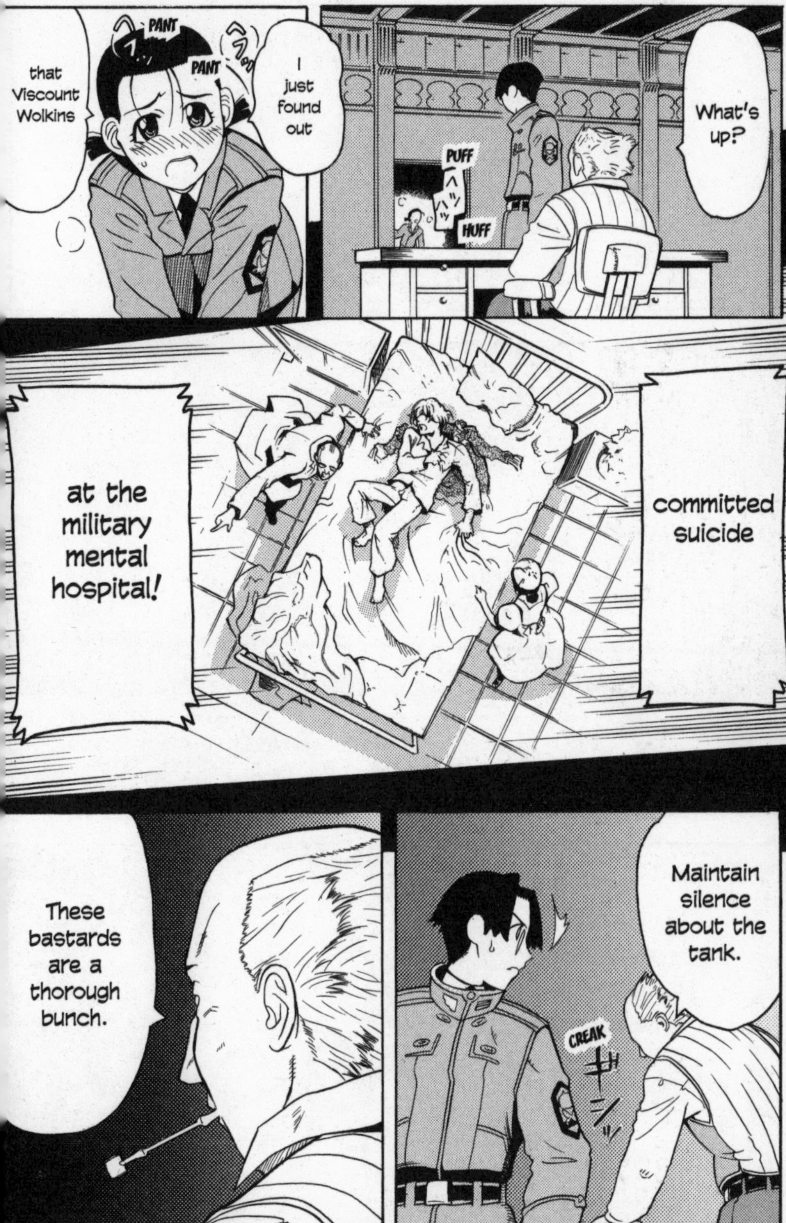
What's up?
PUFF
HUFF
PANT
PANT
I just found out
that Viscount Wolkins
committed suicide
at the military mental hospital!
Maintain silence about the tank.
CREAK
These bastards are a thorough bunch.

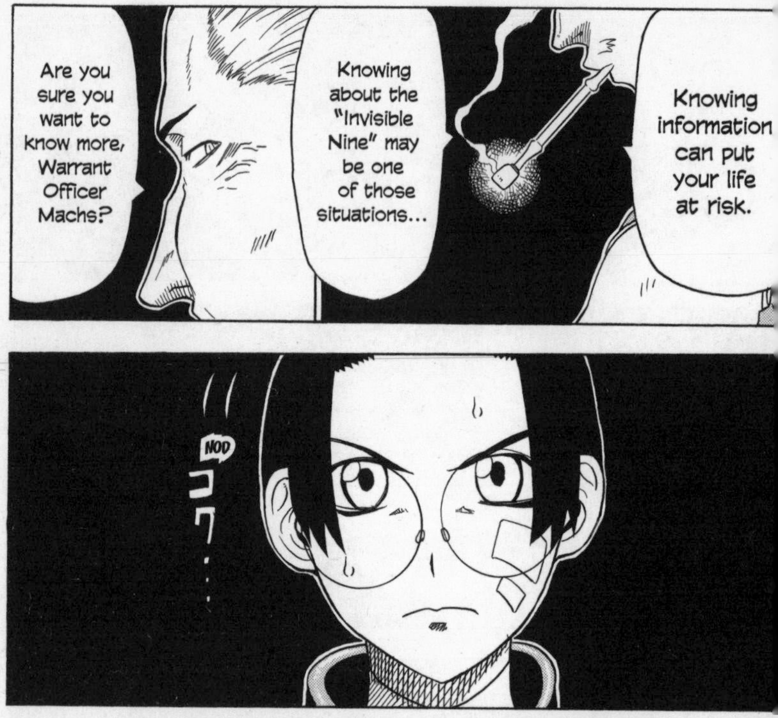
Knowing information can put your life at risk.
Knowing about the "Invisible Nine" may be one of those situations...
Are you sure you want to know more, Warrant Officer Machs?
NOD
コク...

[redacted]

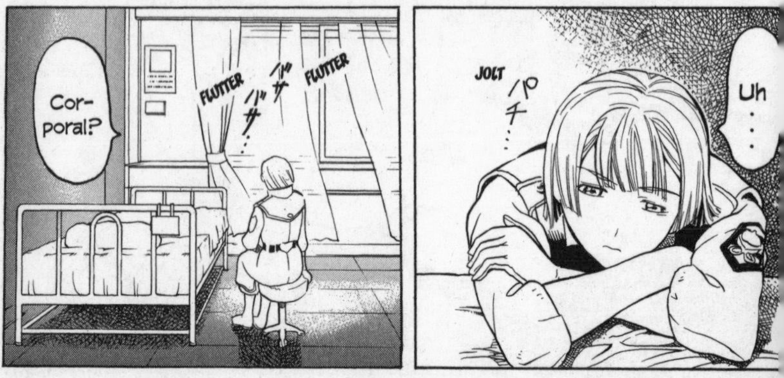
Uh...
JOLT
パチ...
FLUTTER
バサ
バサ...
FLUTTER
Cor-poral?

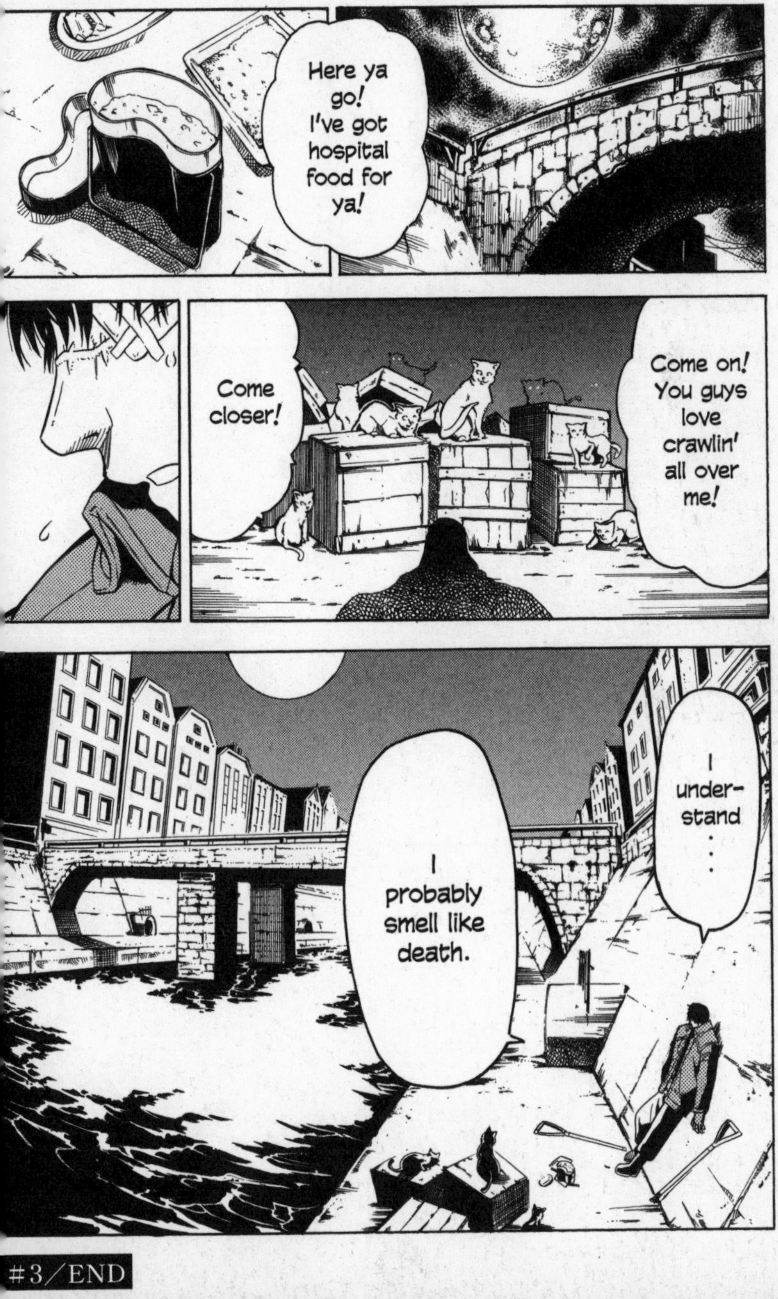
Here ya go! I've got hospital food for ya!
Come on! You guys love crawlin' all over me!
Come closer!
I under-stand . . .
I probably smell like death.

#3/END

PumpkinScissors

Interval

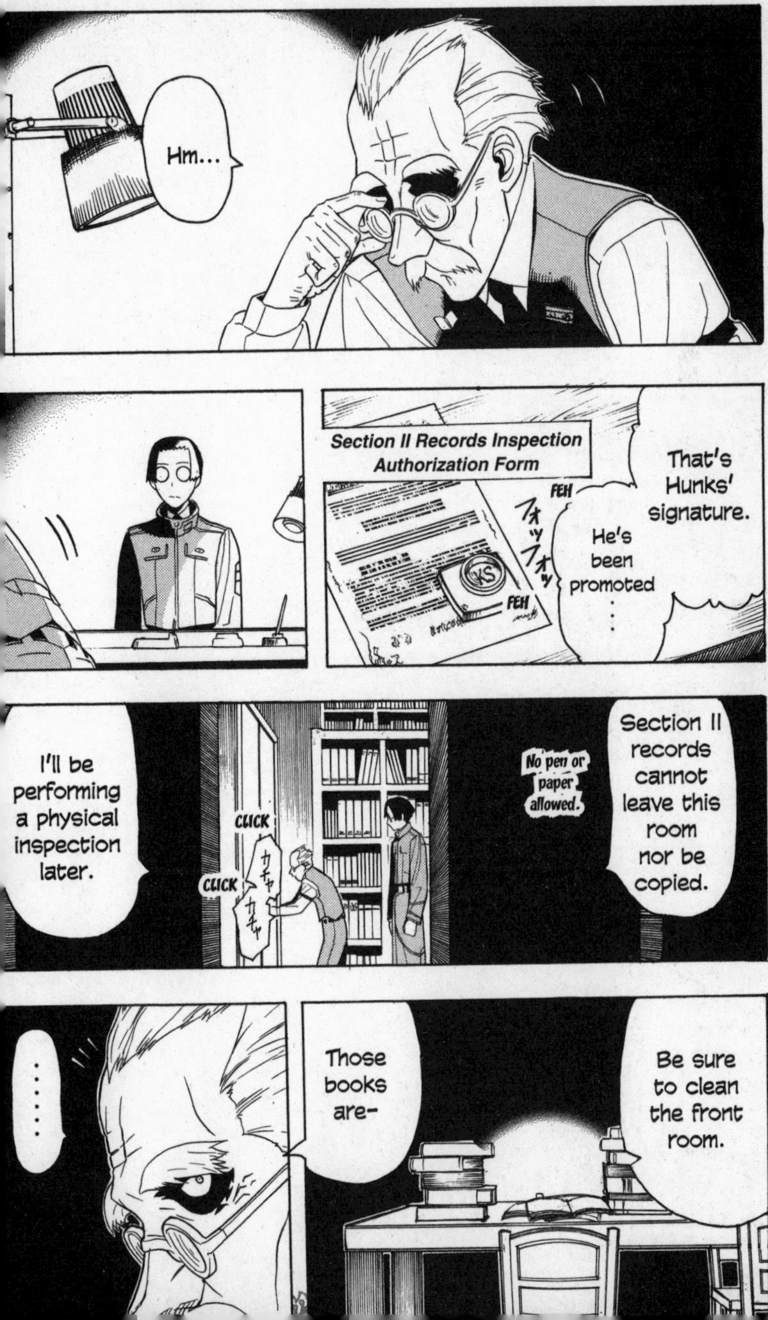

Hm...
Section II Records Inspection Authorization Form
That's Hunks' signature.
FEH
フォッフォッ
He's been promoted...
FEH
Section II records cannot leave this room nor be copied.
No pen or paper allowed.
CLICK
カチャ
CLICK
カチャ
I'll be performing a physical inspection later.
Be sure to clean the front room.
Those books are-
......

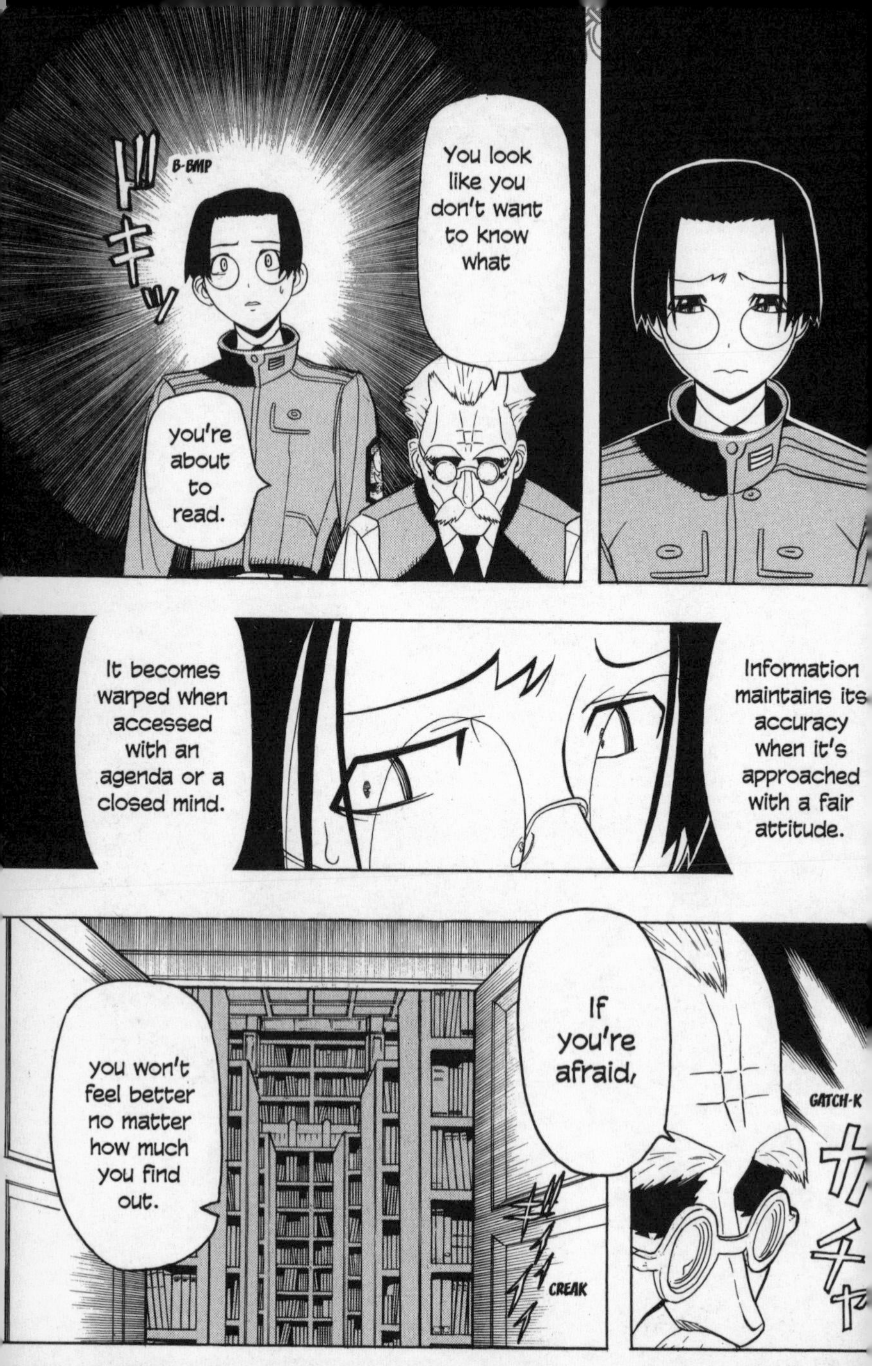
B-BMP
ドキッ
You look like you don't want to know what
you're about to read.
Information maintains its accuracy when it's approached with a fair attitude.
It becomes warped when accessed with an agenda or a closed mind.
If you're afraid,
GATCH-K
カチャ
you won't feel better no matter how much you find out.
CREAK

← NEXT!

PumpkinScissors

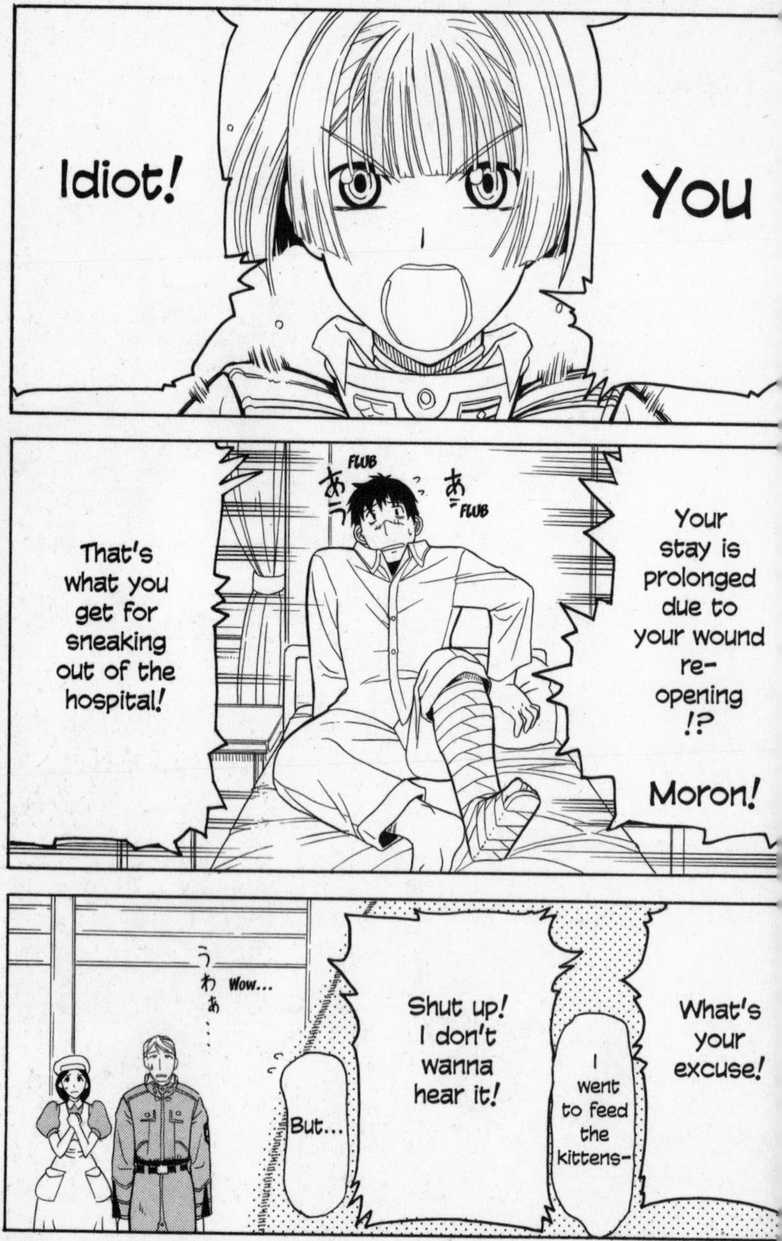
You
Idiot!
Your stay is prolonged due to your wound re-opening!?
Moron!
あ FLUB
あう FLUB
That's what you get for sneaking out of the hospital!
What's your excuse!
I went to feed the kittens-
Shut up! I don't wanna hear it!
But...
うわぁ... Wow...

† Episode 4 Superficial Men

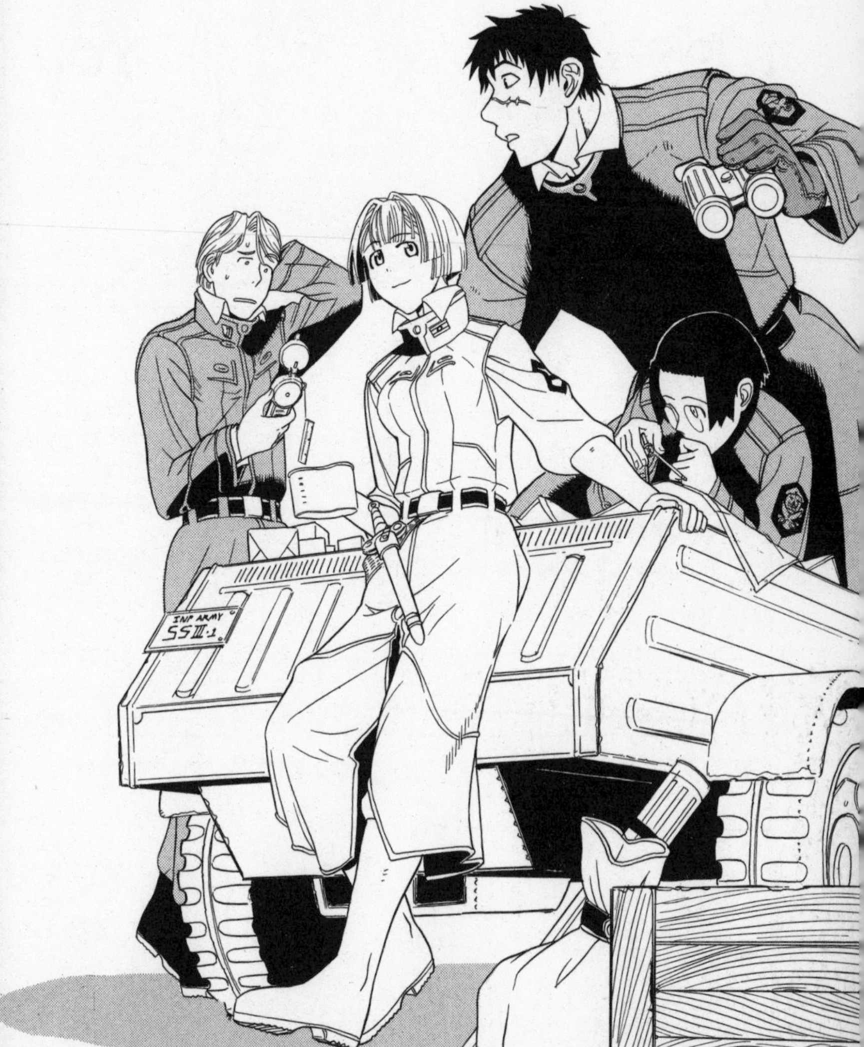
INP ARMY
SSIII·1

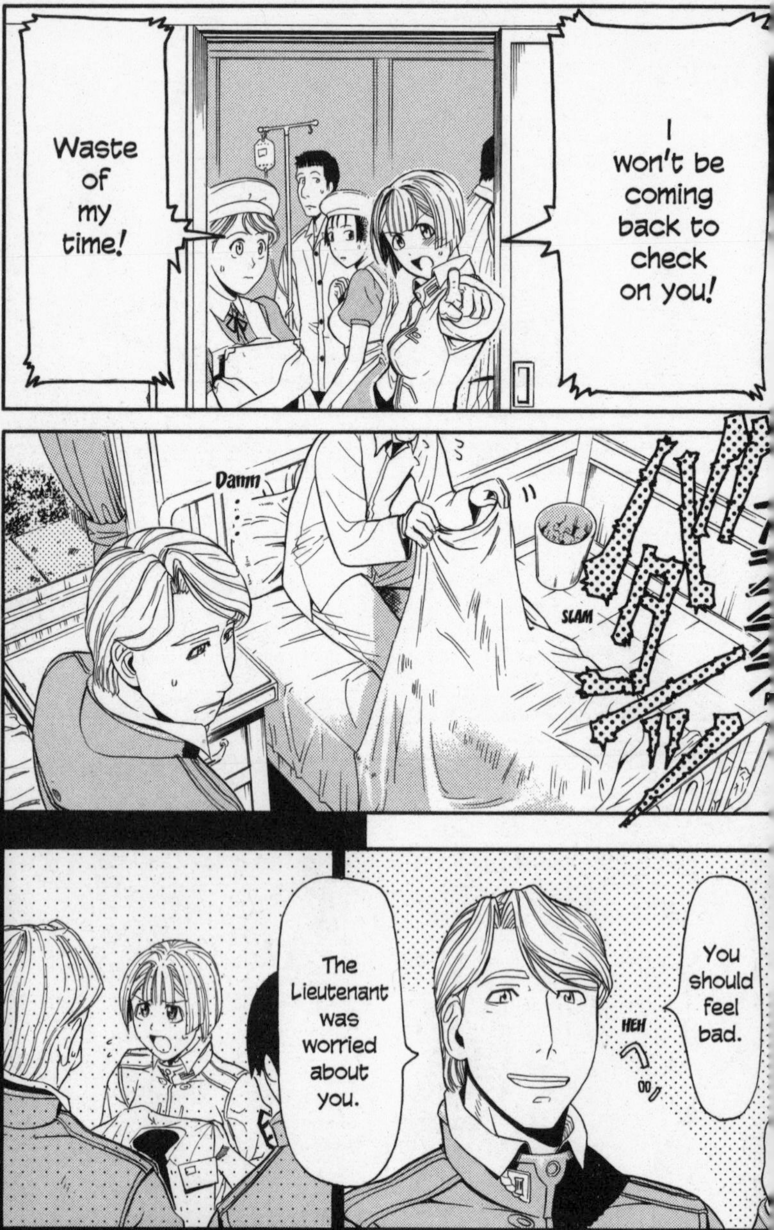
I won't be coming back to check on you!
Waste of my time!
SLAM
Damn
You should feel bad.
HEH
The Lieutenant was worried about you.

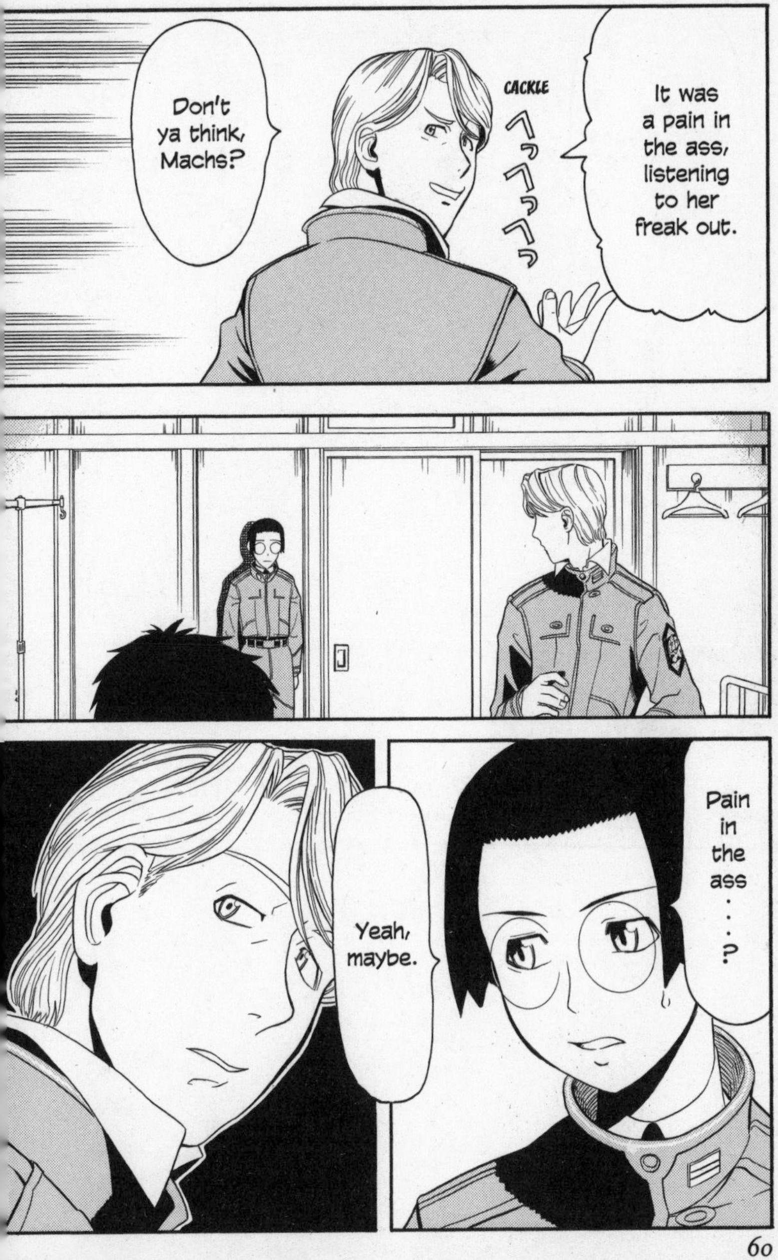
It was a pain in the ass, listening to her freak out.
CACKLE
Don't ya think, Machs?
Pain in the ass . . . ?
Yeah, maybe.

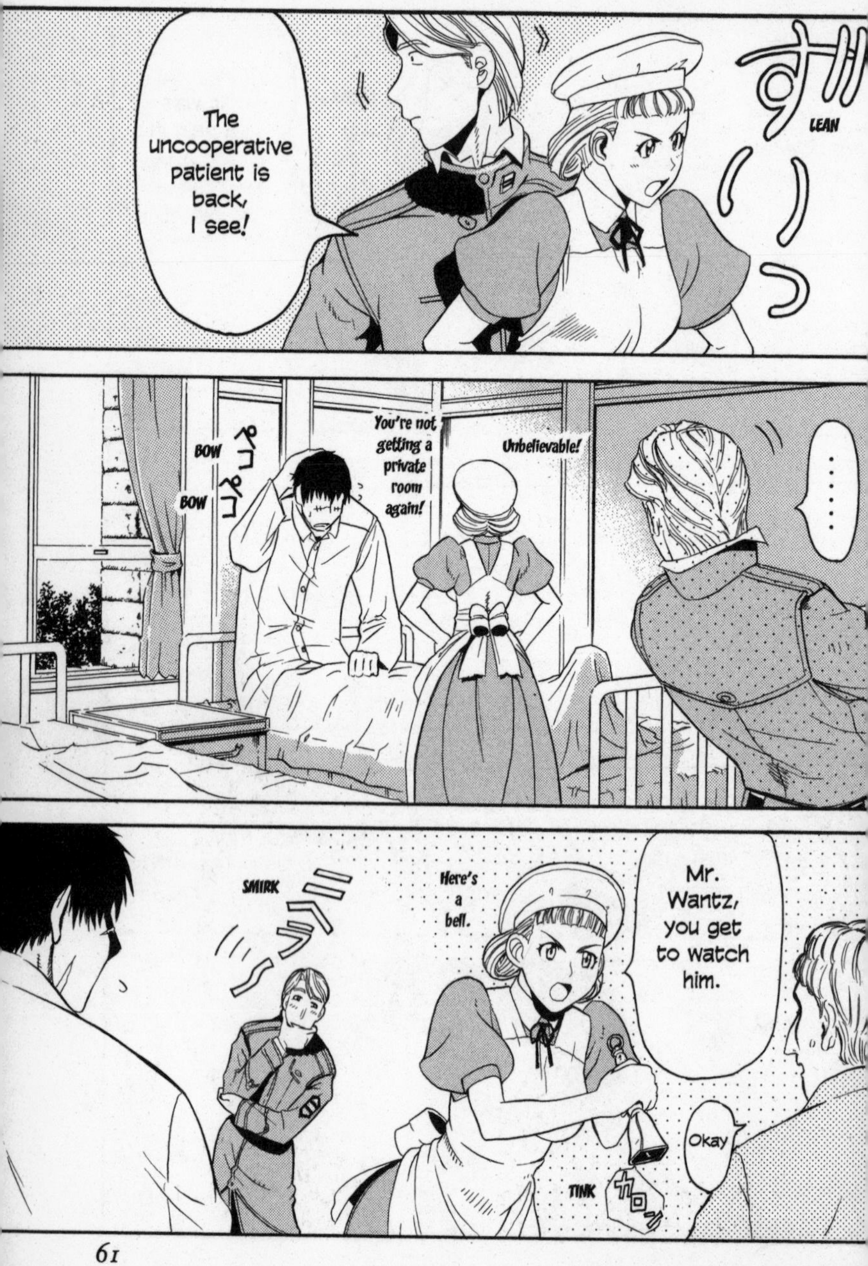

すいっ
LEAN
The uncooperative patient is back, I see!
......
Unbelievable!
You're not getting a private room again!
ペコペコ
BOW
BOW
Mr. Wantz, you get to watch him.
Okay
カロッ
TINK
Here's a bell.
SMIRK

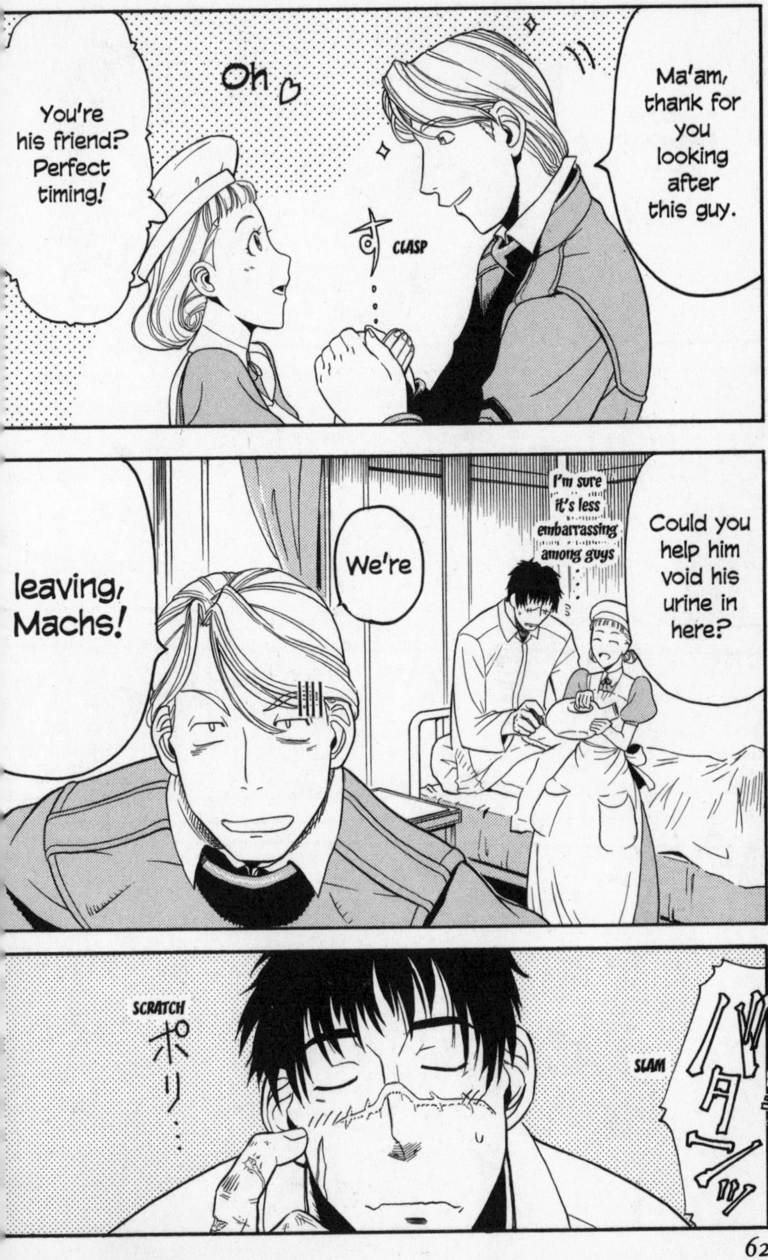
Ma'am, thank for you looking after this guy.
Oh ♡
CLASP
You're his friend? Perfect timing!
Could you help him void his urine in here?
I'm sure it's less embarrassing among guys
We're
leaving, Machs!
ROLLLL
SLAM
SCRATCH

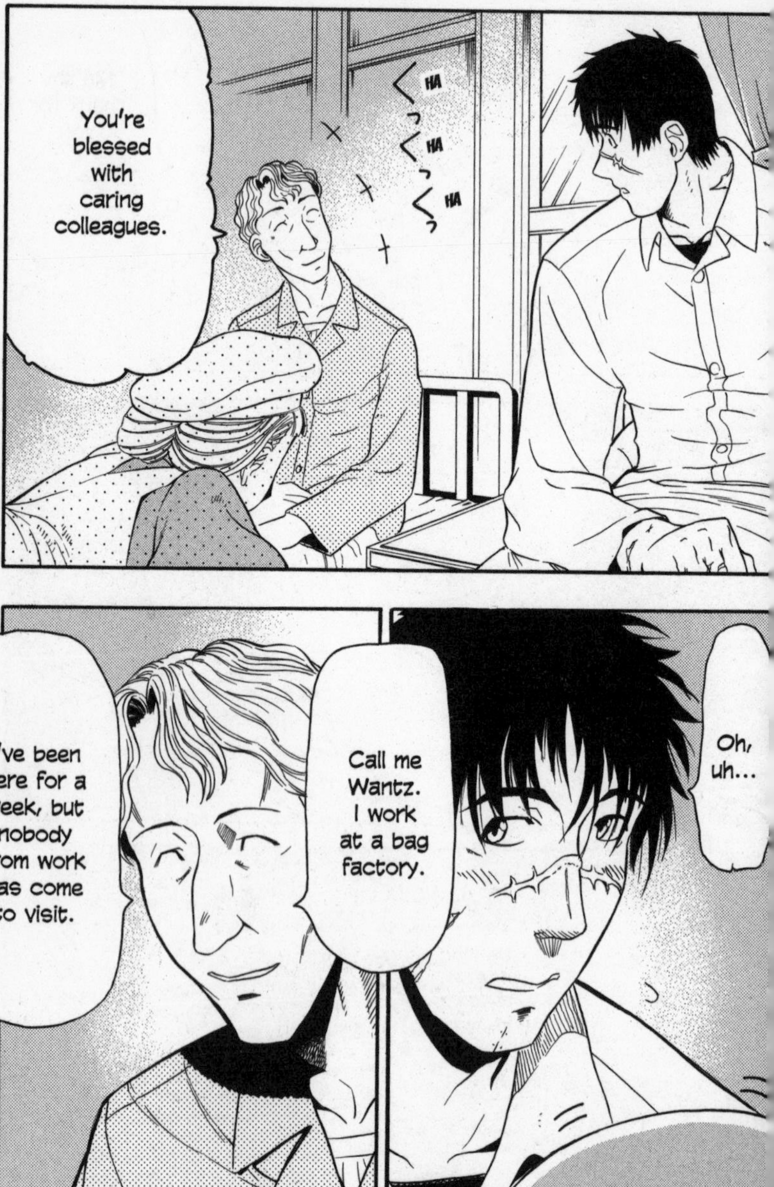
HA
HA
HA
You're blessed with caring colleagues.
Oh, uh...
Call me Wantz. I work at a bag factory.
I've been here for a week, but nobody from work has come to visit.

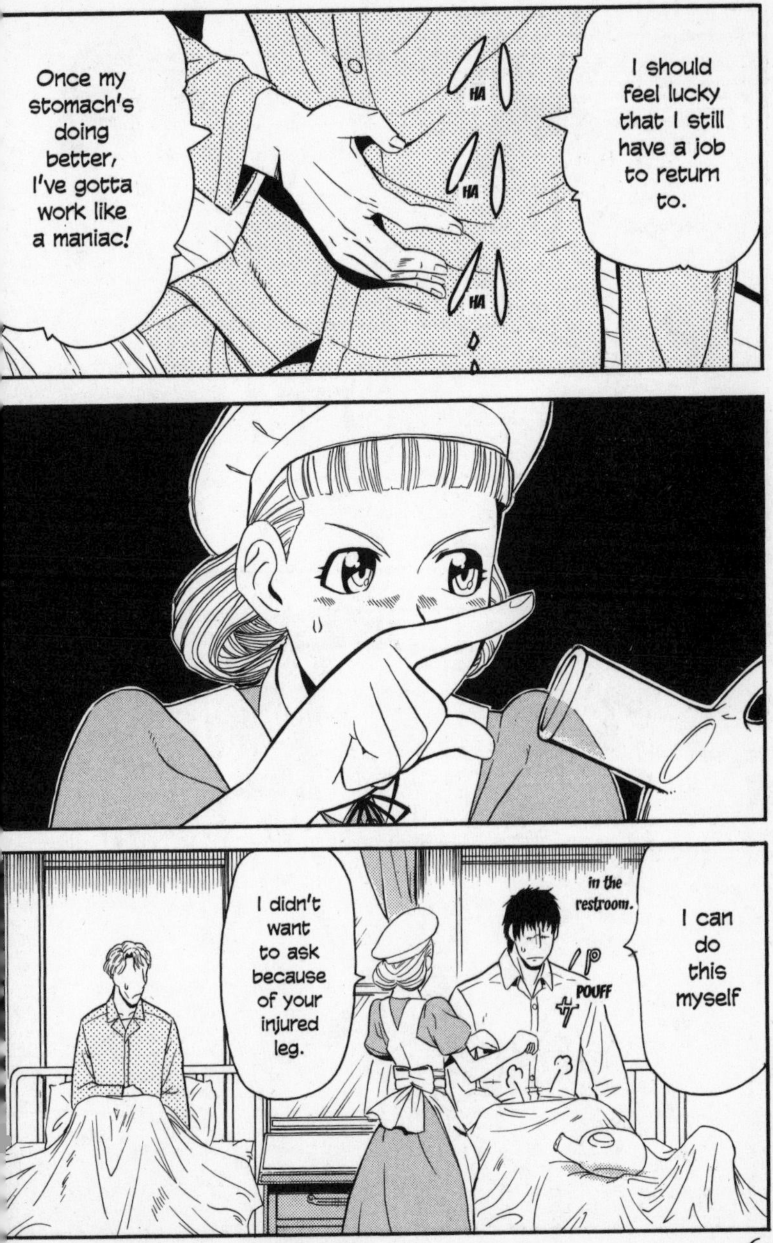
I should feel lucky that I still have a job to return to.
HA
HA
HA
Once my stomach's doing better, I've gotta work like a maniac!
I can do this myself
in the restroom.
POUFF
I didn't want to ask because of your injured leg.

Look for paper cups next to the entrance!

No prob...

I'm sorry! Excuse me.

THUD

Whoa!

Boss!?

How are you, Mr. Wantz?

...em

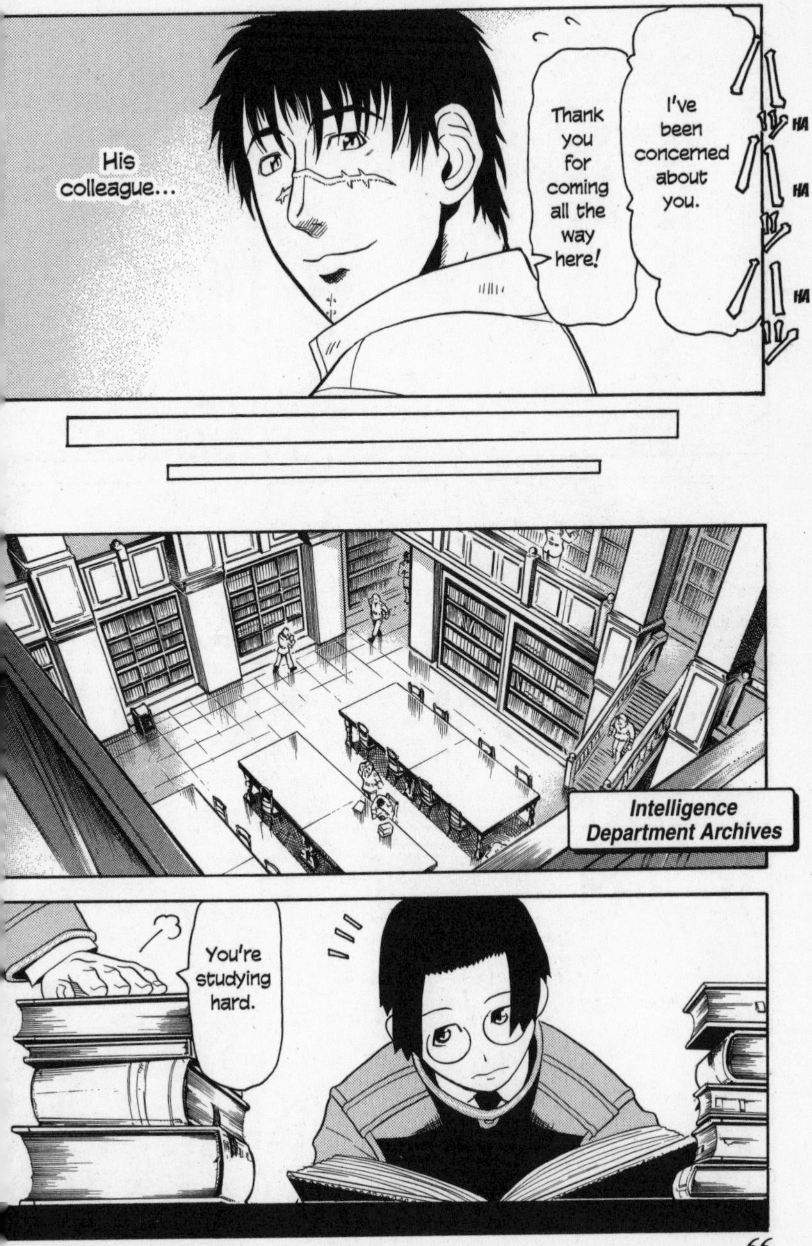
HA
HA
HA
I've been concerned about you.
Thank you for coming all the way here!
His colleague...
Intelligence Department Archives
You're studying hard.

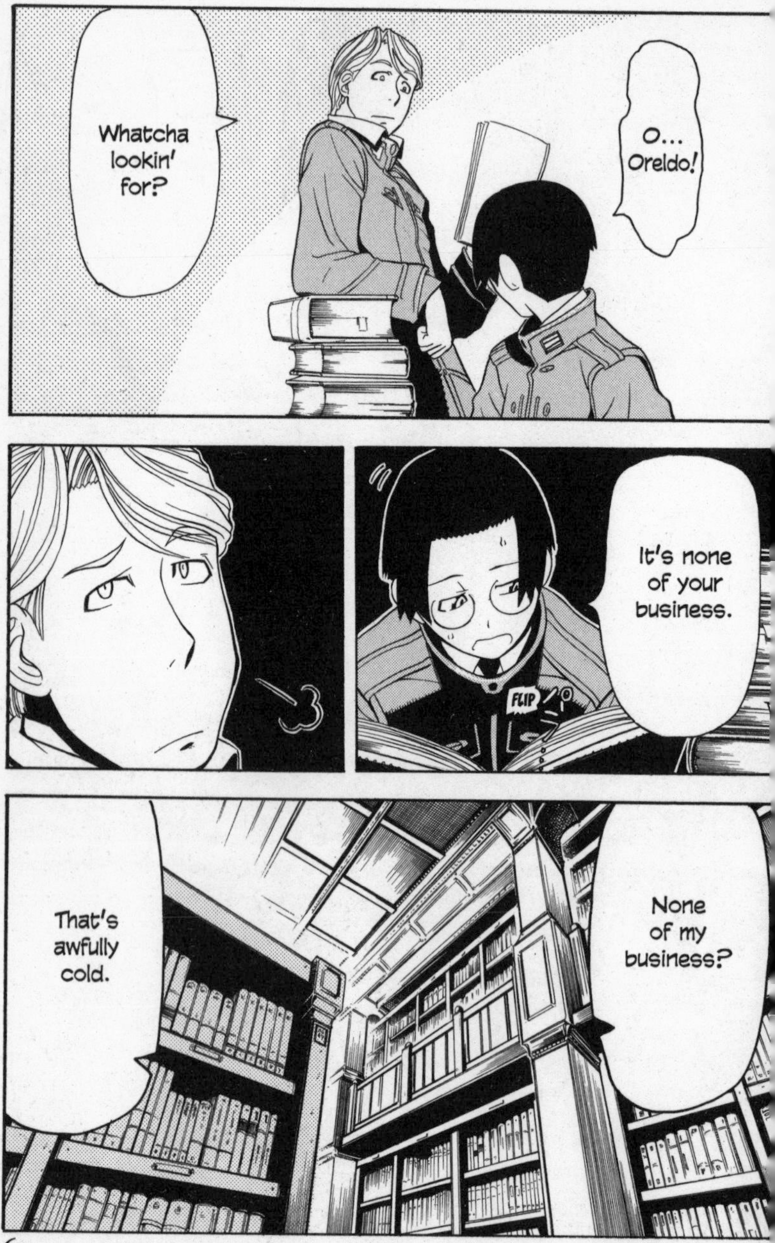
O... Oreldo!
Whatcha lookin' for?
It's none of your business.
FLIP
None of my business?
That's awfully cold.

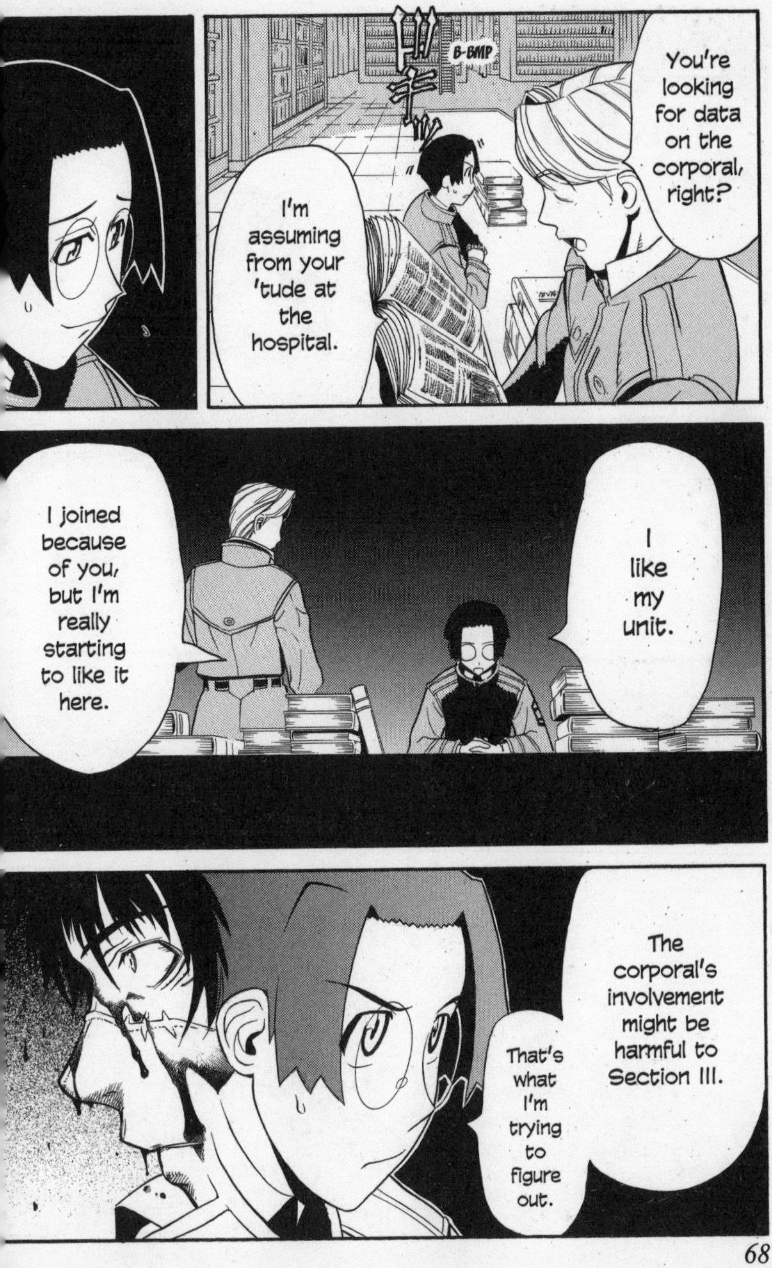
B-BMP
You're looking for data on the corporal, right?
I'm assuming from your 'tude at the hospital.
I like my unit.
I joined because of you, but I'm really starting to like it here.
The corporal's involvement might be harmful to Section III.
That's what I'm trying to figure out.

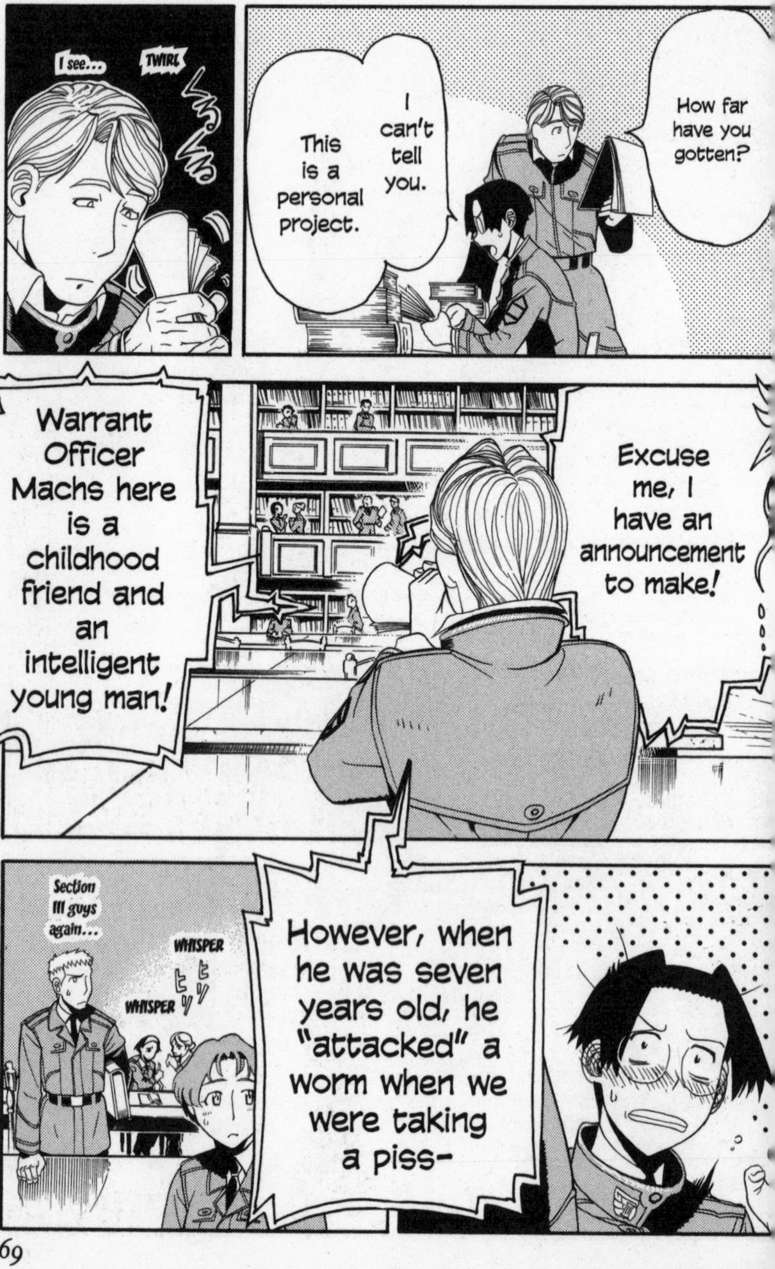
How far have you gotten?
I can't tell you.
This is a personal project.
I see...
TWIRL
Excuse me, I have an announcement to make!
Warrant Officer Machs here is a childhood friend and an intelligent young man!
However, when he was seven years old, he "attacked" a worm when we were taking a piss-
Section III guys again...
WHISPER
WHISPER

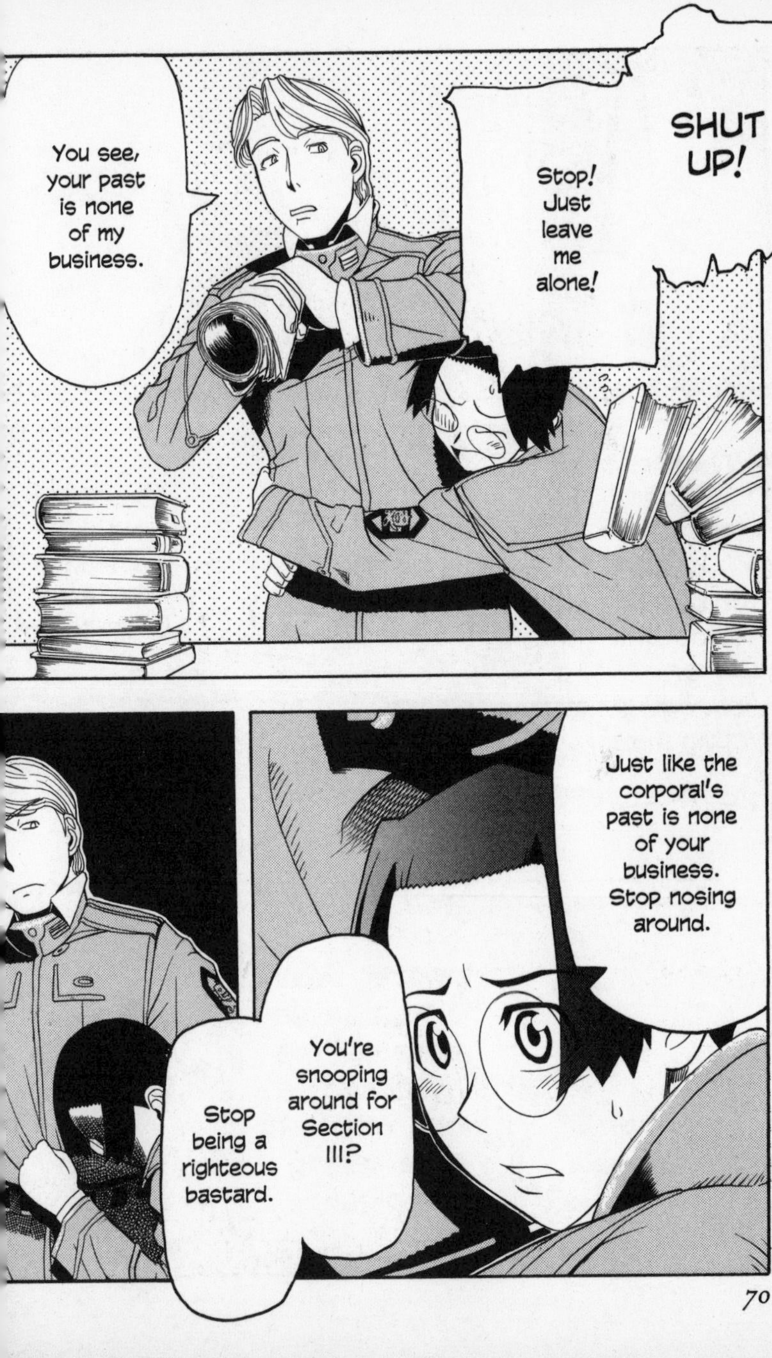
SHUT UP!
Stop! Just leave me alone!
You see, your past is none of my business.
Just like the corporal's past is none of your business. Stop nosing around.
You're snooping around for Section III?
Stop being a righteous bastard.

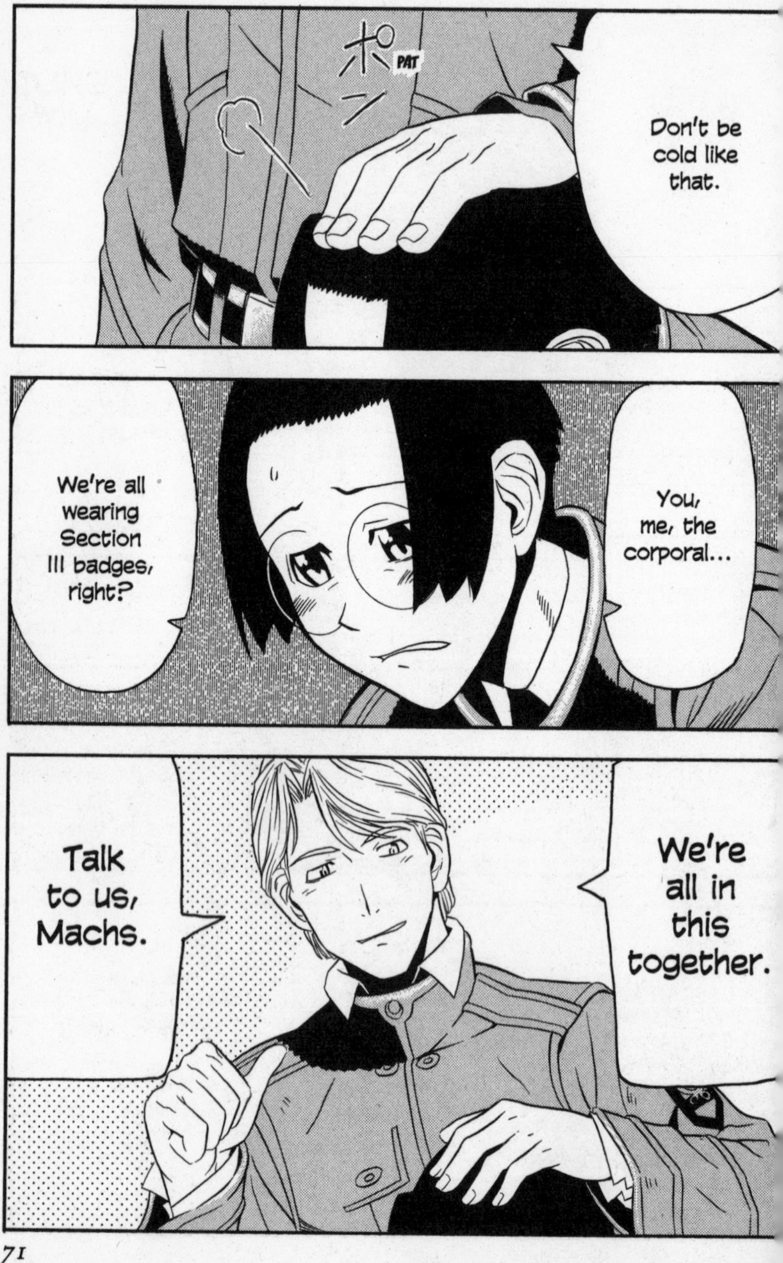
ポン
PAT
Don't be cold like that.
You, me, the corporal...
We're all wearing Section III badges, right?
We're all in this together.
Talk to us, Machs.

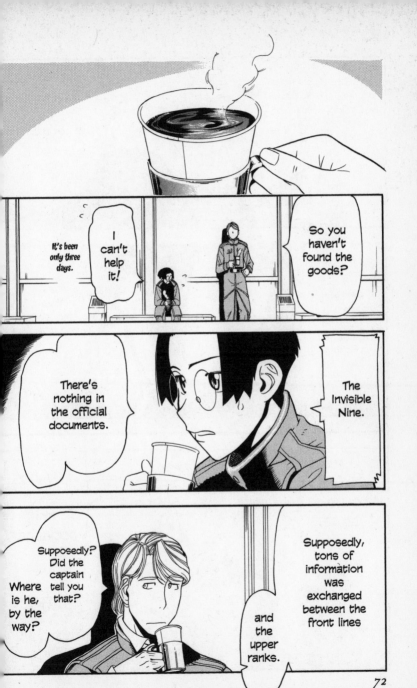

It's been only three days.
I can't help it!
So you haven't found the goods?
There's nothing in the official documents.
The Invisible Nine.
Where is he, by the way?
Supposedly? Did the captain tell you that?
Supposedly, tons of information was exchanged between the front lines
and the upper ranks.

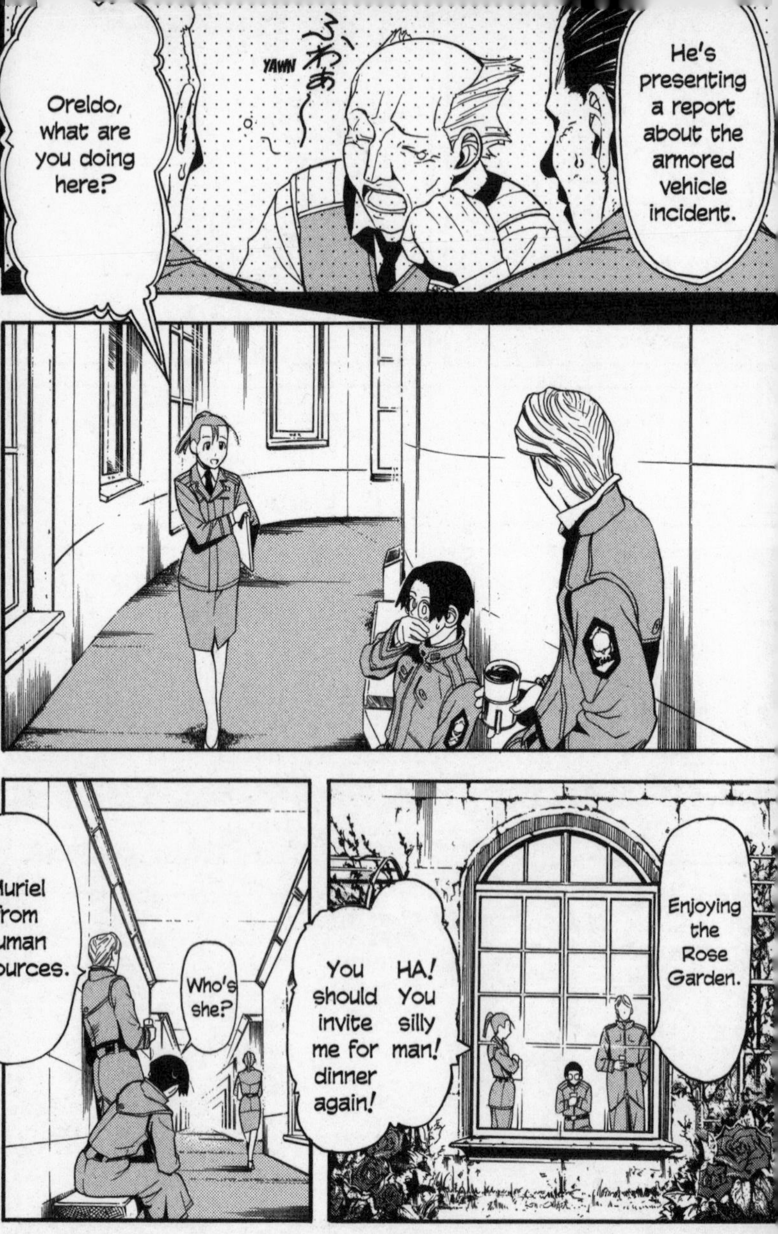

He's presenting a report about the armored vehicle incident.
ふわあ~
YAWN
Oreldo, what are you doing here?
Enjoying the Rose Garden.
HA! You silly man!
You should invite me for dinner again!
Who's she?
Muriel from human resources.

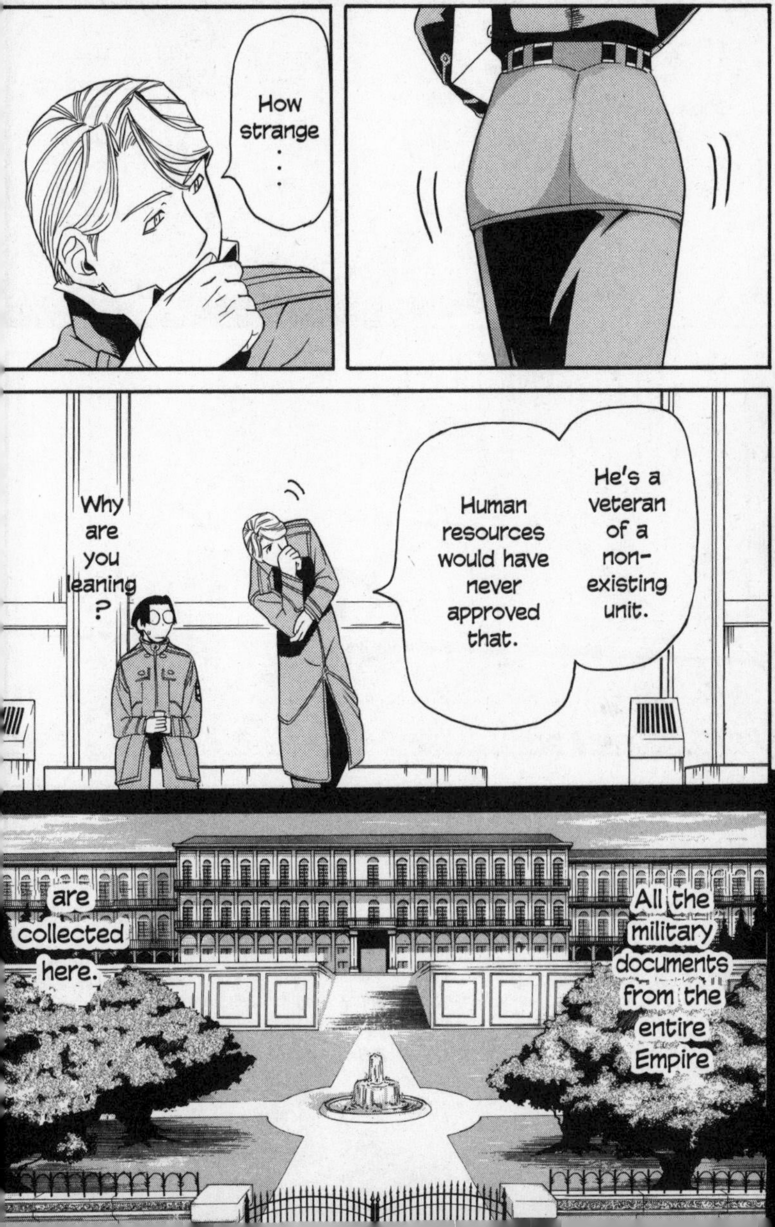
How strange . . .
He's a veteran of a non-existing unit.
Human resources would have never approved that.
Why are you leaning?
All the military documents from the entire Empire
are collected here.

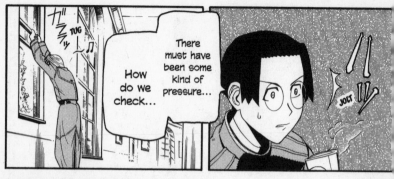

JOLT
There must have been some kind of pressure...
How do we check...
TUG
SNAP
SMIRK
I'll take care of this.
Oreldo, I can't!
People will be back soon!
Stop!
Human Resources Department

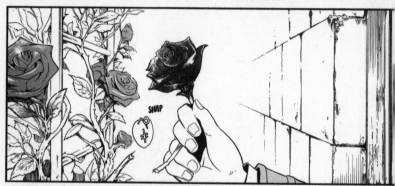

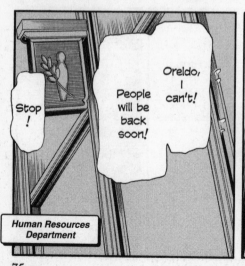

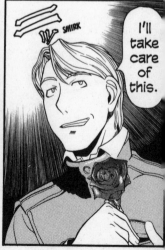

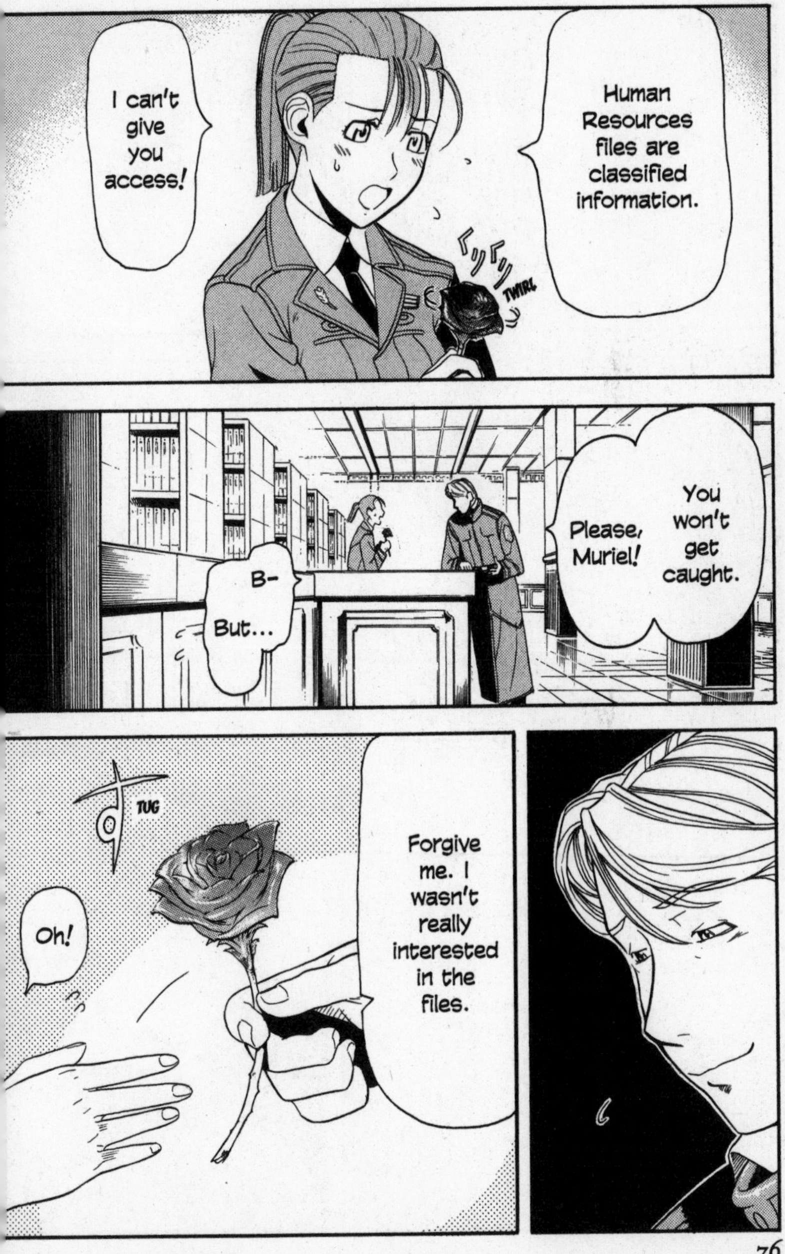
Human Resources files are classified information.
I can't give you access!
TWIRL
Please, Muriel! You won't get caught.
B- But...
Forgive me. I wasn't really interested in the files.
TUG
Oh!

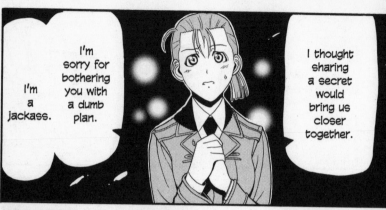

I thought sharing a secret would bring us closer together.
I'm sorry for bothering you with a dumb plan.
I'm a jackass.
.....
Good-bye.
Make sure you're
done before the others come back.

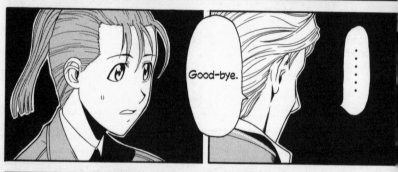

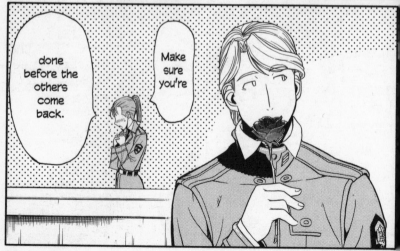

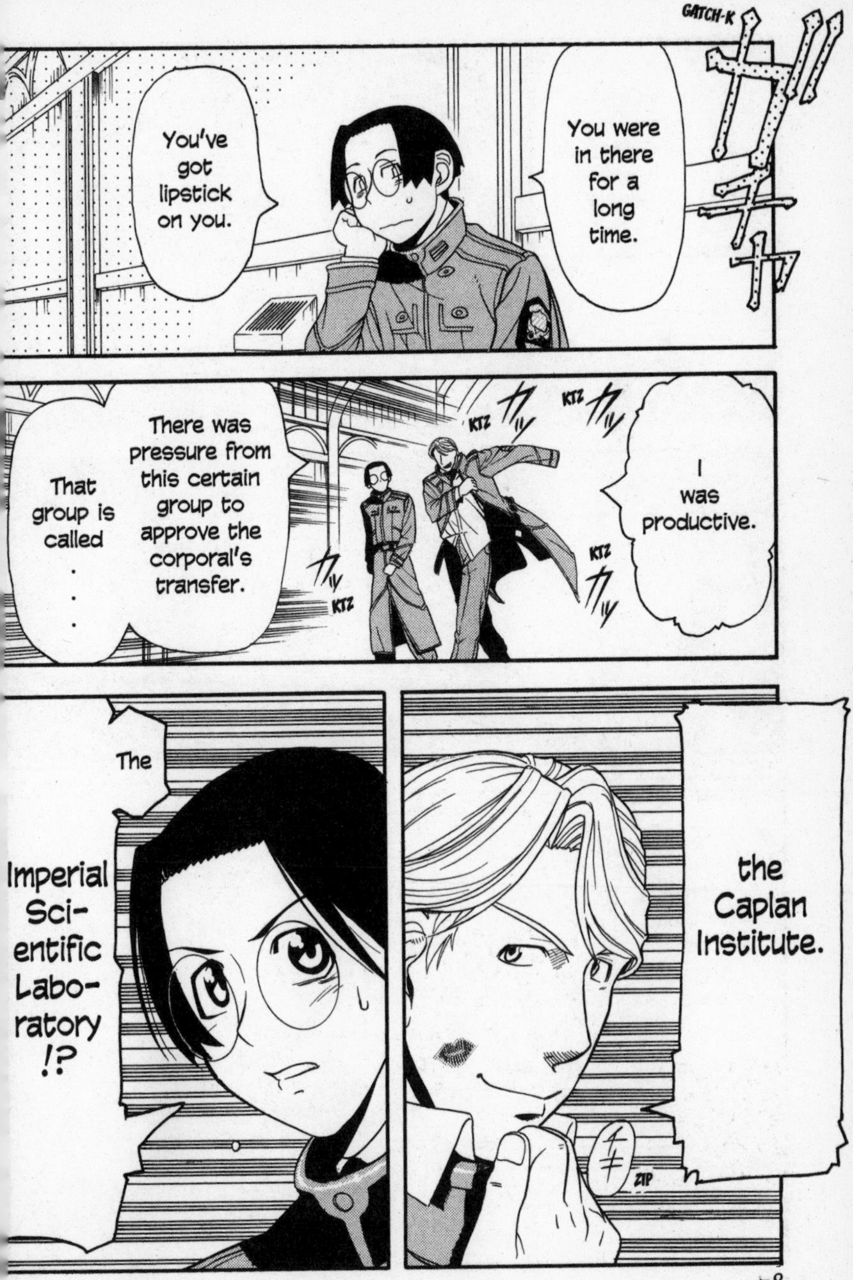
GATCH-K
You were in there for a long time.
You've got lipstick on you.
KTZ
KTZ
KTZ
KTZ
I was productive.
There was pressure from this certain group to approve the corporal's transfer.
That group is called . . .
the Caplan Institute.
ZIP
The
Imperial Sci-entific Labo-ratory !?

They'll have more information on the corporal...

I'm sorry, Oreldo.

SQUEEZE

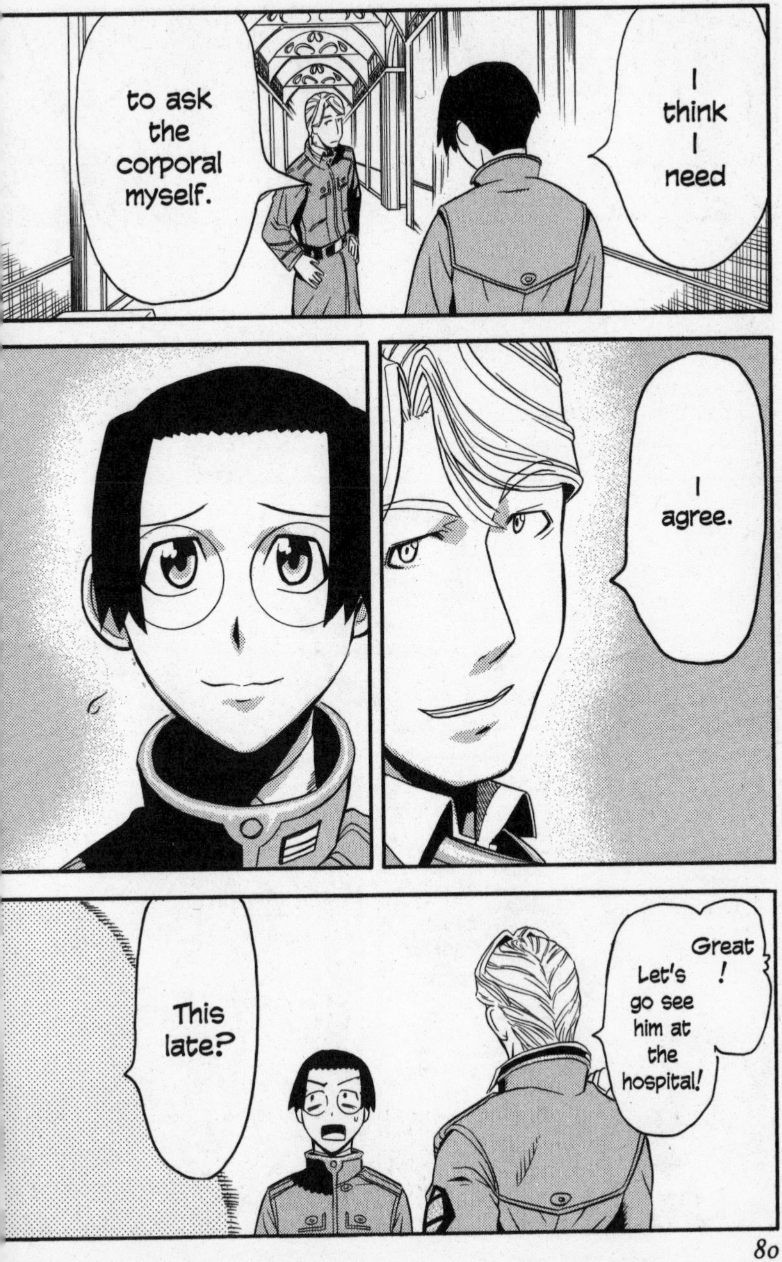
I think I need
to ask the corporal myself.
I agree.
Great!
Let's go see him at the hospital!
This late?

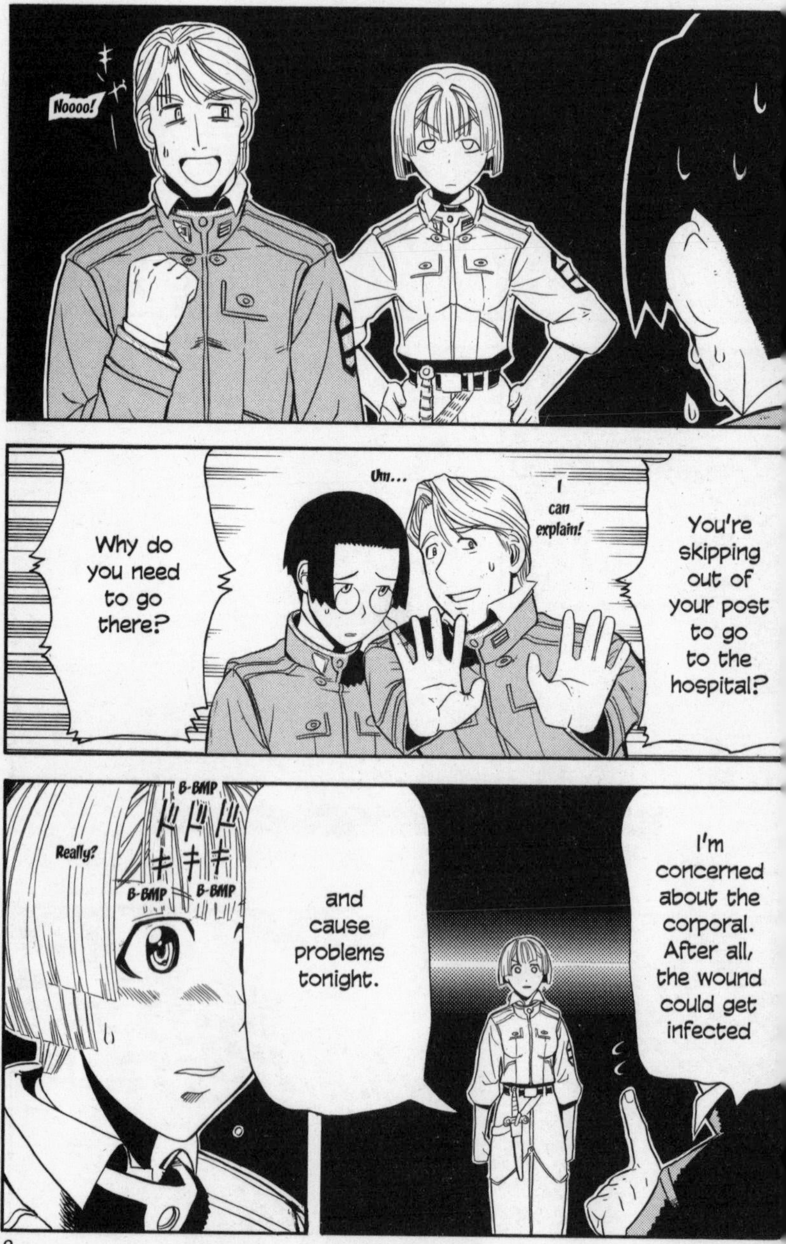
Noooo!
You're skipping out of your post to go to the hospital?
I can explain!
Um...
Why do you need to go there?
I'm concerned about the corporal. After all, the wound could get infected
and cause problems tonight.
B-BMP
B-BMP
B-BMP
Really?

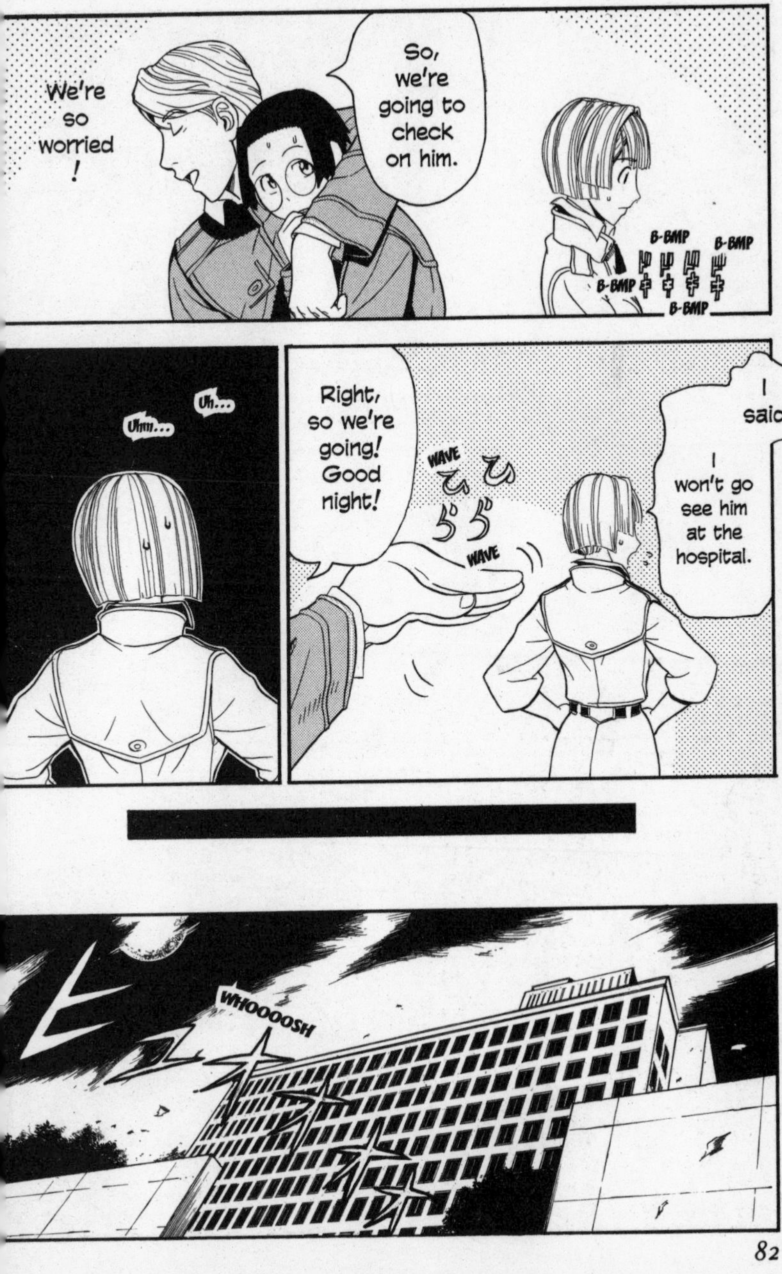
So, we're going to check on him.
We're so worried!
B-BMP B-BMP B-BMP B-BMP
I said
I won't go see him at the hospital.
Right, so we're going! Good night!
WAVE
WAVE
Uh...
Umm...
WHOOOOSH

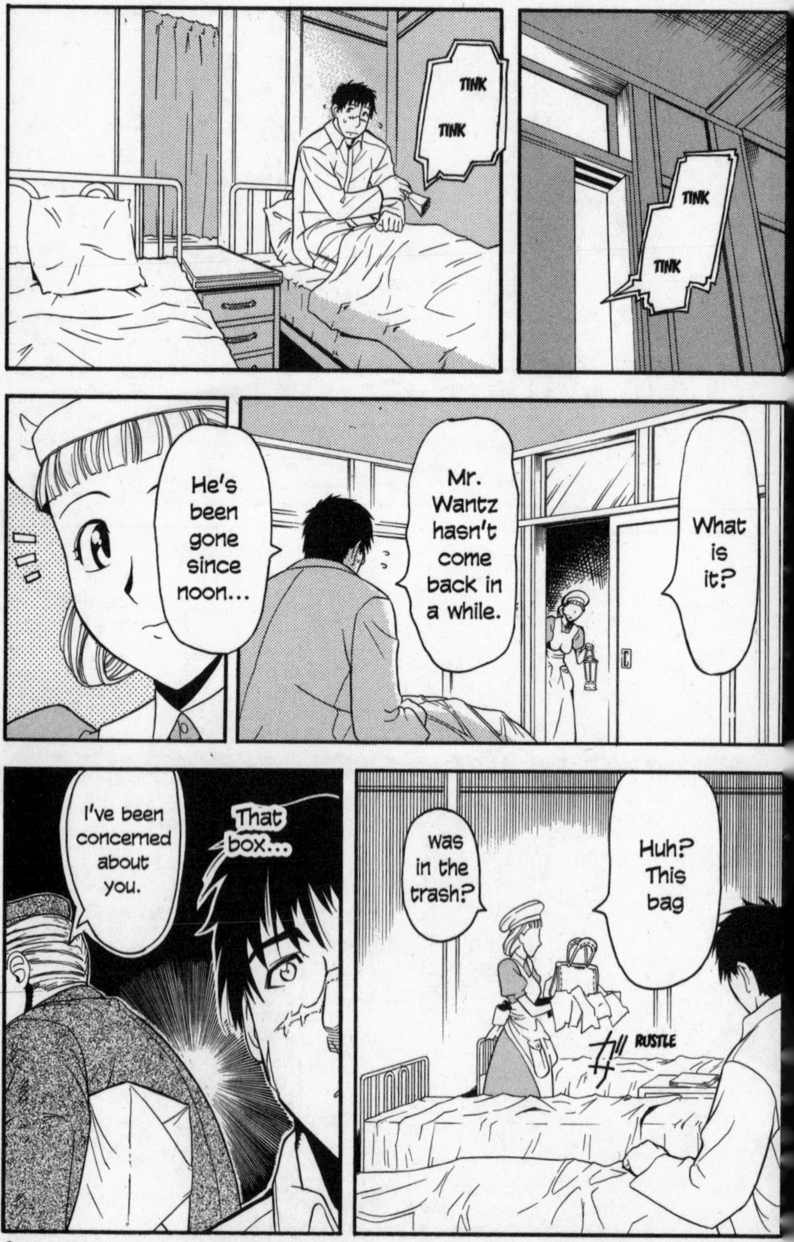
TINK
TINK
TINK
TINK
What is it?
Mr. Wantz hasn't come back in a while.
He's been gone since noon...
Huh? This bag
was in the trash?
RUSTLE
That box...
I've been concerned about you.

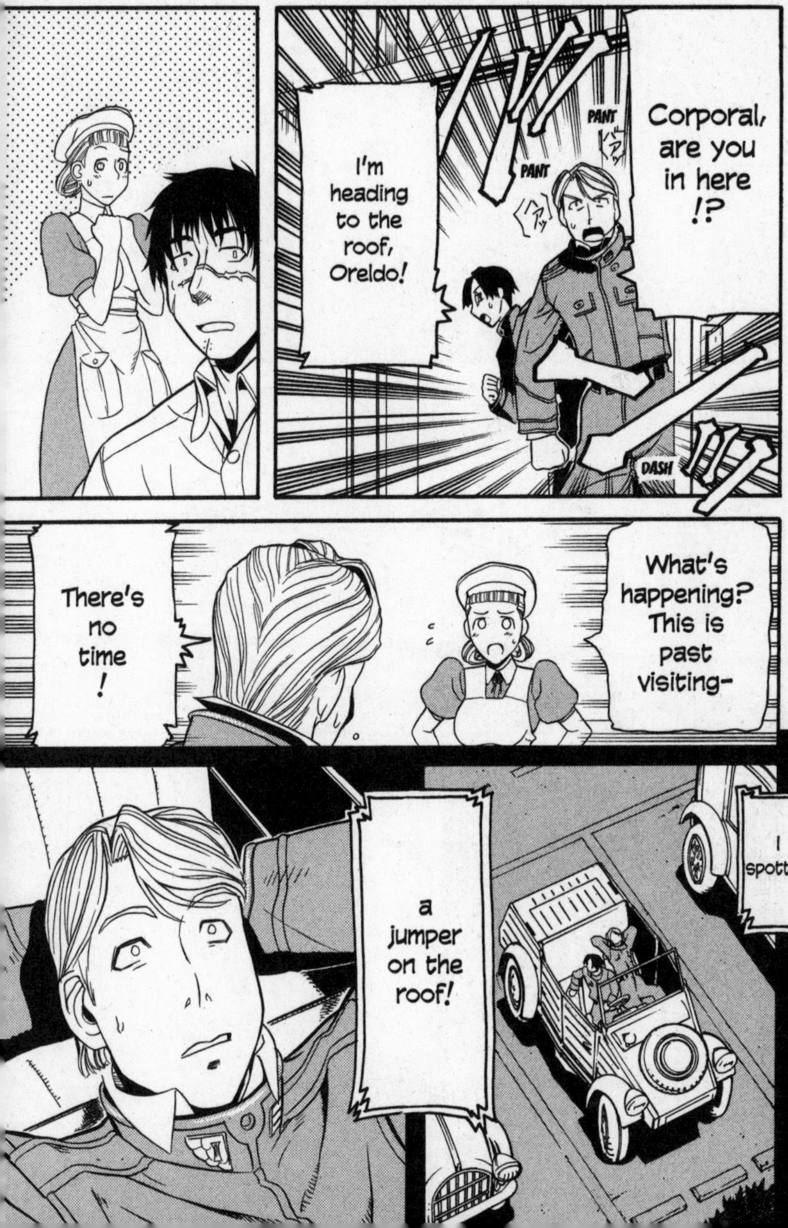
Corporal, are you in here!?
PANT
PANT
I'm heading to the roof, Oreldo!
DASH
What's happening? This is past visiting-
There's no time!
I spotted
a jumper on the roof!

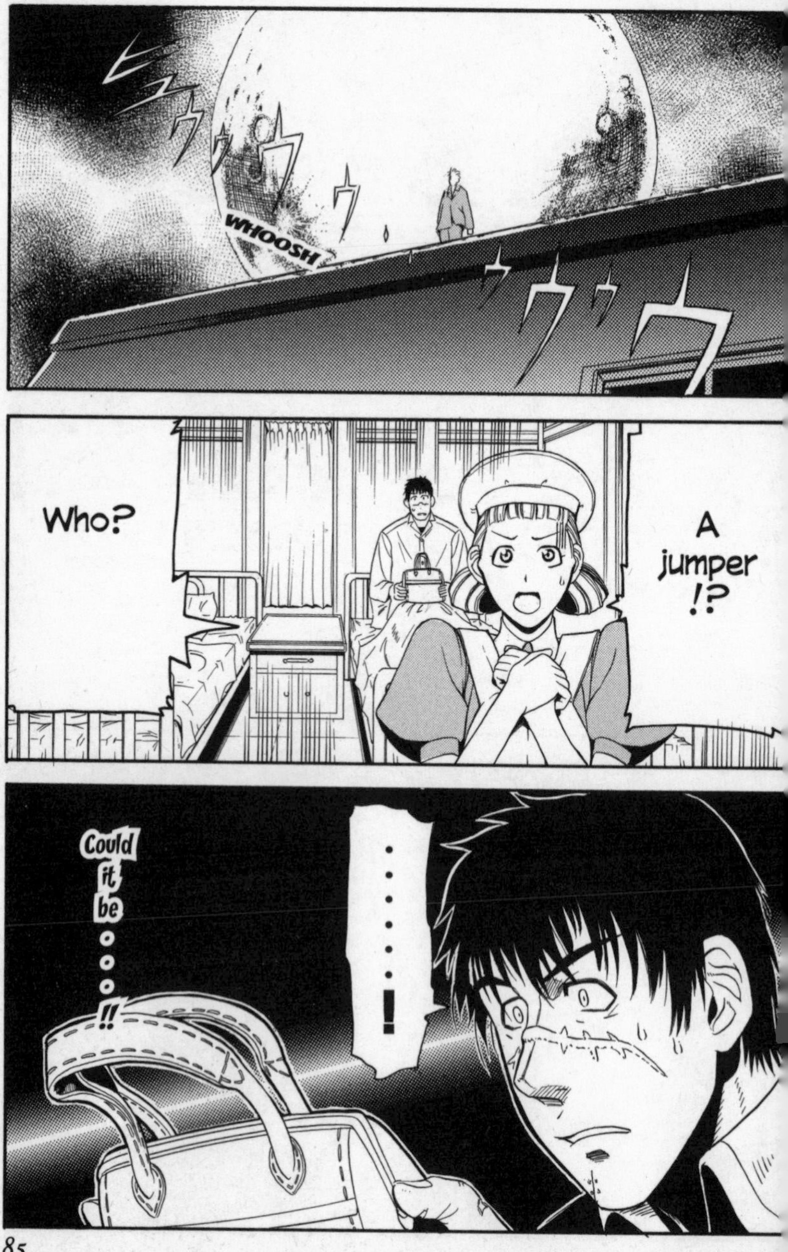
WHOOSH
A jumper!?
Who?
......!
Could it be...!!

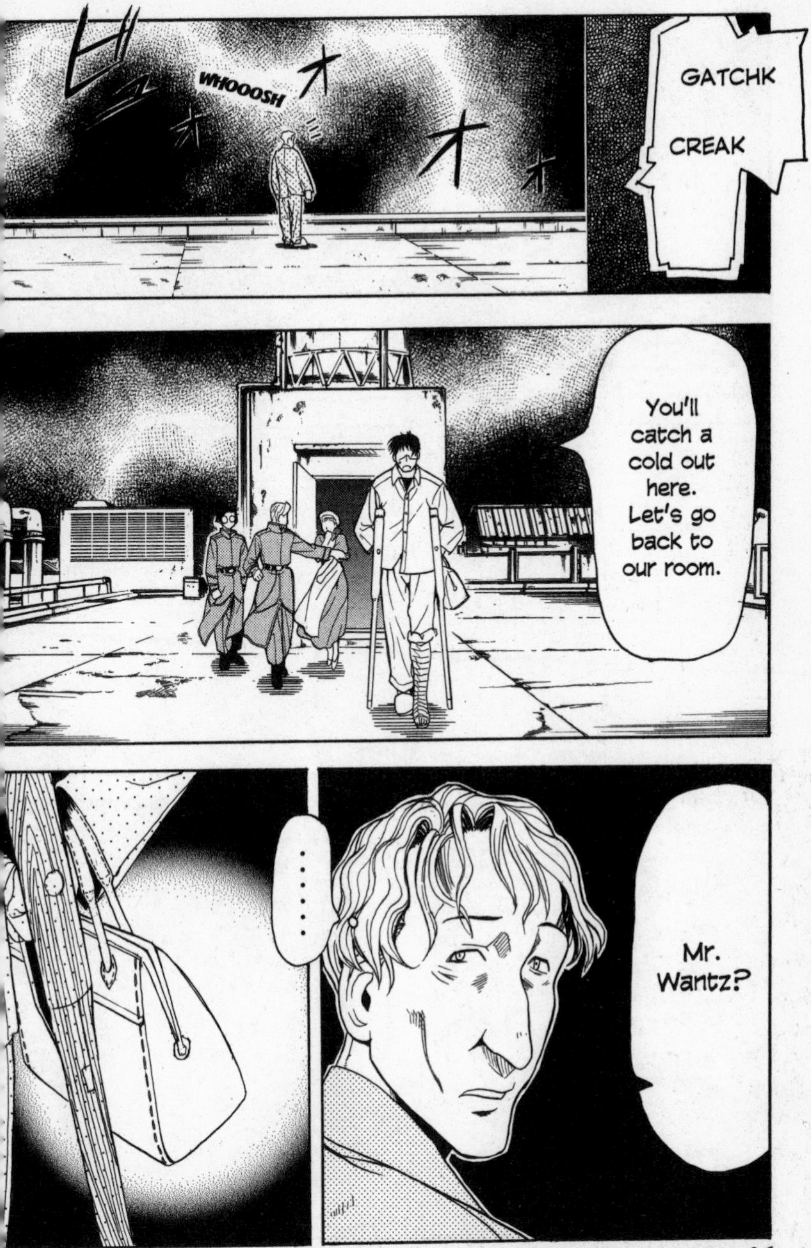
GATCHK
CREAK
WHOOOSH
You'll catch a cold out here. Let's go back to our room.
Mr. Wantz?
......

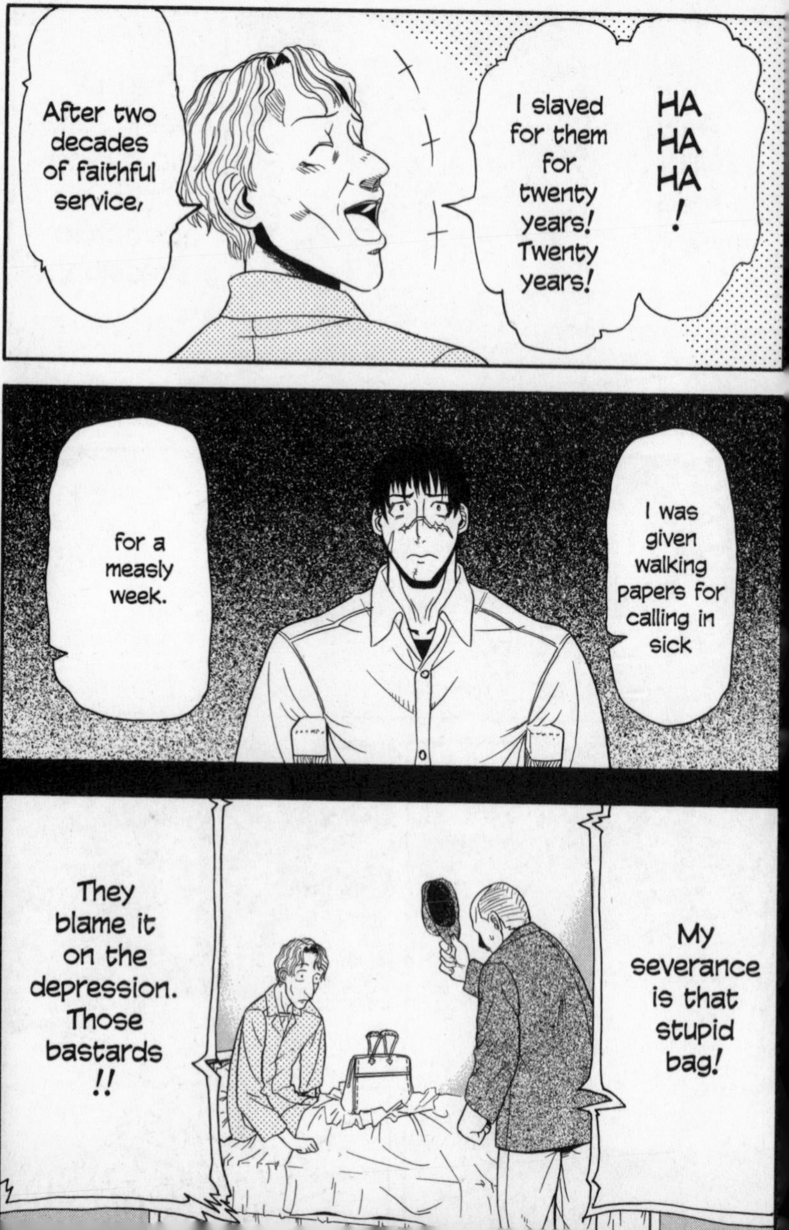
HA HA HA!
I slaved for them for twenty years! Twenty years!
After two decades of faithful service,
I was given walking papers for calling in sick
for a measly week.
My severance is that stupid bag!
They blame it on the depression. Those bastards!!

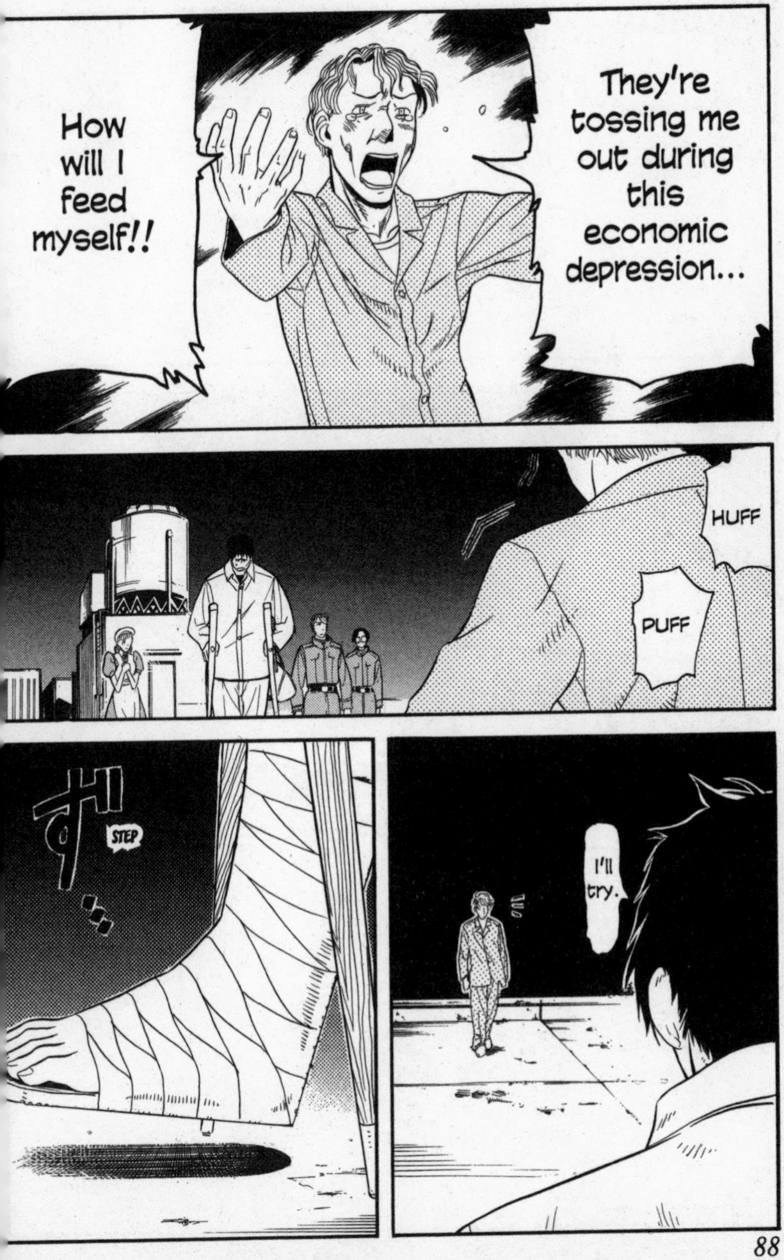
They're tossing me out during this economic depression...
How will I feed myself!!
HUFF
PUFF
I'll try.
す
STEP

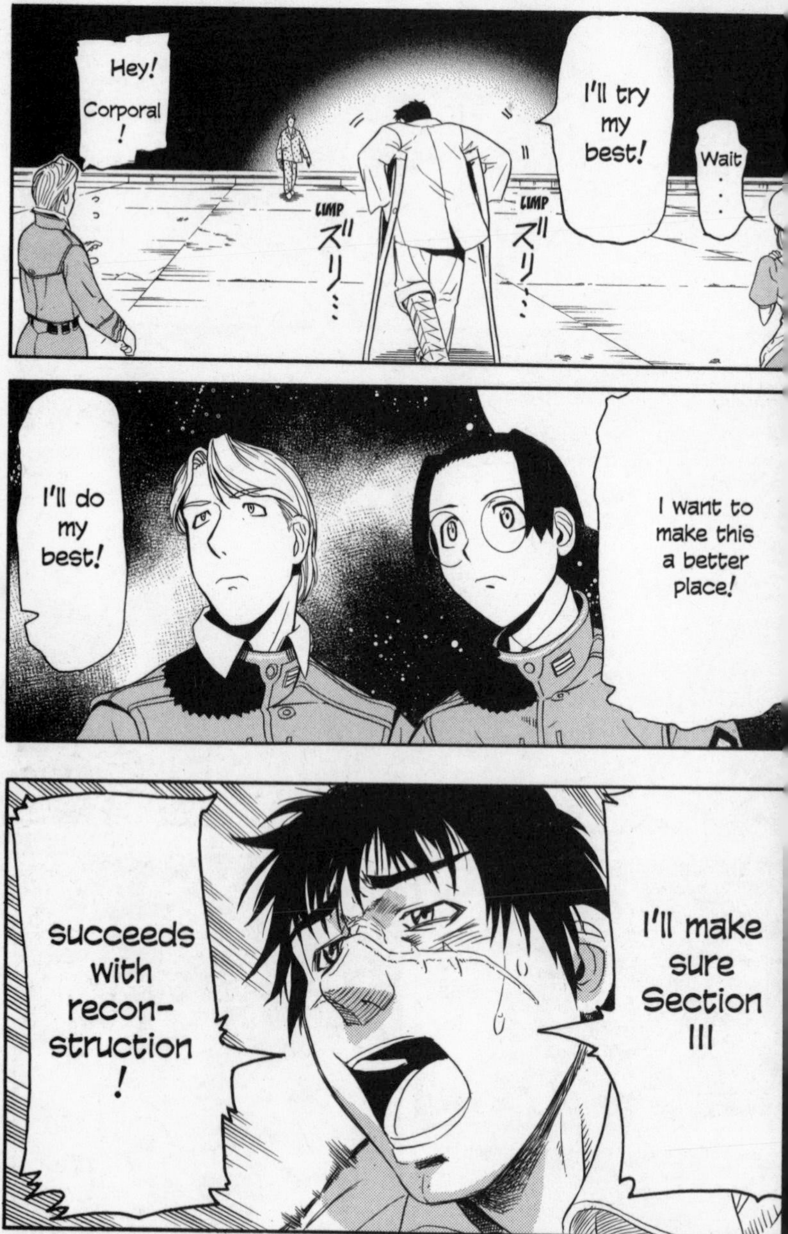
Wait...
I'll try my best!
LIMP
ズリ…
LIMP
ズリ…
Hey! Corporal!
I want to make this a better place!
I'll do my best!
I'll make sure Section III
succeeds with recon-struction!

TWITCH

Stop!

Don't come any closer!

WHIOOOOSH

I can't help him!

WHIOOOO

FLAP
FLAP

He's too far...

B-BMP

B-BMP

B-BMP

B-BMP

Can I run fast enough?
Can I run at all?
ズキン
STABB
ズキン
STABB
ガクガク
SHAKE
SHAKE
No. I can't ignore the pain.
My knees are shaking from fear...
SQUEEZE
I can go on a murderous rampage
when I have my lantern.

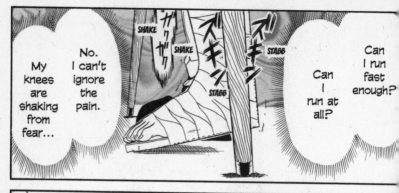

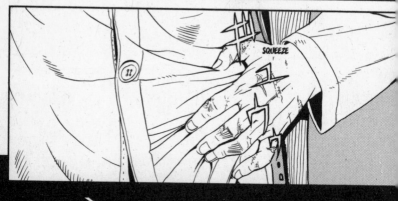

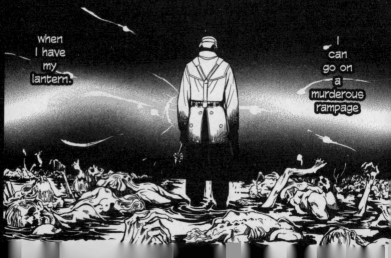

Without my lantern,

I'm useless.

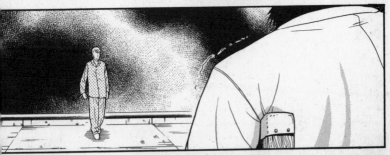

You're a kind man. We may be roommates,

but this doesn't concern you.

Let me be.

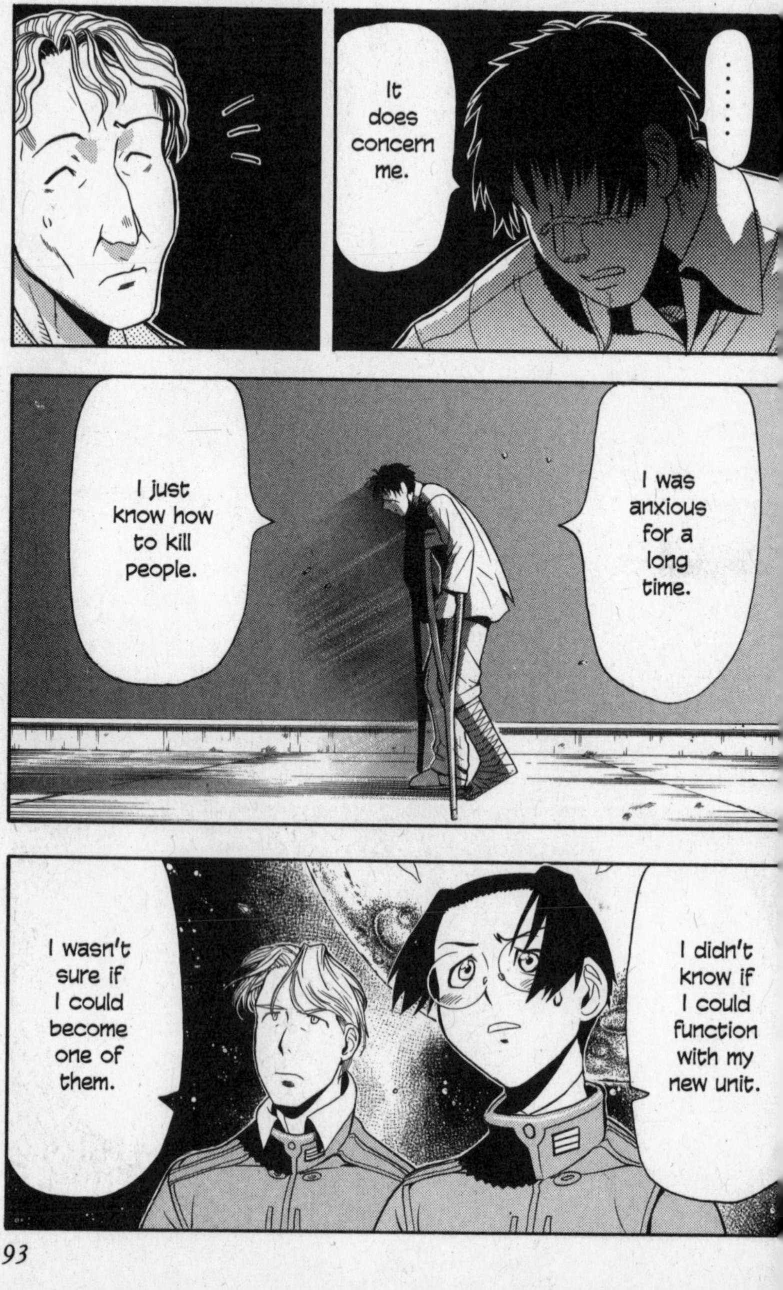
......
It does concern me.
I was anxious for a long time.
I just know how to kill people.
I didn't know if I could function with my new unit.
I wasn't sure if I could become one of them.

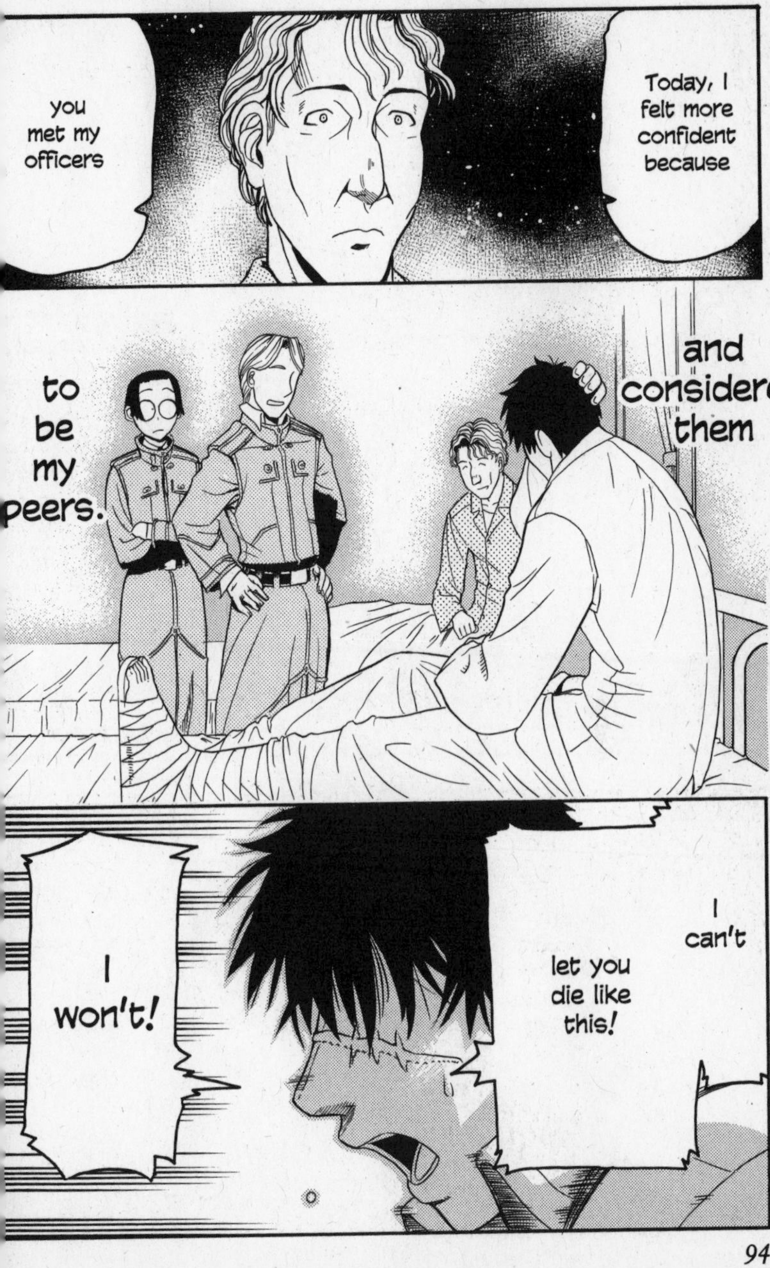
Today, I felt more confident because
you met my officers
and considered them
to be my peers.
I can't
let you die like this!
I won't!

You're being selfish...

I'm sorry.

I made a difference to you, even though we just met earlier today.

HAHA

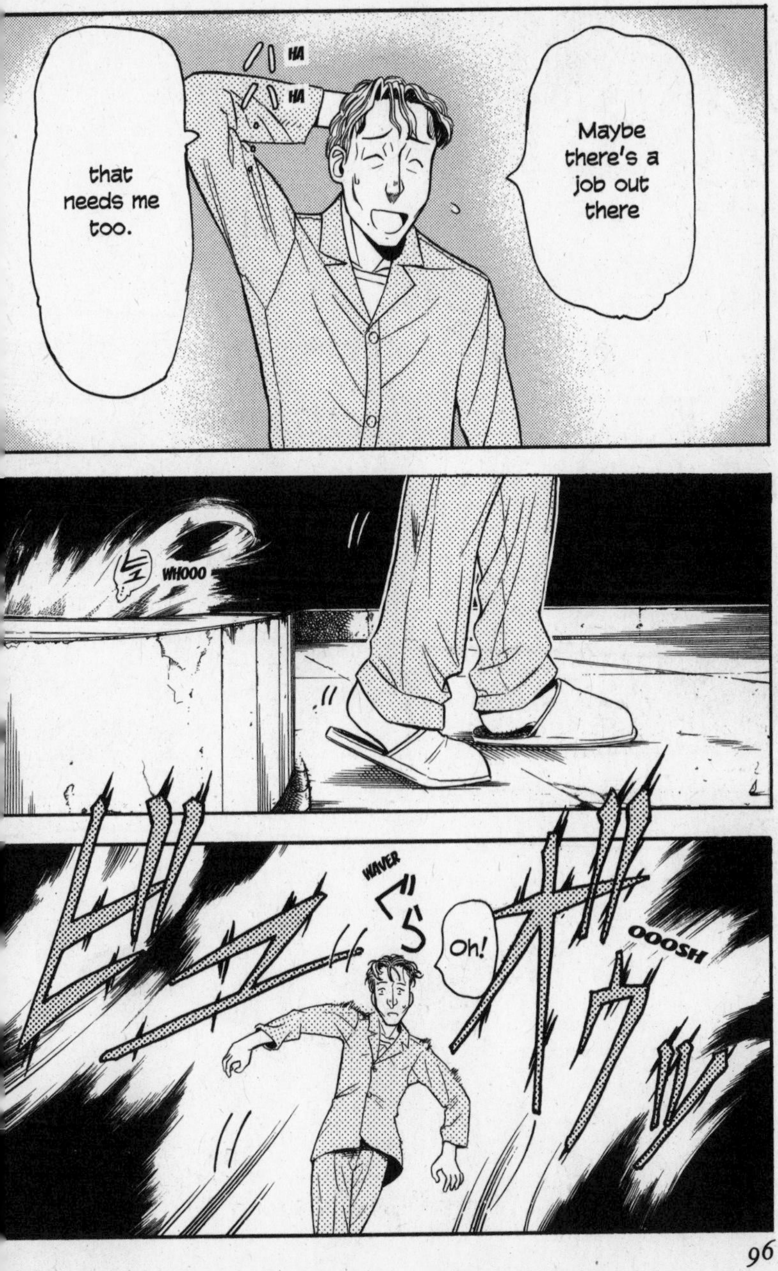
Maybe there's a job out there
HA
HA
that needs me too.
WHOOO
OOOSH
Oh!
WAVER

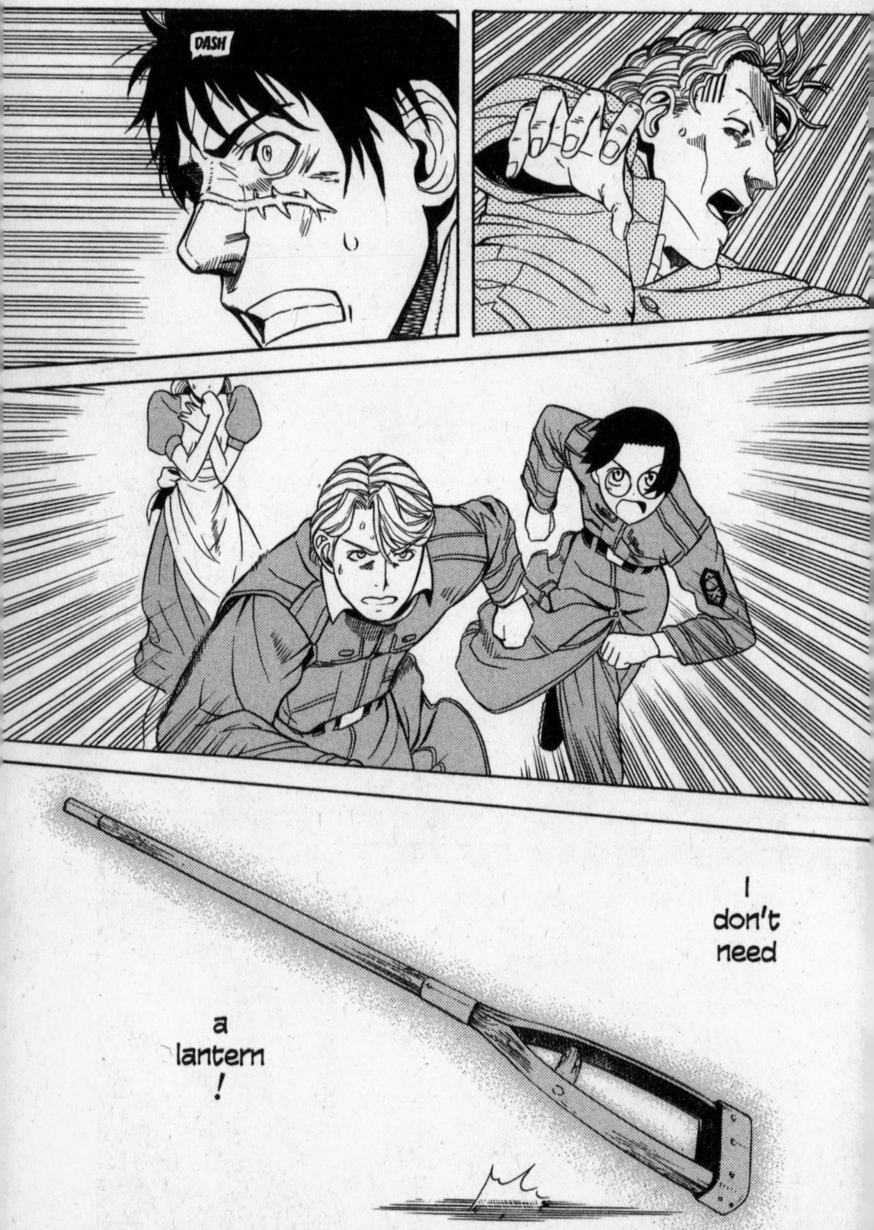
DASH
I don't need
a lantern!

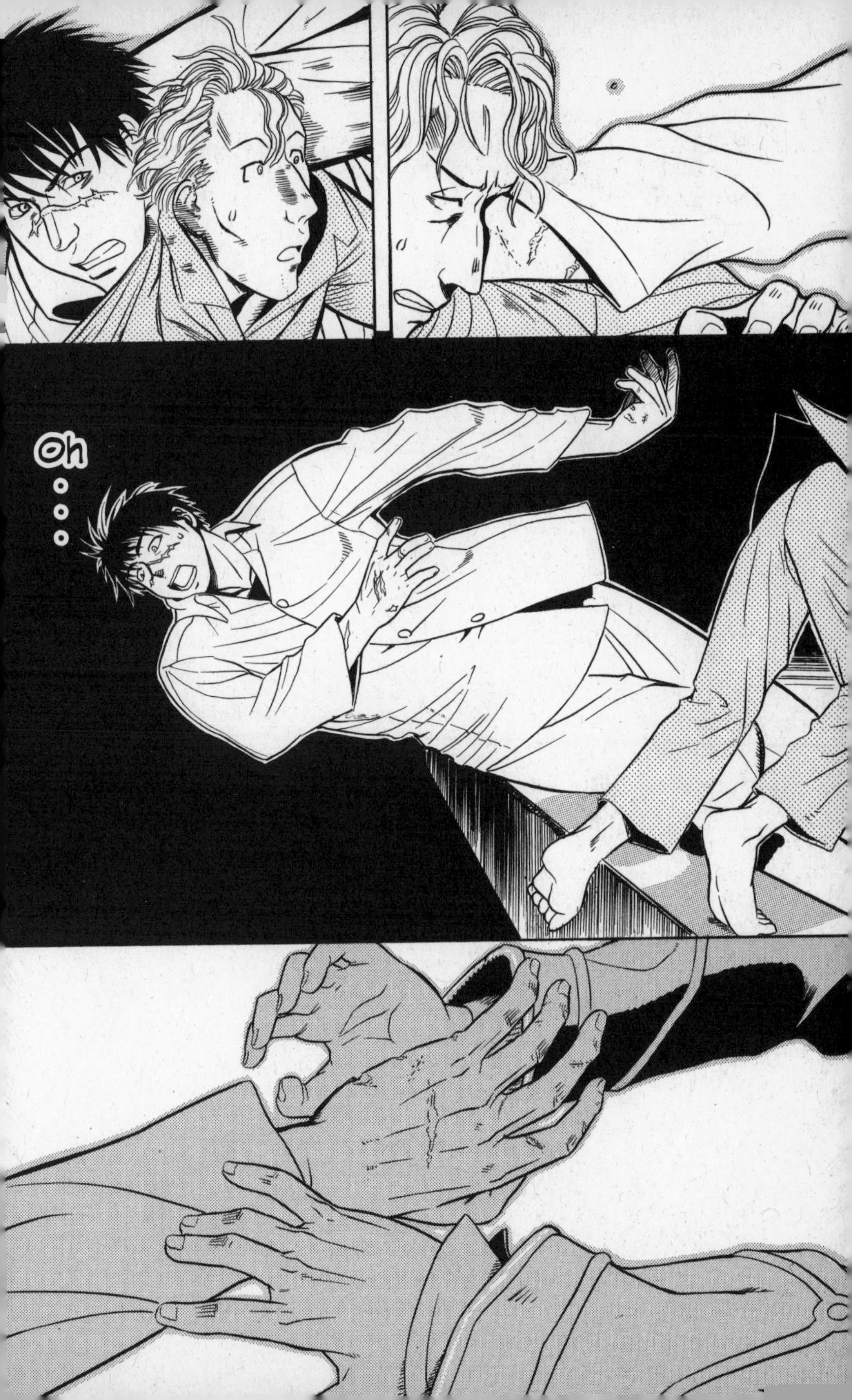
Oh...

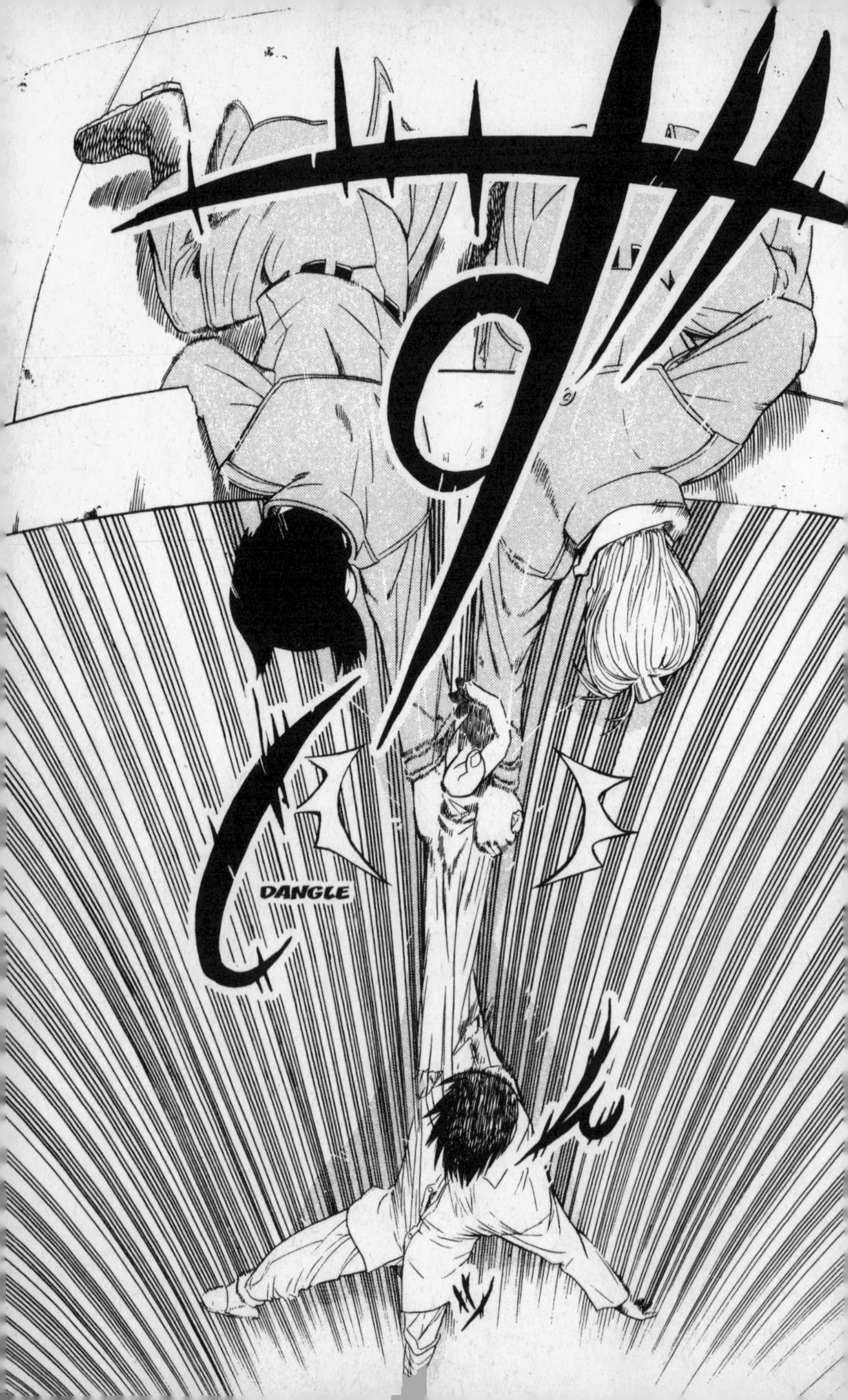
DANGLE

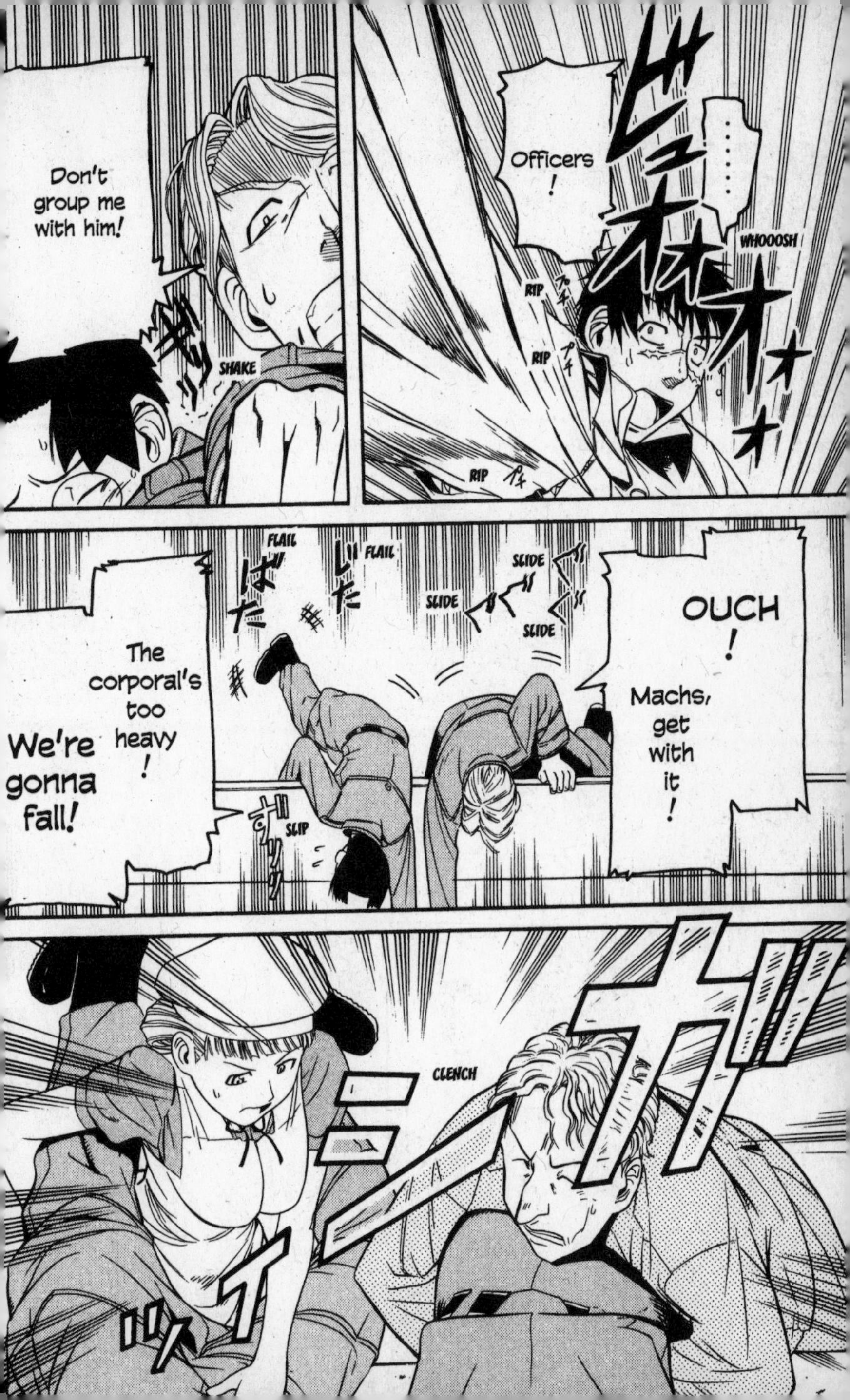
Officers!
WHOOOSH
RIP
RIP
RIP
Don't group me with him!
SHAKE
OUCH!
Machs, get with it!
SLIDE
SLIDE
SLIDE
FLAIL
FLAIL
The corporal's too heavy!
We're gonna fall!
SLIP
CLENCH

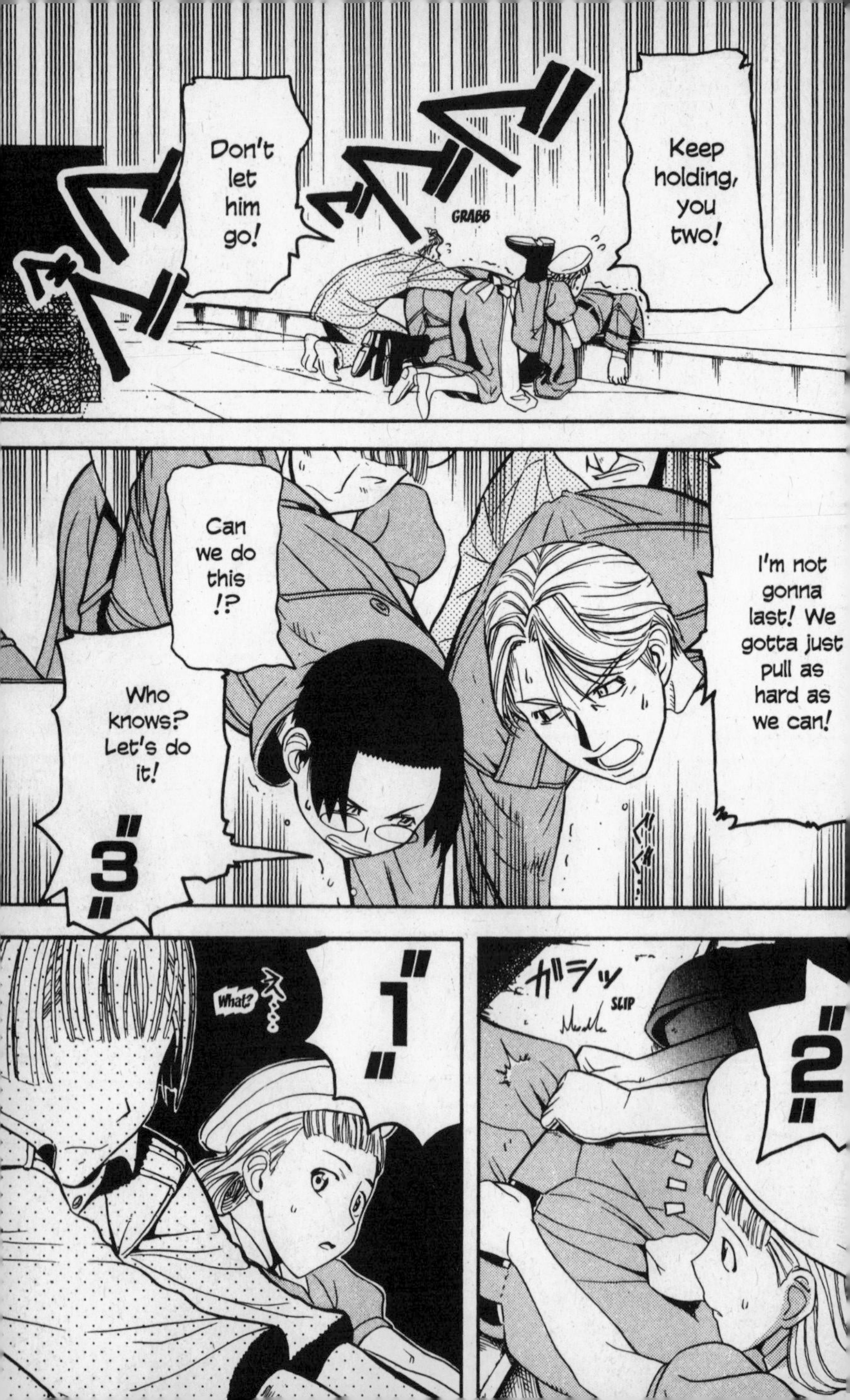
Keep holding, you two!
GRABB
Don't let him go!
I'm not gonna last! We gotta just pull as hard as we can!
Can we do this!?
Who knows? Let's do it!
"3"
"2"
SLIP
"1"
What?

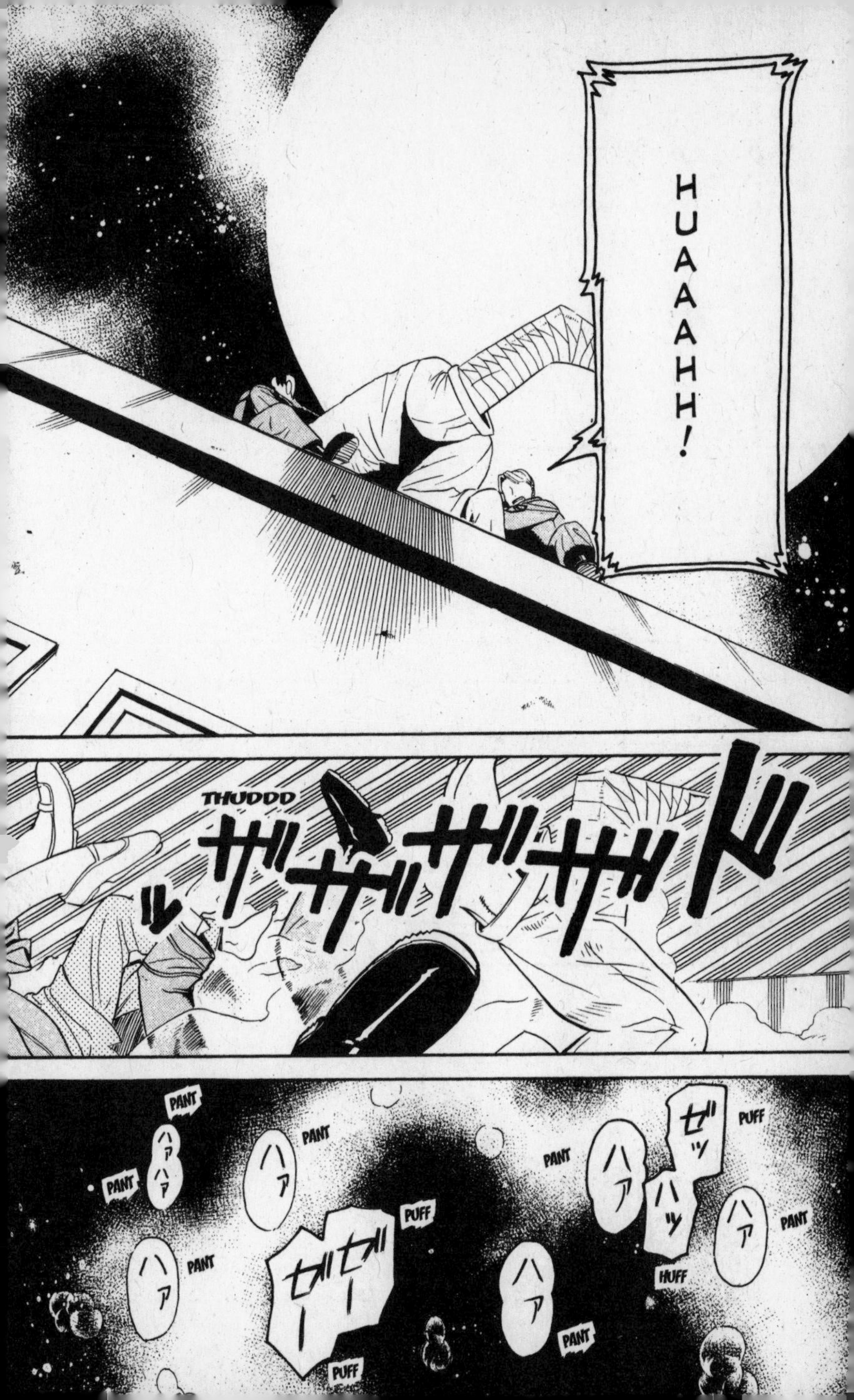
HUAAAAHH!
THUDDD
PUFF
ゼッ
PANT
ハァ
ハァ
PANT
ハッ
HUFF
ハァ
PANT
PUFF
ぜーぜー
PUFF
PANT
ハァ
PANT
PANT
ハァハァ
PANT
ハァ
PANT

WHEEZE

PANT

Hey, Corporal...

It's my fault.

We're supposed to be the mellow Section III!

PANT

PANT

PANT

Yes?

PANT

PANT

Never mind!

What?

PANT

PANT

I'm sorry for suspecting you.

......

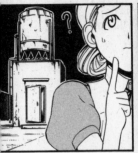

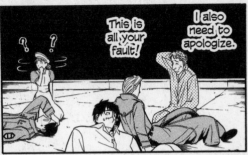

I also need to apologize.
This is all your fault!
Heh, he's doing just fine.

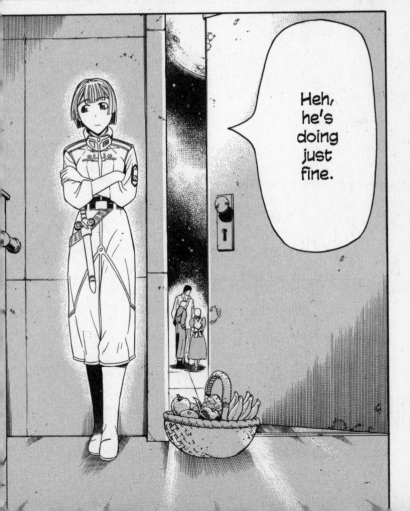

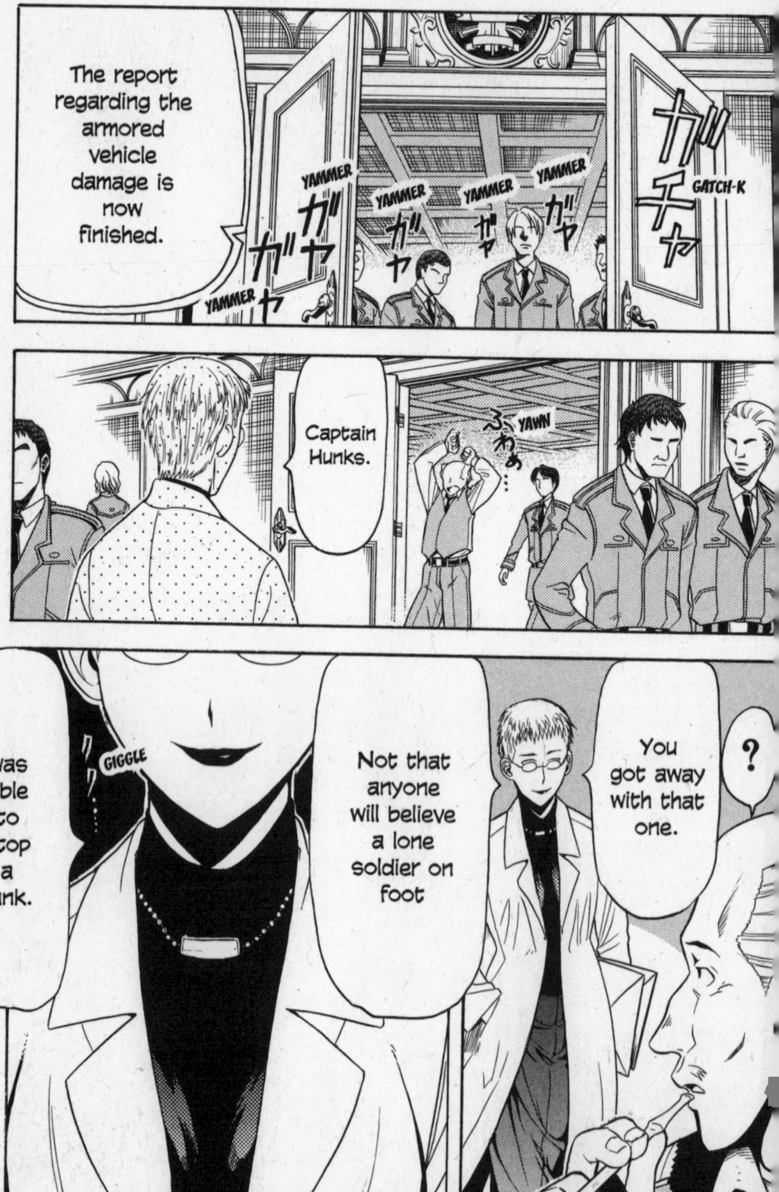
ガチャ
GATCH-K
YAMMER
YAMMER
YAMMER
YAMMER
YAMMER
The report regarding the armored vehicle damage is now finished.
YAWN
Captain Hunks.
?
You got away with that one.
Not that anyone will believe a lone soldier on foot
GIGGLE
was able to stop a tank.

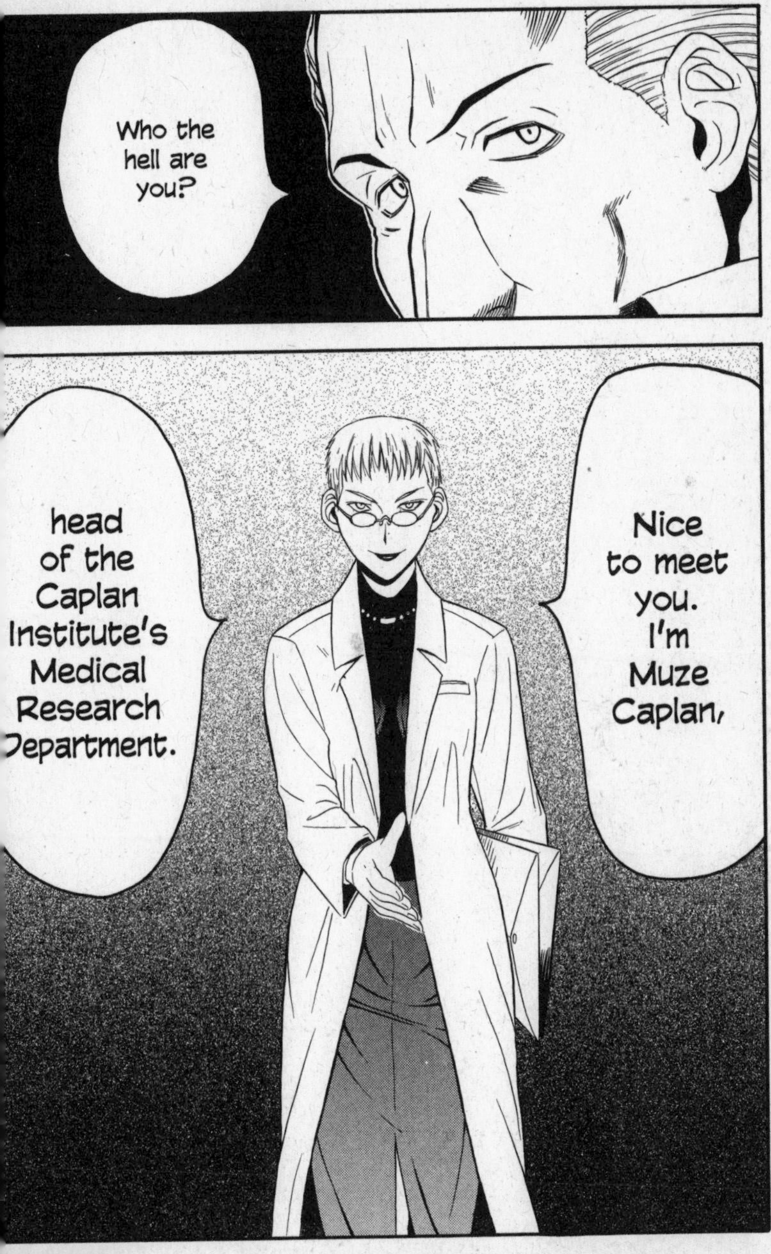
Who the hell are you?
Nice to meet you. I'm Muze Caplan,
head of the Caplan Institute's Medical Research Department.

#4/END

PumpkinScissors

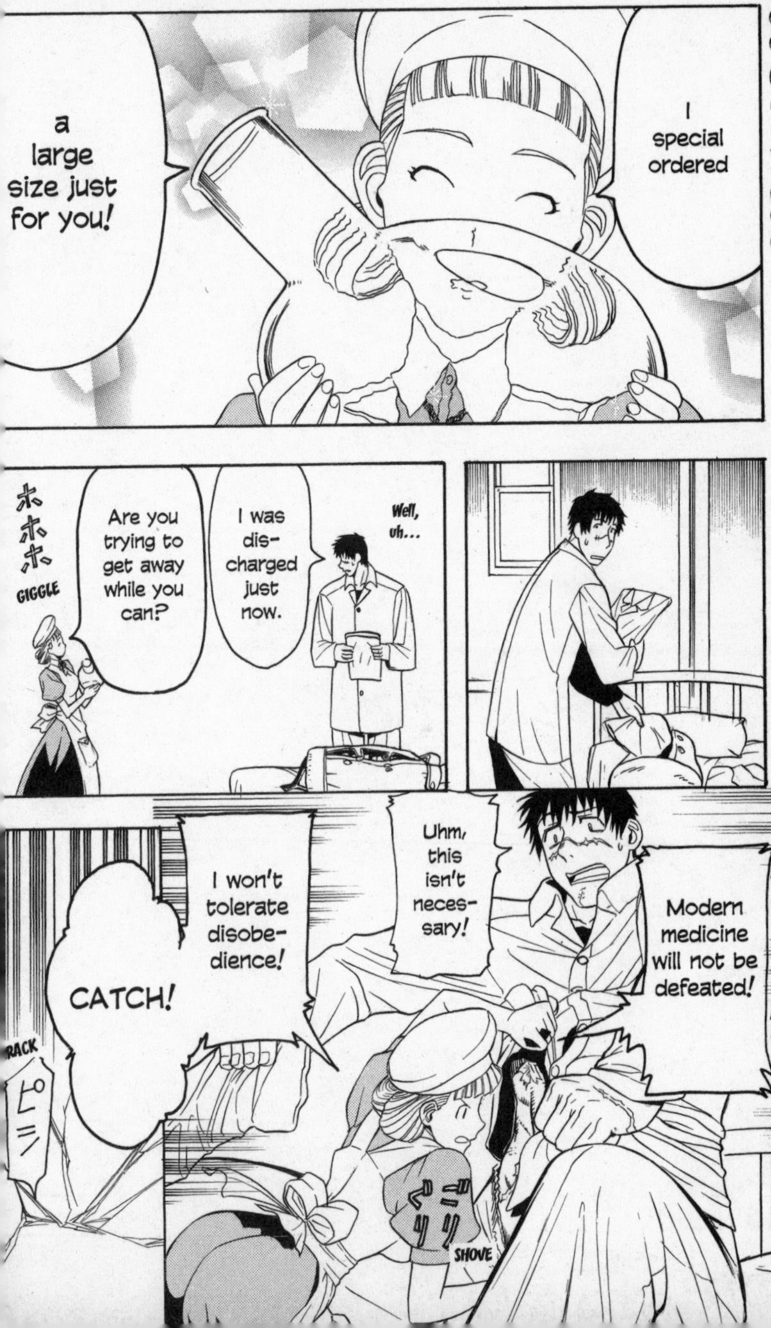
I special ordered
a large size just for you!
Well, uh...
I was dis-charged just now.
Are you trying to get away while you can?
ホホホ
GIGGLE
じた
FLAIL
ばた
FLAIL
Modern medicine will not be defeated!
Uhm, this isn't neces-sary!
I won't tolerate disobe-dience!
CATCH!
RACK
ピシ
ぐいー
SHOVE

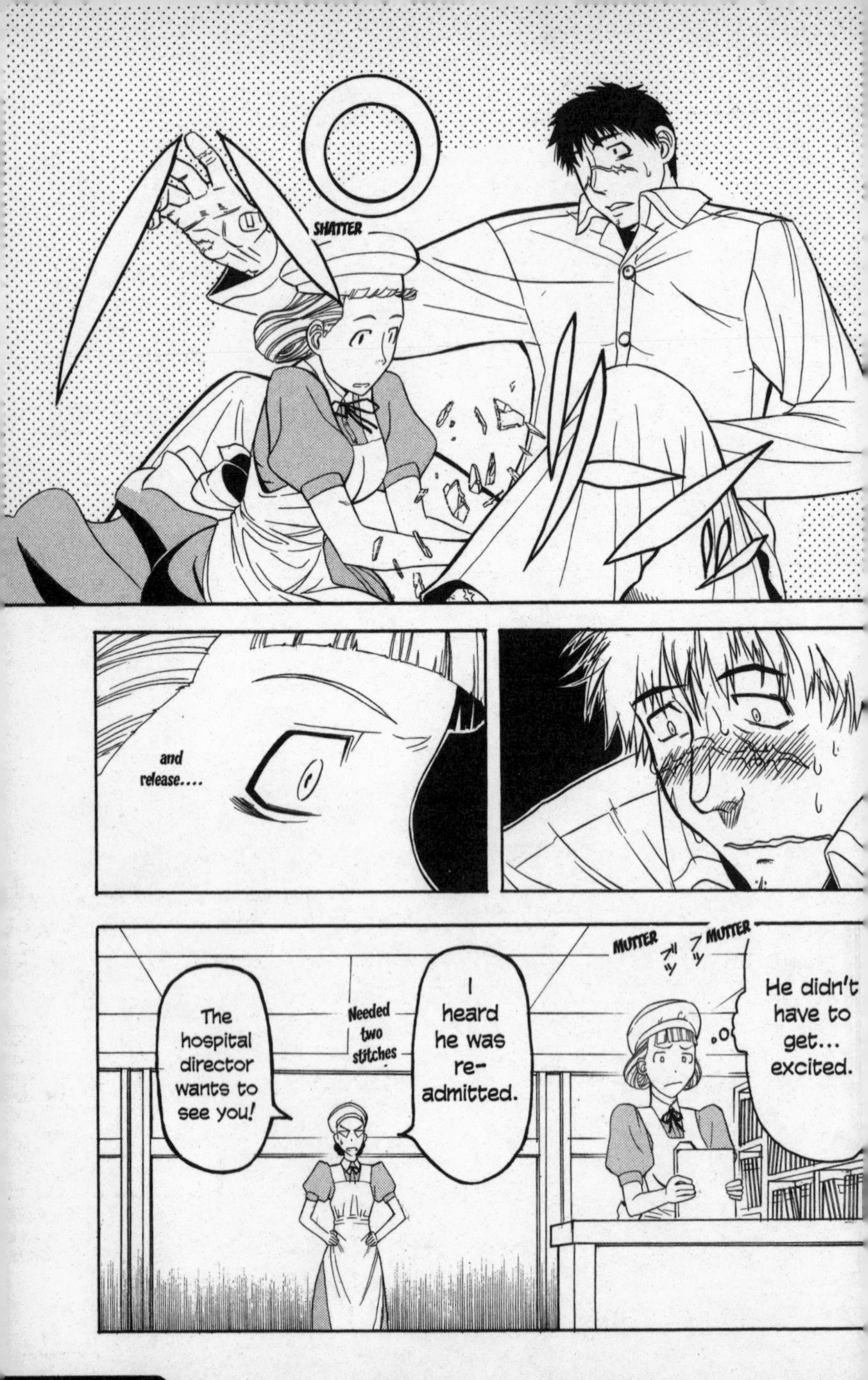
SHATTER
and release....
MUTTER MUTTER
ブツ ブツ
He didn't have to get... excited.
I heard he was re-admitted.
Needed two stitches
The hospital director wants to see you!

← NEXT!

PumpkinScissors

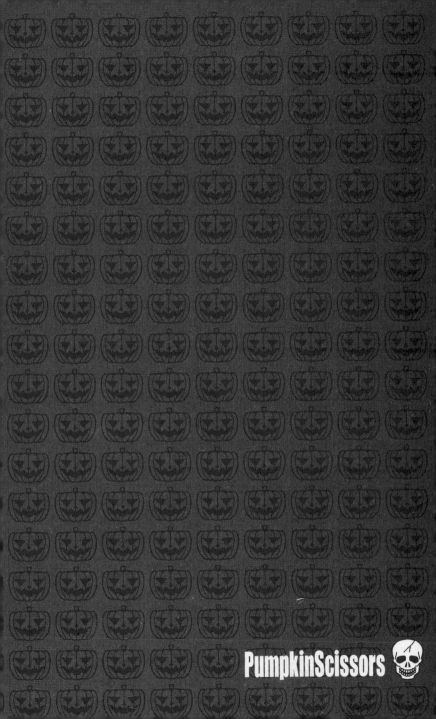

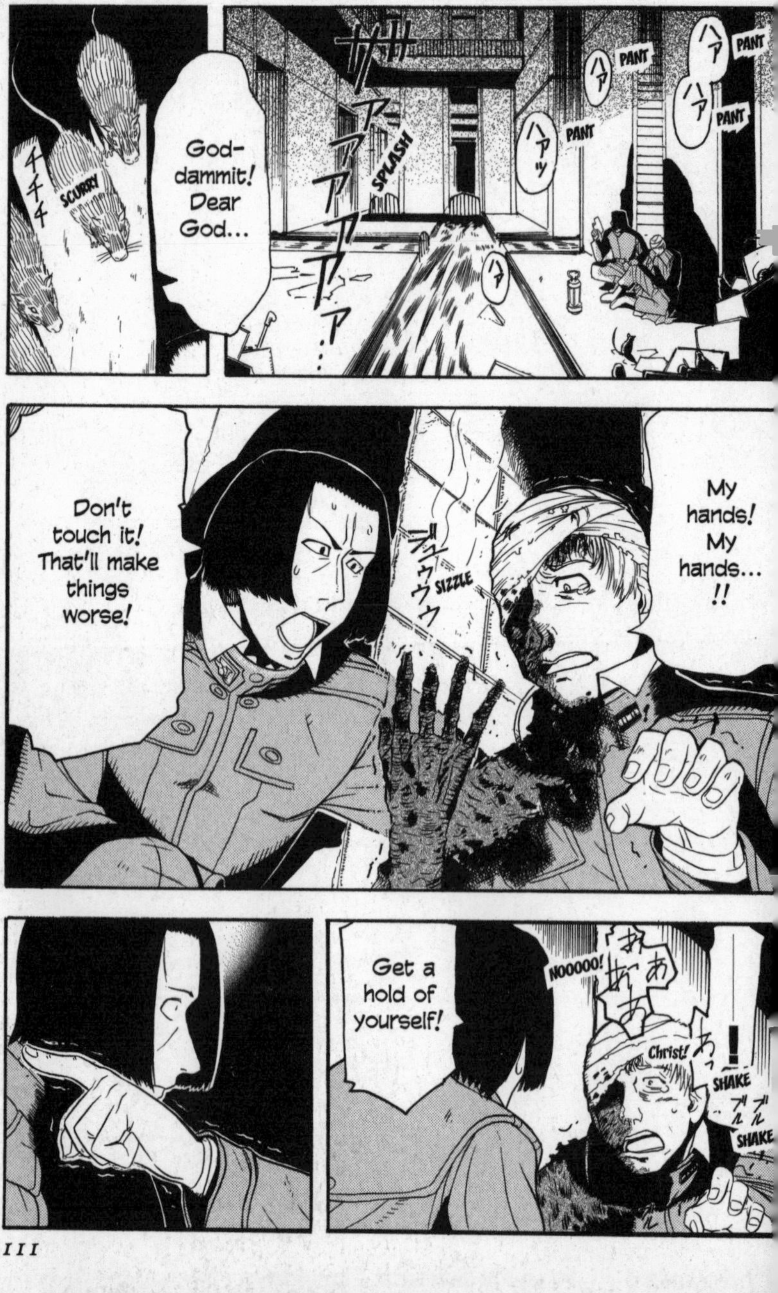
PANT
PANT
PANT
PANT
SPLASH
God-dammit! Dear God...
SCURRY
My hands! My hands...!!
SIZZLE
Don't touch it! That'll make things worse!
NOOOOO!
Christ!
SHAKE
SHAKE
Get a hold of yourself!

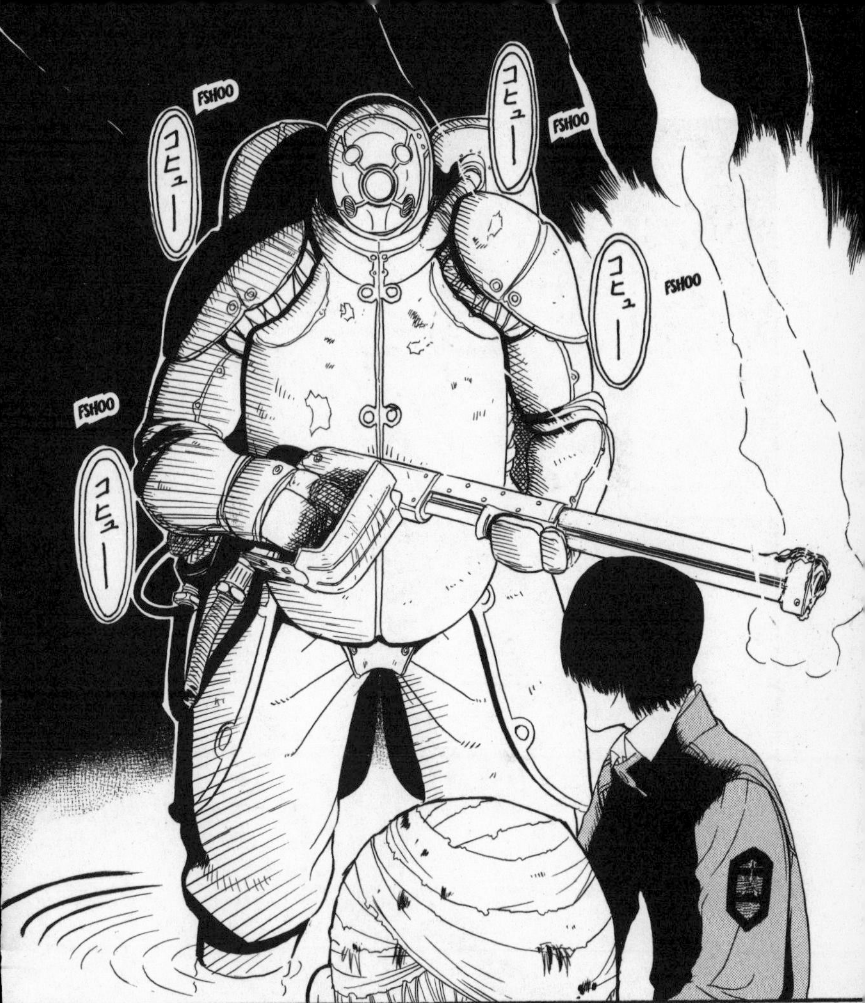
コヒュー
FSHOO
FSHOO
コヒュー
コヒュー
FSHOO
FSHOO
コヒュー

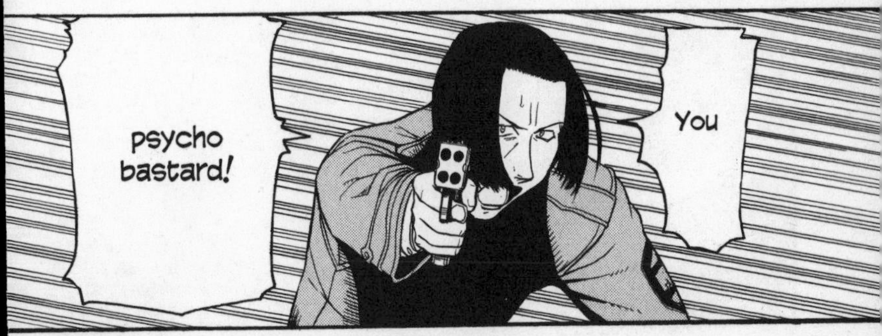
You
psycho bastard!

Episode 5 Pumpkin Scissors: Pumpkin

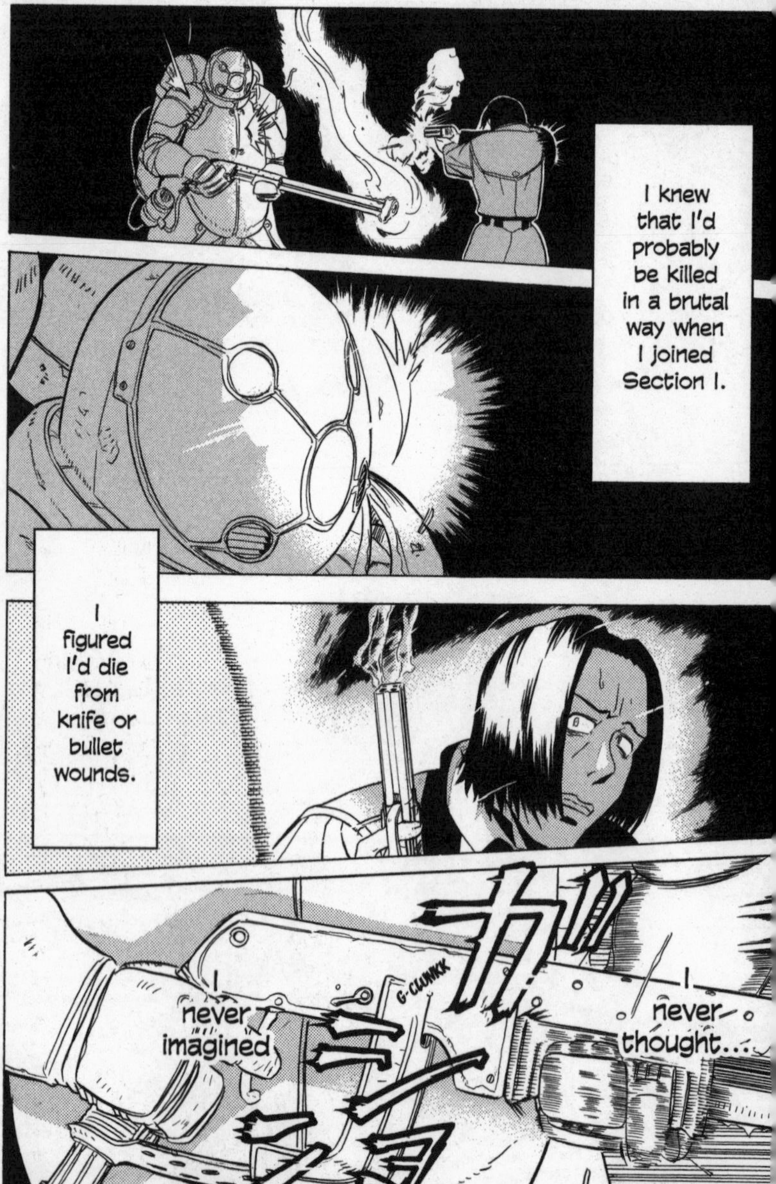

I knew that I'd probably be killed in a brutal way when I joined Section 1.
I figured I'd die from knife or bullet wounds.
G-CLUNKK
I never thought...
I never imagined

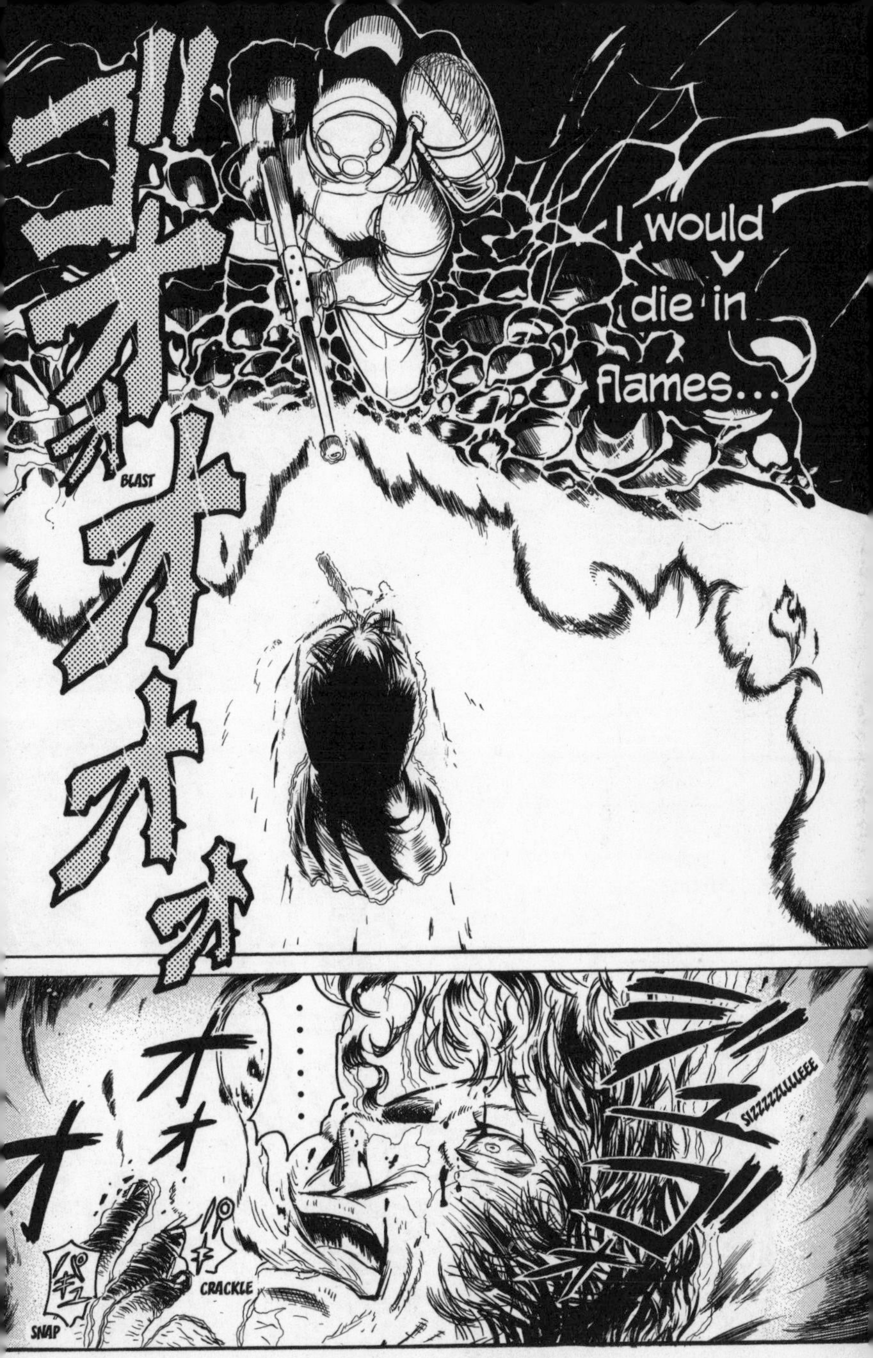
I would die in flames...
BLAST
SIZZZZZZLLLLEEE
......
CRACKLE
SNAP

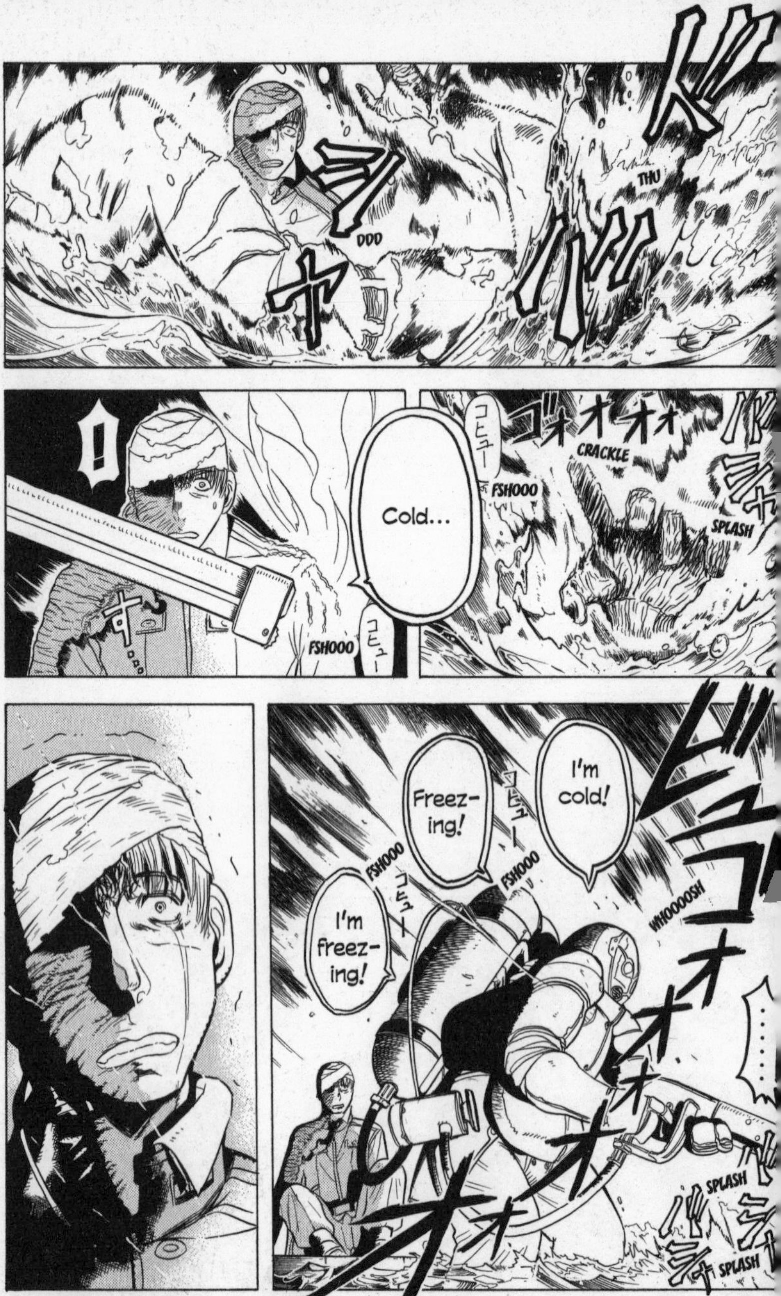
THU
DDD
CRACKLE
SPLASH
FSHOOO
Cold...
FSHOOO
I'm cold!
Freez-ing!
FSHOOO
FSHOOO
I'm freez-ing!
WHOOOOSH
SPLASH
SPLASH

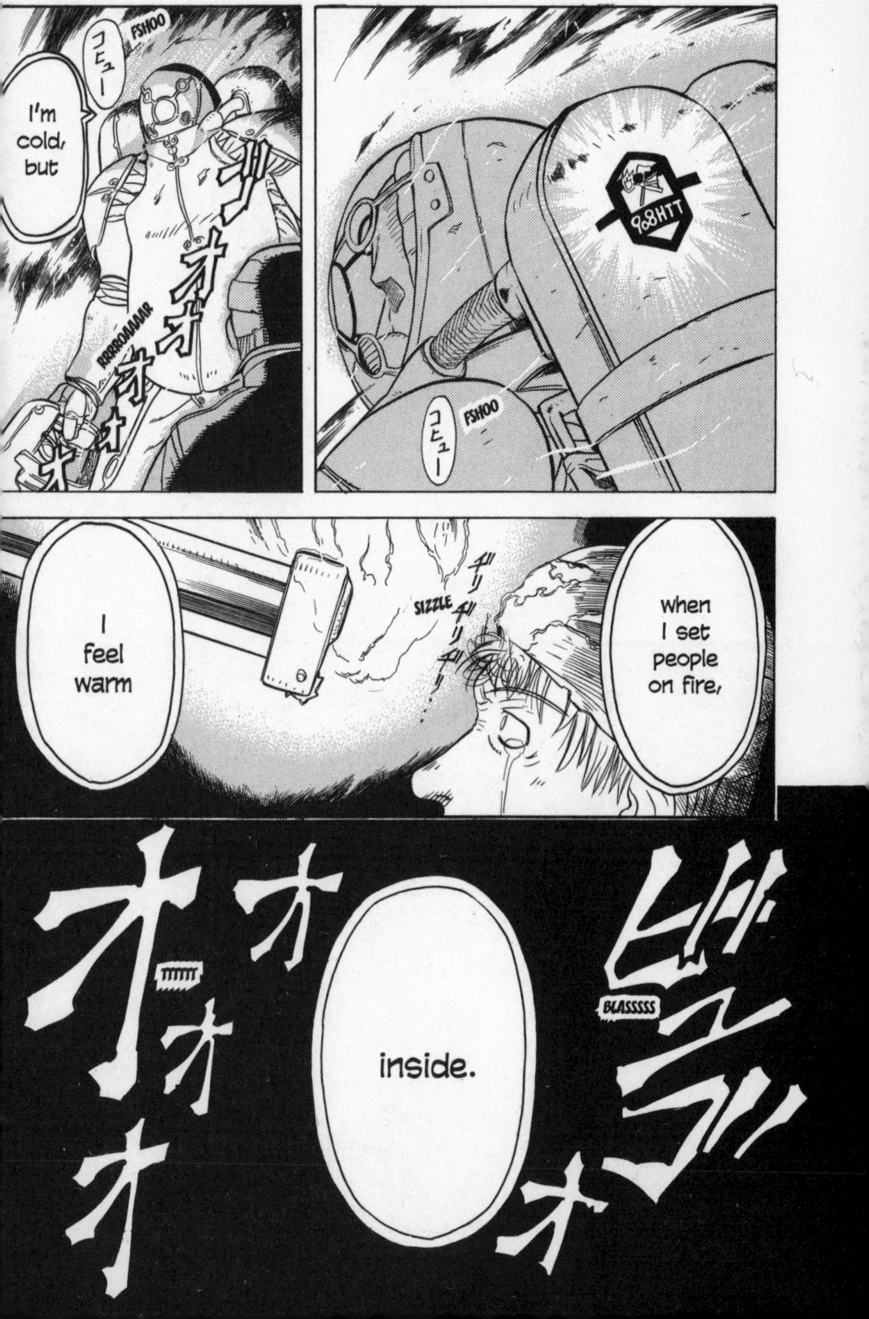
コヒュー
FSHOO
FSHOO
コヒュー
I'm cold, but
RRRROAAAAR
when I set people on fire,
SIZZLE
I feel warm
BLASSSSS
inside.
TTTTTT

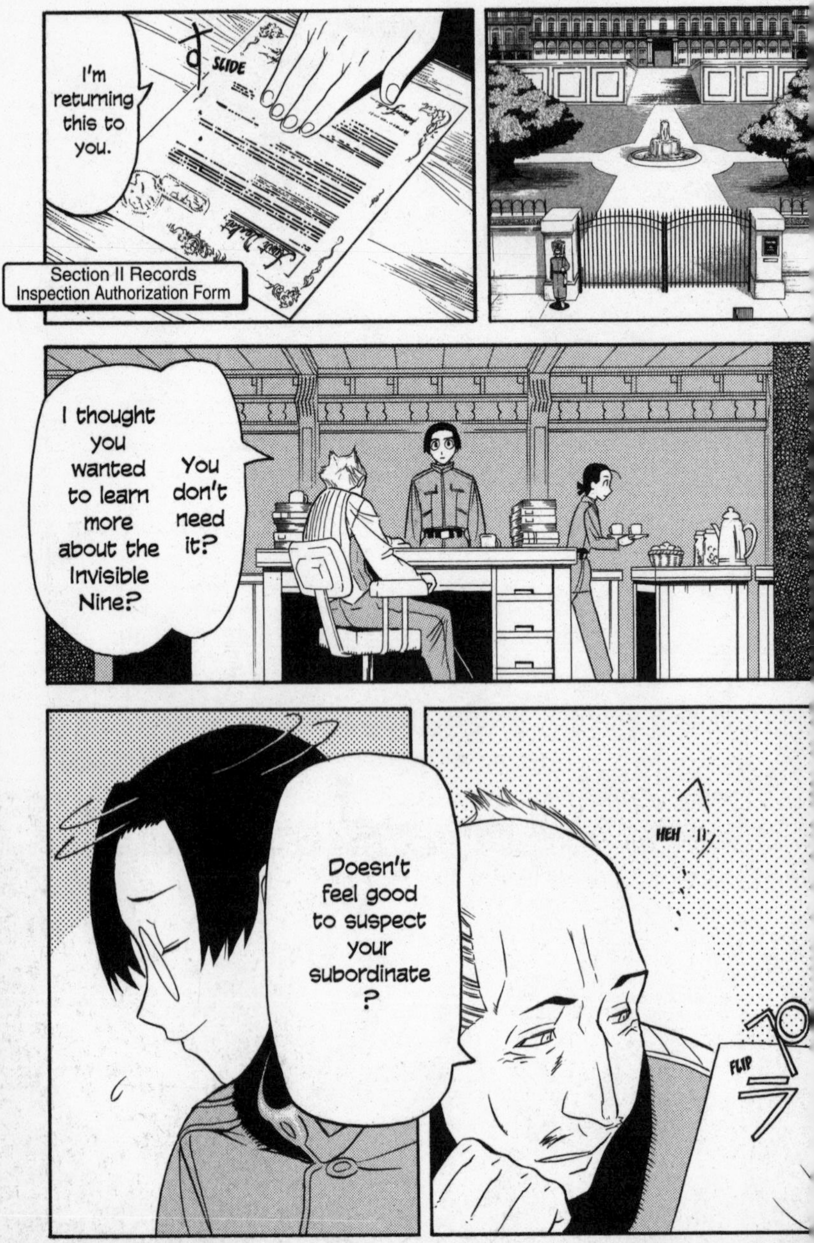
SLIDE
I'm returning this to you.
Section II Records Inspection Authorization Form
You don't need it?
I thought you wanted to learn more about the Invisible Nine?
HEH
FLIP
Doesn't feel good to suspect your subordinate?

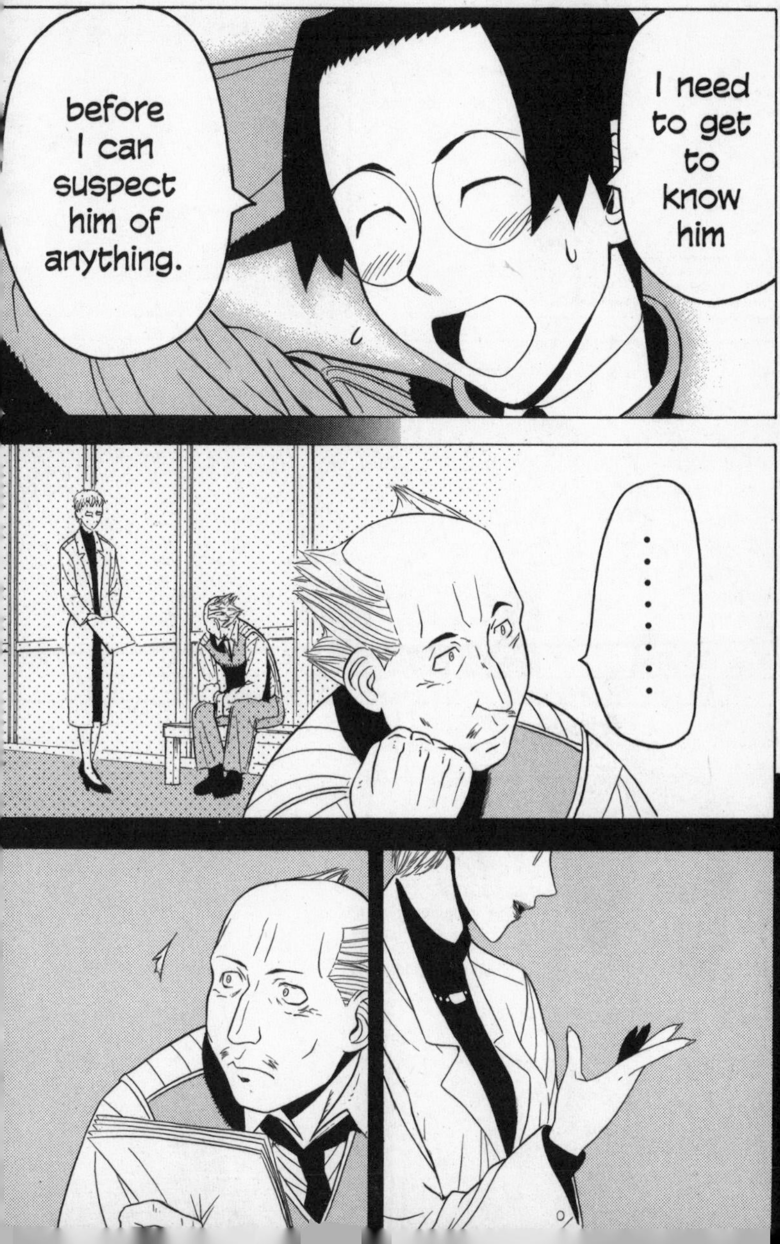
I need to get to know him
before I can suspect him of anything.
....

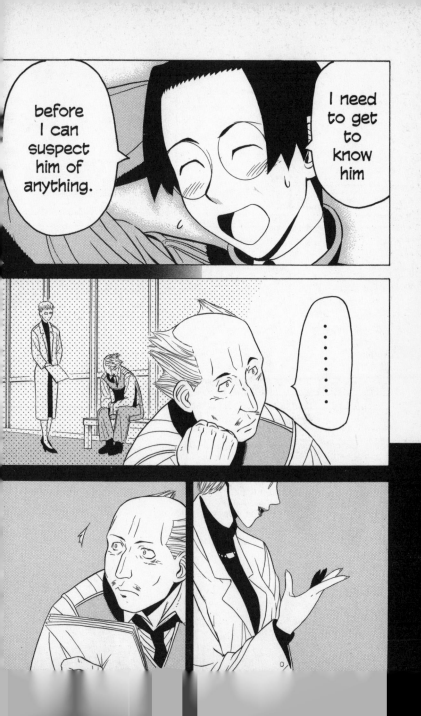

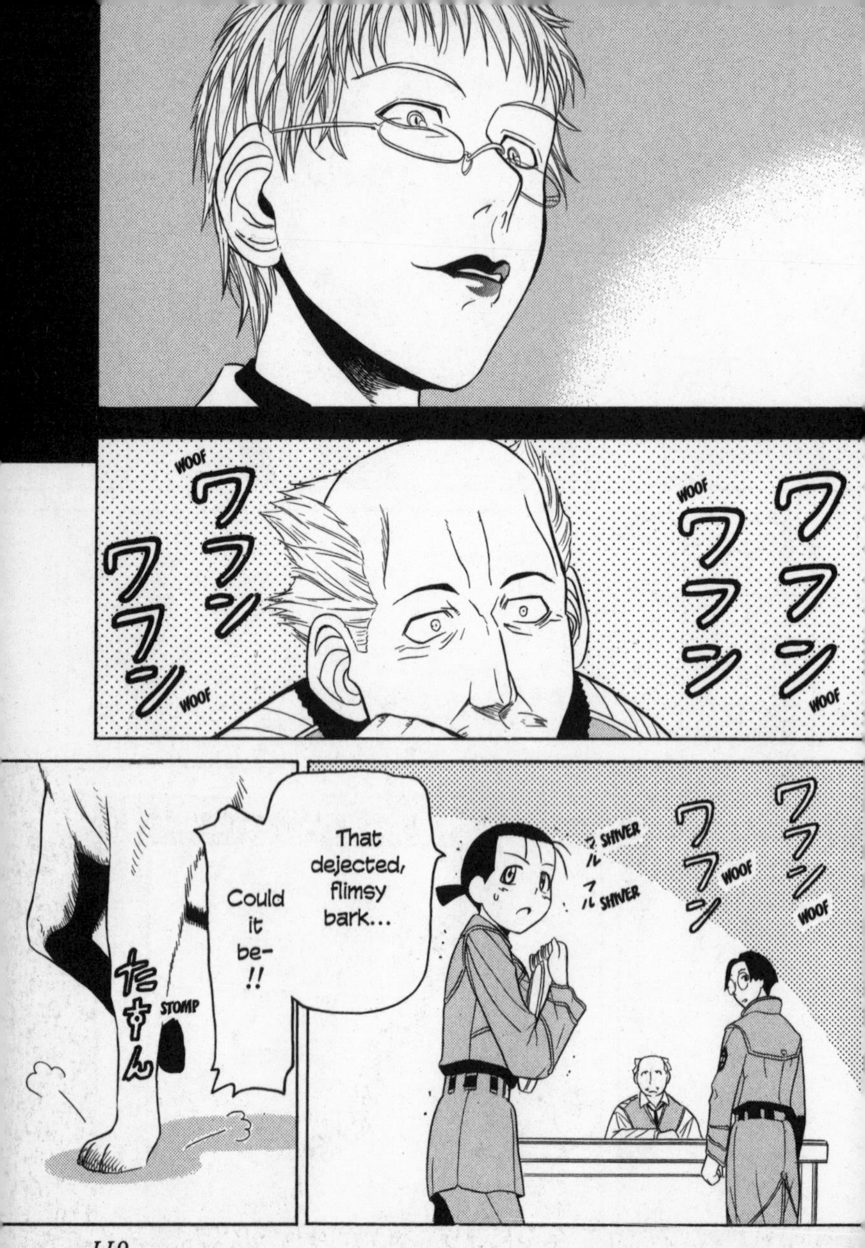
WOOF
ワフン
WOOF
ワフン
WOOF
ワフン
WOOF
ワフン
ワフン
WOOF
ワフン
WOOF
フル SHIVER
フル SHIVER
That dejected, flimsy bark...
Could it be-!!
たすん
STOMP

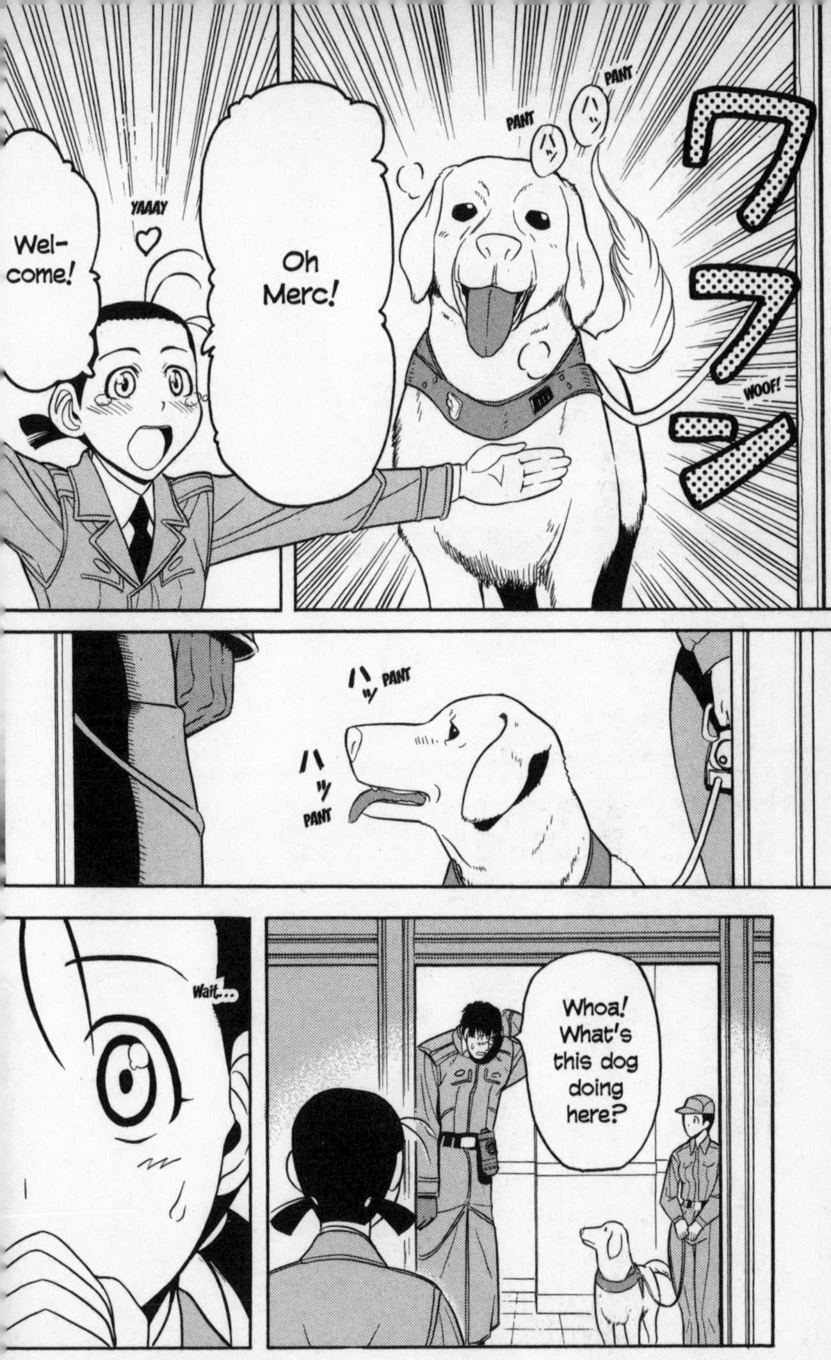
WOOF!
PANT
PANT
Oh Merc!
YAAAY
Wel-come!
PANT
PANT
Whoa! What's this dog doing here?
Wait...

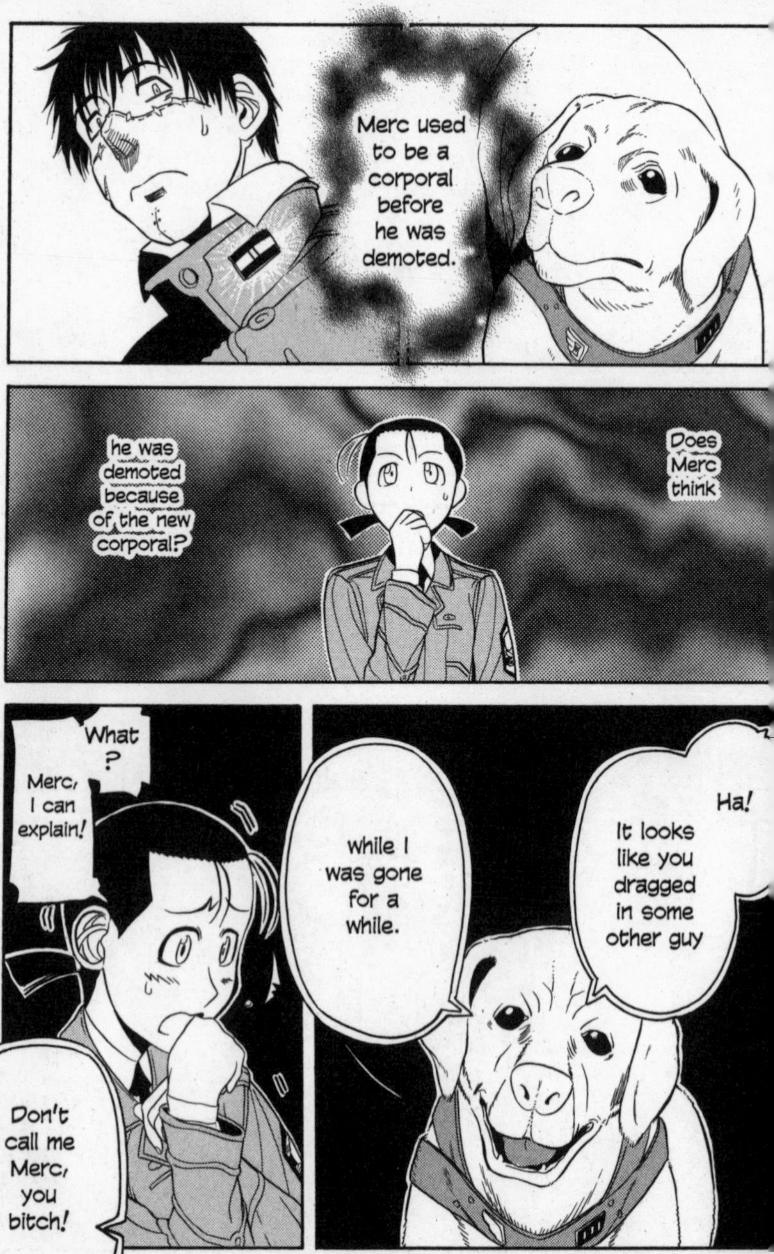
Merc used to be a corporal before he was demoted.
Does Merc think
he was demoted because of the new corporal?
Ha!
It looks like you dragged in some other guy
while I was gone for a while.
What?
Merc, I can explain!
Don't call me Merc, you bitch!

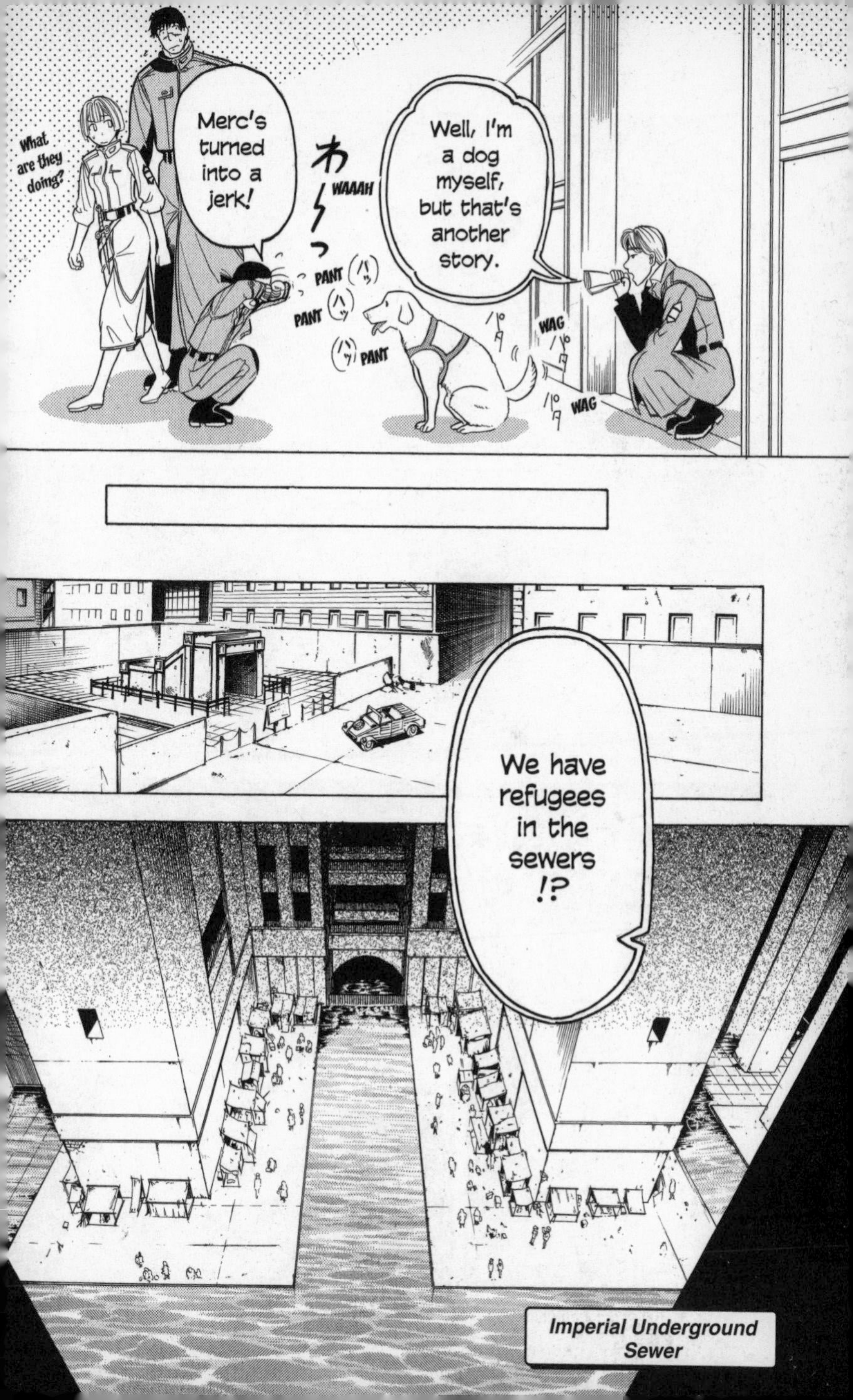
Well, I'm a dog myself, but that's another story.
WAG
WAG
PANT
PANT
PANT
WAAAH
Merc's turned into a jerk!
What are they doing?
We have refugees in the sewers !?
Imperial Underground Sewer

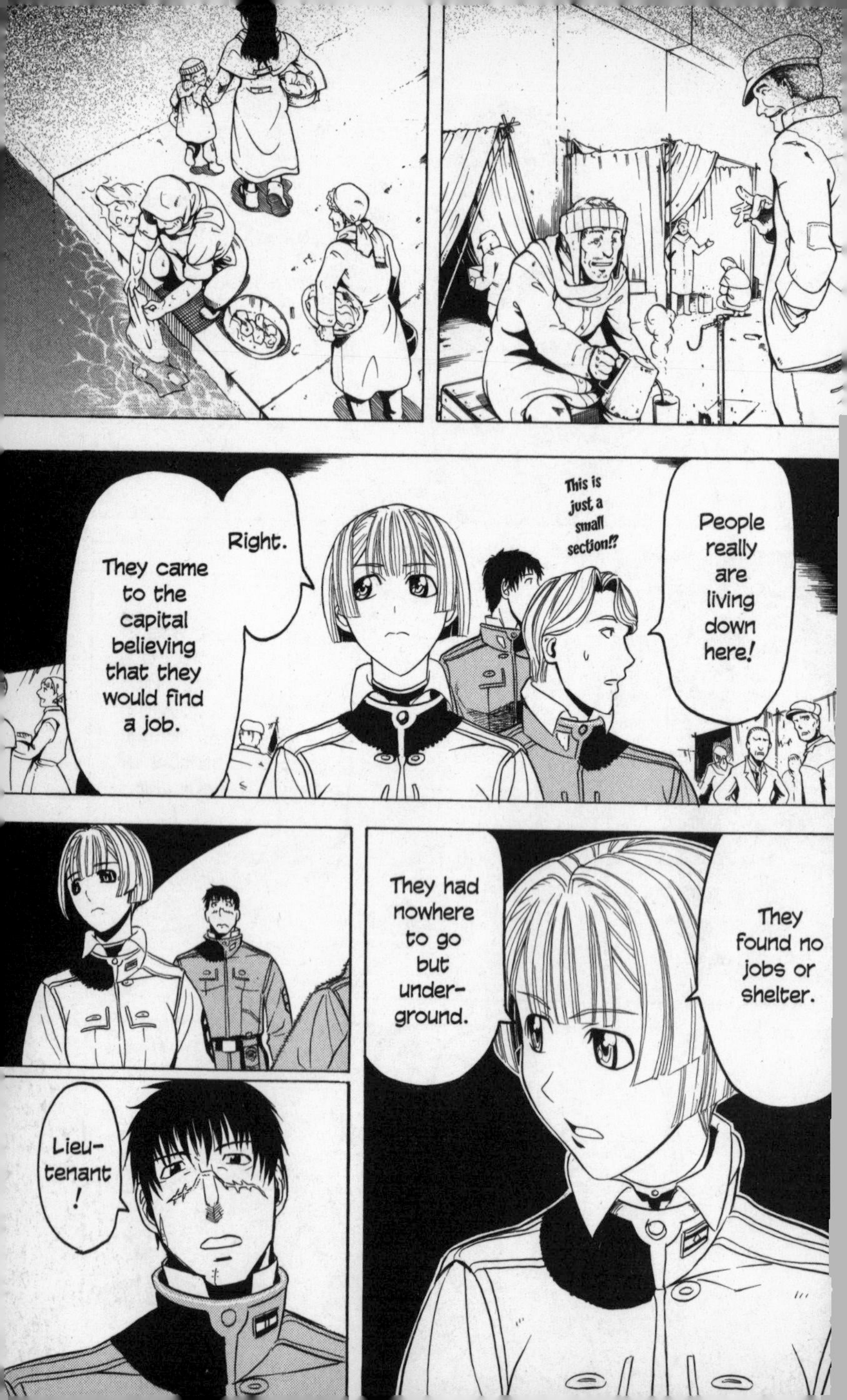

People really are living down here!
This is just a small section!?
Right.
They came to the capital believing that they would find a job.
They found no jobs or shelter.
They had nowhere to go but under-ground.
Lieu-tenant!

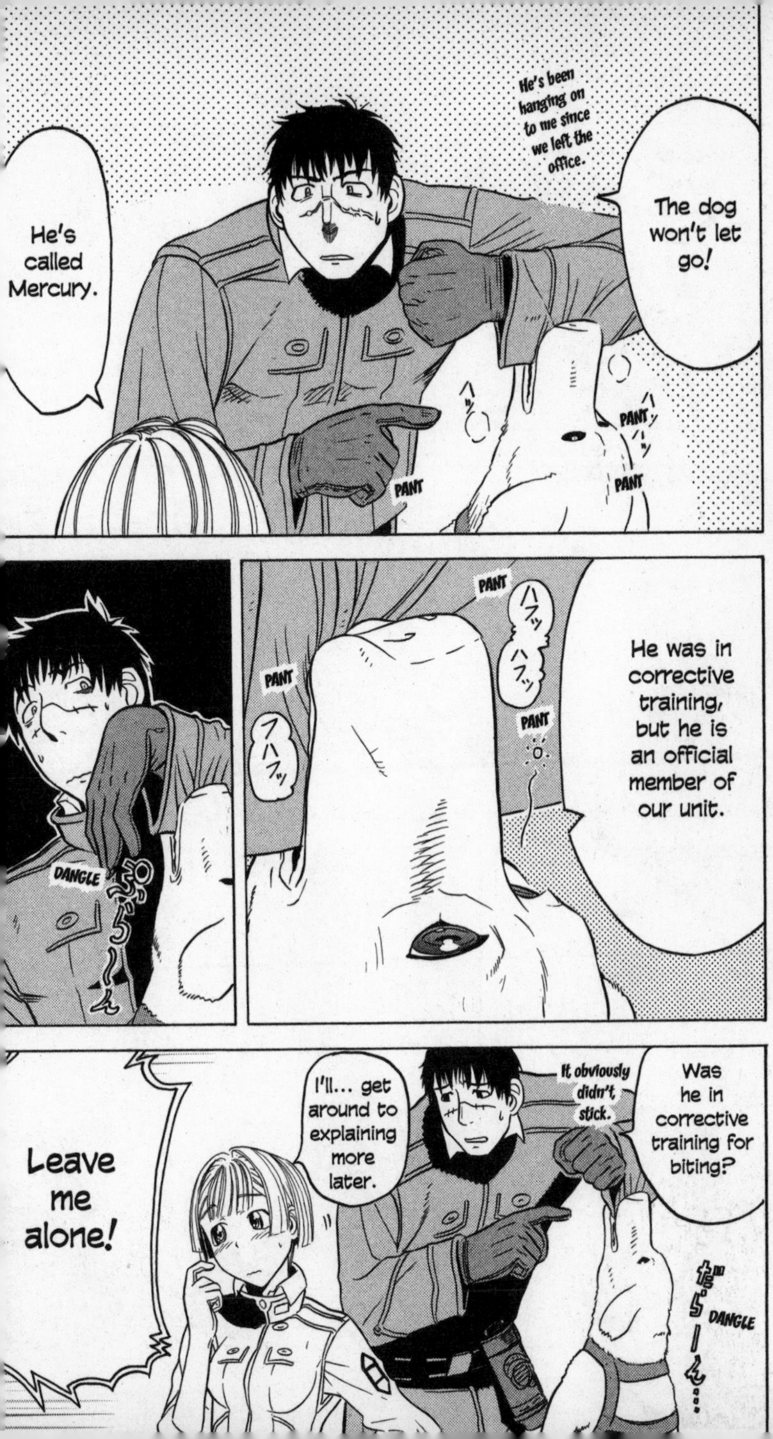
The dog won't let go!
He's been hanging on to me since we left the office.
He's called Mercury.
PANT
PANT
PANT
PANT
ハフッ ハフッ
PANT
フハフッ
He was in corrective training, but he is an official member of our unit.
DANGLE
ぶら～ん
Was he in corrective training for biting?
It obviously didn't stick.
I'll... get around to explaining more later.
Leave me alone!
だら～ん…
DANGLE

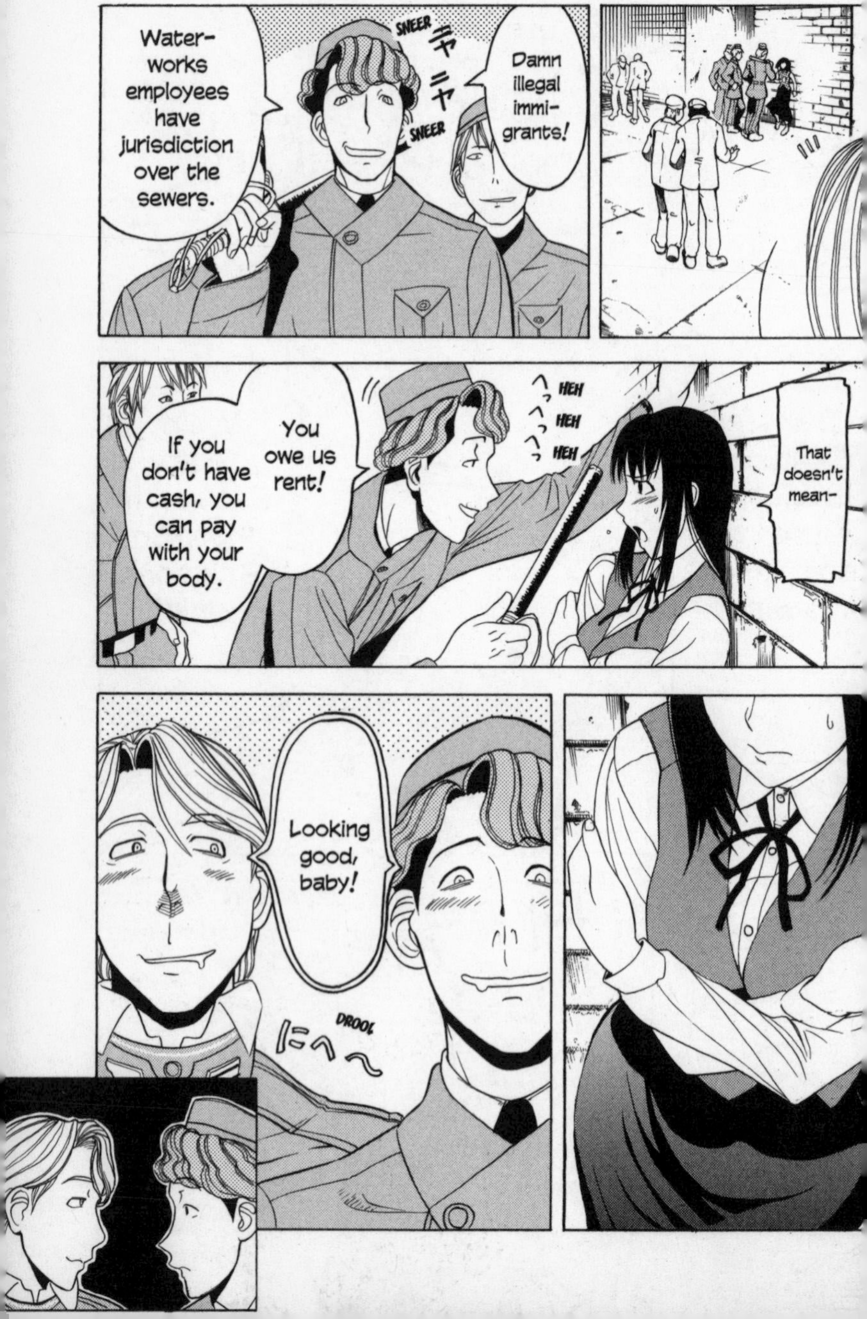

Damn illegal immigrants!
SNEER ニヤ ニヤ SNEER
Water-works employees have jurisdiction over the sewers.
That doesn't mean-
HEH HEH HEH ヘッヘッヘッ
You owe us rent!
If you don't have cash, you can pay with your body.
Looking good, baby!
DROOL にへ〜

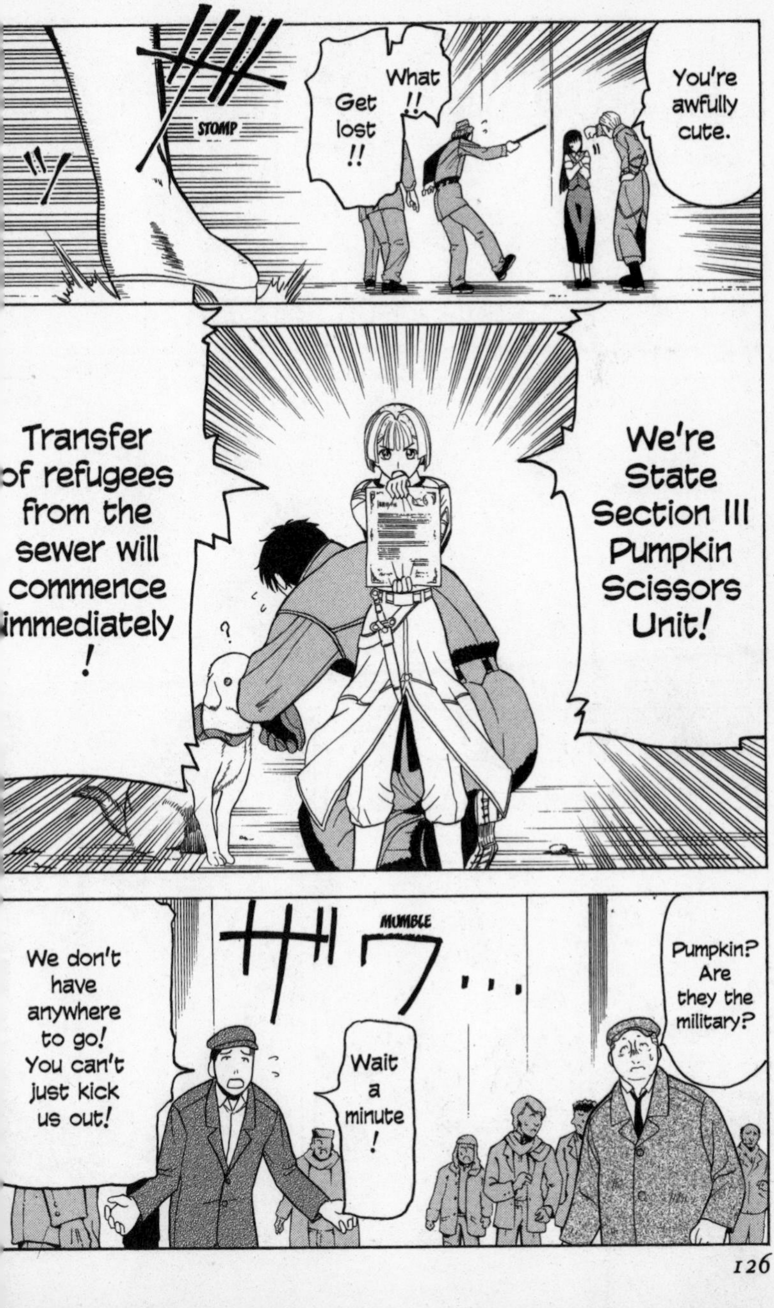
You're awfully cute.
What!!
Get lost!!
STOMP
We're State Section III Pumpkin Scissors Unit!
Transfer of refugees from the sewer will commence immediately!
Pumpkin? Are they the military?
MUMBLE
Wait a minute!
We don't have anywhere to go! You can't just kick us out!

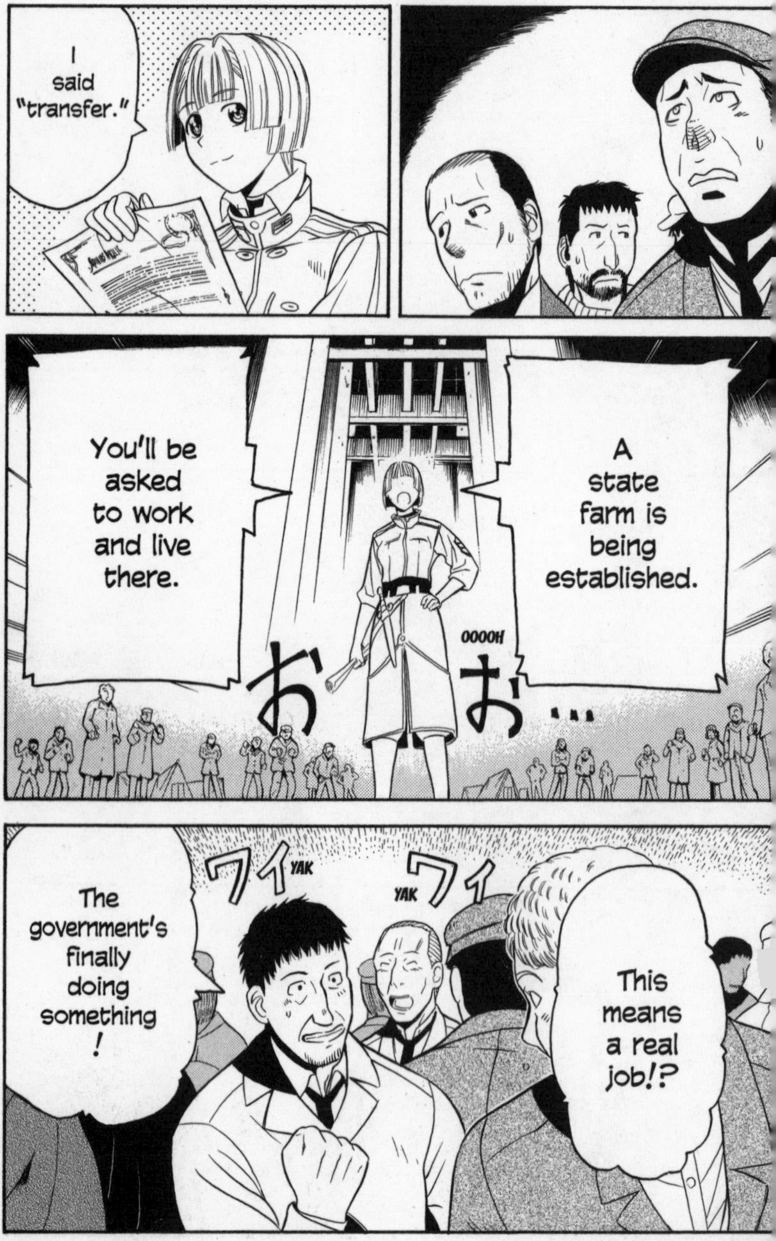
I said "transfer."
A state farm is being established.
You'll be asked to work and live there.
OOOOH
おお...
This means a real job!?
ワイ YAK
ワイ YAK
The government's finally doing something!

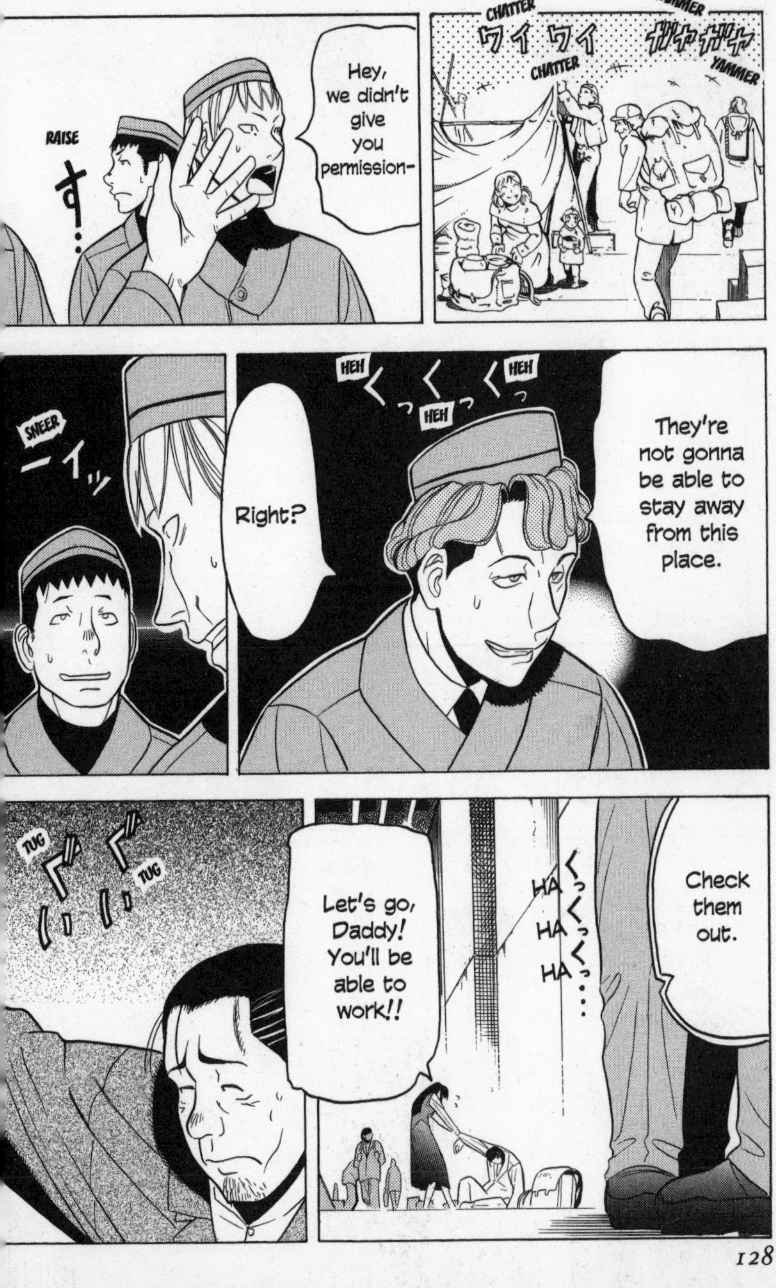
CHATTER
ワイワイ
YAMMER
ガヤガヤ
CHATTER
YAMMER
Hey, we didn't give you permission-
RAISE
す…
They're not gonna be able to stay away from this place.
HEH
HEH
HEH
Right?
SNEER
ニイッ
Check them out.
HA
HA
HA
Let's go, Daddy! You'll be able to work!!
TUG
TUG

Why don't you want to leave this hellhole?

Lieutenant!

A group over there

is refusing to leave!

HEE HEE HEE

KTZ

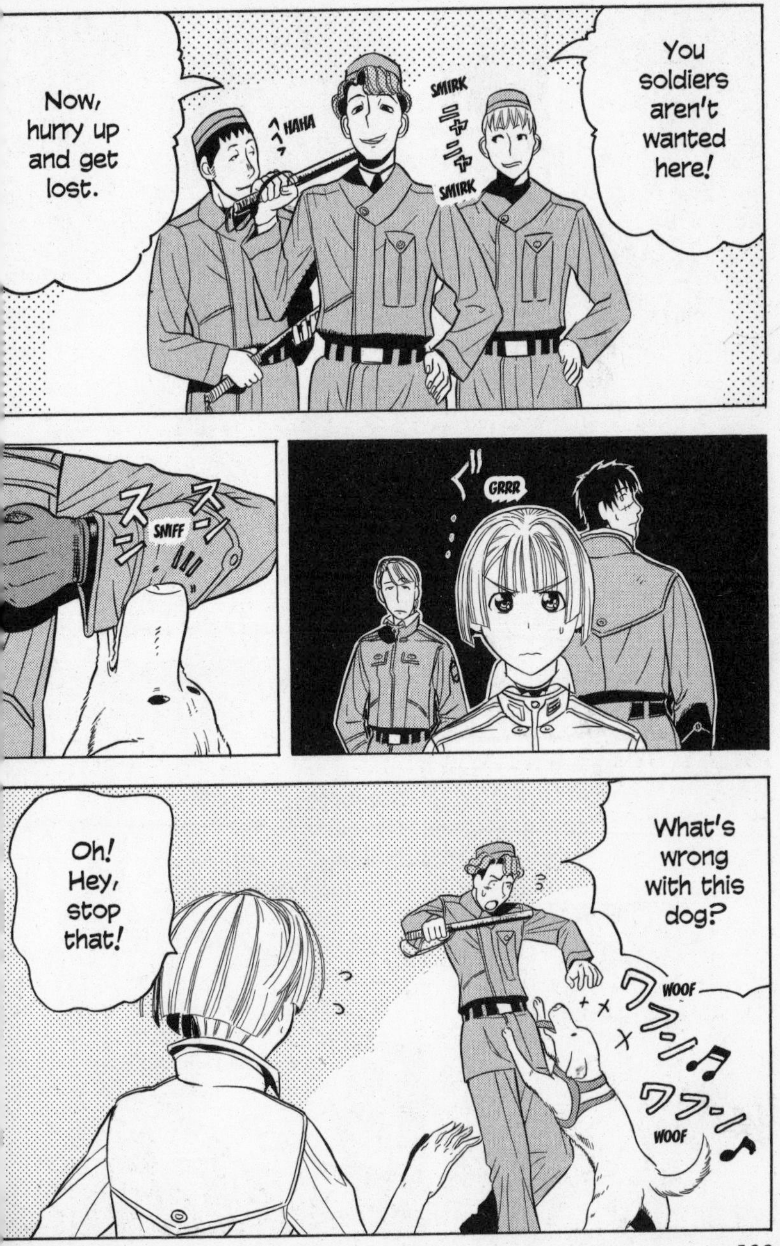
You soldiers aren't wanted here!
SMIRK
SMIRK
HAHA
Now, hurry up and get lost.
GRRR
SNIFF
What's wrong with this dog?
WOOF
WOOF
Oh! Hey, stop that!

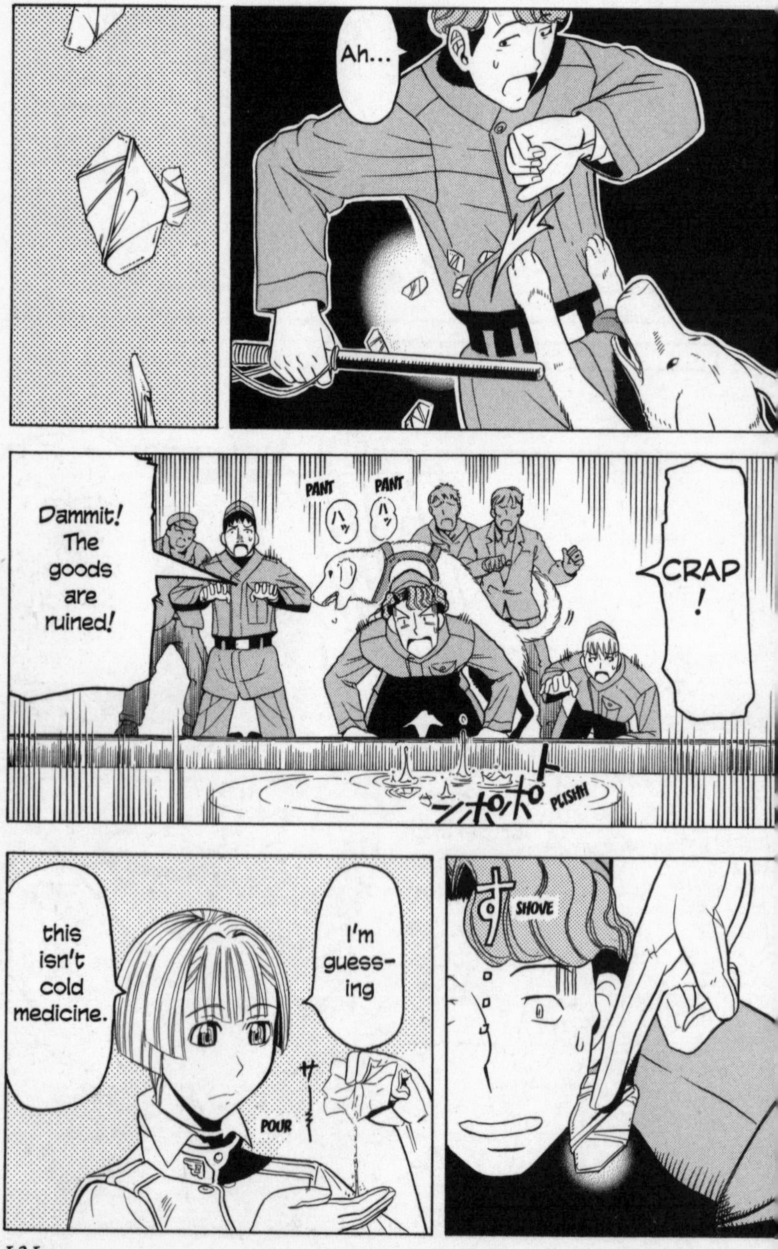
Ah...
CRAP!
PANT
PANT
ハッ
ハッ
Dammit! The goods are ruined!
PLISHH
す
SHOVE
I'm guessing-
this isn't cold medicine.
サー
POUR

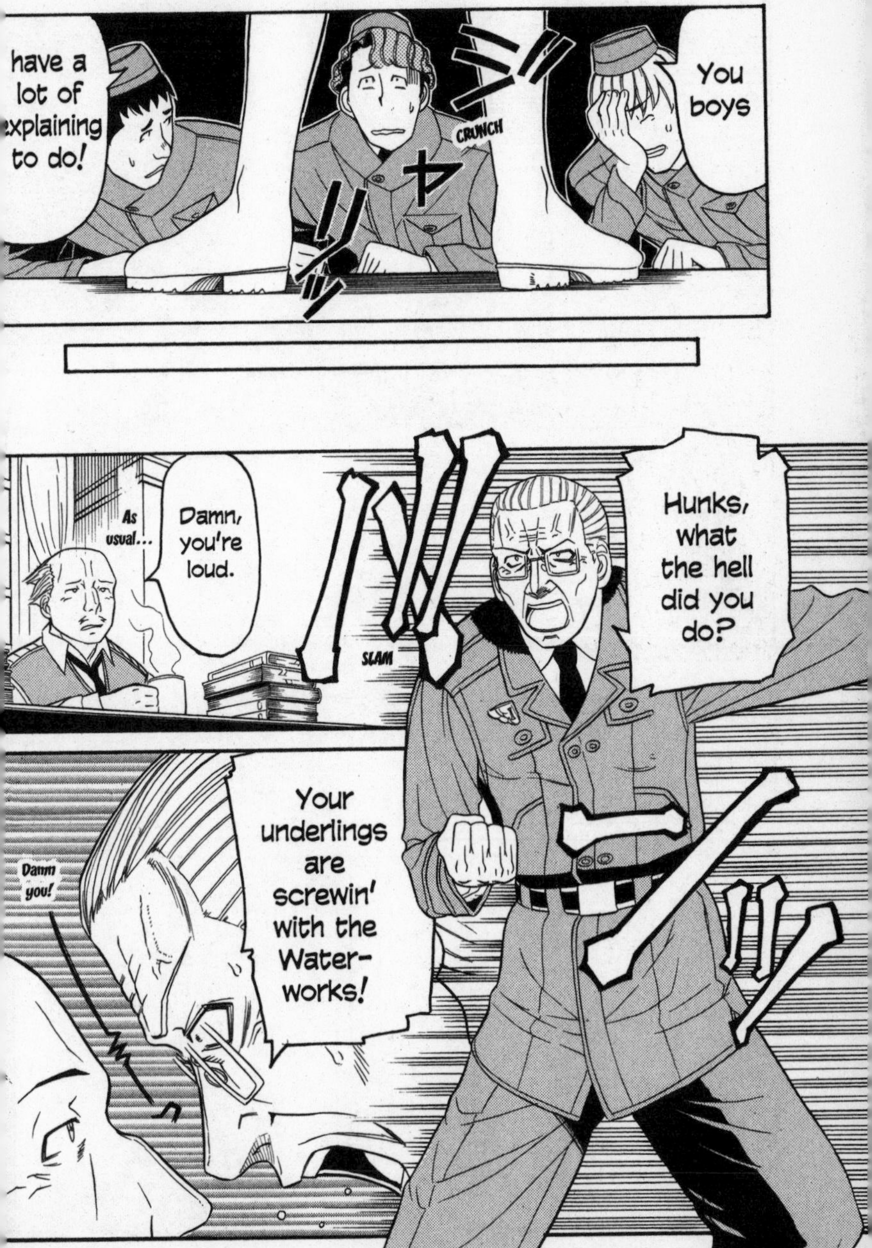
You boys
CRUNCH
have a lot of explaining to do!
Hunks, what the hell did you do?
SLAM
Damn, you're loud.
As usual...
Your underlings are screwin' with the Water-works!
Damn you!

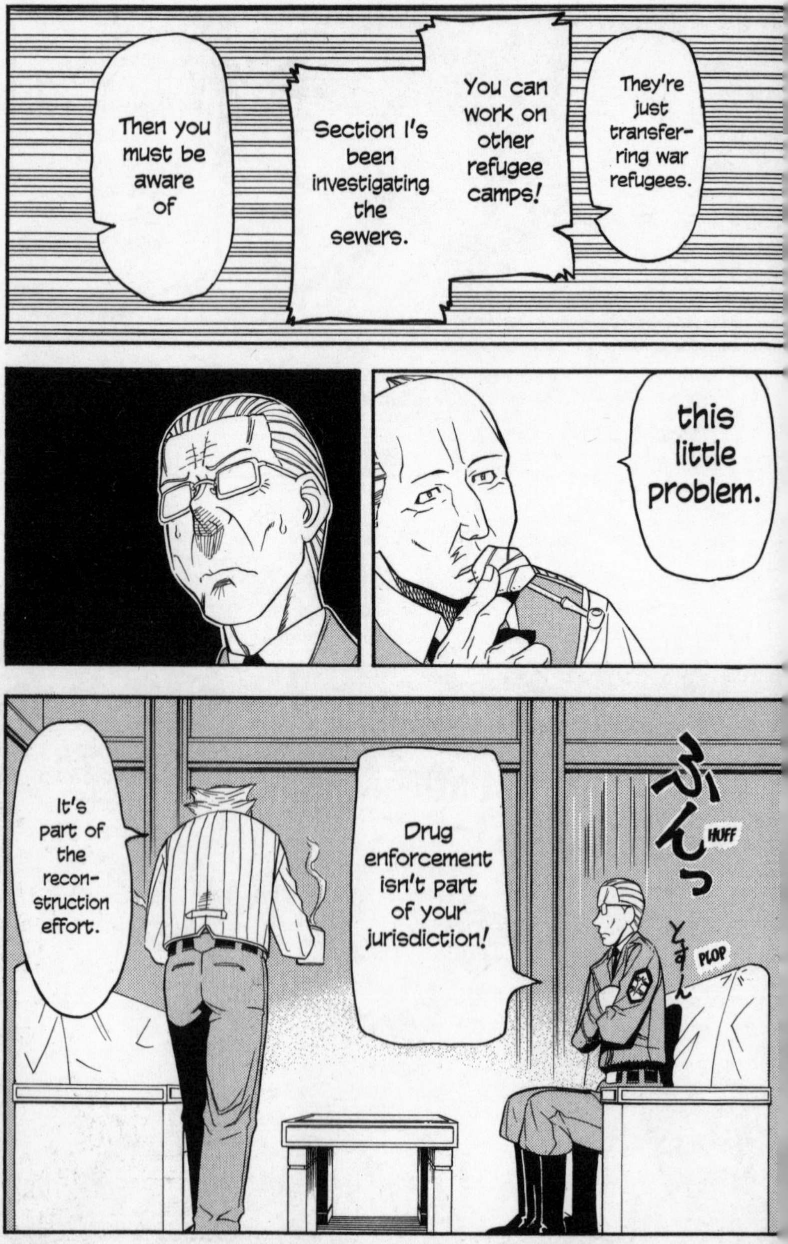
They're just transfer-ring war refugees.
You can work on other refugee camps!
Section 1's been investigating the sewers.
Then you must be aware of
this little problem.
ふんっ
HUFF
とすん
PLOP
Drug enforcement isn't part of your jurisdiction!
It's part of the recon-struction effort.

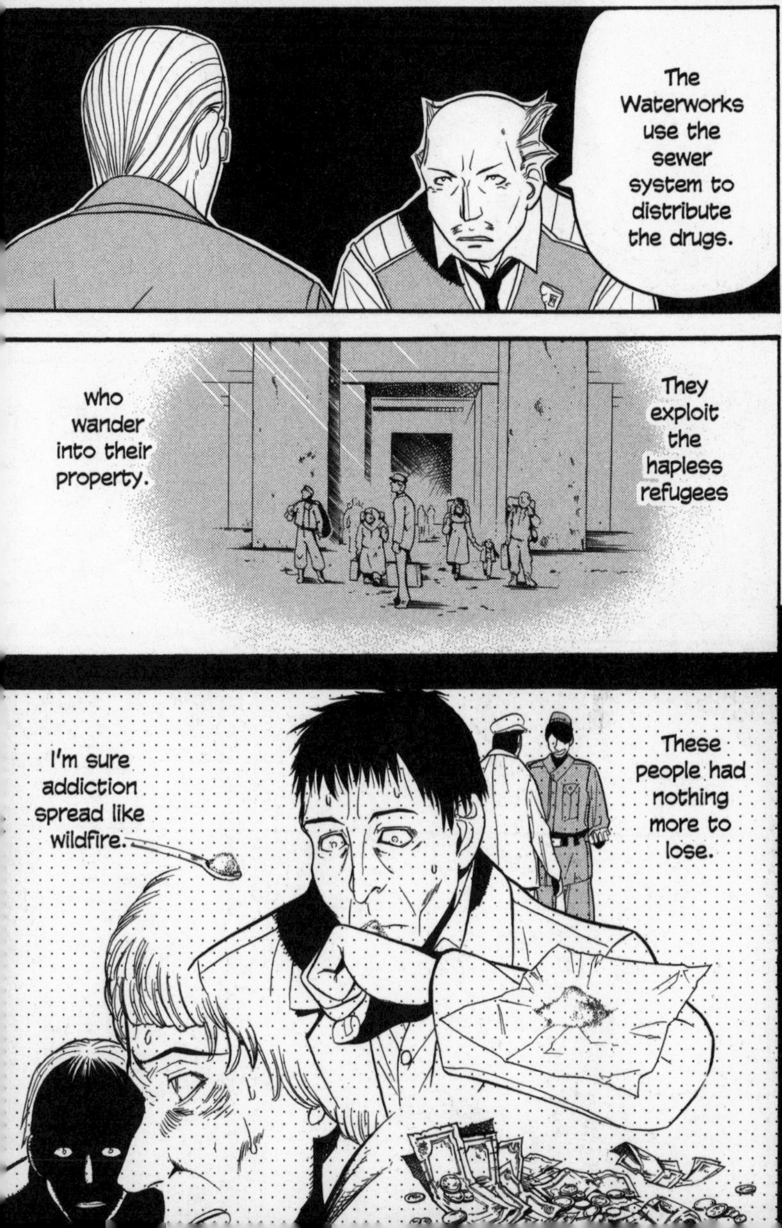
The Waterworks use the sewer system to distribute the drugs.
They exploit the hapless refugees
who wander into their property.
These people had nothing more to lose.
I'm sure addiction spread like wildfire.

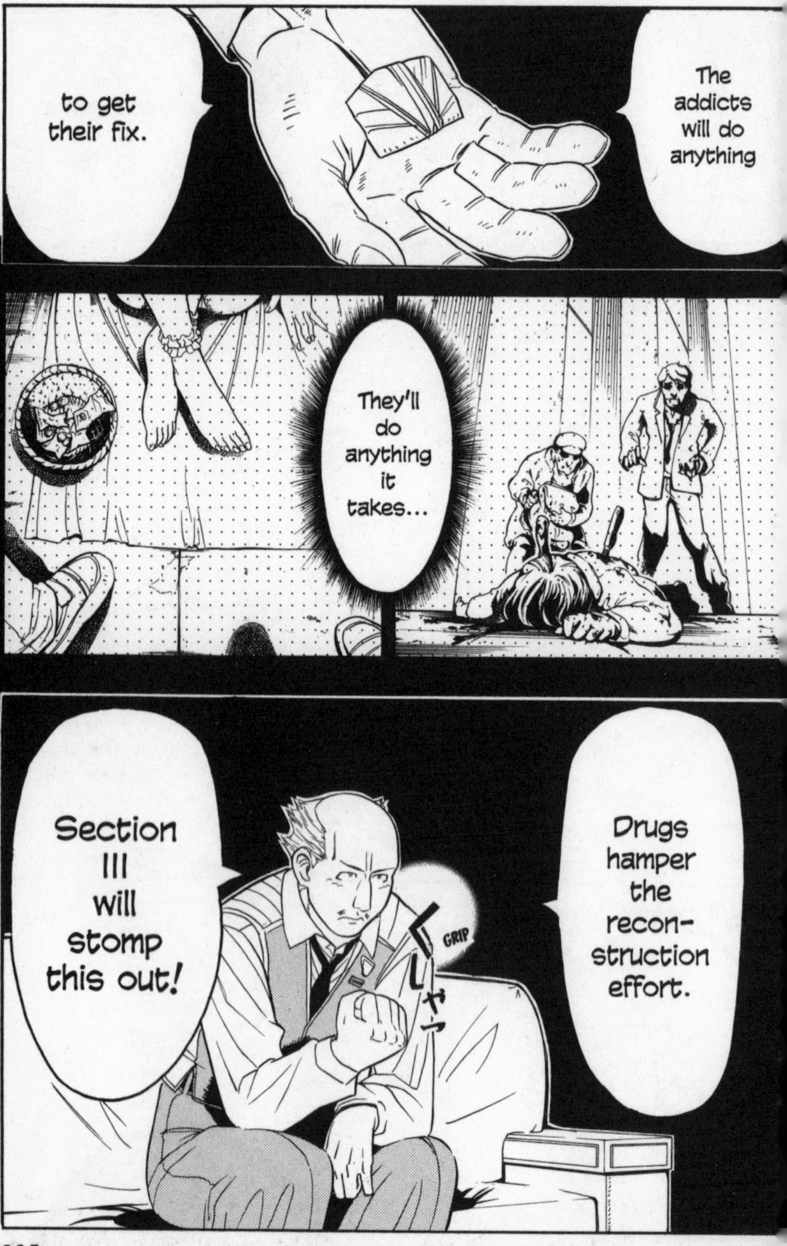
The addicts will do anything
to get their fix.
They'll do anything it takes...
Drugs hamper the recon-struction effort.
GRIP
Section III will stomp this out!

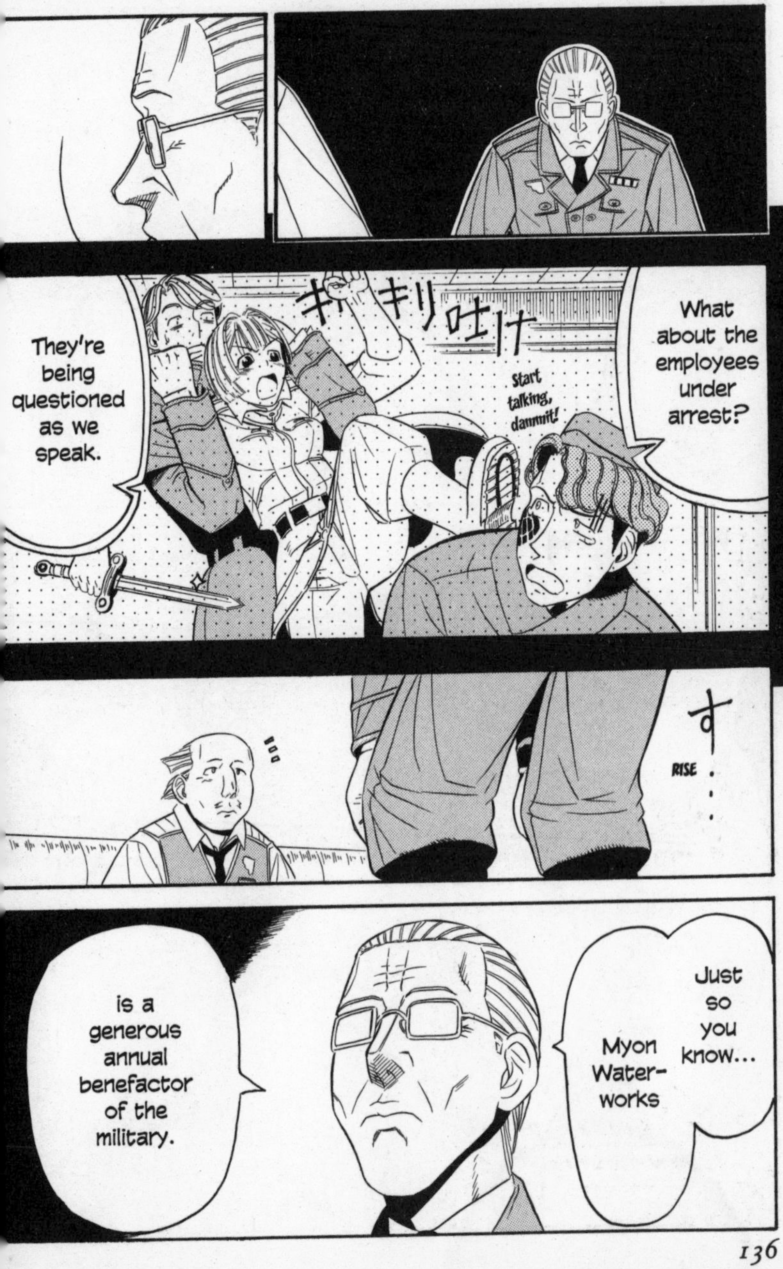
What about the employees under arrest?
キリキリ吐け
Start talking, dammit!
They're being questioned as we speak.
す
RISE . . .
Just so you know...
Myon Water-works
is a generous annual benefactor of the military.

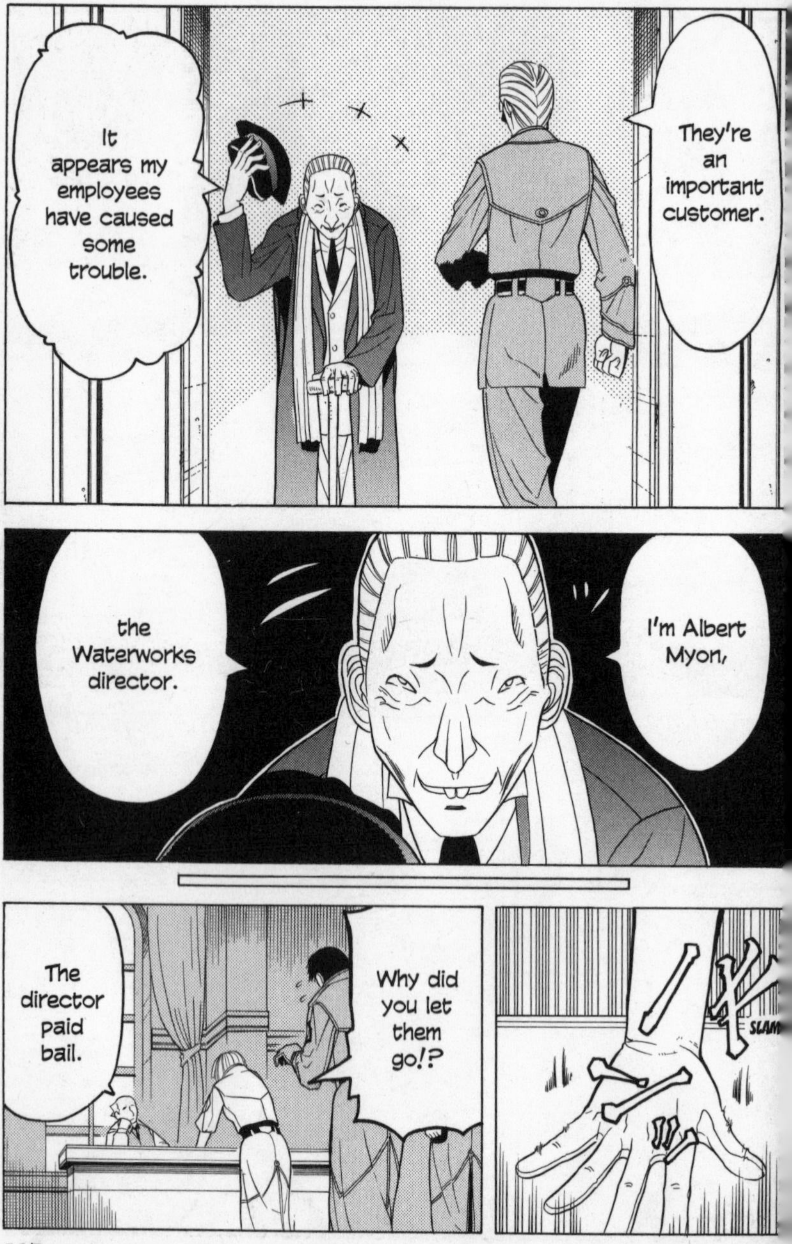
They're an important customer.
It appears my employees have caused some trouble.
I'm Albert Myon,
the Waterworks director.
SLAM
Why did you let them go!?
The director paid bail.

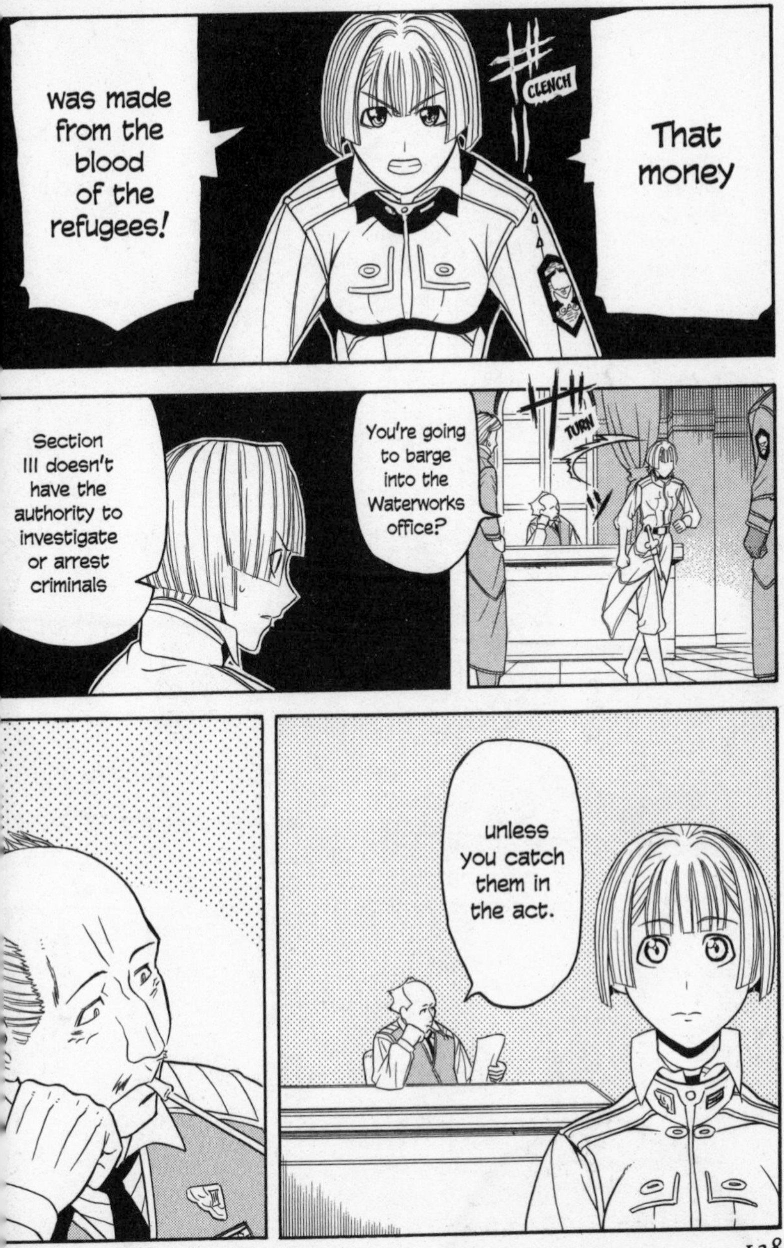
CLENCH
That money
was made from the blood of the refugees!
TURN
You're going to barge into the Waterworks office?
Section III doesn't have the authority to investigate or arrest criminals
unless you catch them in the act.

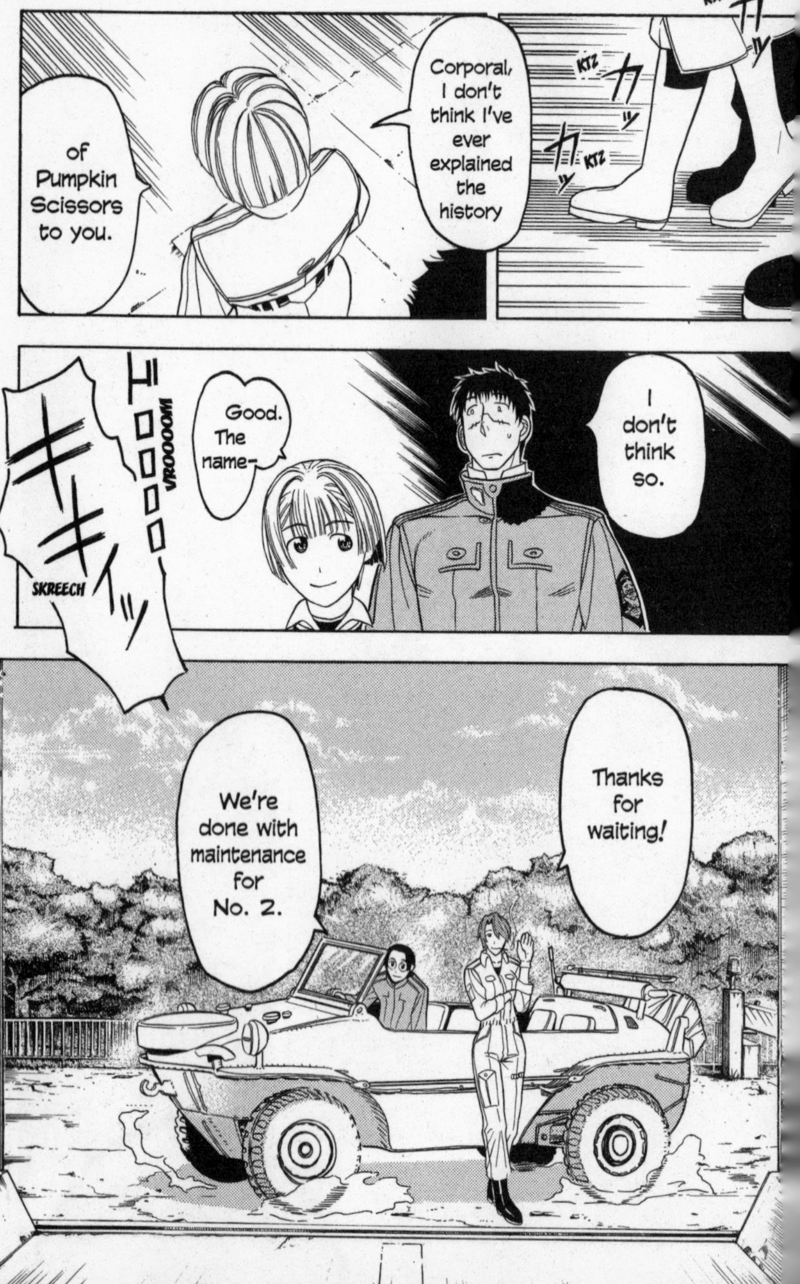
KTZ
KTZ
KTZ
Corporal, I don't think I've ever explained the history
of Pumpkin Scissors to you.
I don't think so.
Good. The name—
VROOOOM
SKREECH
Thanks for waiting!
We're done with maintenance for No. 2.

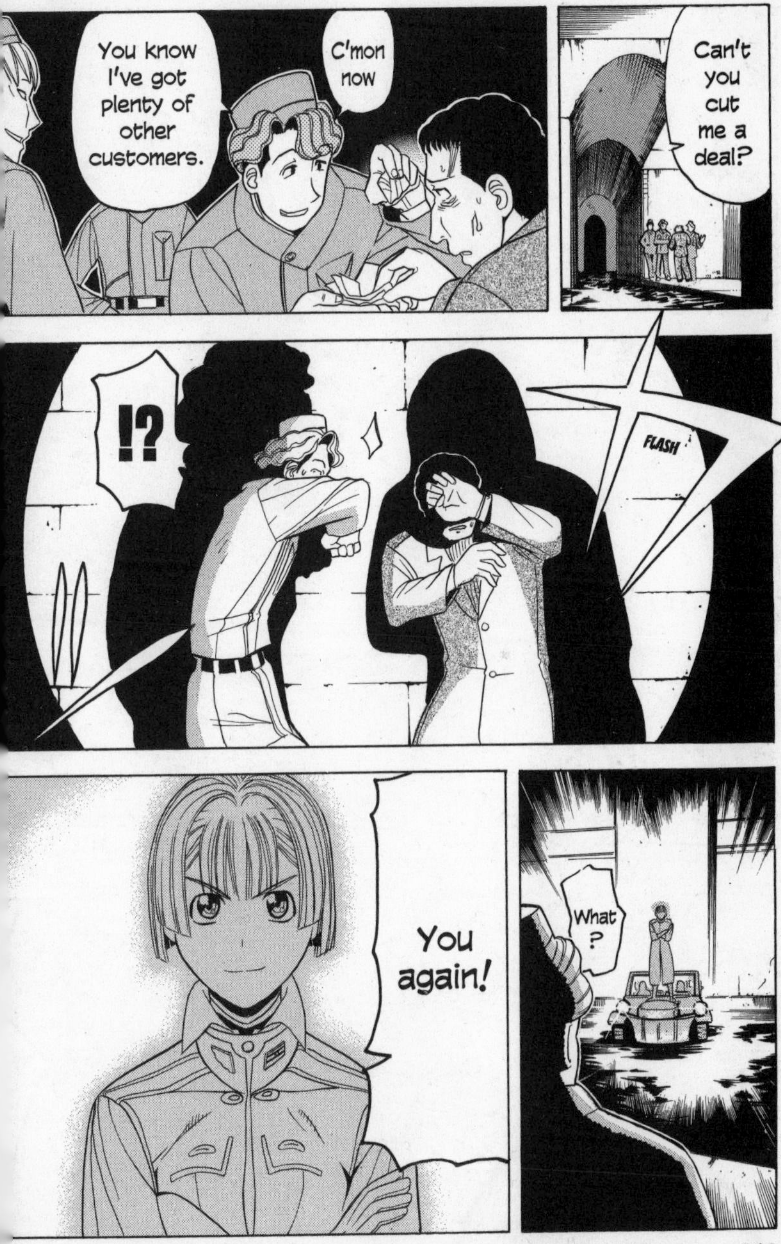
Can't you cut me a deal?
C'mon now
You know I've got plenty of other customers.
FLASH
!?
What?
You again!

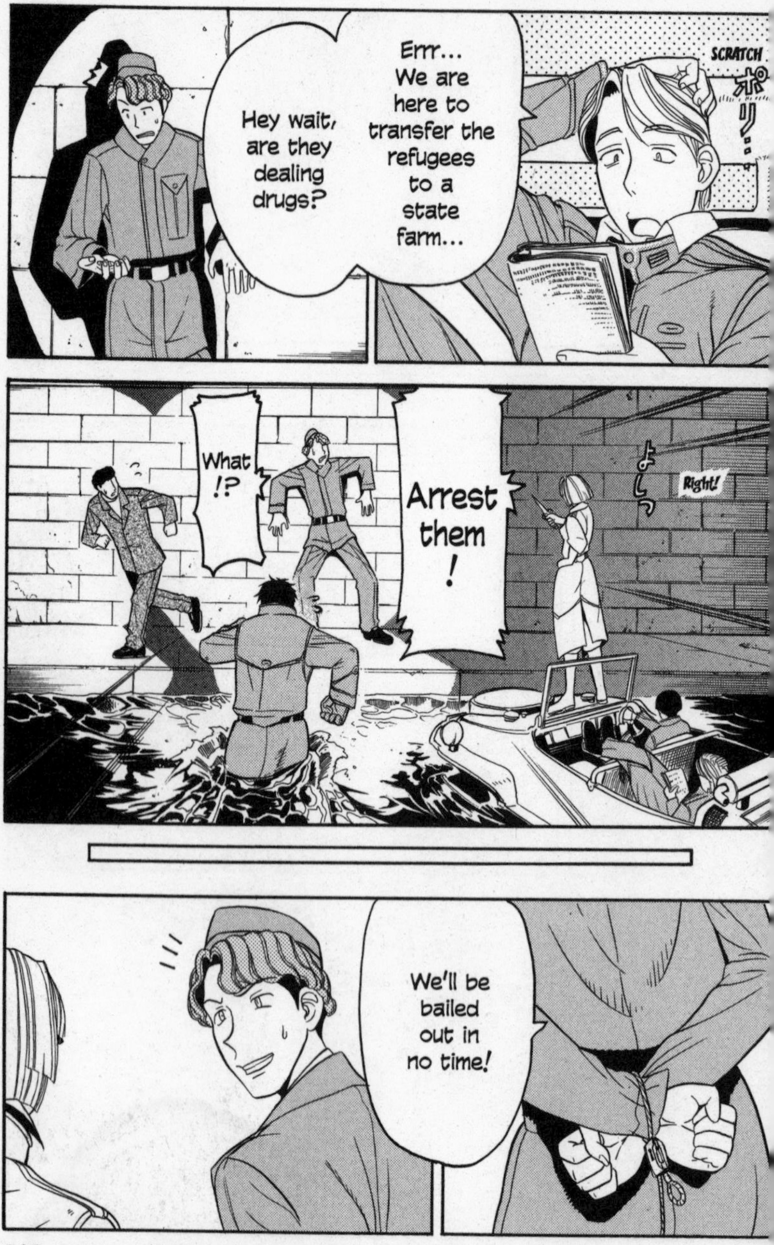
SCRATCH
ポリ…
Errr... We are here to transfer the refugees to a state farm...
Hey wait, are they dealing drugs?
Arrest them!
よしっ
Right!
What!?
We'll be bailed out in no time!

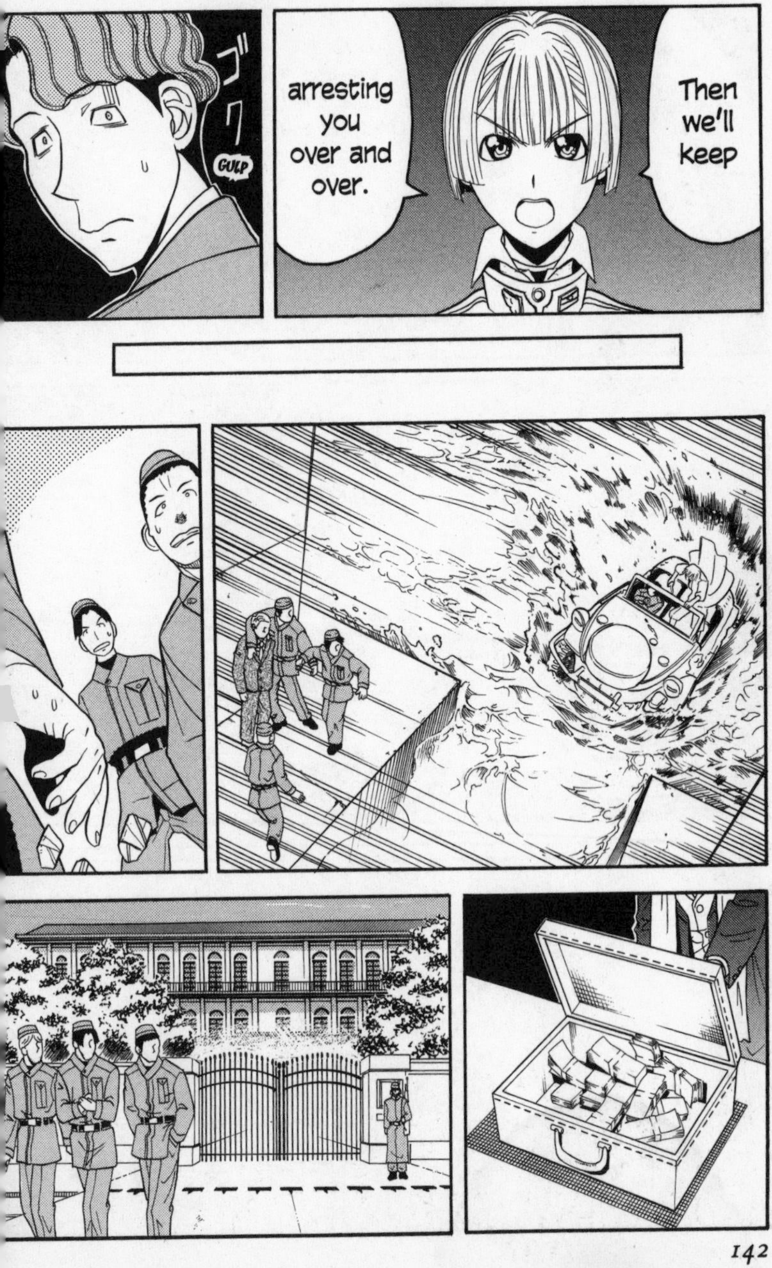
Then we'll keep
arresting you over and over.
ゴク
GULP

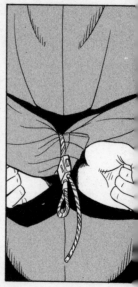

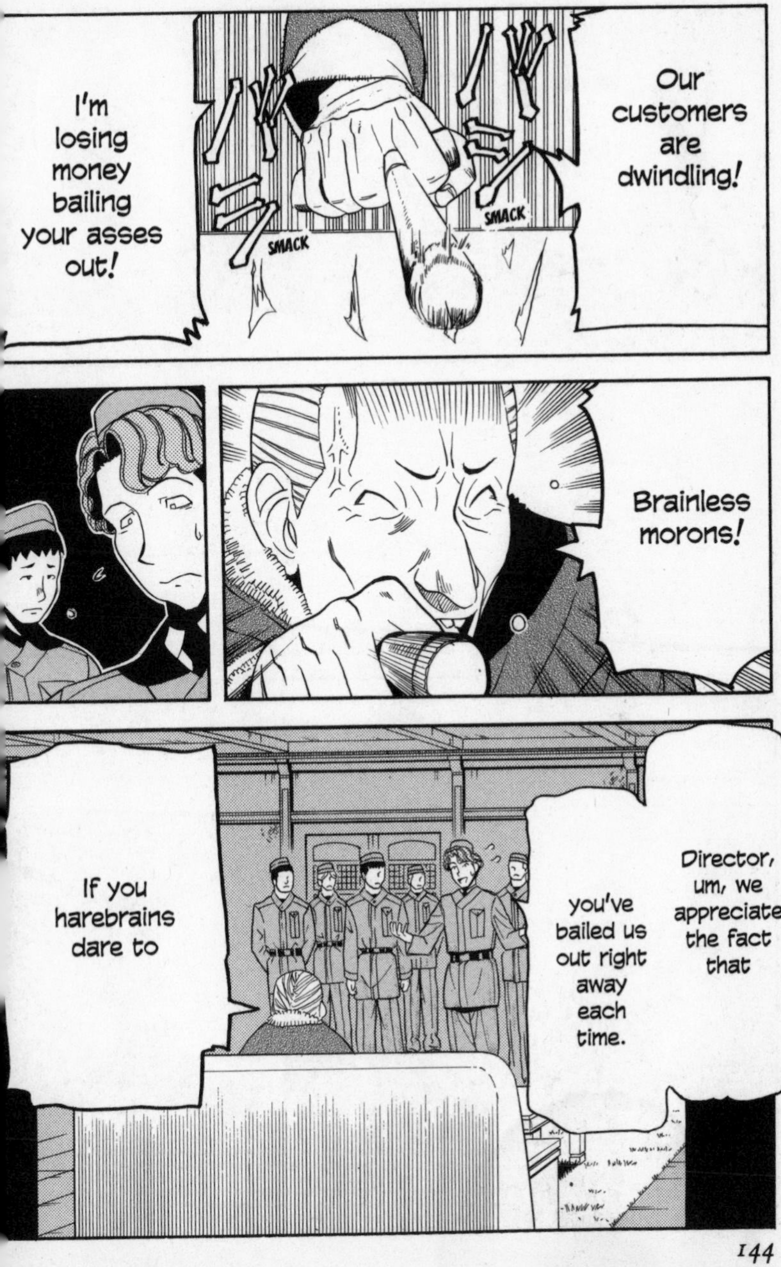
Our customers are dwindling!
SMACK
SMACK
I'm losing money bailing your asses out!
Brainless morons!
Director, um, we appreciate the fact that
you've bailed us out right away each time.
If you harebrains dare to

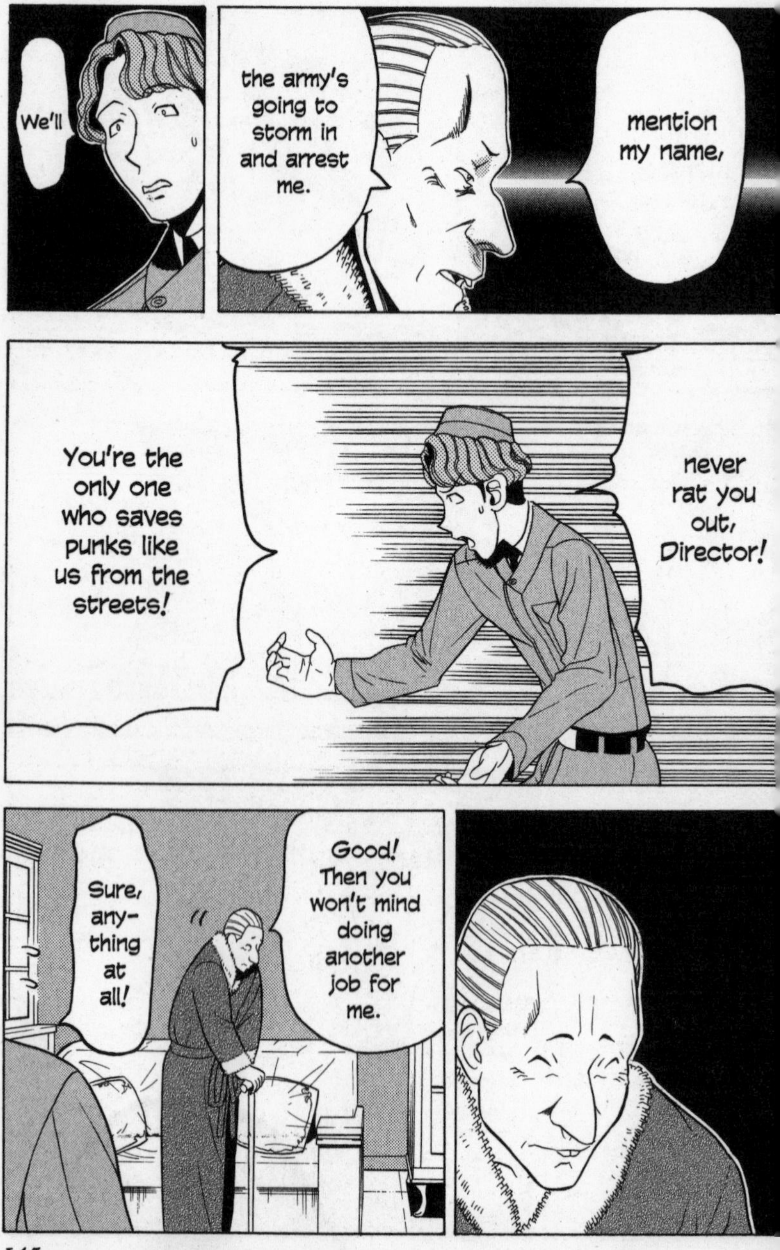
mention my name,
the army's going to storm in and arrest me.
We'll
never rat you out, Director!
You're the only one who saves punks like us from the streets!
Good! Then you won't mind doing another job for me.
Sure, any-thing at all!

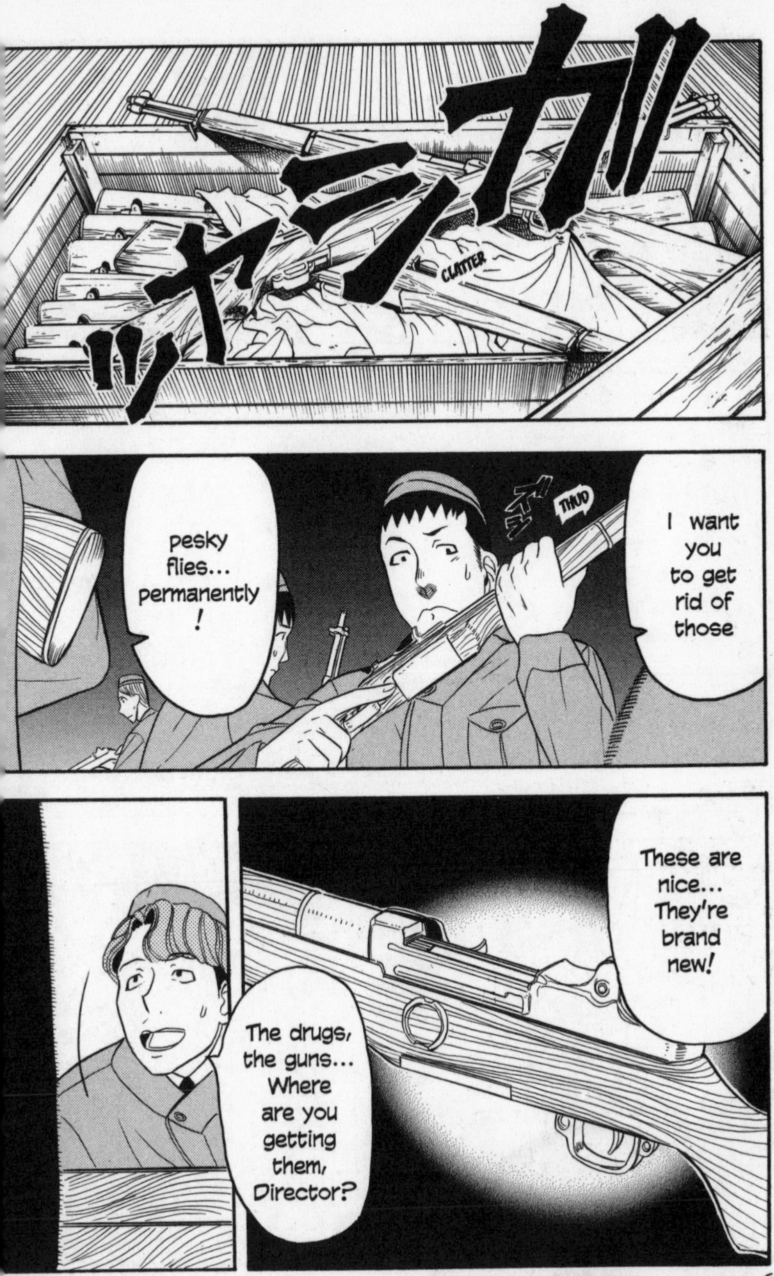
CLATTER
THUD
I want you to get rid of those
pesky flies... permanently!
These are nice... They're brand new!
The drugs, the guns... Where are you getting them, Director?

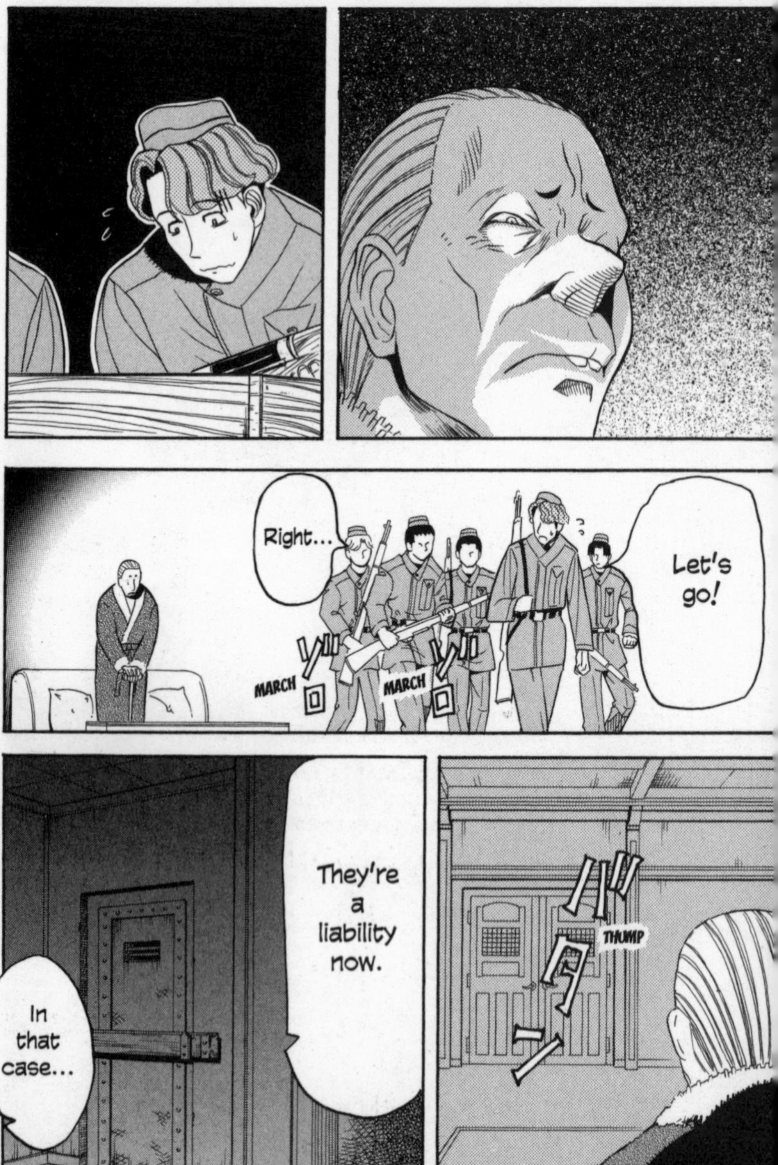
Let's go!
Right...
MARCH
MARCH
THUMP
They're a liability now.
In that case...

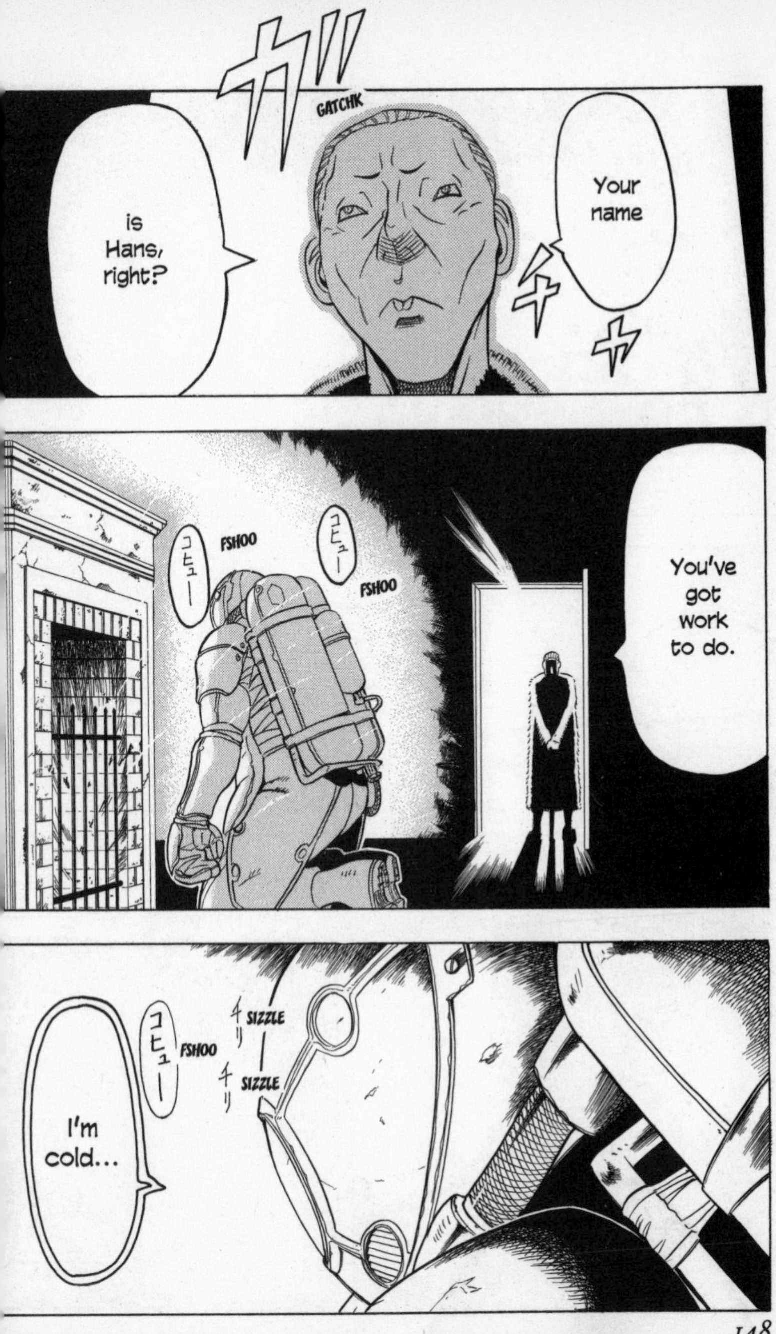
ガッ
GATCHK
Your name
is Hans, right?
You've got work to do.
コヒュー
FSHOO
コヒュー
FSHOO
チリ
SIZZLE
チリ
SIZZLE
コヒュー
FSHOO
I'm cold...

You were going to tell me the other day...

VROOOM

SPLISH

SPLISH!

SPLISH!

SPLASH

Merc! Nooo!

He was um... a little too randy with the messenger dogs from Section 1.

Oh? About Mercury?

I was talking about the unit's history.

RAISE

Why didn't you say so!?

I'm sorry!

VROOC

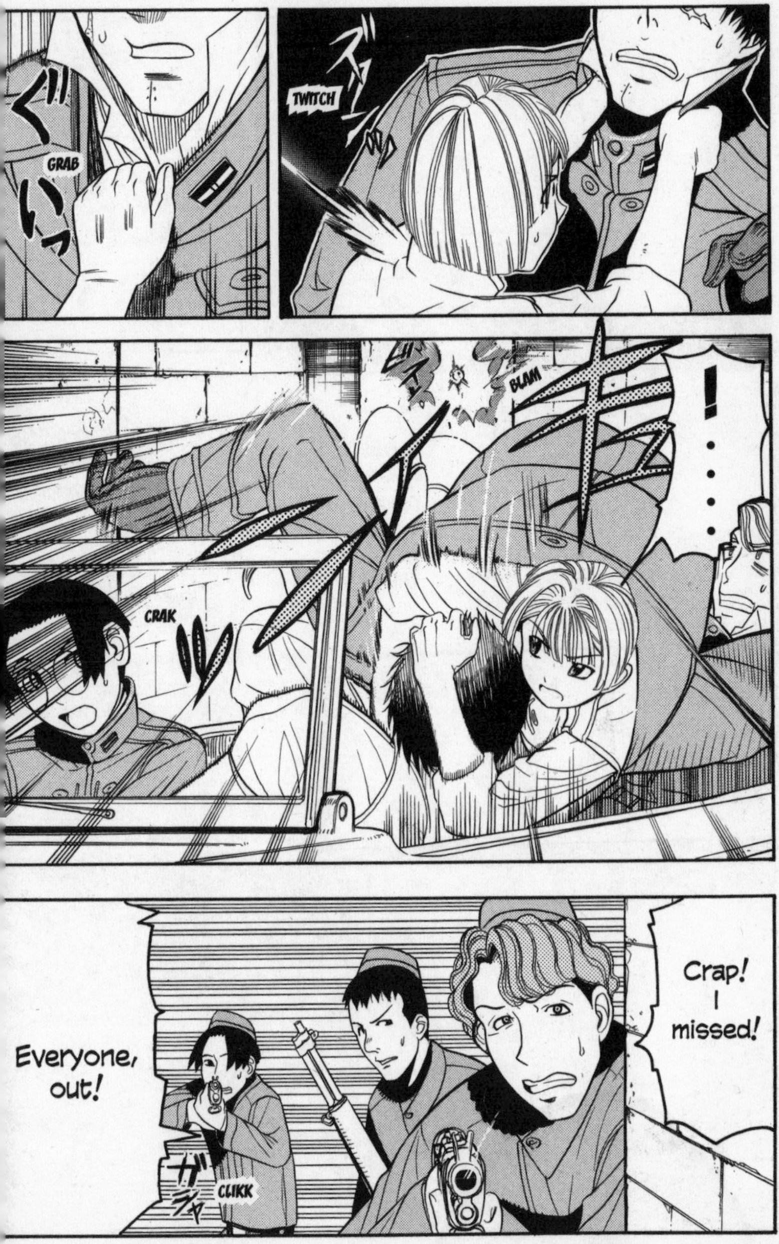
TWITCH
GRAB
!....
BLAM
CRAK
Crap! I missed!
Everyone, out!
CLIKK

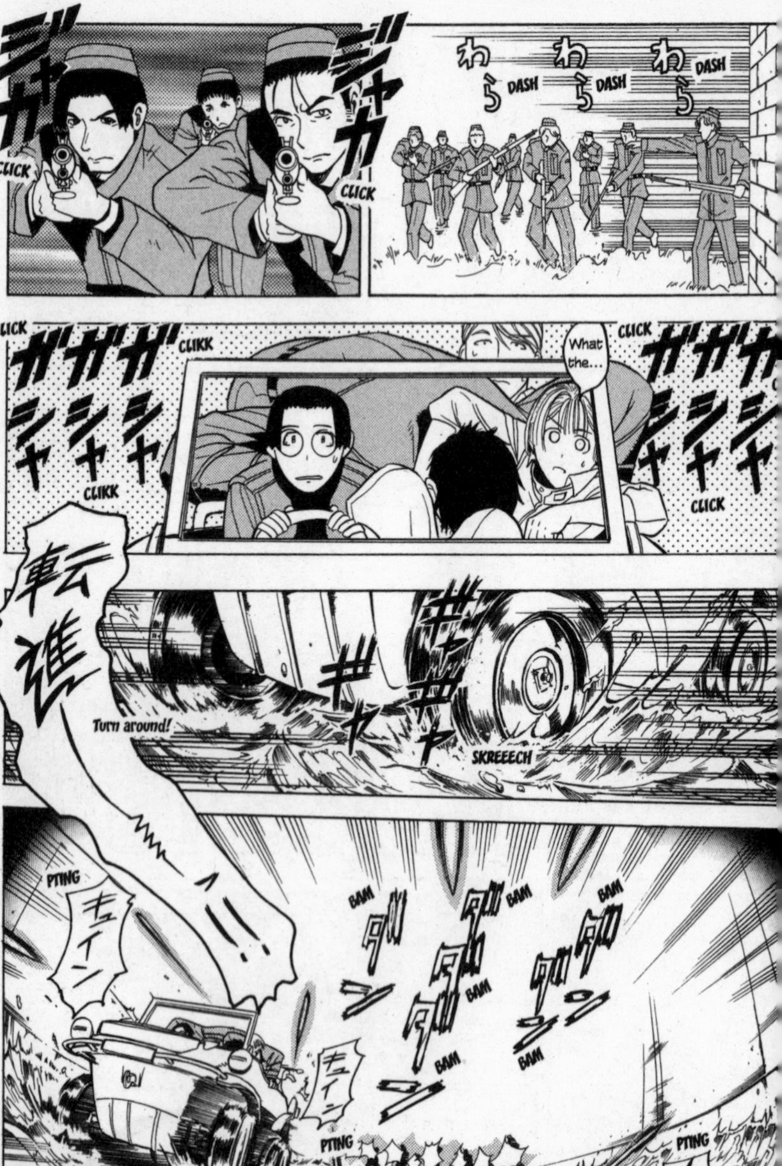

わら DASH
わら DASH
わら DASH
ジャカ
CLICK
ジャカ
CLICK
CLICK
ガシャガシャガシャ
CLICK
What the...
CLICK
CLIKK
ガシャガシャガシャ
CLIKK
ギャギャ
SKREEECH
転進
Turn around!
BAM
ダン
BAM
ダン
BAM
ダン
BAM
ダン
BAM
ダン
BAM
ダン
PTING
キュイン
PTING
キュイン
PTING
キュイン

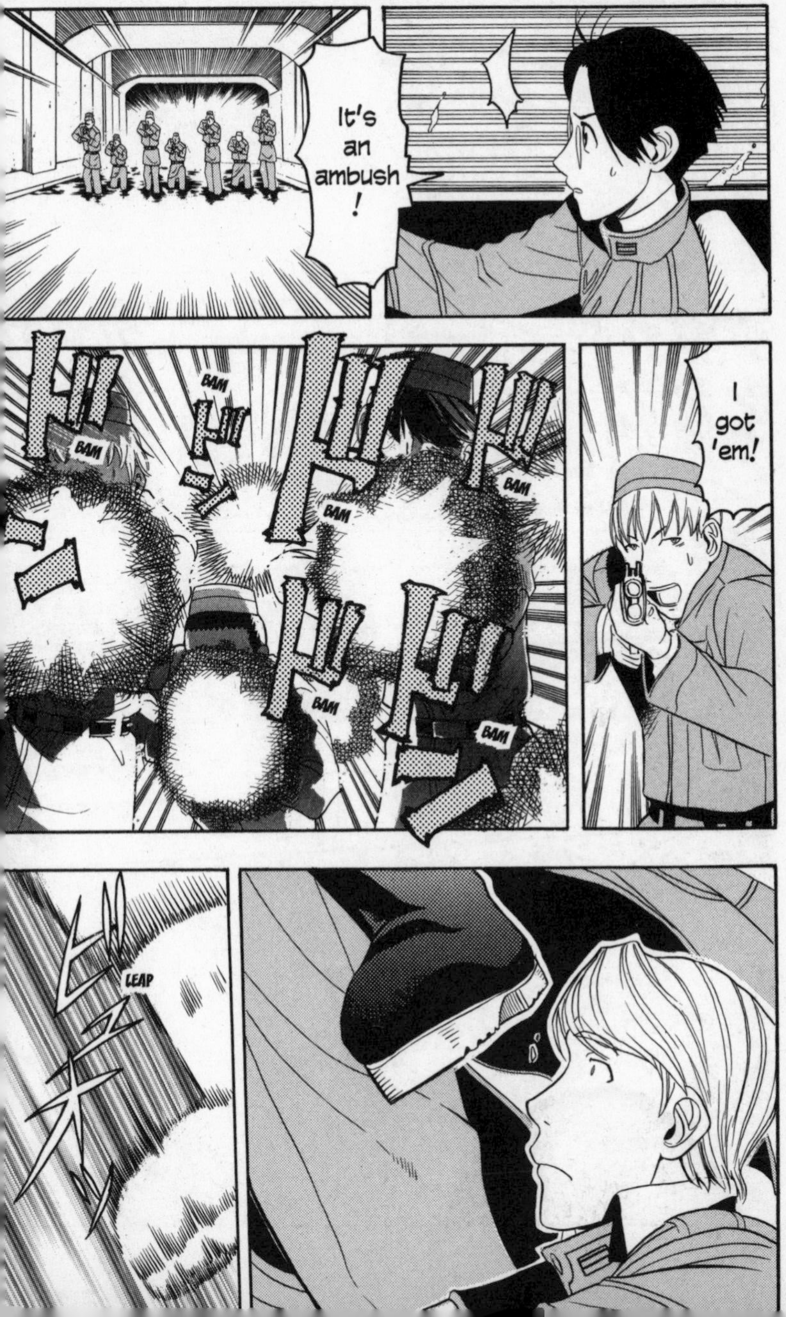
It's an ambush!
BAM
BAM
BAM
BAM
BAM
BAM
I got 'em!
LEAP

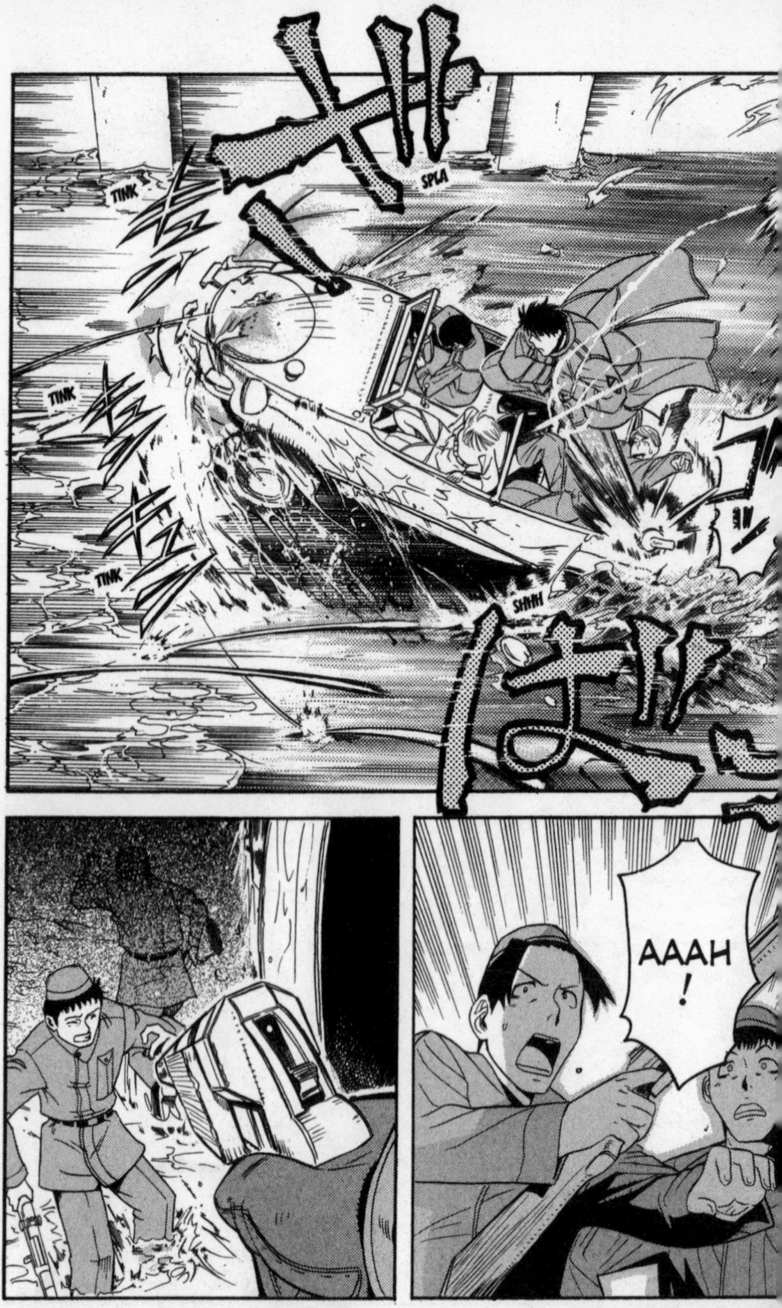
SPLA
TINK
TINK
TINK
SHHH
AAAH!

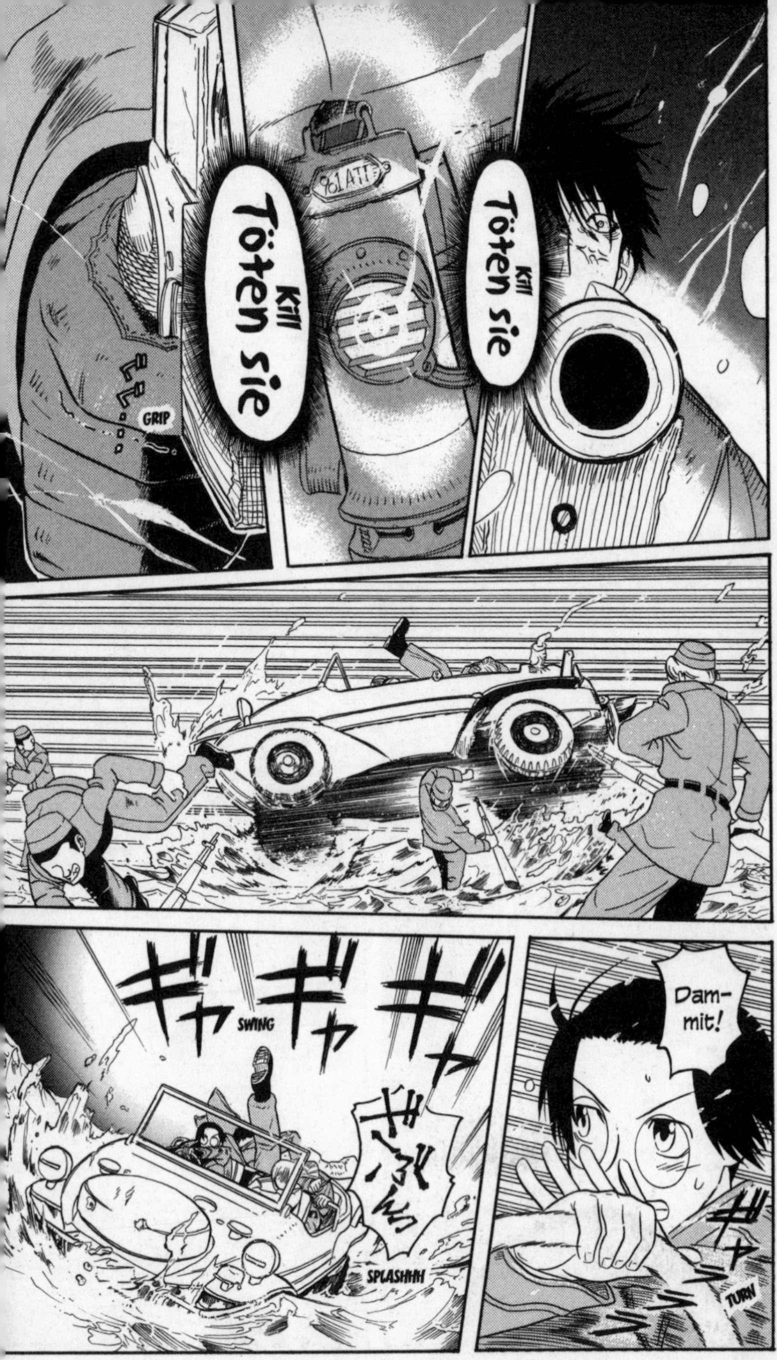
Töten sie
Kill
Töten sie
Kill
GRIP
Dam-
mit!
TURN
SWING
SPLASHHH

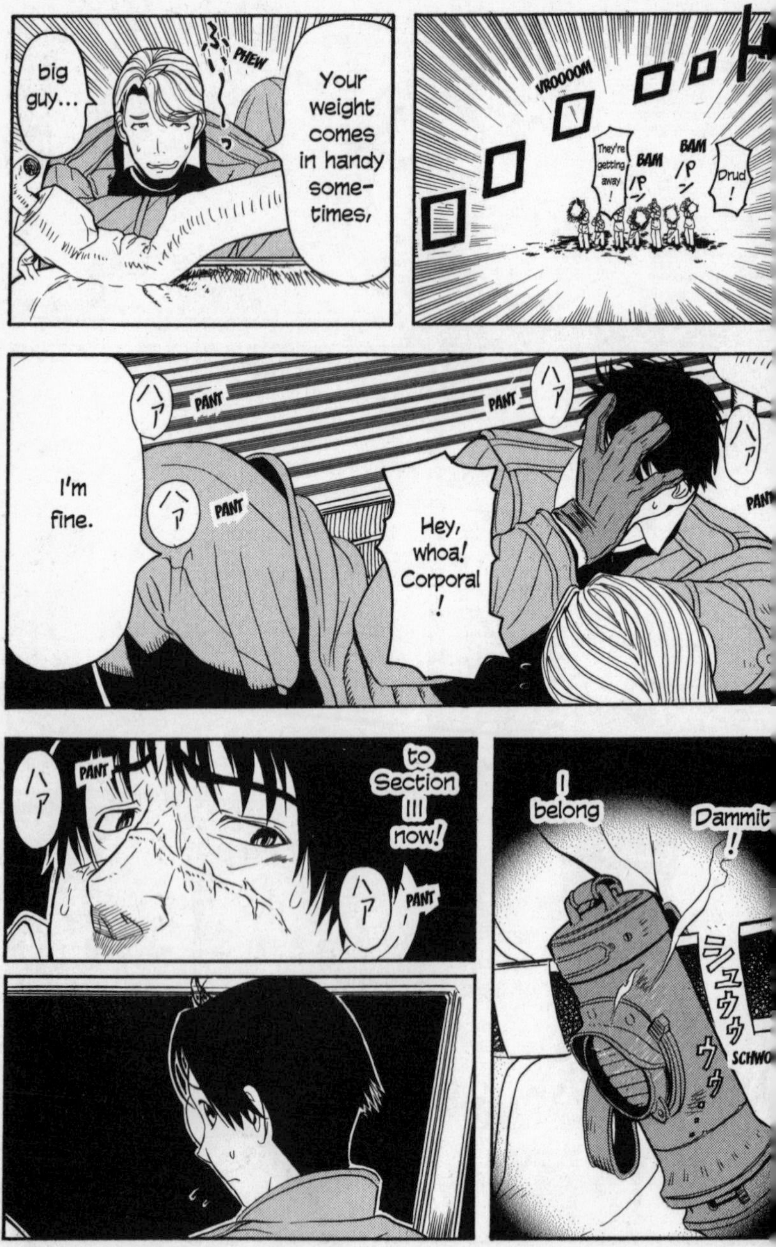
VROOOOM
Drud!
BAM
BAM
They're getting away!
PHEW
Your weight comes in handy some-times,
big guy...
ハァ
PAN
ハァ
PANT
Hey, whoa! Corporal!
ハァ
PANT
I'm fine.
ハァ
PANT
Dammit!
I belong
シュウウウゥ
SCHWO
to Section III now!
ハァ
PANT
ハァ
PANT

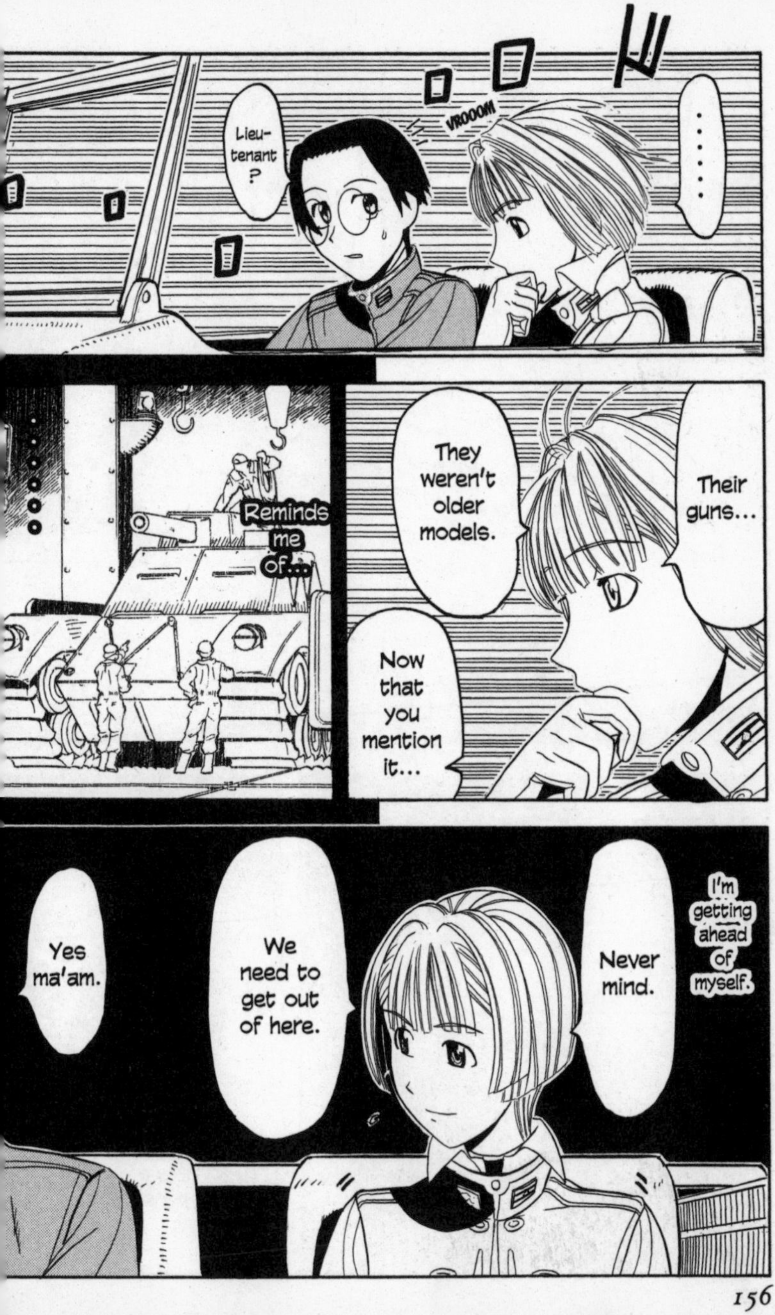

. . . . . .
VROOOM
Lieu-tenant?
Their guns...
They weren't older models.
Now that you mention it...
Reminds me of...
. . . . . .
I'm getting ahead of myself.
Never mind.
We need to get out of here.
Yes ma'am.

...
CLICK
SHWOO
G-CLUNKK
FLARE
CRACKLE

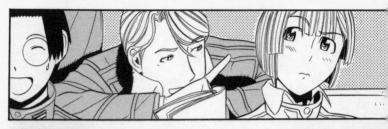

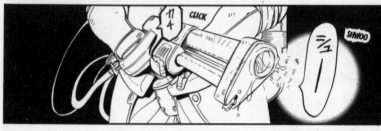

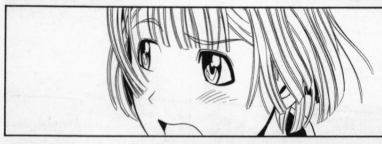

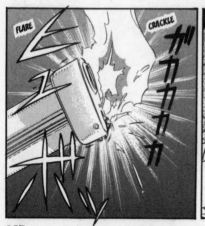

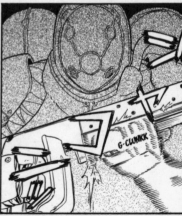

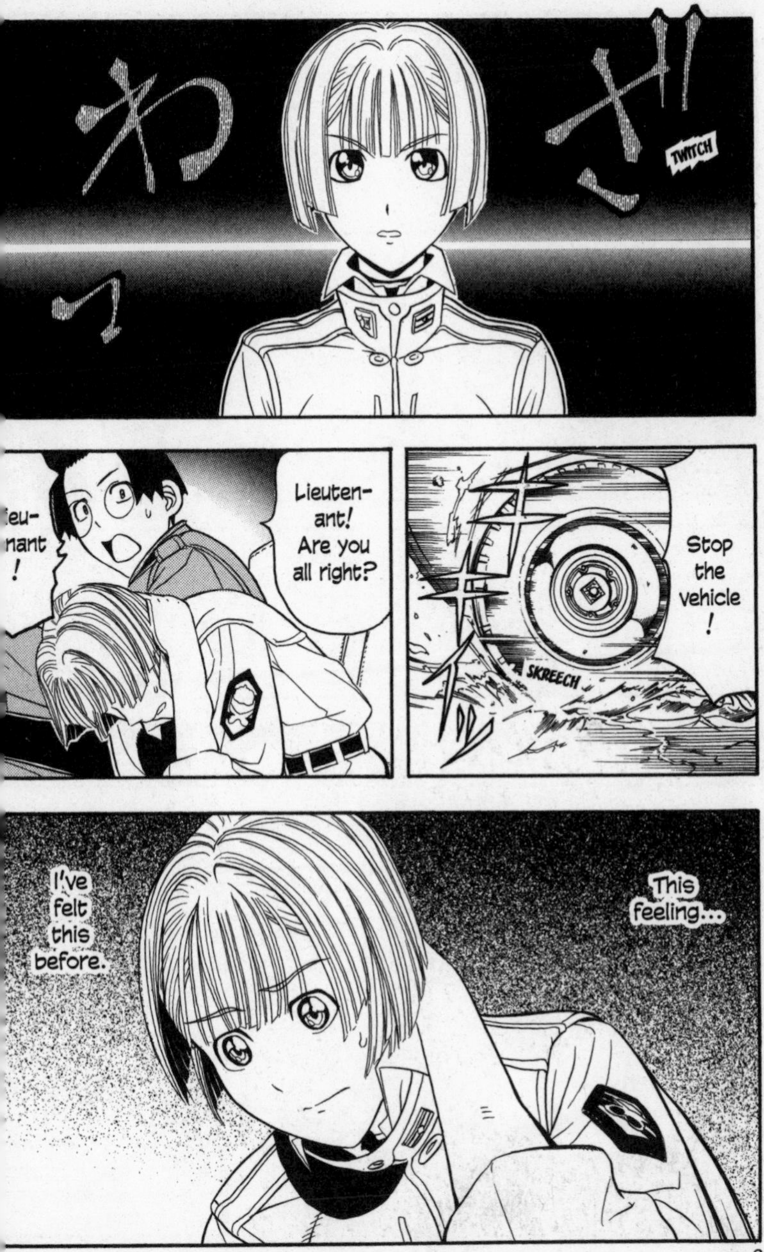
TWITCH
Lieuten-ant! Are you all right?
ieu-nant!
Stop the vehicle!
SKREECH
This feeling...
I've felt this before.

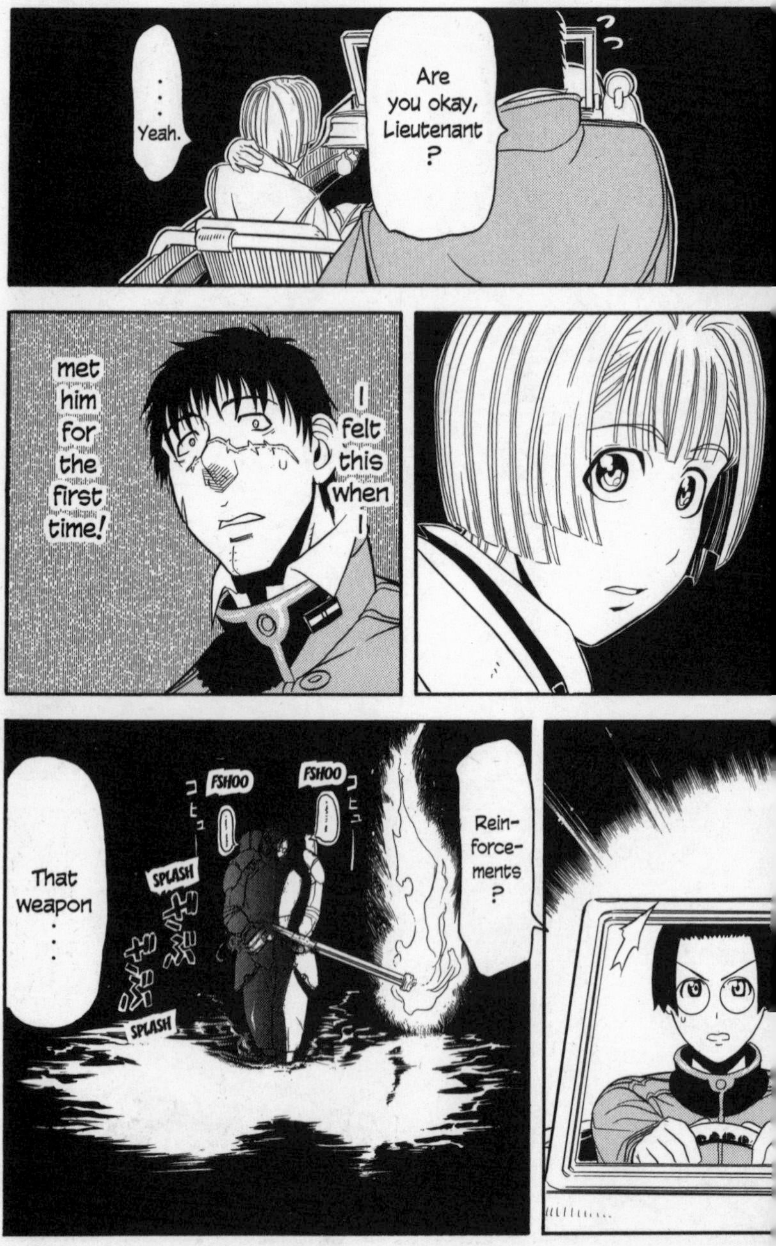
Are you okay, Lieutenant?
. . . Yeah.
I felt this when I met him for the first time!
Rein-force-ments?
FSHOO
FSHOO
SPLASH
SPLASH
That weapon . . .

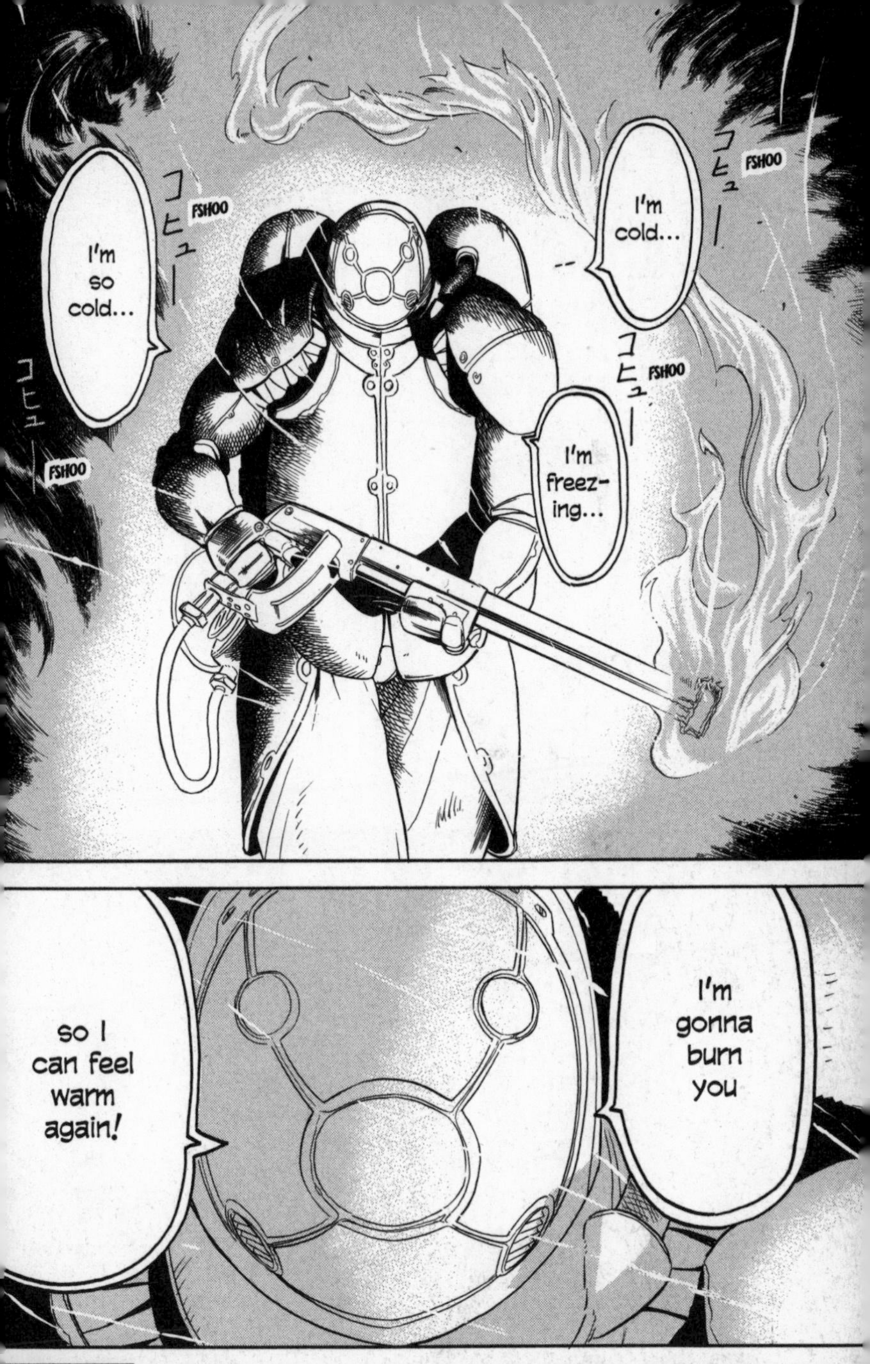
コヒュー
FSHOO
I'm cold...
コヒュー
FSHOO
I'm so cold...
コヒュー
FSHOO
I'm freezing...
コヒュー
FSHOO
I'm gonna burn you
so I can feel warm again!

#5/END

PumpkinScissors

PumpkinScissors

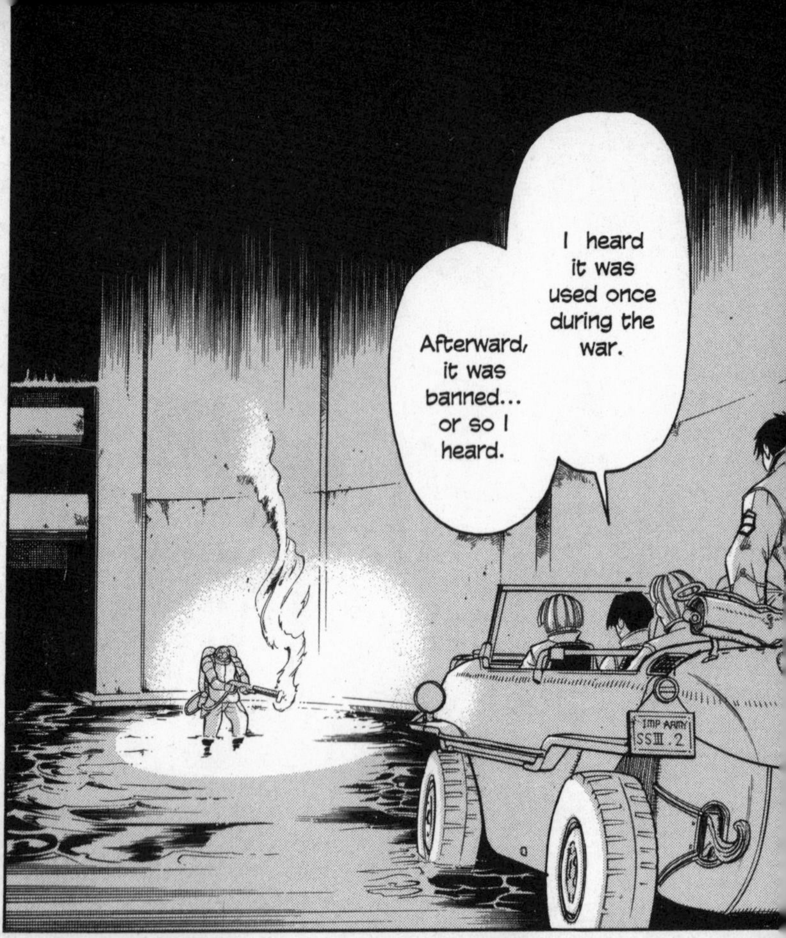
I heard it was used once during the war.
Afterward, it was banned... or so I heard.
IMP ARMY SSIII.2

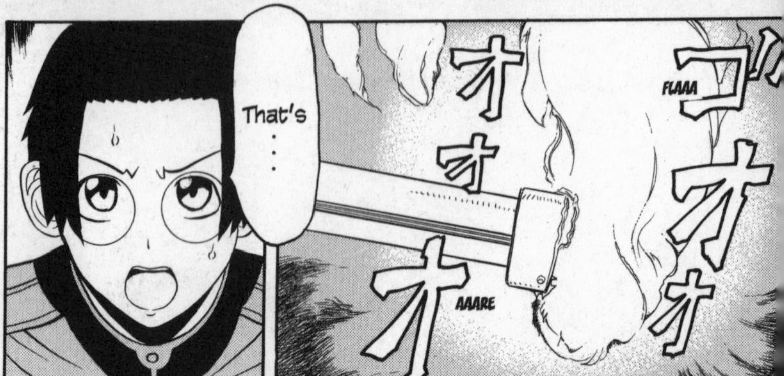
FLAAA
AAARE
That's ...

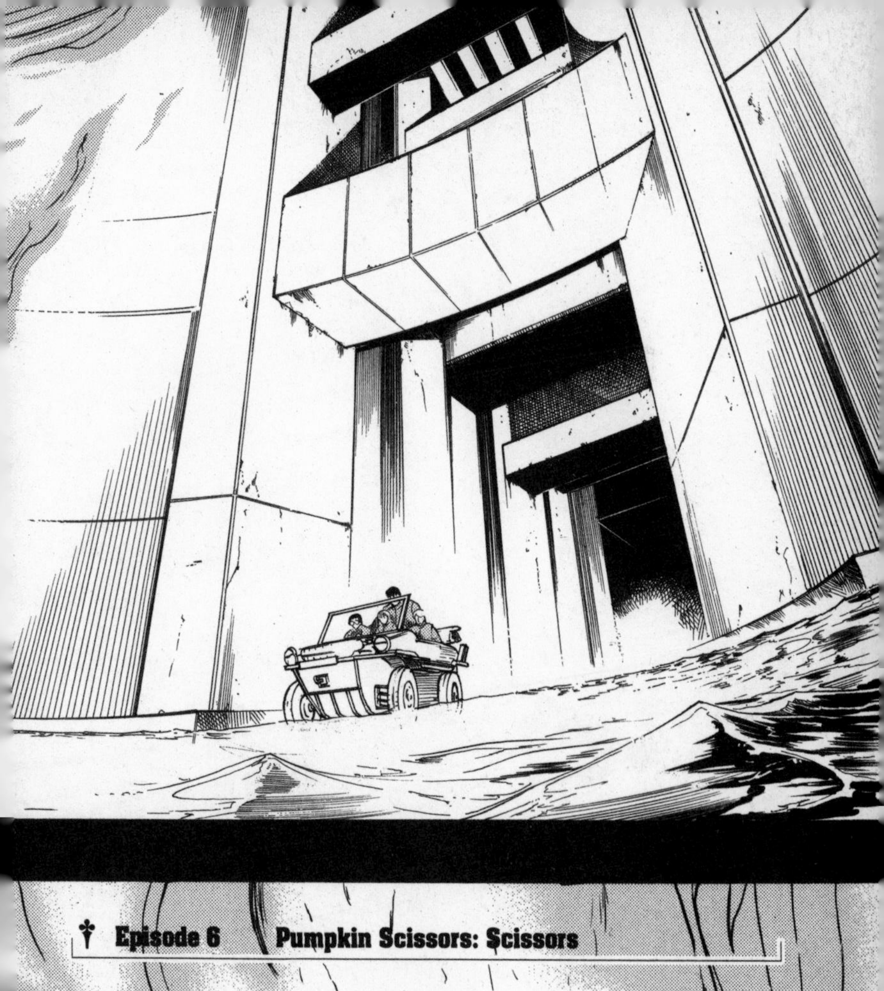

Episode 6 Pumpkin Scissors: Scissors

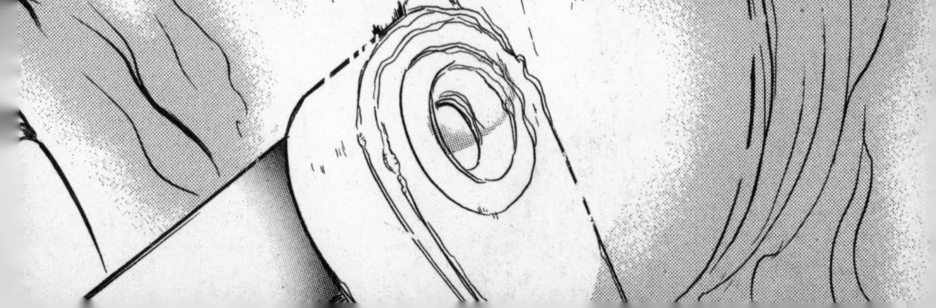

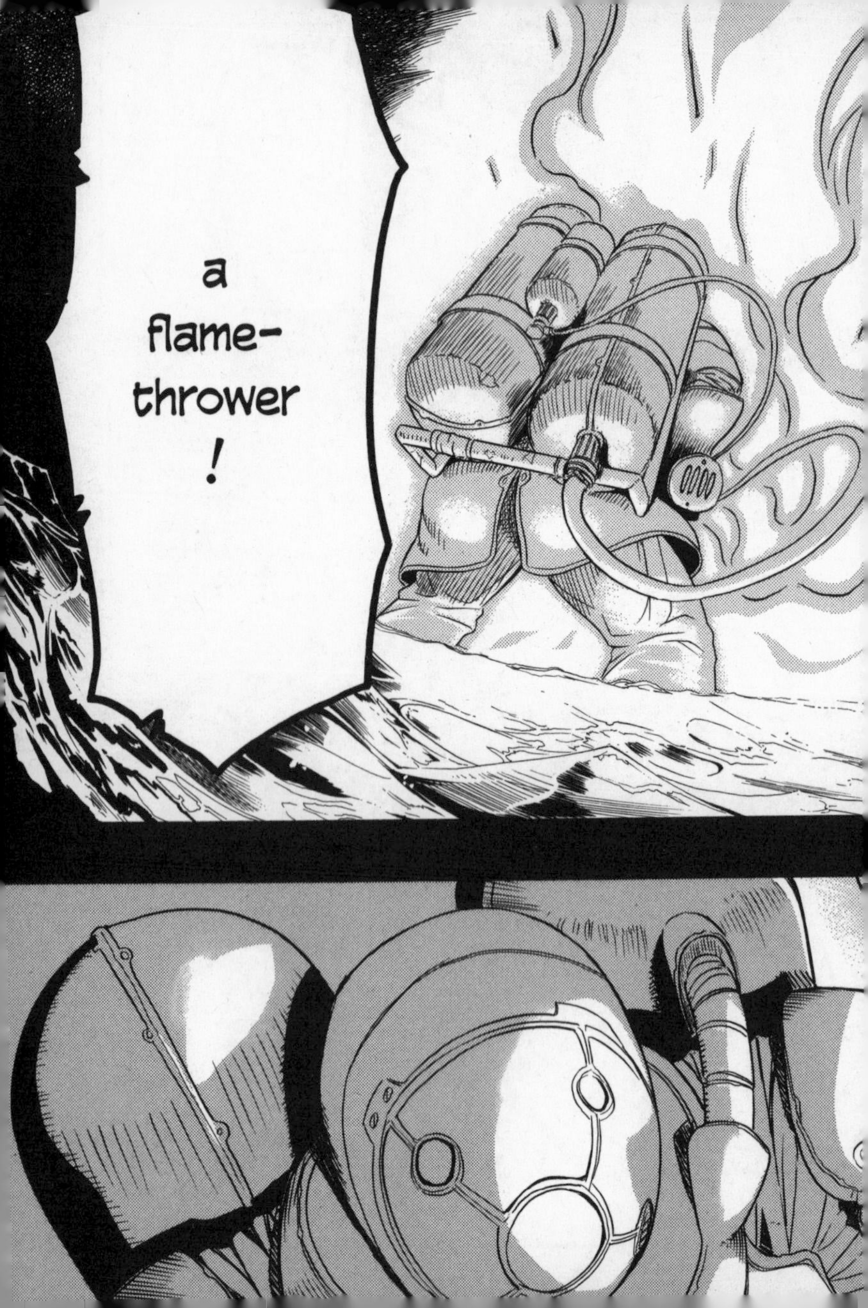
a flame-thrower!

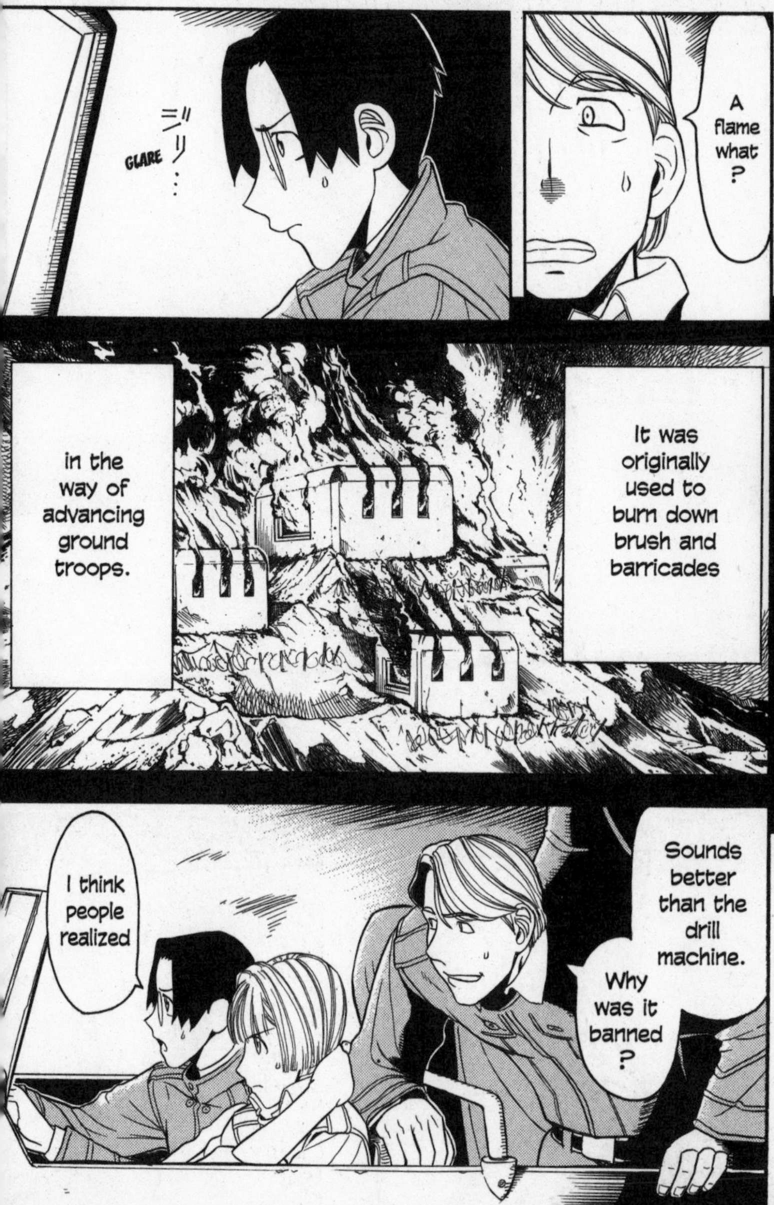
A flame what?
ジリ…
GLARE
It was originally used to burn down brush and barricades
in the way of advancing ground troops.
Sounds better than the drill machine.
Why was it banned?
I think people realized

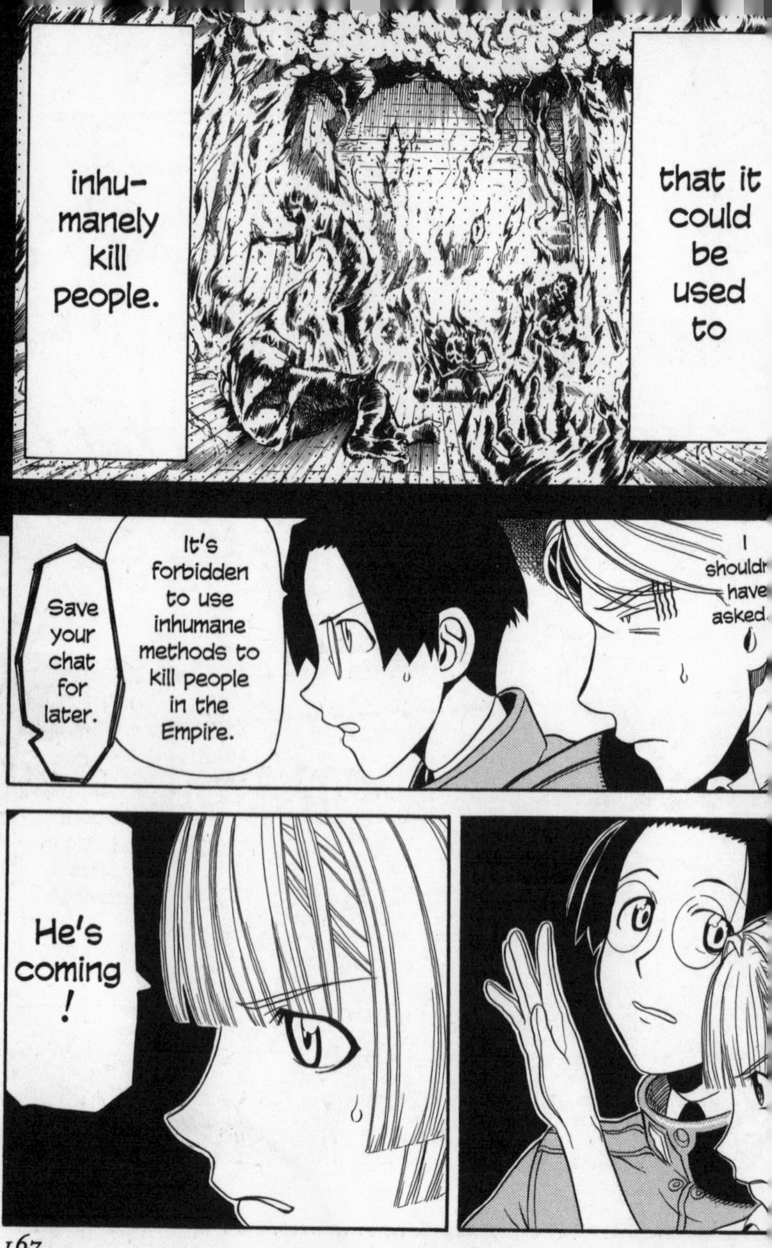
that it could be used to
inhu-manely kill people.
I shouldn have asked.
It's forbidden to use inhumane methods to kill people in the Empire.
Save your chat for later.
He's coming!

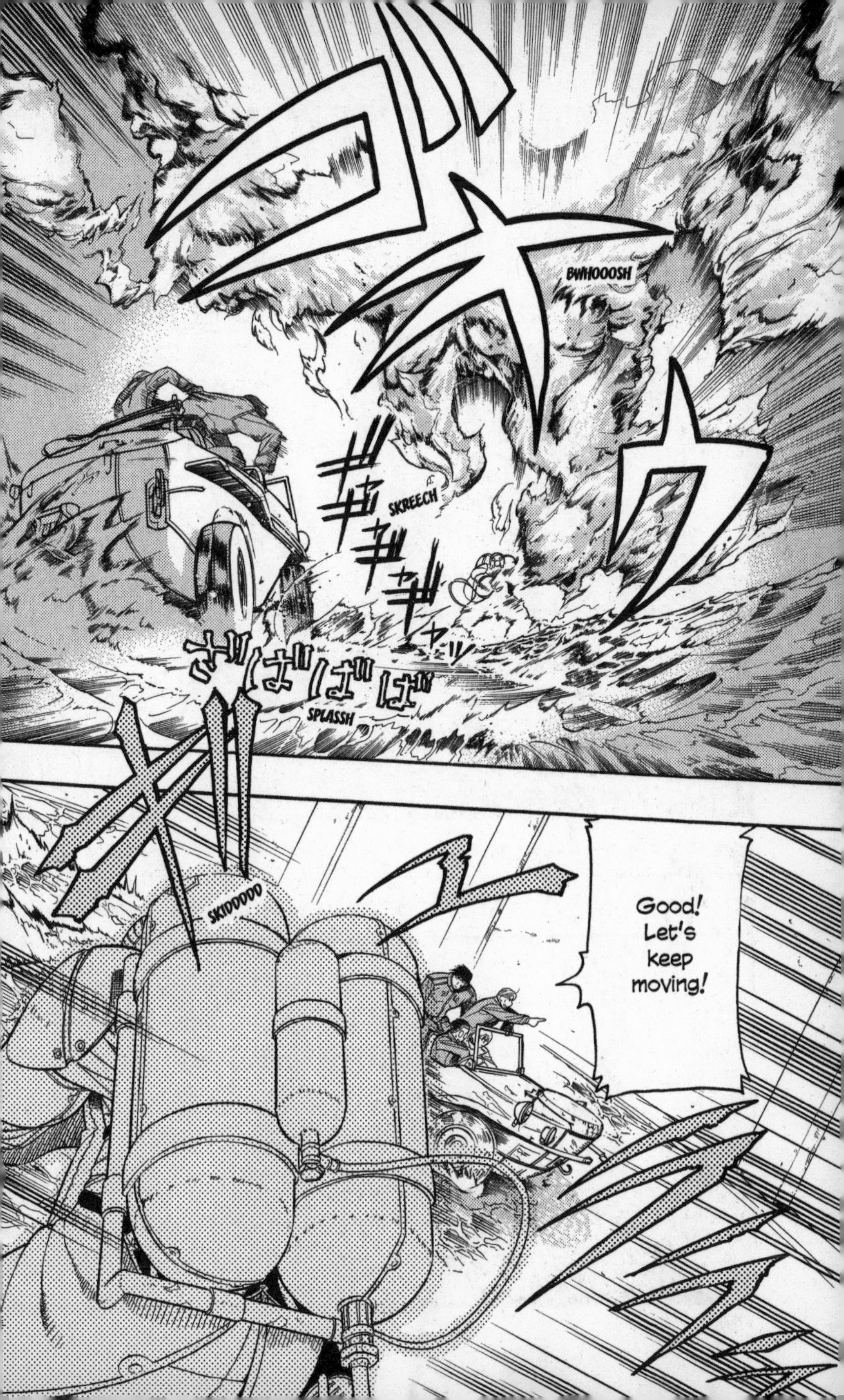

BWHOOOSH
SKREECH
SPLASSH
SKIDDOOO
Good! Let's keep moving!

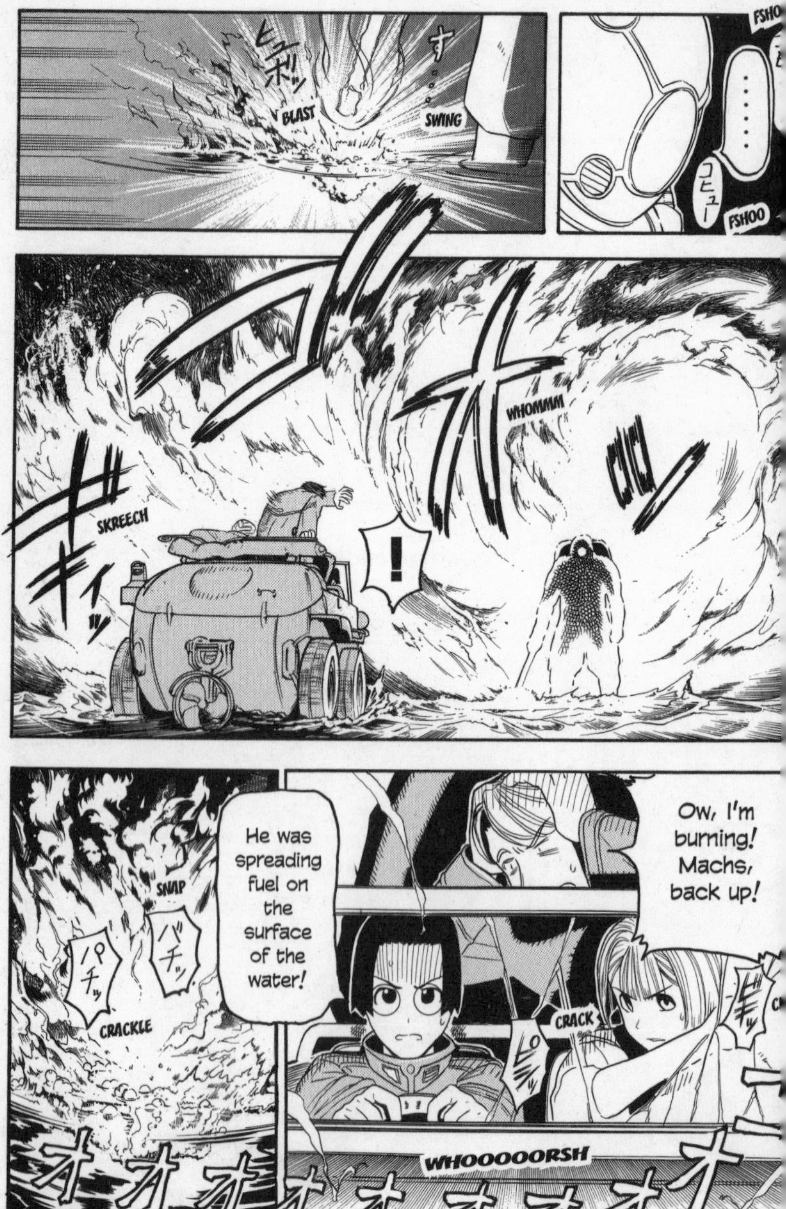
FSHOO
......
FSHOO
BLAST
SWING
WHOMMM
SKREECH
!
Ow, I'm burning! Machs, back up!
He was spreading fuel on the surface of the water!
CRACK
WHOOOOORSH
SNAP
CRACKLE

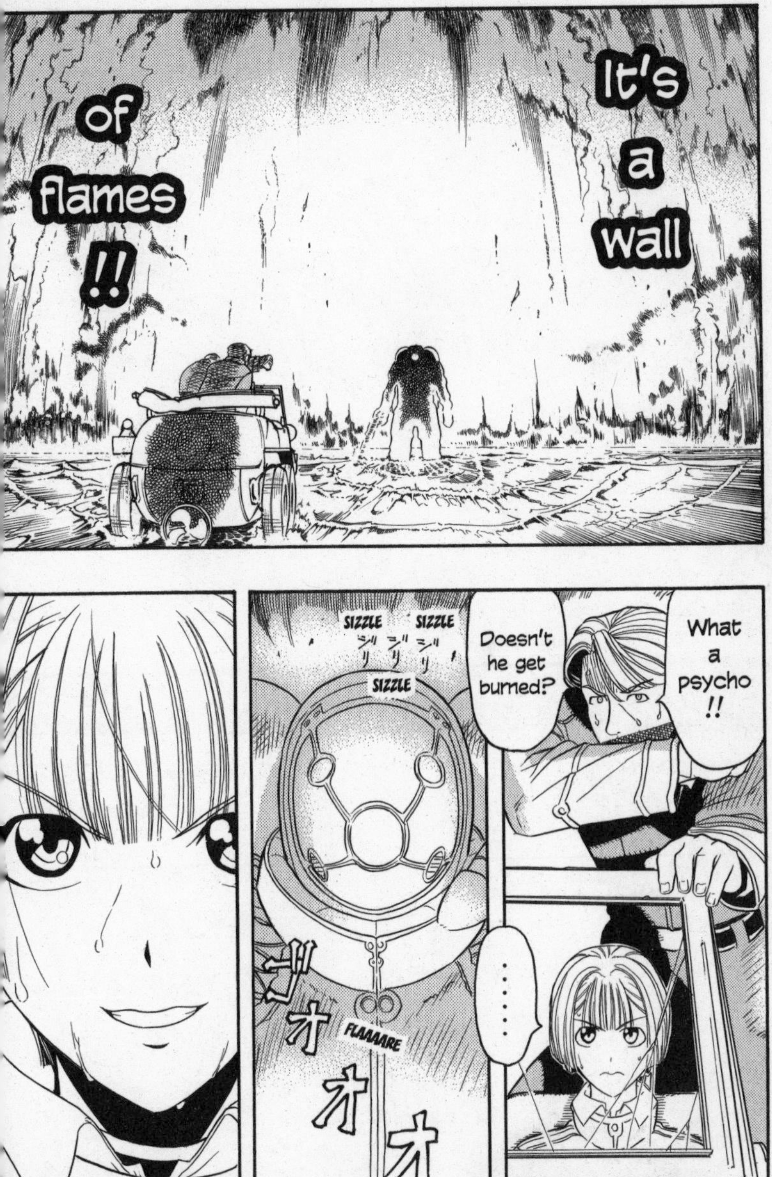
It's a wall
of flames!!
What a psycho!!
Doesn't he get burned?
......
SIZZLE SIZZLE
SIZZLE
ジリジリジリ
ゴオオオ
FLAAAARE

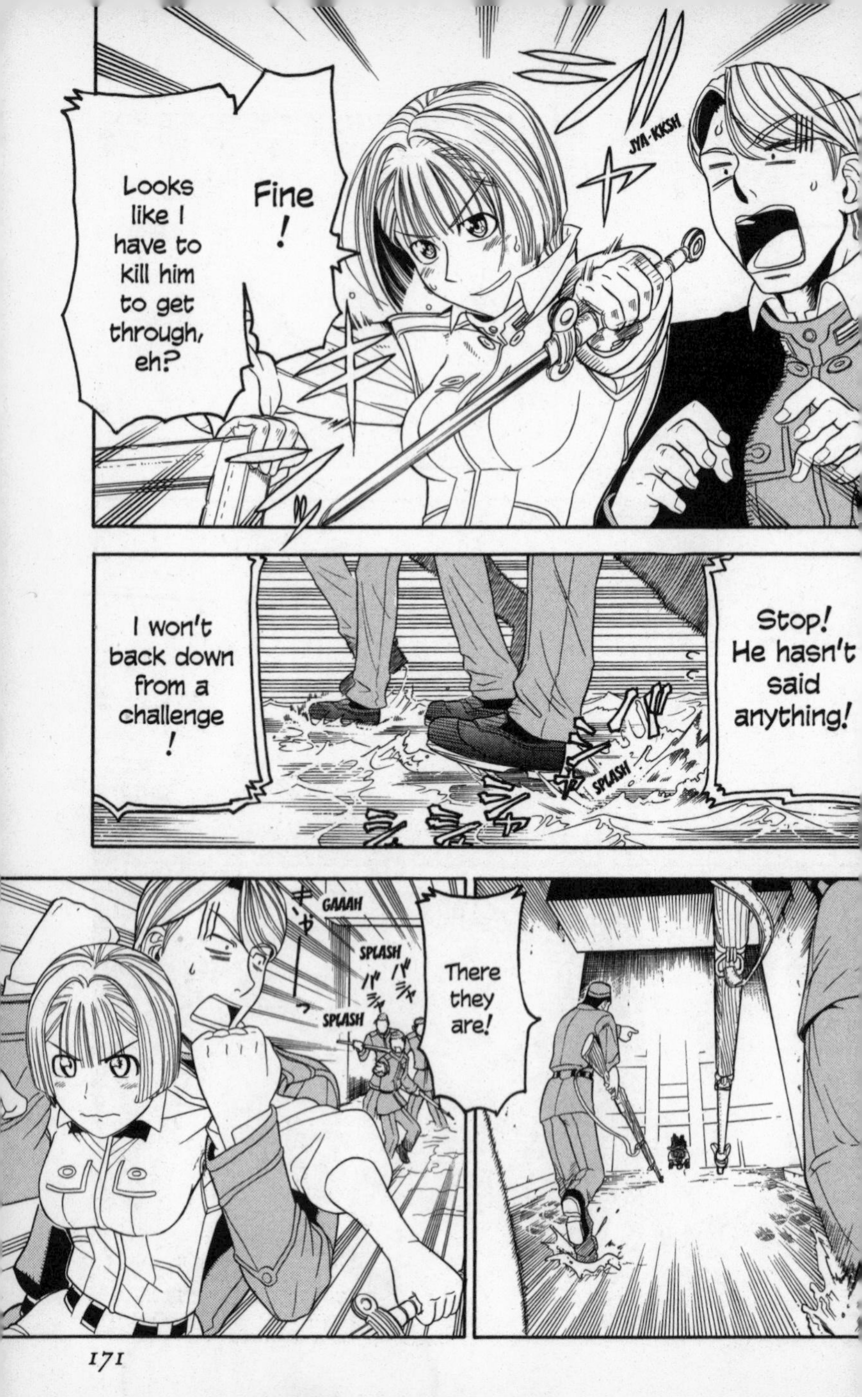
JYA-KKSH
Fine!
Looks like I have to kill him to get through, eh?
Stop! He hasn't said anything!
SPLASH
I won't back down from a challenge!
There they are!
GAAAH
SPLASH
SPLASH

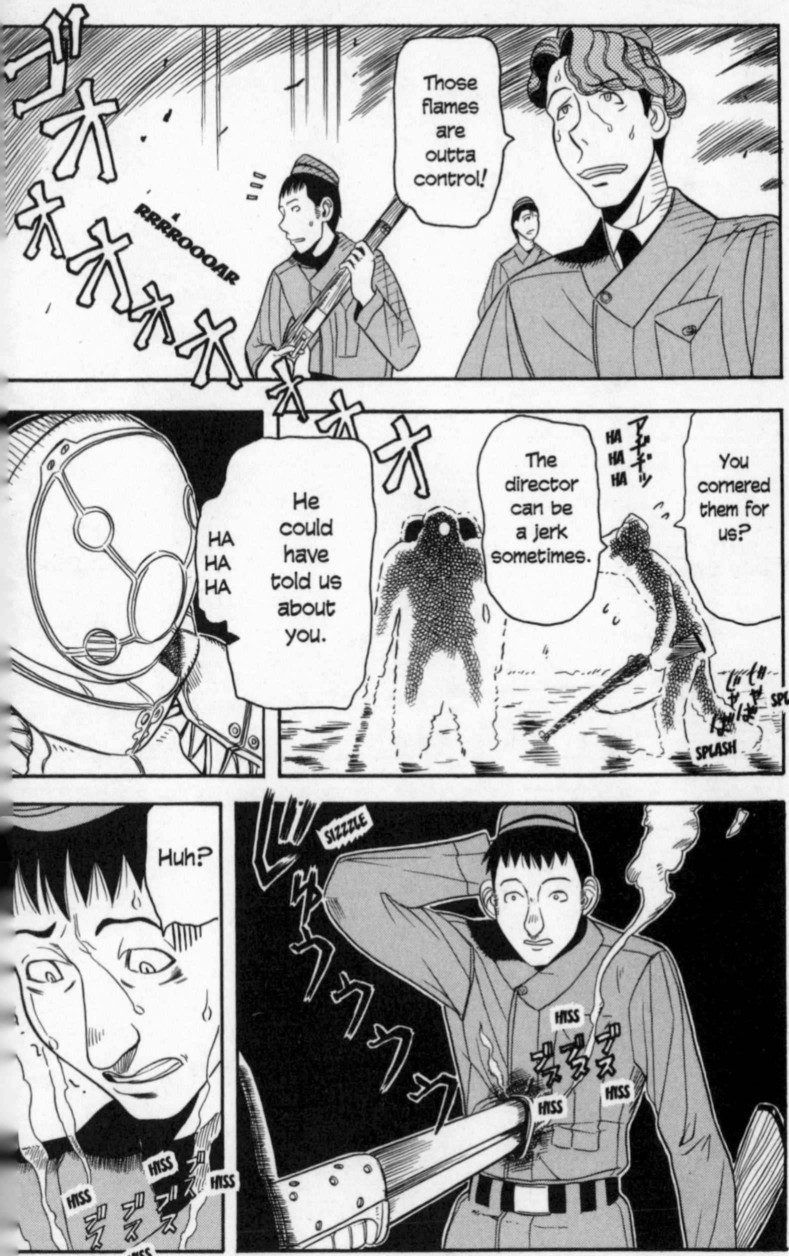
Those flames are outta control!
RRRROOOAR
You cornered them for us?
The director can be a jerk sometimes.
HA HA HA
SPLASH
SPLASH
He could have told us about you.
HA HA HA
SIZZZLE
HISS
HISS
HISS
Huh?
HISS
HISS
HISS
HISS

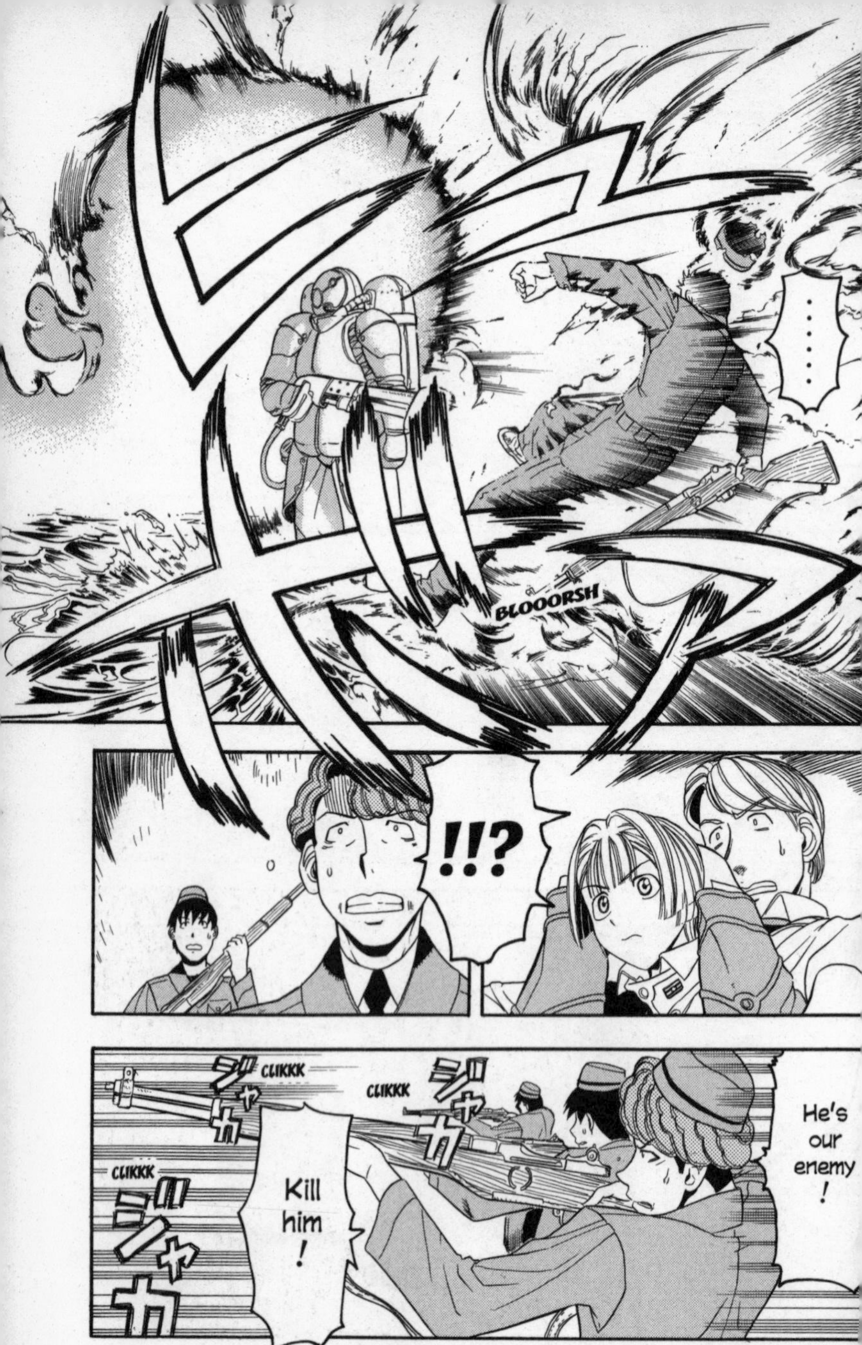
......
BLOOORSH
!!?
He's our enemy!
Kill him!
CLIKKK
CLIKKK
CLIKKK

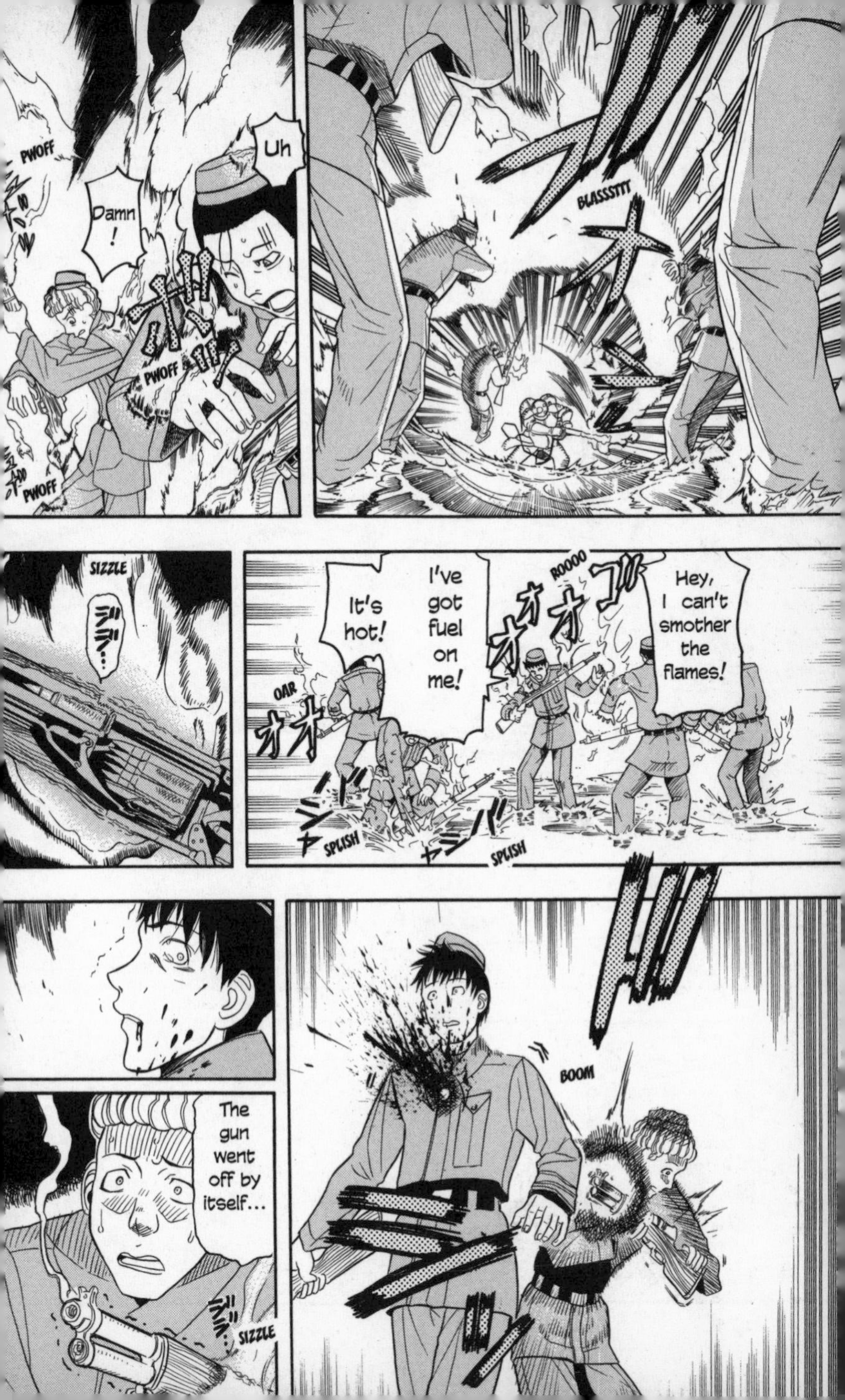
BLASSSTTT
Uh
Damn!
PWOFF
PWOFF
PWOFF
Hey, I can't smother the flames!
ROOOO
I've got fuel on me!
It's hot!
OAR
SPLISH
SPLISH
SIZZLE
BOOM
The gun went off by itself...
SIZZLE

PTINK
PTINK
THUMK
BLAMMMMMMMMMMM
THUMK
PWHOOOSH
I can't... breathe...
STAGGER
FLARRRE
SIZZLE
BLASSST
HISS
HISS

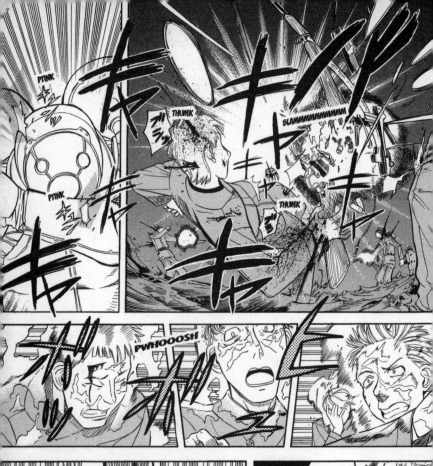

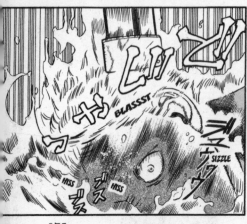

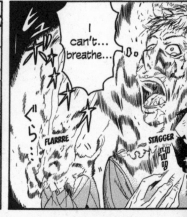

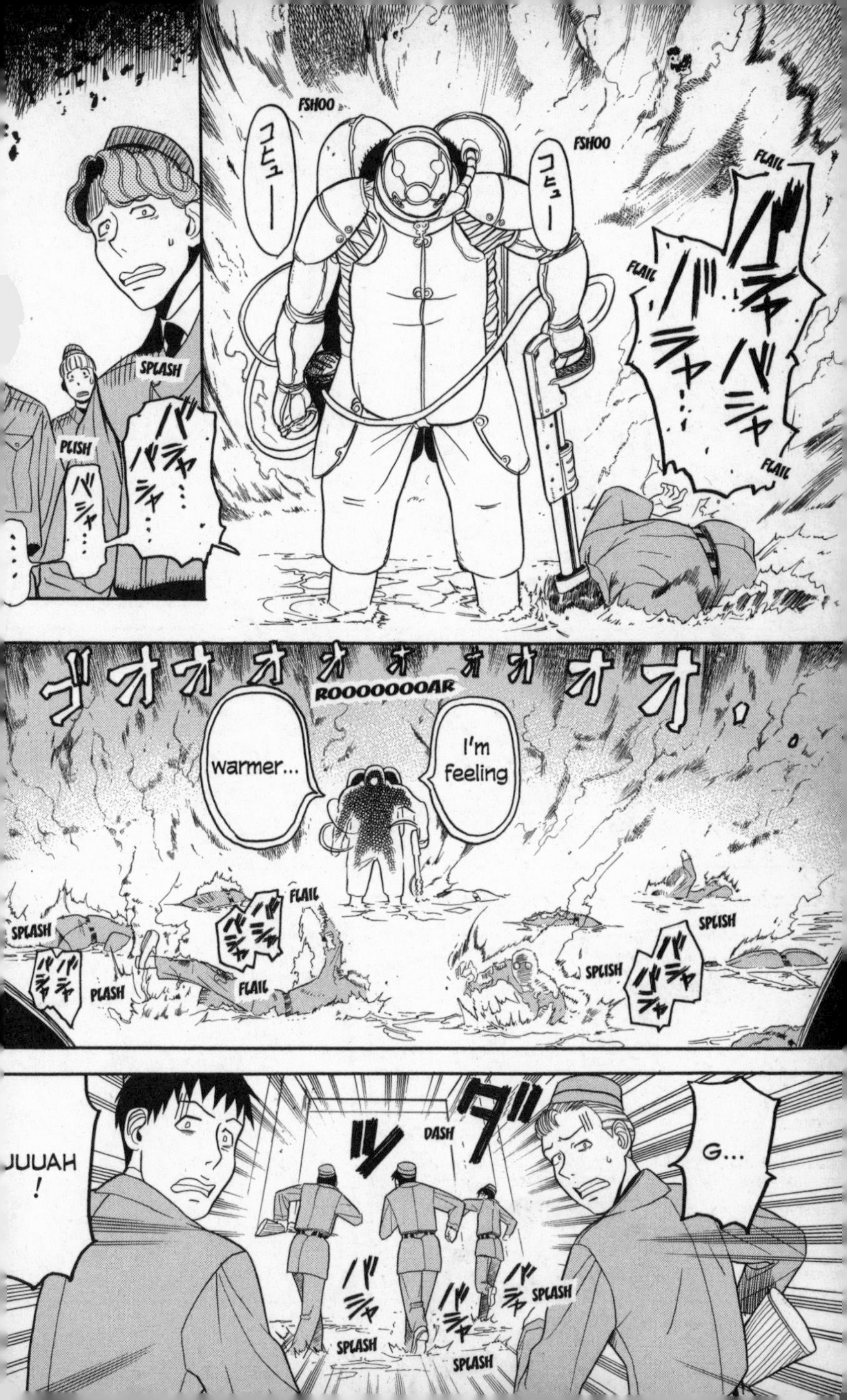
FSHOO
コヒュー
FSHOO
コヒュー
FLAIL
バシャバシャ
バシャ…
FLAIL
FLAIL
SPLASH
バシャバシャ…
PLISH
バシャ…
…
ゴオオオオオオオオオ。
ROOOOOOOAR
I'm feeling
warmer…
SPLISH
バシャバシャ
SPLISH
FLAIL
バシャバシャ
FLAIL
SPLASH
バシャバシャ
PLASH
G…
ダッ
DASH
バシャ
SPLASH
バシャ
SPLASH
バシャ
SPLASH
JUUAH!

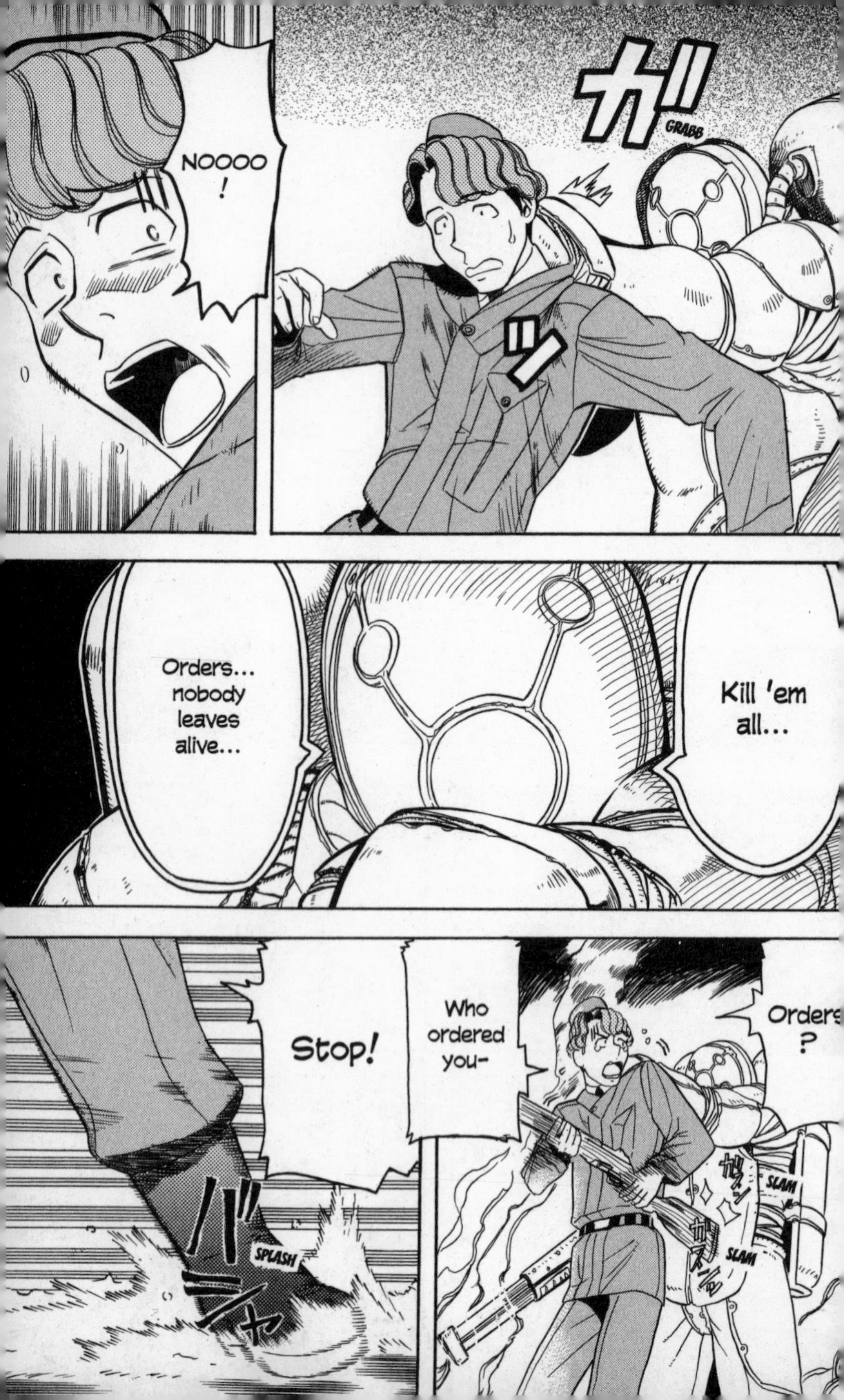
ガ
GRABB
NOOOO!
Kill 'em all...
Orders... nobody leaves alive...
Orders?
Who ordered you-
SLAM
SLAM
Stop!
SPLASH

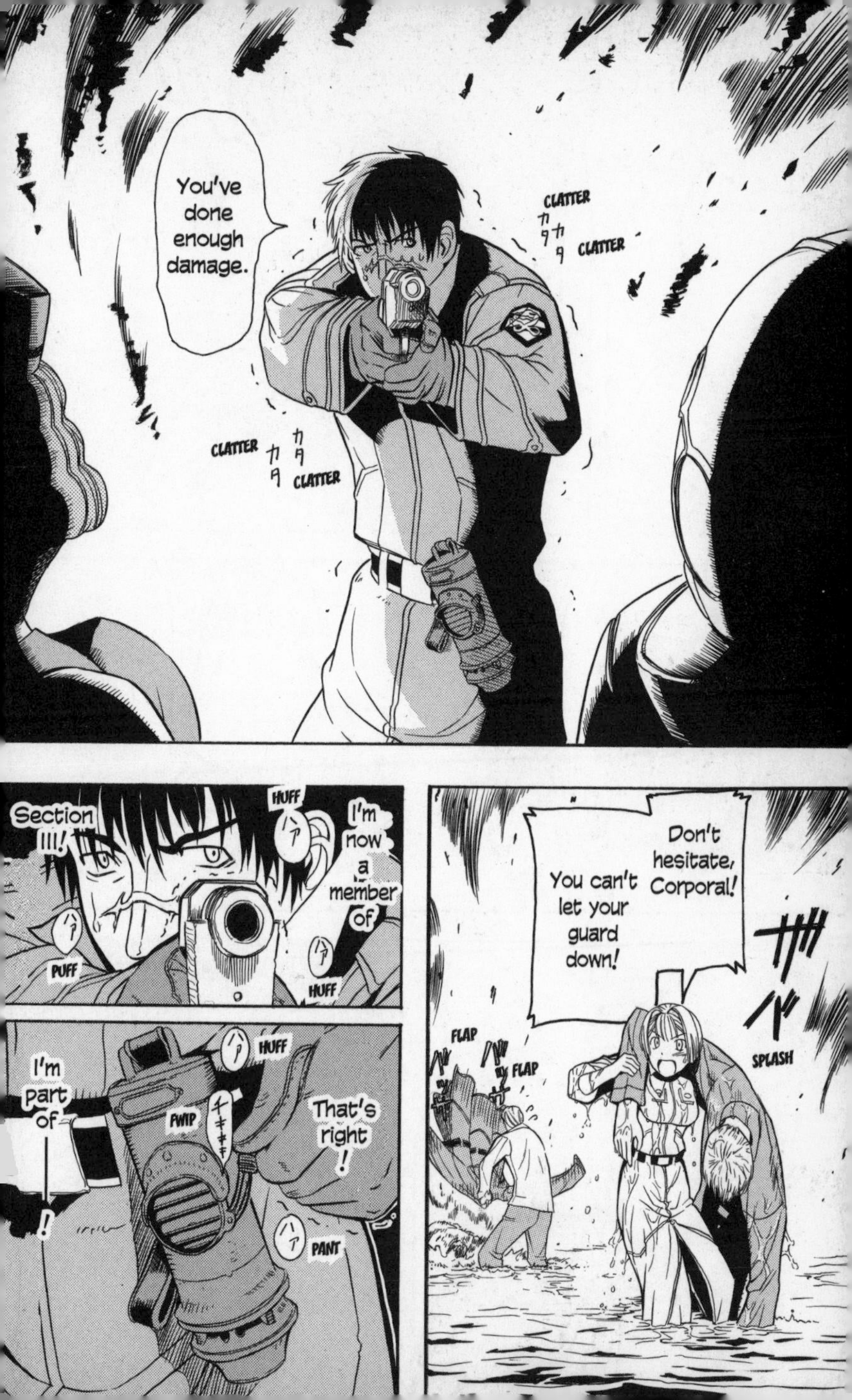
You've done enough damage.
CLATTER
カタ
CLATTER
カタ
CLATTER
カタ
CLATTER
カタ
Don't hesitate, Corporal!
You can't let your guard down!
SPLASH
FLAP
FLAP
HUFF
I'm now a member of
Section IIII!
PUFF
HUFF
HUFF
That's right!
I'm part of —!
FWIP
PANT

That lantern's used by unit 901!

901ATT

FSHOO コヒュー FSHOO コヒュー

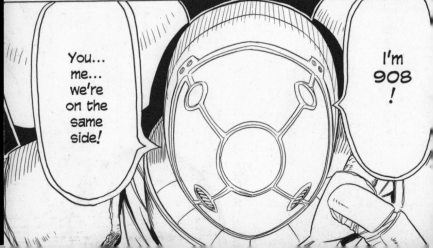

You... me... we're on the same side!

I'm 908!

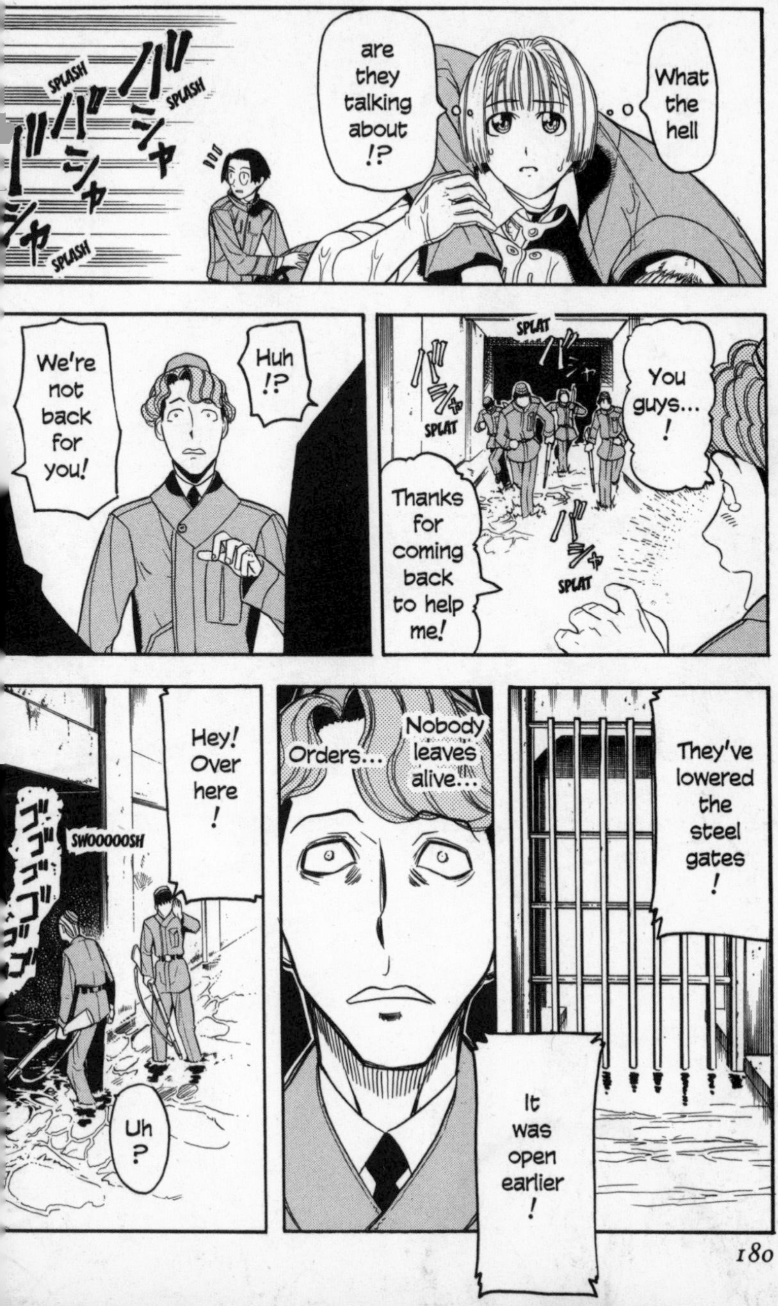
What the hell
are they talking about!?
SPLASH
SPLASH
SPLASH
You guys...!
Thanks for coming back to help me!
SPLAT
SPLAT
SPLAT
Huh!?
We're not back for you!
They've lowered the steel gates!
It was open earlier!
Nobody leaves alive...
Orders...
Hey! Over here!
Uh?
SWOOOOOSH

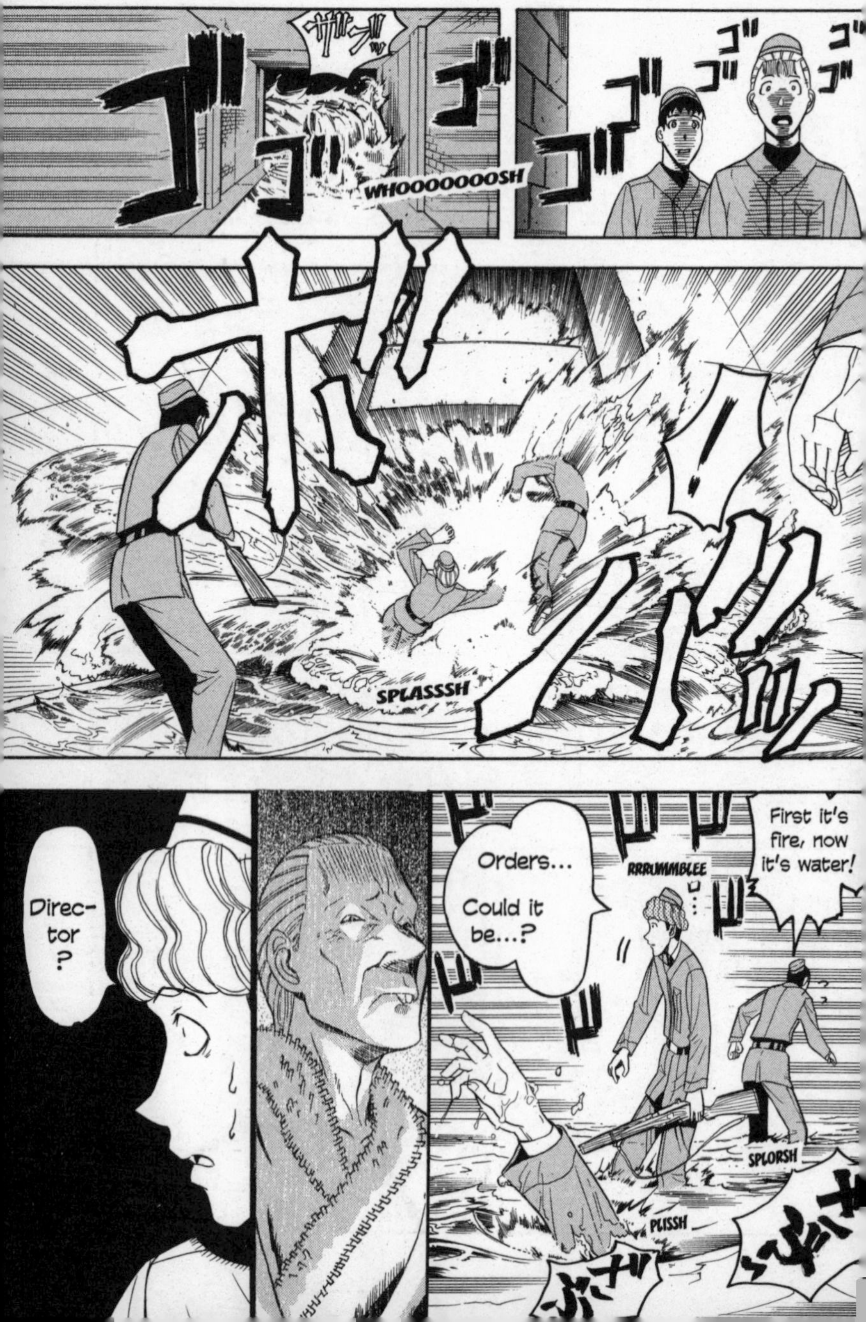

WHOOOOOOOOSH
SPLASSSH
First it's fire, now it's water!
RRRUMMBLEE
Orders... Could it be...?
SPLORSH
PLISSH
Direc-tor?

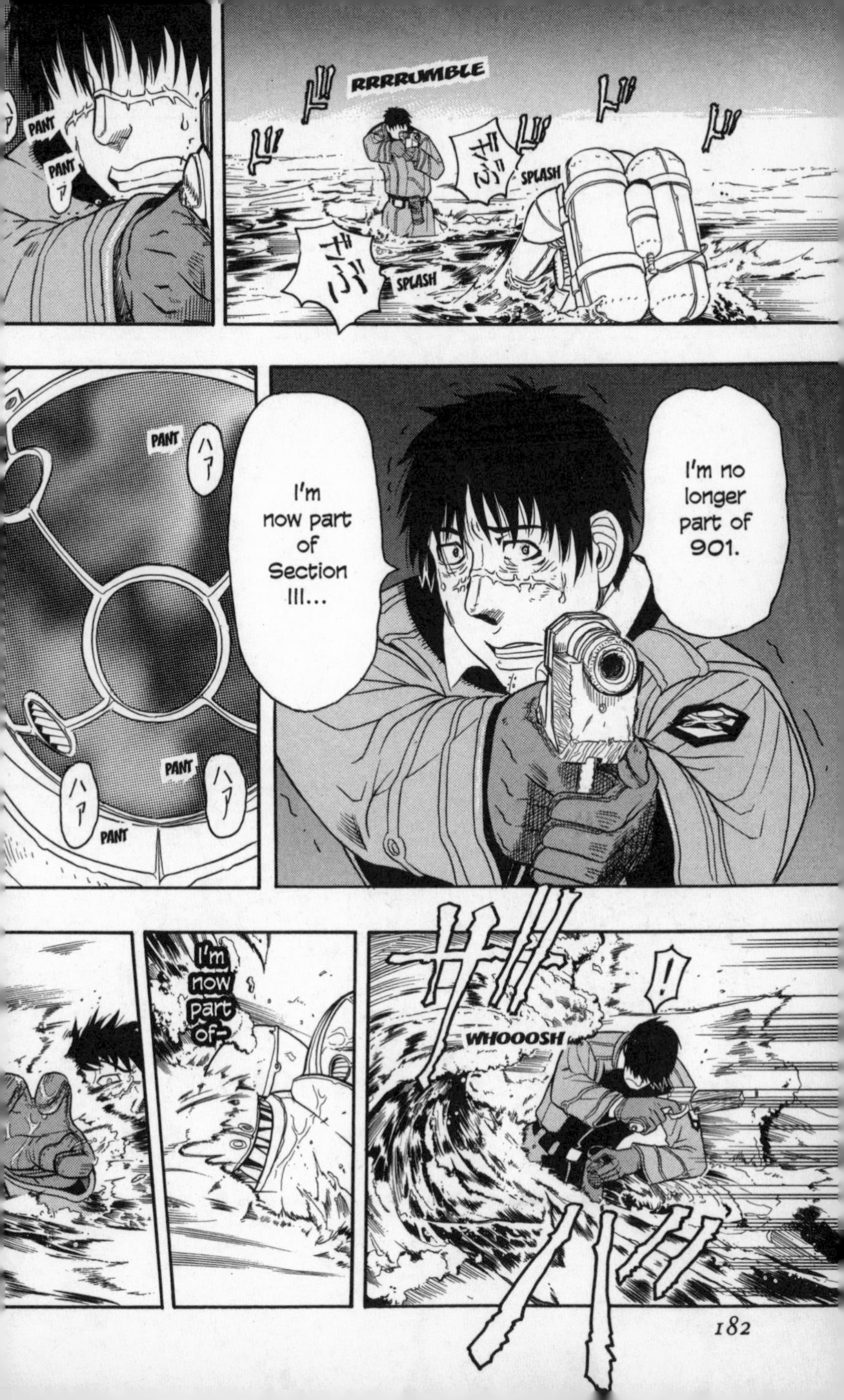
RRRRUMBLE
ザブ
SPLASH
ザブ
SPLASH
PANT
PANT
I'm no longer part of 901.
I'm now part of Section III...
PANT
PANT
PANT
!
WHOOOSH
I'm now part of-

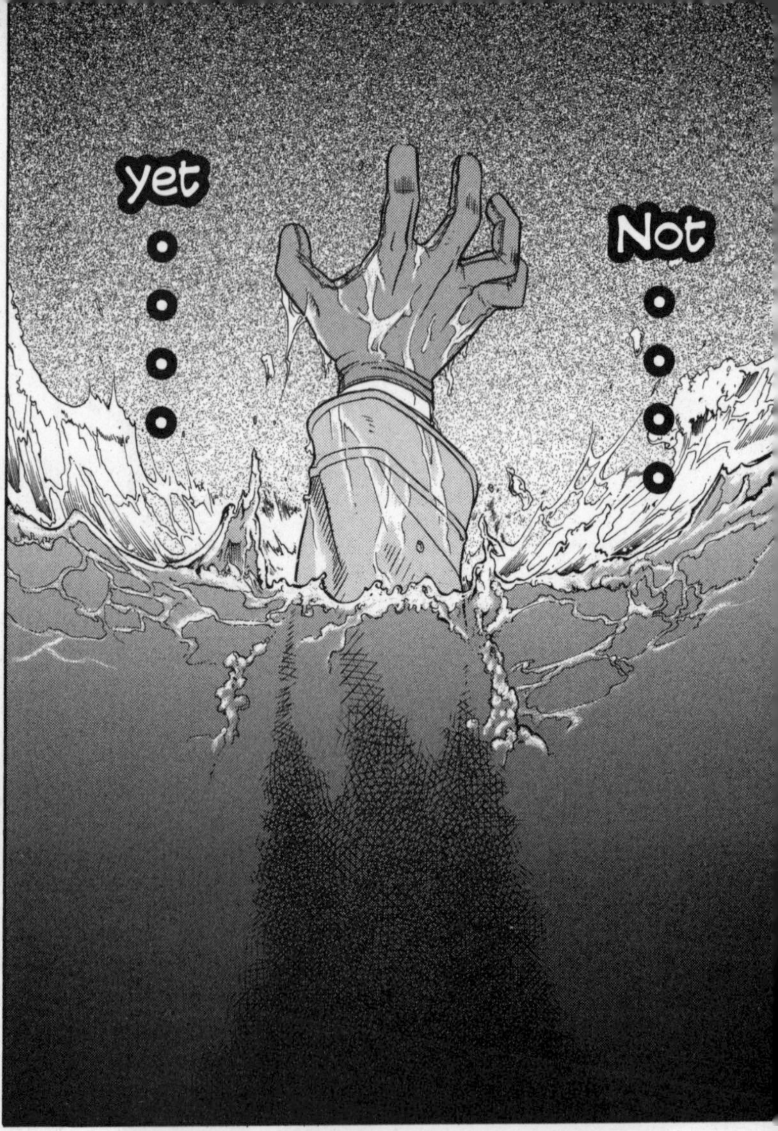
Not....
yet....

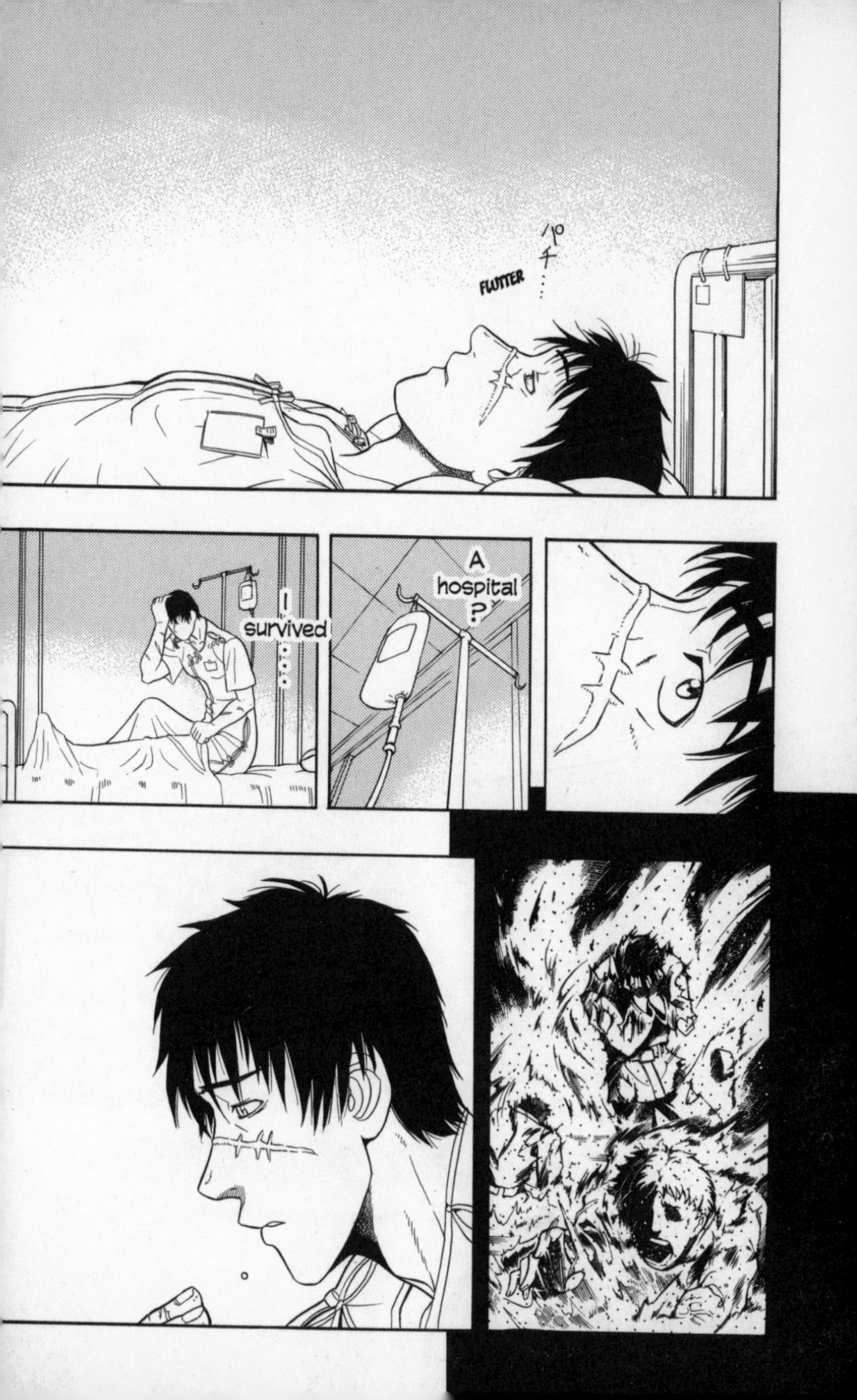
パチ…
FLUTTER
A hospital?
I survived....

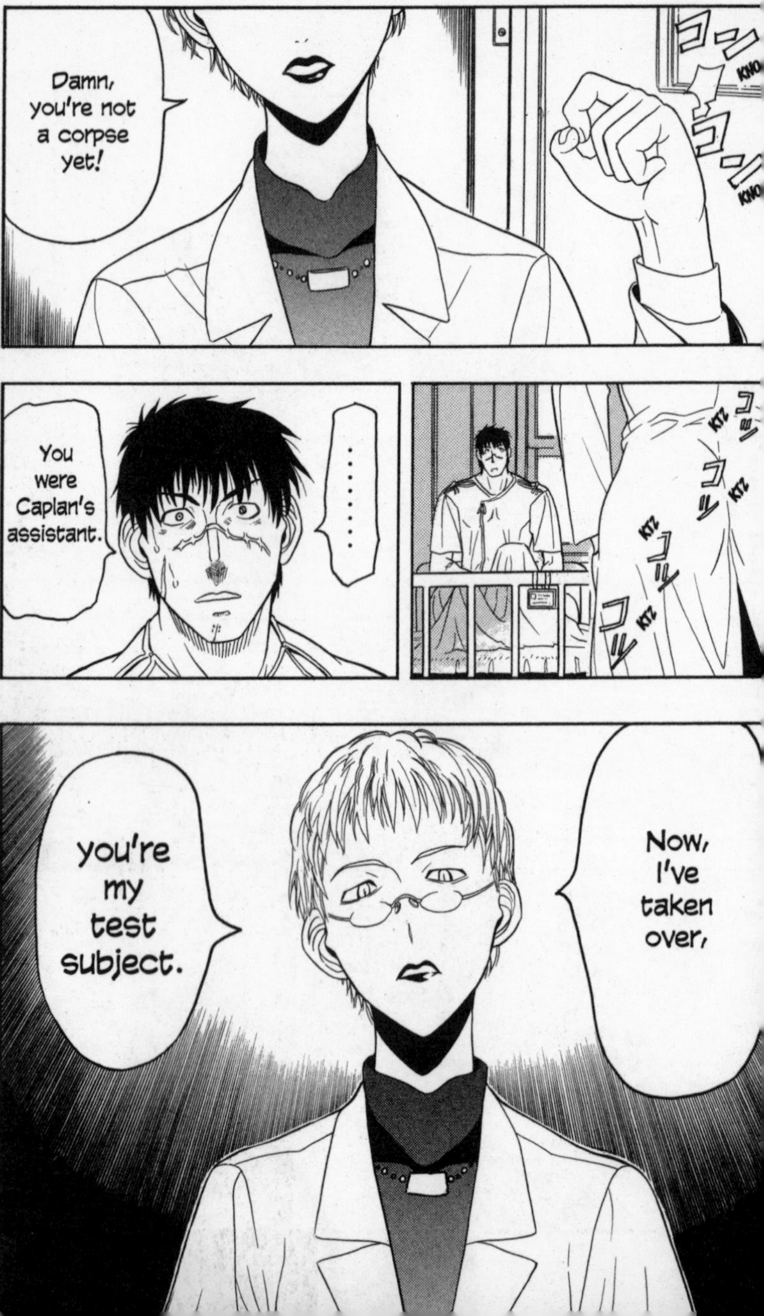
KNO
KNO
Damn, you're not a corpse yet!
KTZ
KTZ
KTZ
KTZ
......
You were Caplan's assistant.
Now, I've taken over,
you're my test subject.

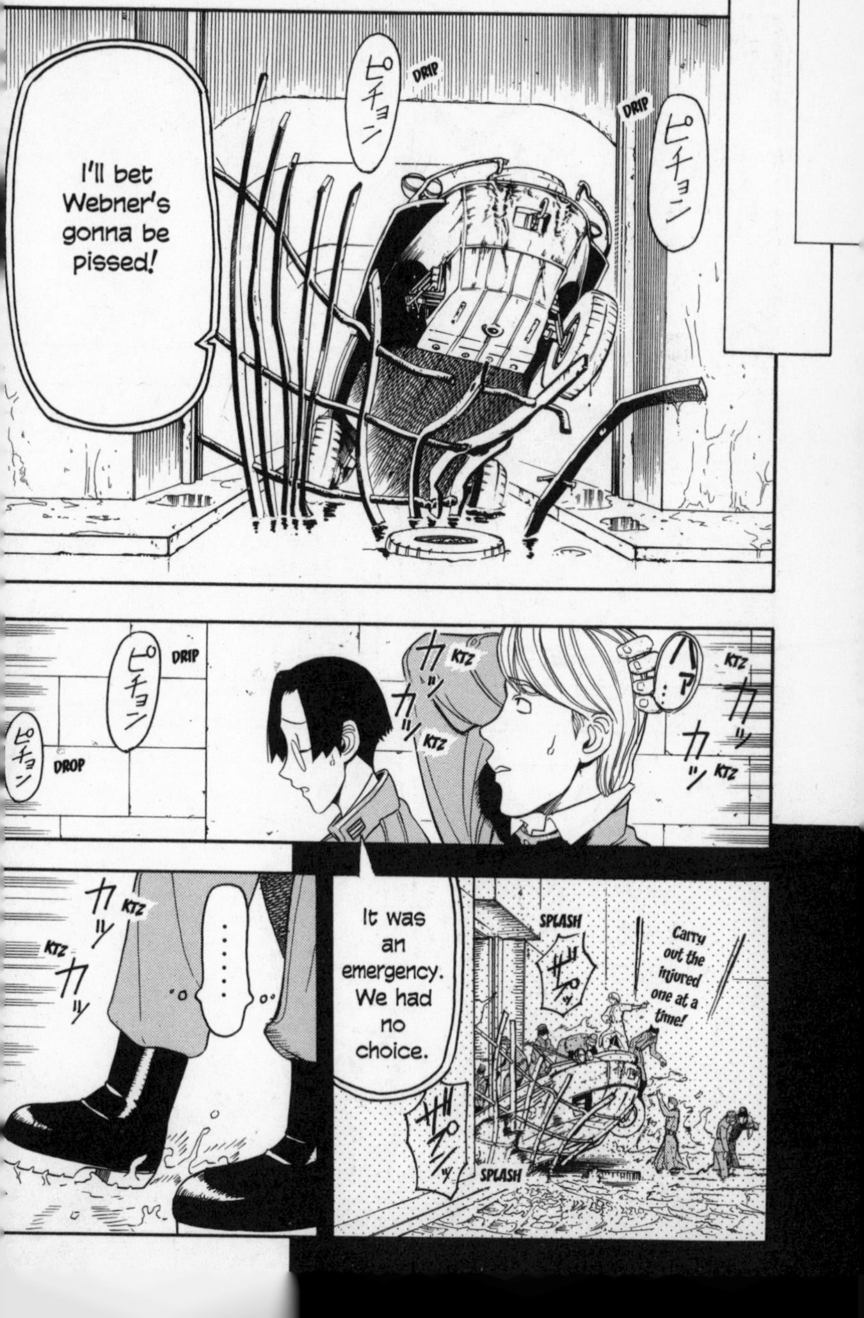

DRIP
ピチョン
DRIP
ピチョン
I'll bet Webner's gonna be pissed!
KTZ
カッ
カッ
KTZ
ハア…
KTZ
カッ
カッ
KTZ
DRIP
ピチョン
DROP
ピチョン
Carry out the injured one at a time!
SPLASH
It was an emergency. We had no choice.
SPLASH
……
KTZ
カッ
KTZ
カッ

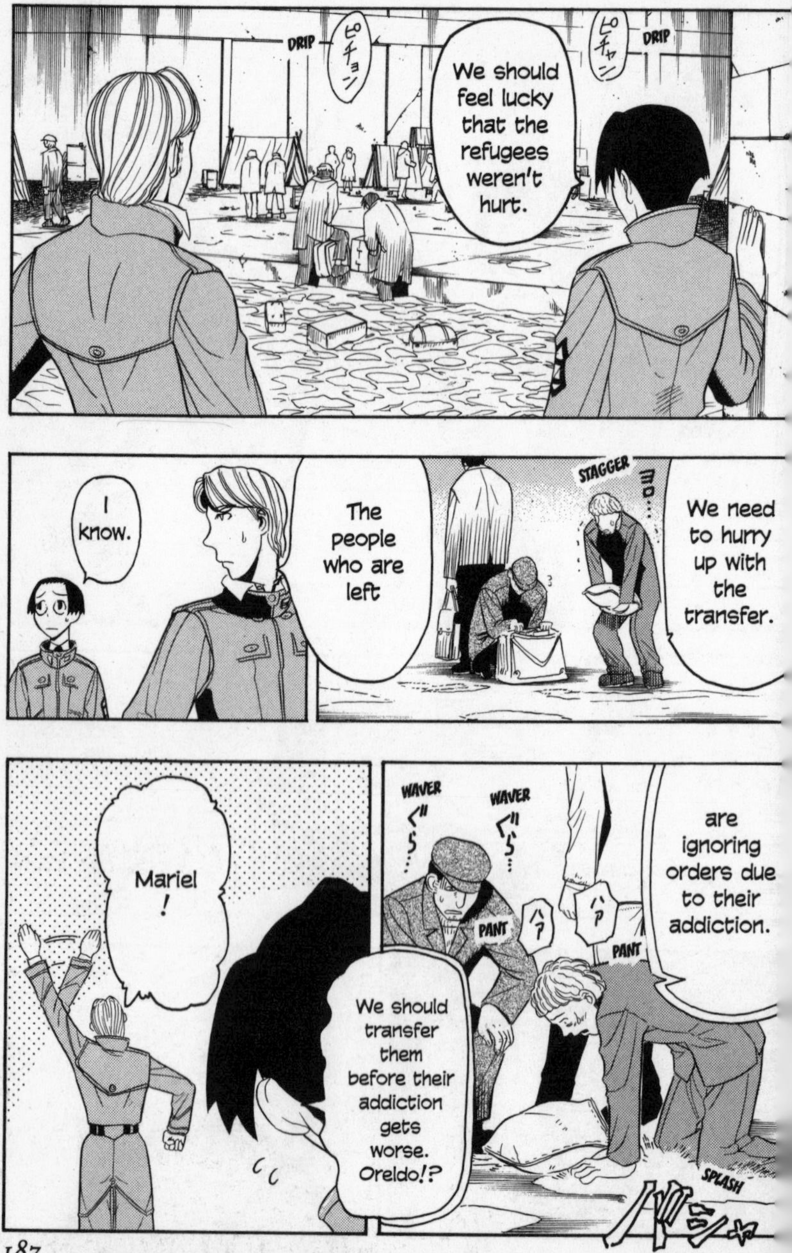
DRIP
ピチャン
We should feel lucky that the refugees weren't hurt.
DRIP
ピチョン
We need to hurry up with the transfer.
STAGGER
ヨロ…
The people who are left
I know.
are ignoring orders due to their addiction.
WAVER
ぐら…
WAVER
ぐら…
PANT
ハァ
PANT
ハァ
We should transfer them before their addiction gets worse. Oreldo!?
SPLASH
バシャ
Mariel!

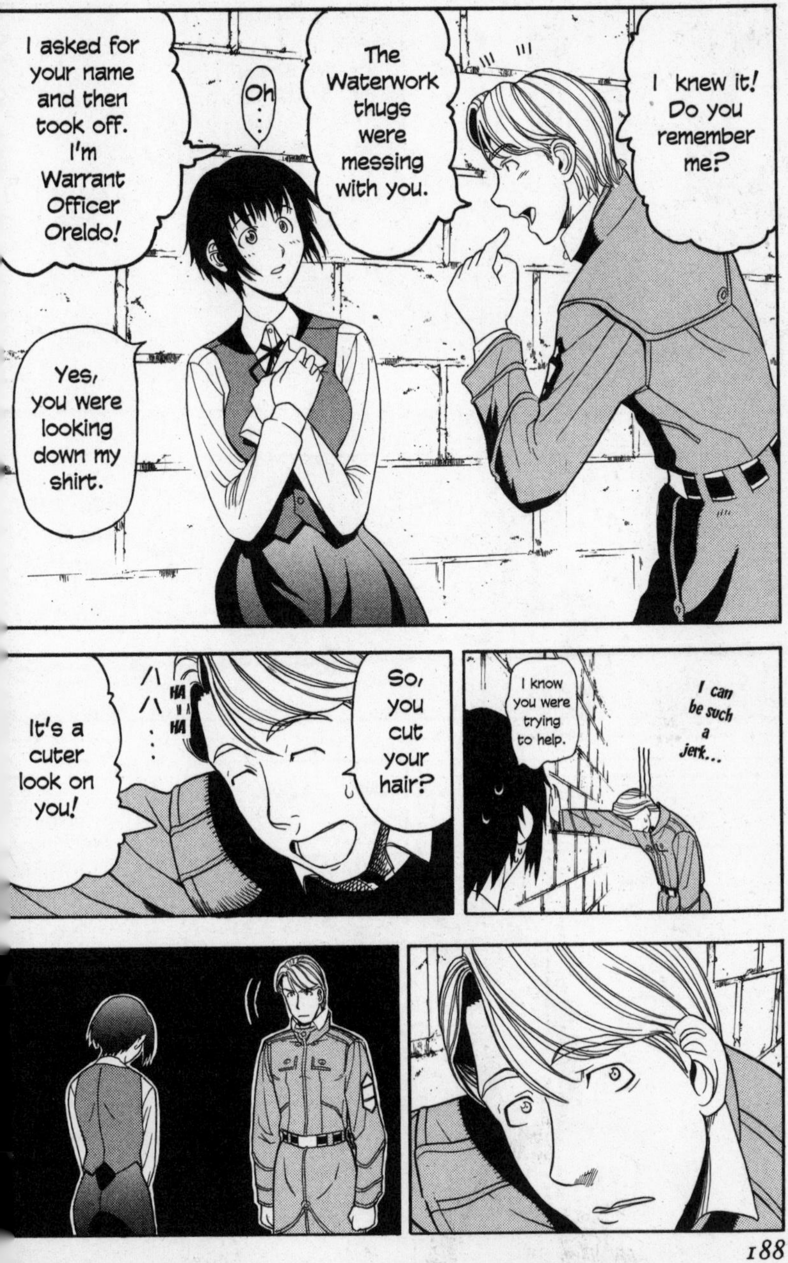
I knew it! Do you remember me?
The Waterwork thugs were messing with you.
Oh...
I asked for your name and then took off. I'm Warrant Officer Oreldo!
Yes, you were looking down my shirt.
I can be such a jerk...
I know you were trying to help.
So, you cut your hair?
HA HA...
It's a cuter look on you!

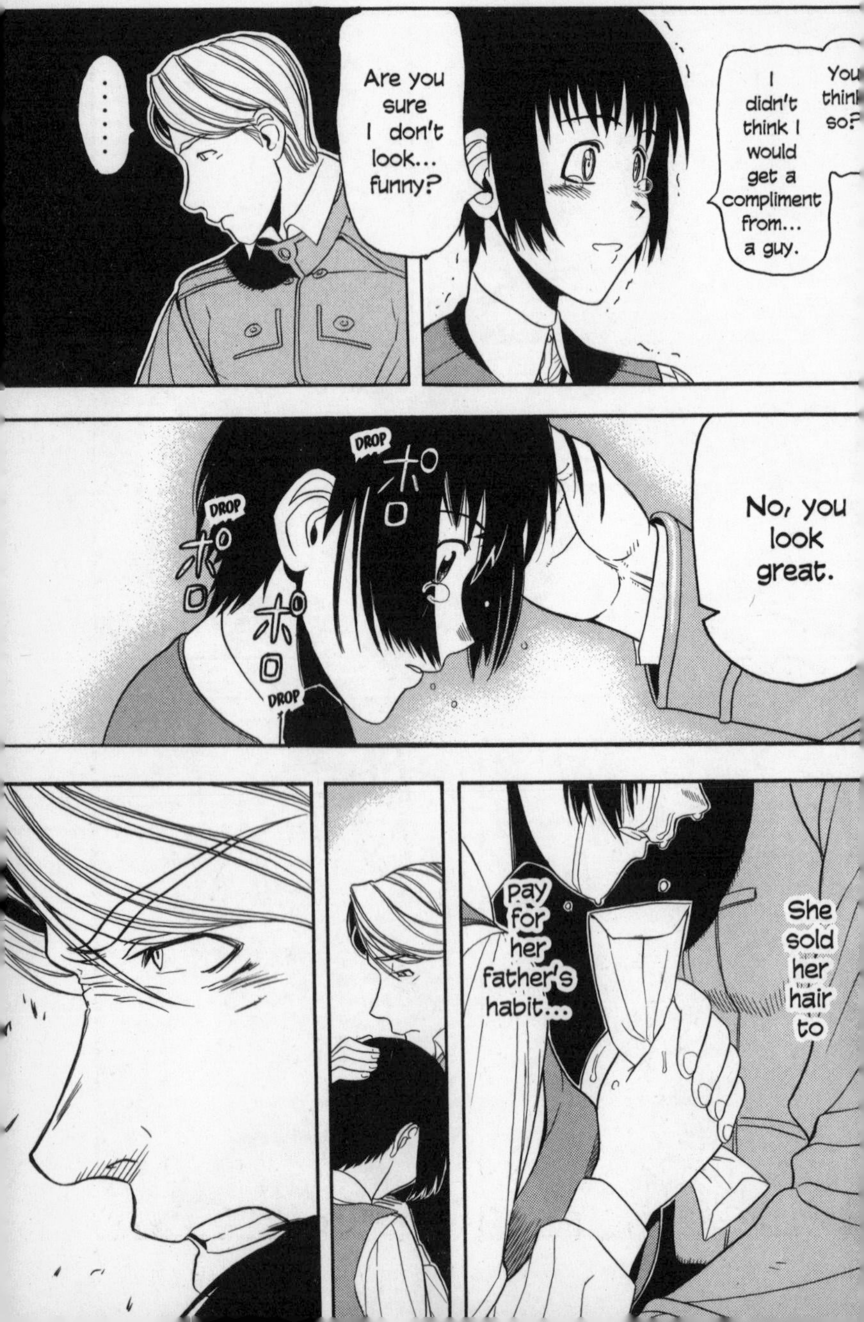
You think so?
I didn't think I would get a compliment from... a guy.
Are you sure I don't look... funny?
......
No, you look great.
DROP
ポロ
DROP
ポロ
ポロ
DROP
She sold her hair to
pay for her father's habit...

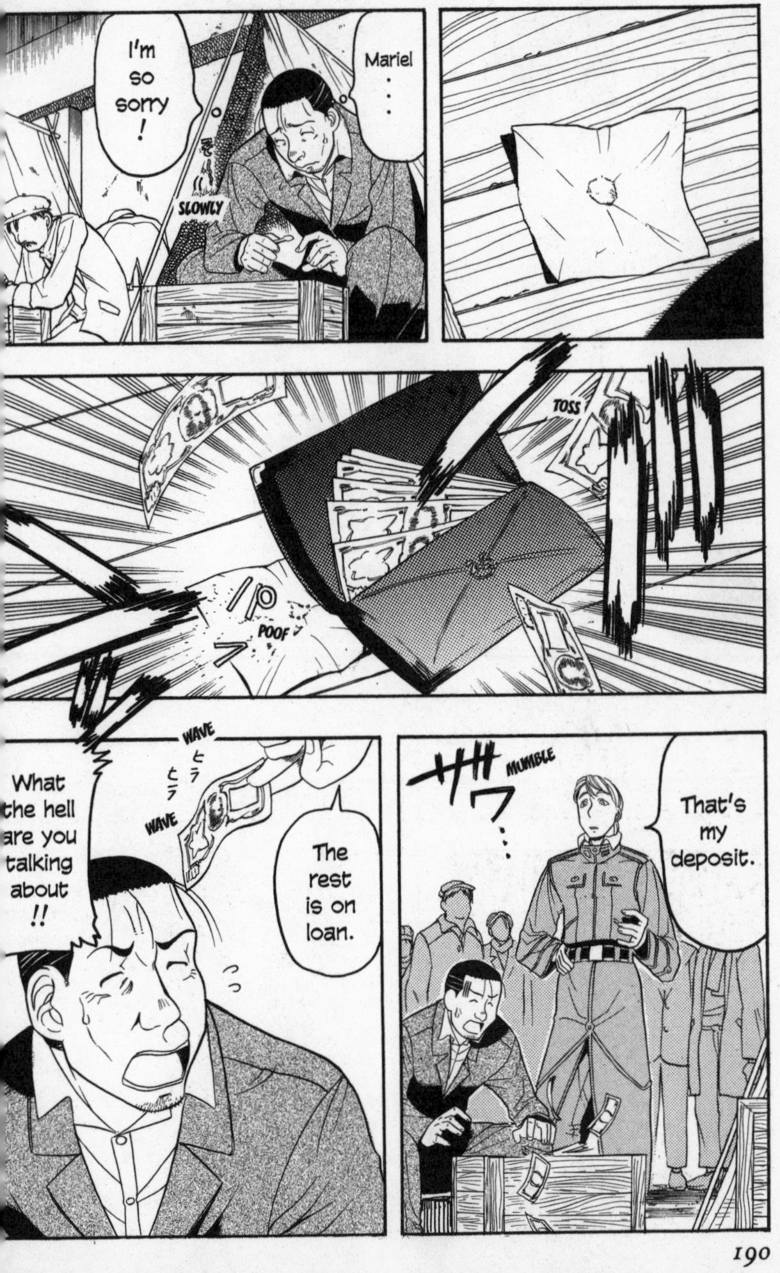
Mariel . . .
SLOWLY
I'm so sorry!
TOSS
POOF
That's my deposit.
MUMBLE
The rest is on loan.
WAVE
WAVE
What the hell are you talking about!!

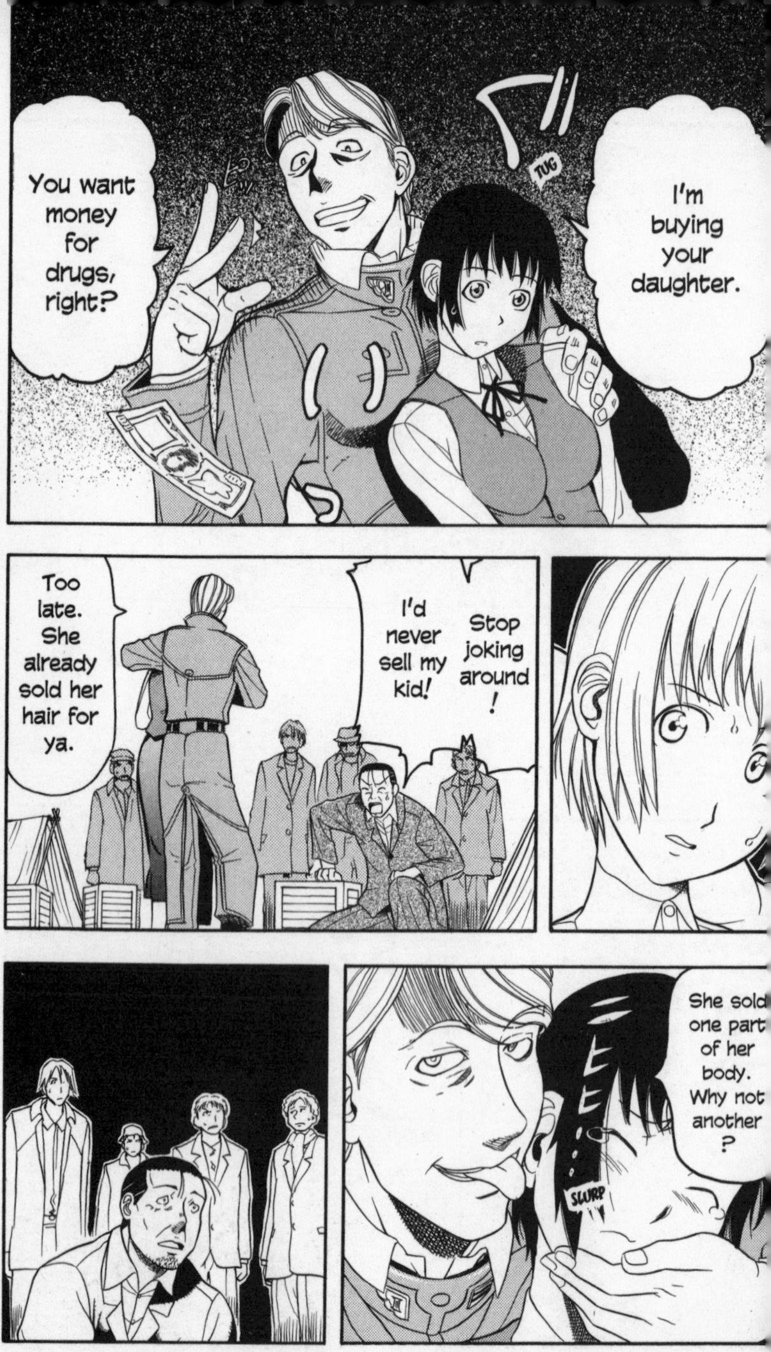
TUG
I'm buying your daughter.
You want money for drugs, right?
Stop joking around!
I'd never sell my kid!
Too late. She already sold her hair for ya.
She sold one part of her body. Why not another?
SLURP

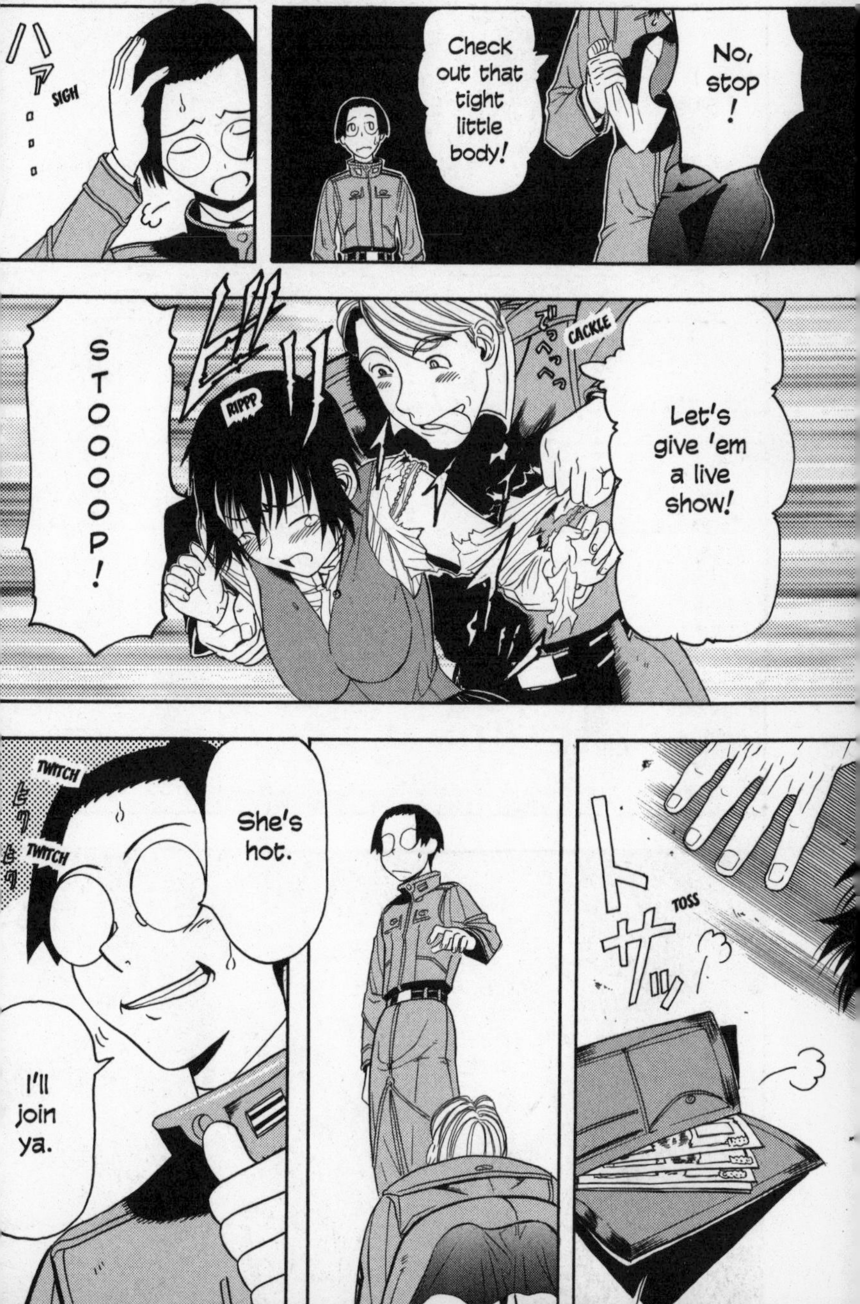
No, stop!
Check out that tight little body!
ハァ…
SIGH
CACKLE
Let's give 'em a live show!
RIPPP
STOOOOOP!
トサッ
TOSS
She's hot.
TWITCH
TWITCH
I'll join ya.

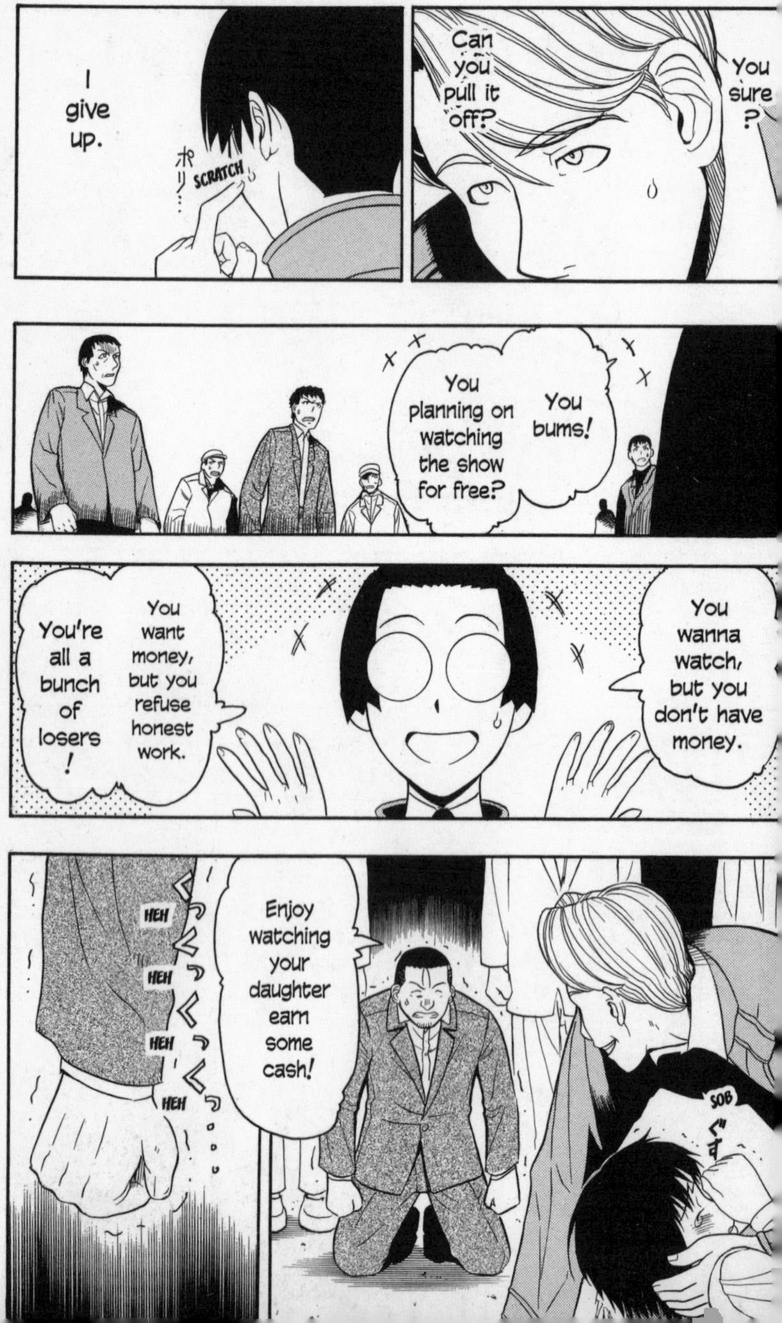
You sure?
Can you pull it off?
I give up.
ポリ…
SCRATCH
You bums!
You planning on watching the show for free?
You wanna watch, but you don't have money.
You want money, but you refuse honest work.
You're all a bunch of losers!
SOB
ぐす
Enjoy watching your daughter earn some cash!
HEH
HEH
HEH
HEH

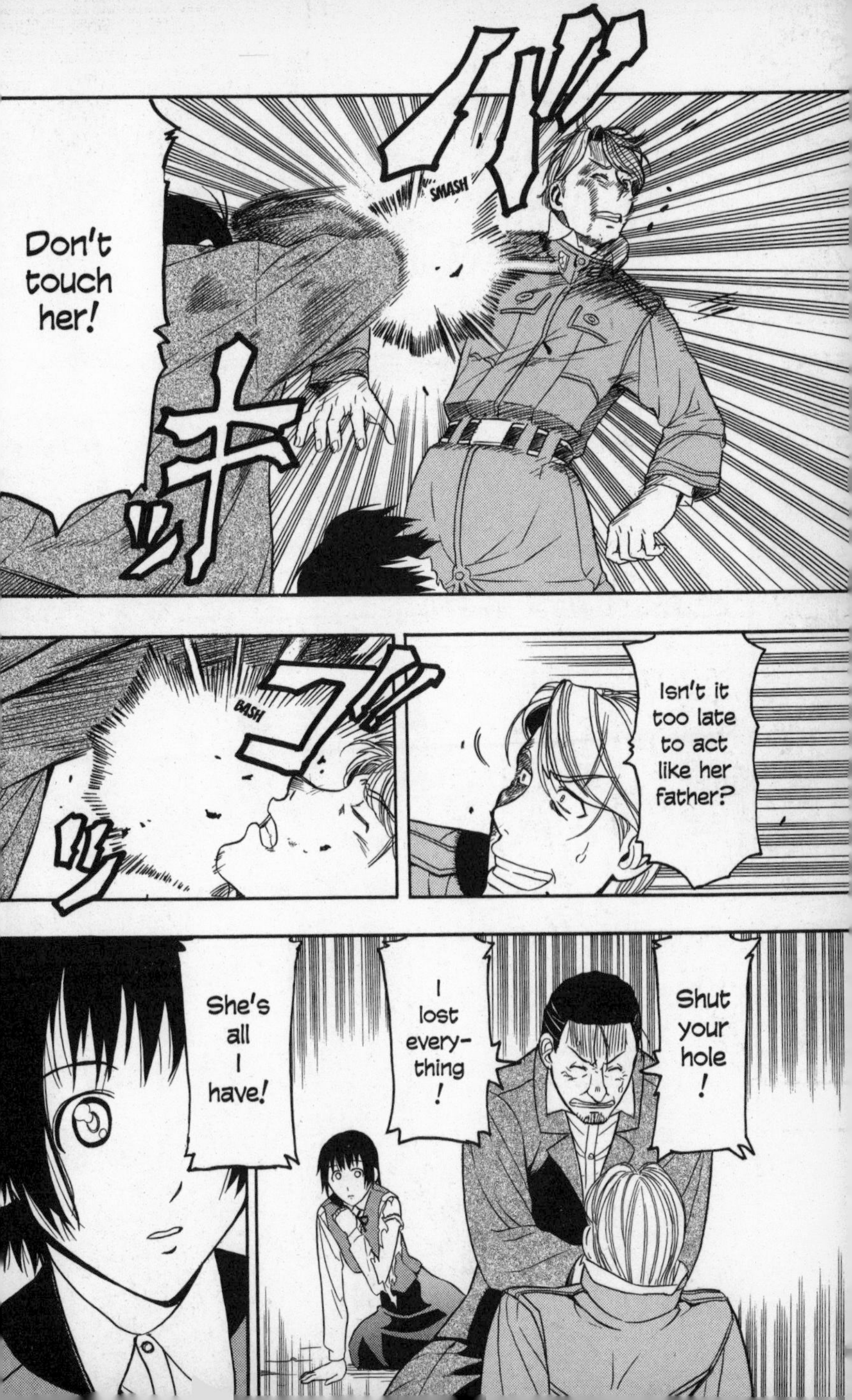
SMASH
Don't touch her!
Isn't it too late to act like her father?
BASH
Shut your hole!
I lost everything!
She's all I have!

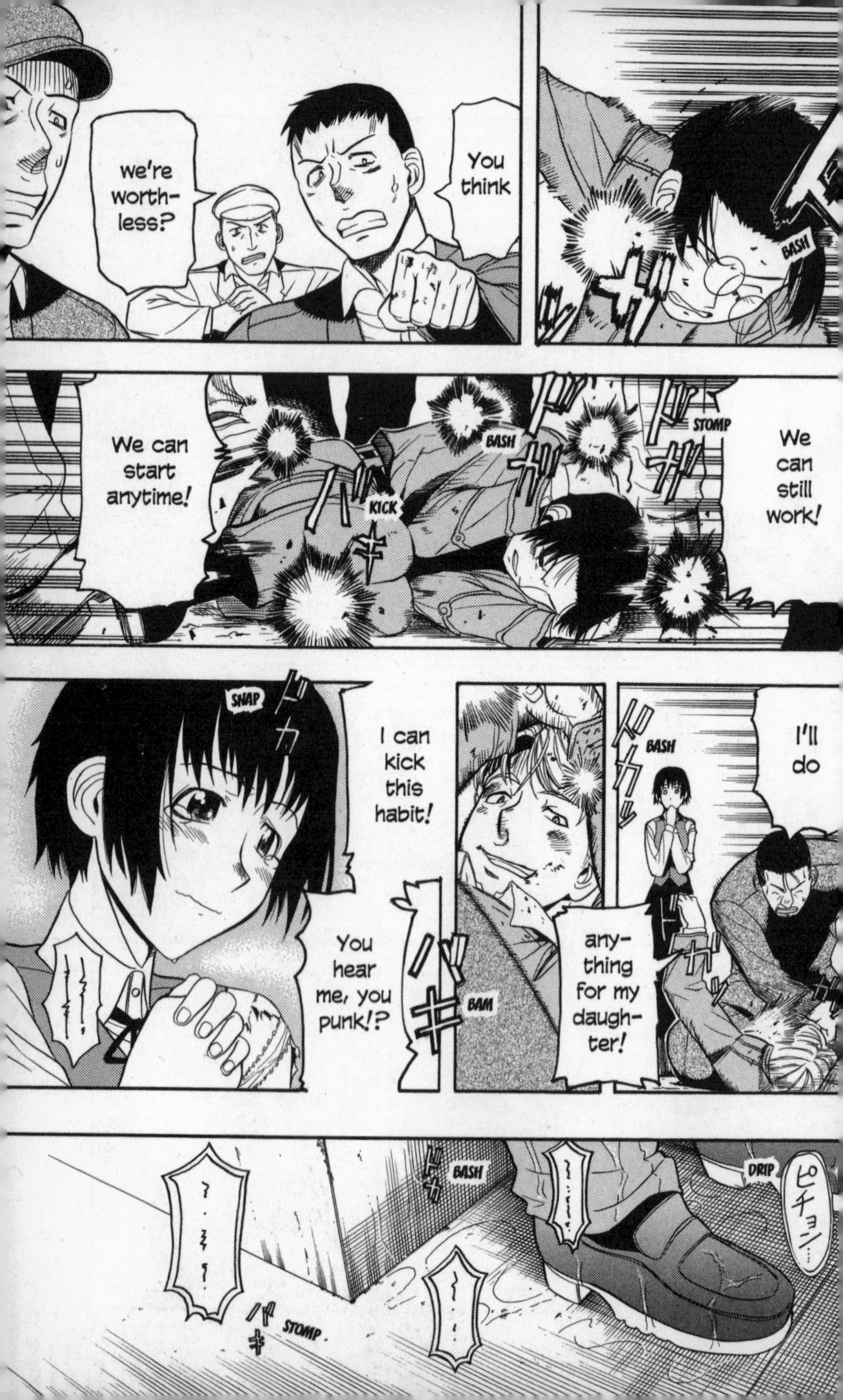

BASH
You think
we're worth-less?
We can still work!
STOMP
BASH
KICK
We can start anytime!
I'll do
BASH
any-thing for my daugh-ter!
BAM
I can kick this habit!
SNAP
You hear me, you punk!?
DRIP
ピチョン…
BASH
STOMP

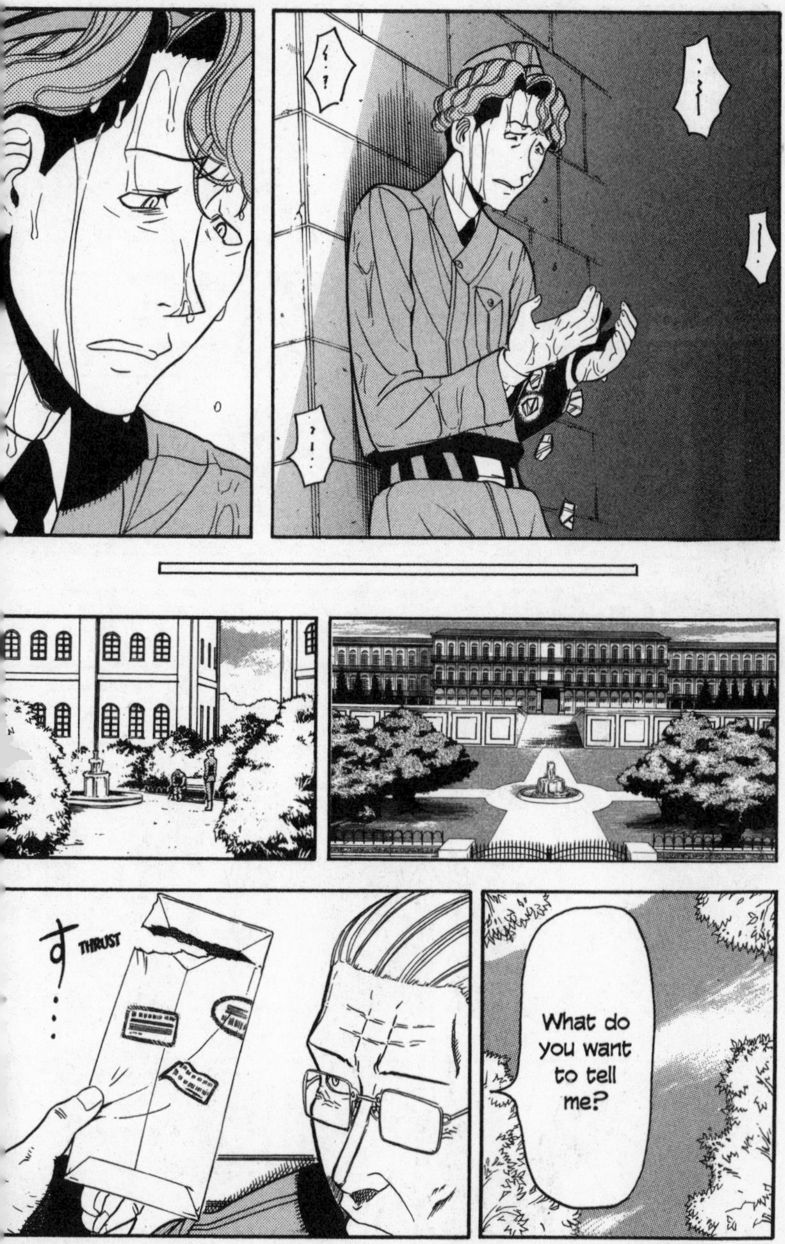
What do you want to tell me?
す
THRUST

That was mailed to our unit.

?

RUSTLE
RUSTLE
カシャ
カシャ

I believe it's a warning.

カシャ

CLIK

So, your covert operation was a failure.

SQUEEZE
キュ...

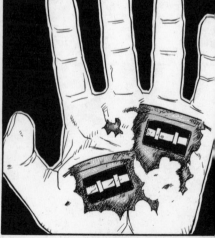

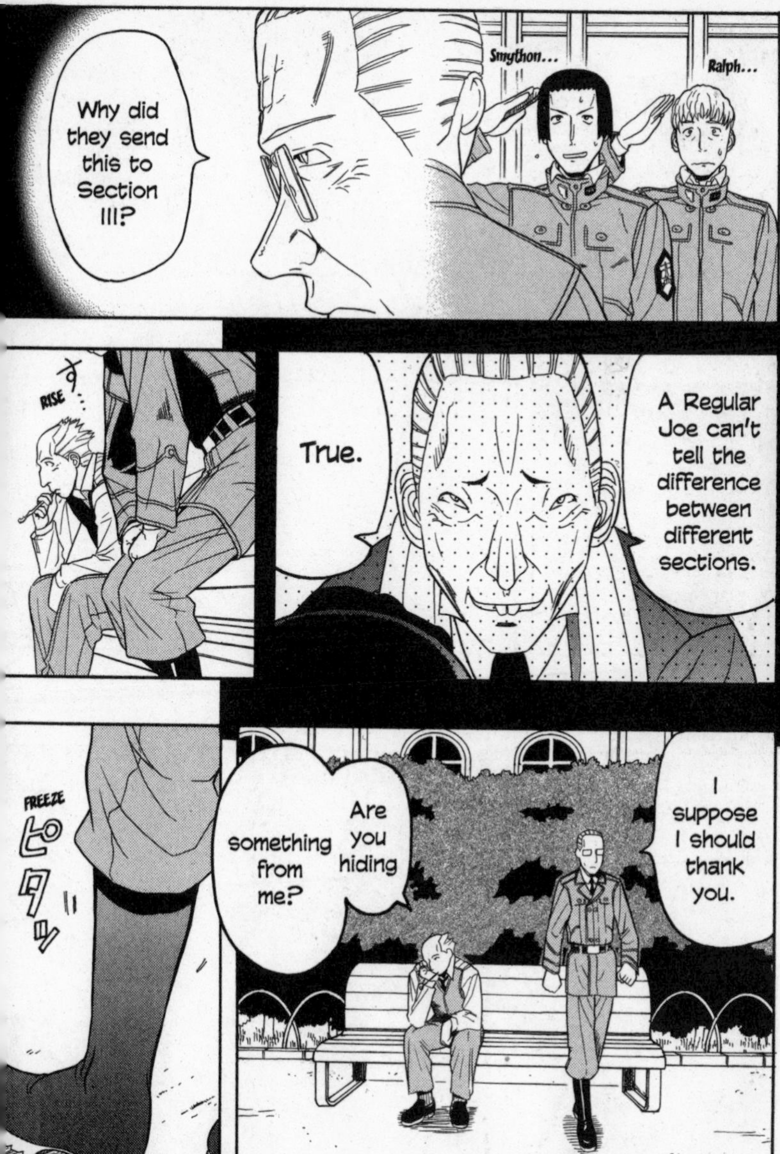
Ralph...
Smython...
Why did they send this to Section III?
A Regular Joe can't tell the difference between different sections.
True.
RISE
す
I suppose I should thank you.
Are you hiding something from me?
FREEZE
ピタッ

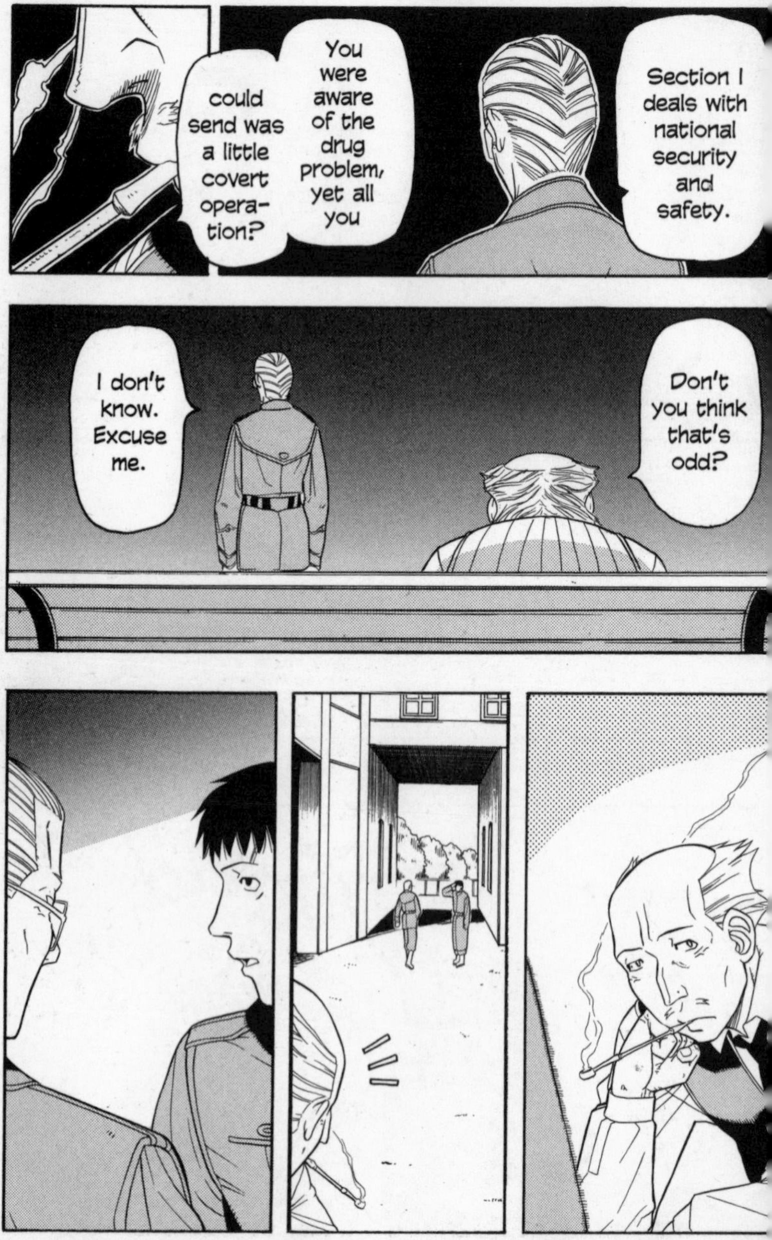
Section 1 deals with national security and safety.
You were aware of the drug problem, yet all you
could send was a little covert operation?
Don't you think that's odd?
I don't know. Excuse me.

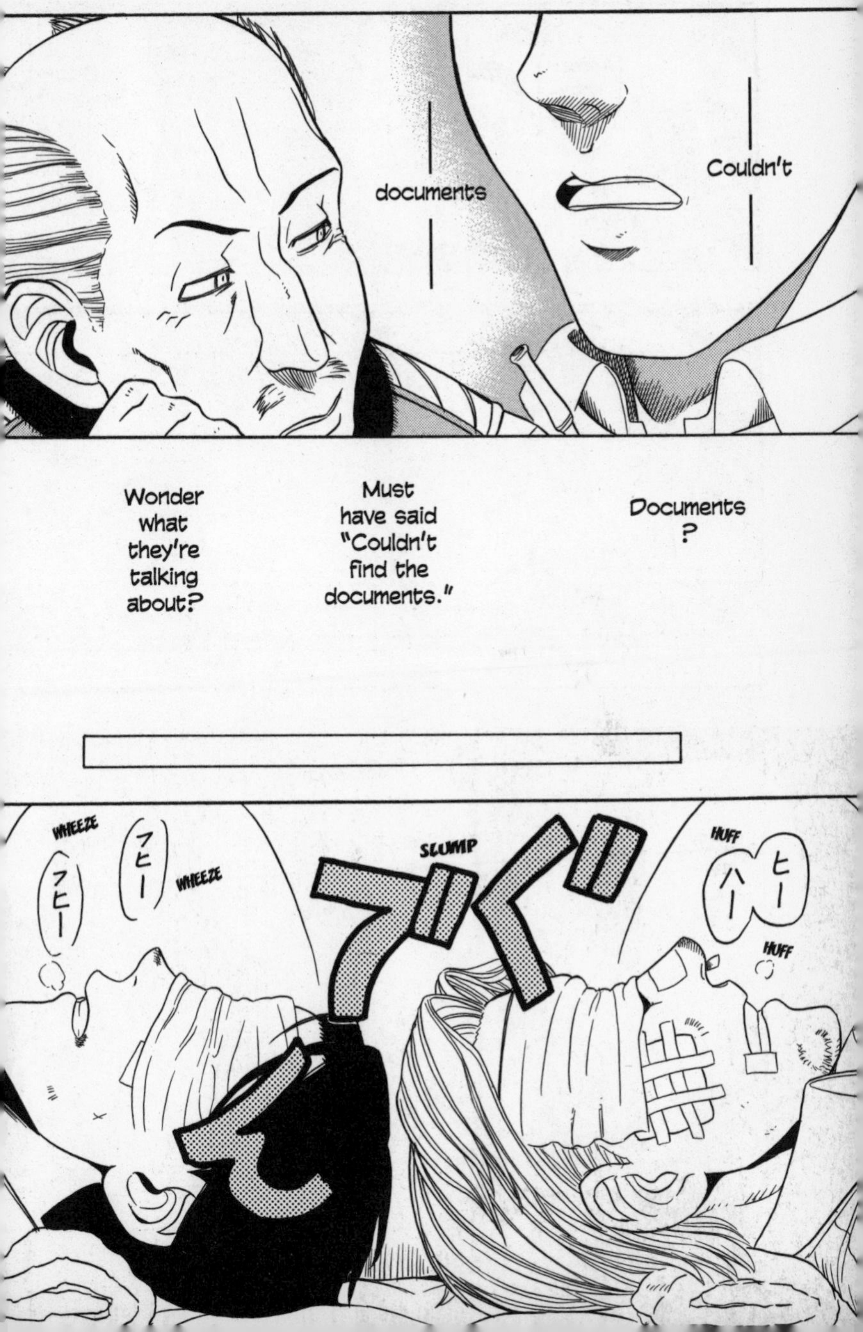
Couldn't
documents
Documents ?
Must have said "Couldn't find the documents."
Wonder what they're talking about?
HUFF
ヒーハー
HUFF
SLUMP
WHEEZE
フヒー
WHEEZE
フヒー

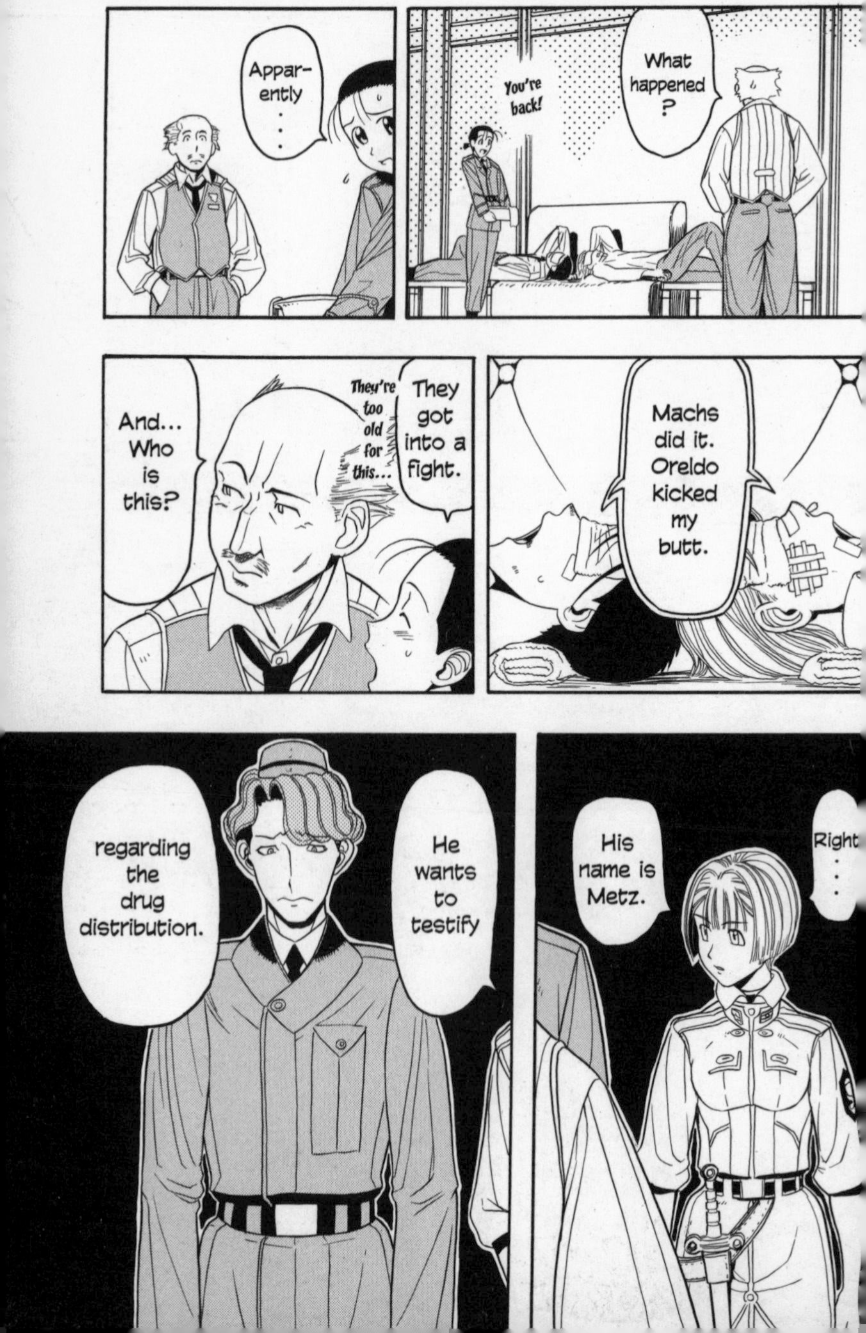
What happened?
You're back!
Appar-ently . . .
Machs did it. Oreldo kicked my butt.
They got into a fight.
They're too old for this...
And... Who is this?
Right . . .
His name is Metz.
He wants to testify
regarding the drug distribution.

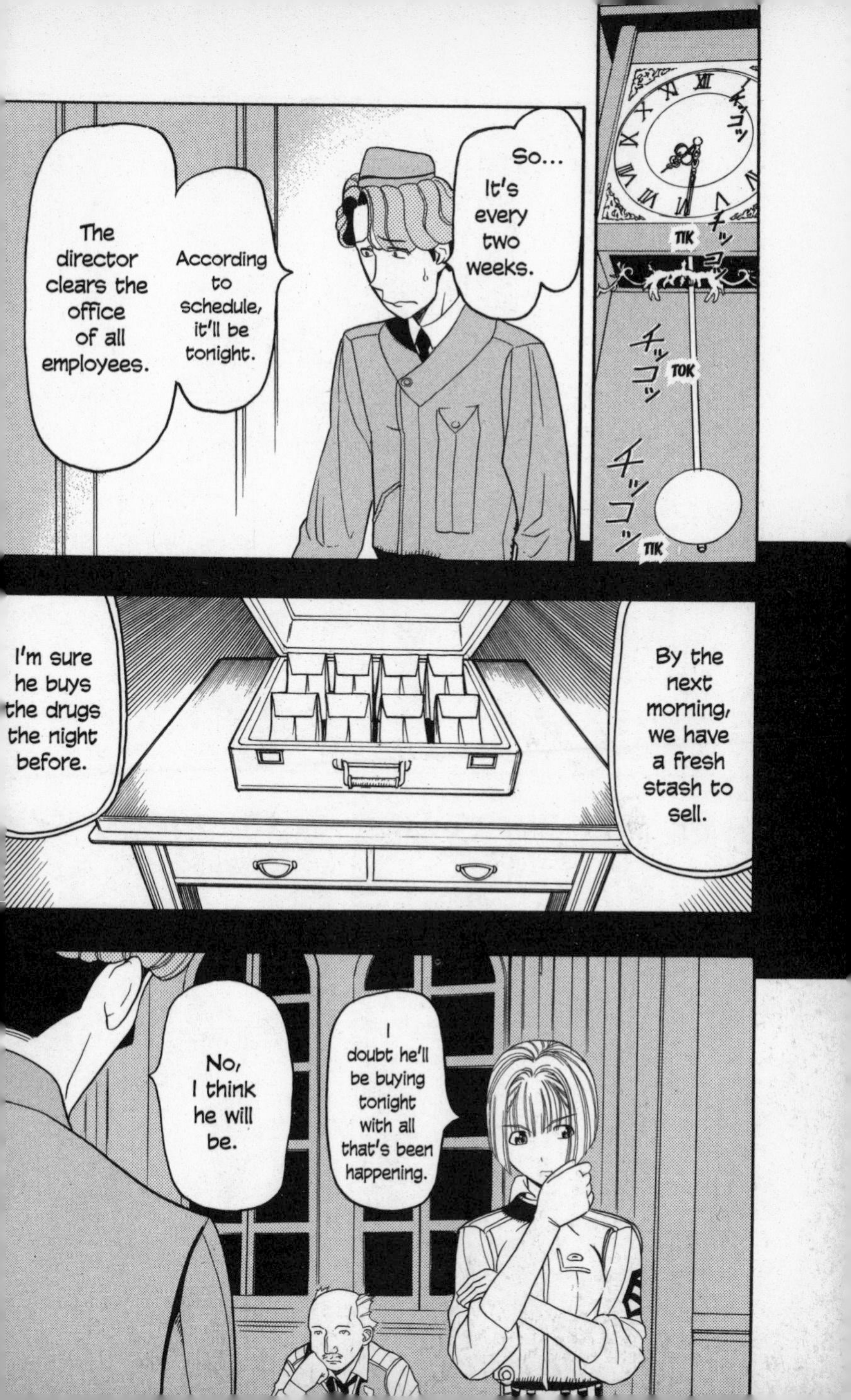

チッコッ
TIK
チッコッ
TOK
チッコッ
TIK
So... It's every two weeks.
According to schedule, it'll be tonight.
The director clears the office of all employees.
By the next morning, we have a fresh stash to sell.
I'm sure he buys the drugs the night before.
I doubt he'll be buying tonight with all that's been happening.
No, I think he will be.

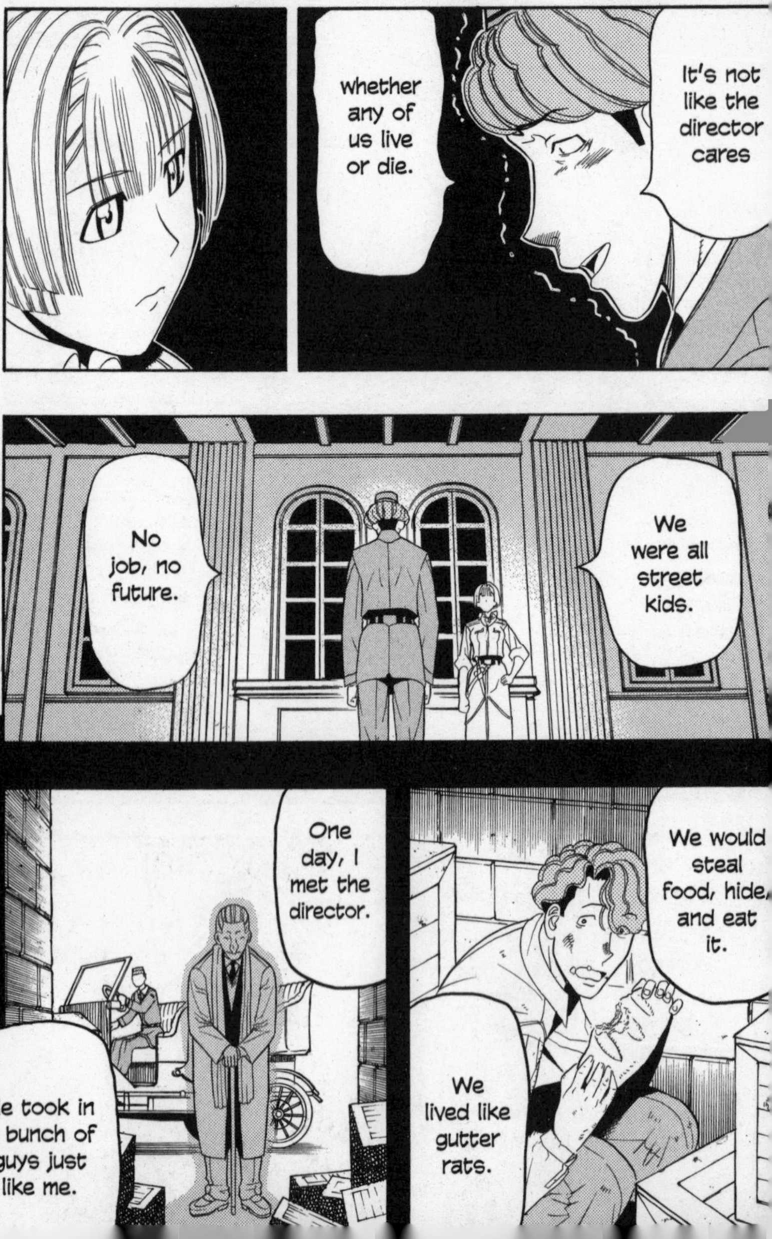
It's not like the director cares
whether any of us live or die.
We were all street kids.
No job, no future.
We would steal food, hide, and eat it.
We lived like gutter rats.
One day, I met the director.
He took in a bunch of guys just like me.

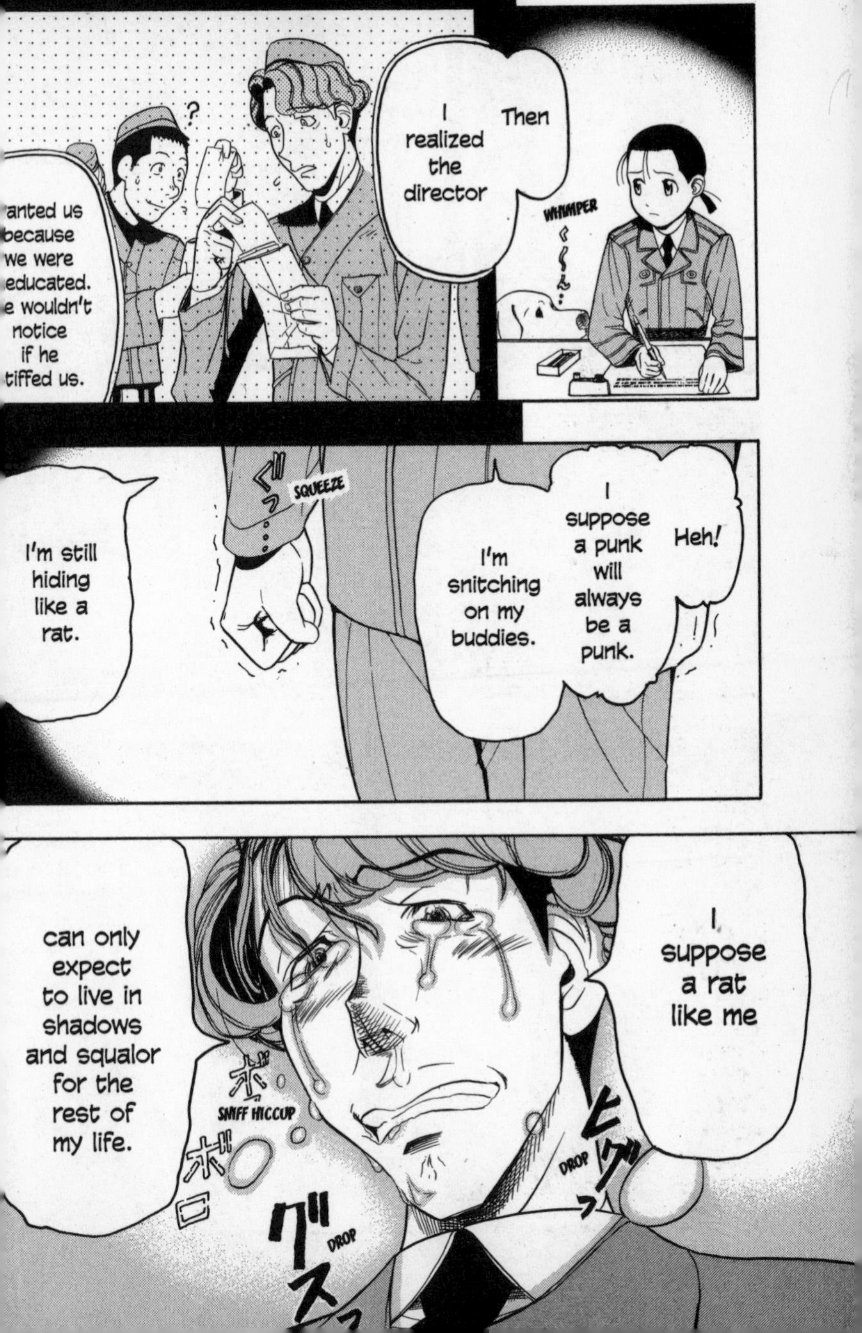
Then I realized the director
WHIMPER
?
anted us because we were educated. e wouldn't notice if he tiffed us.
Heh!
I suppose a punk will always be a punk.
I'm snitching on my buddies.
SQUEEZE
I'm still hiding like a rat.
I suppose a rat like me
DROP
SNIFF HICCUP
can only expect to live in shadows and squalor for the rest of my life.
DROP

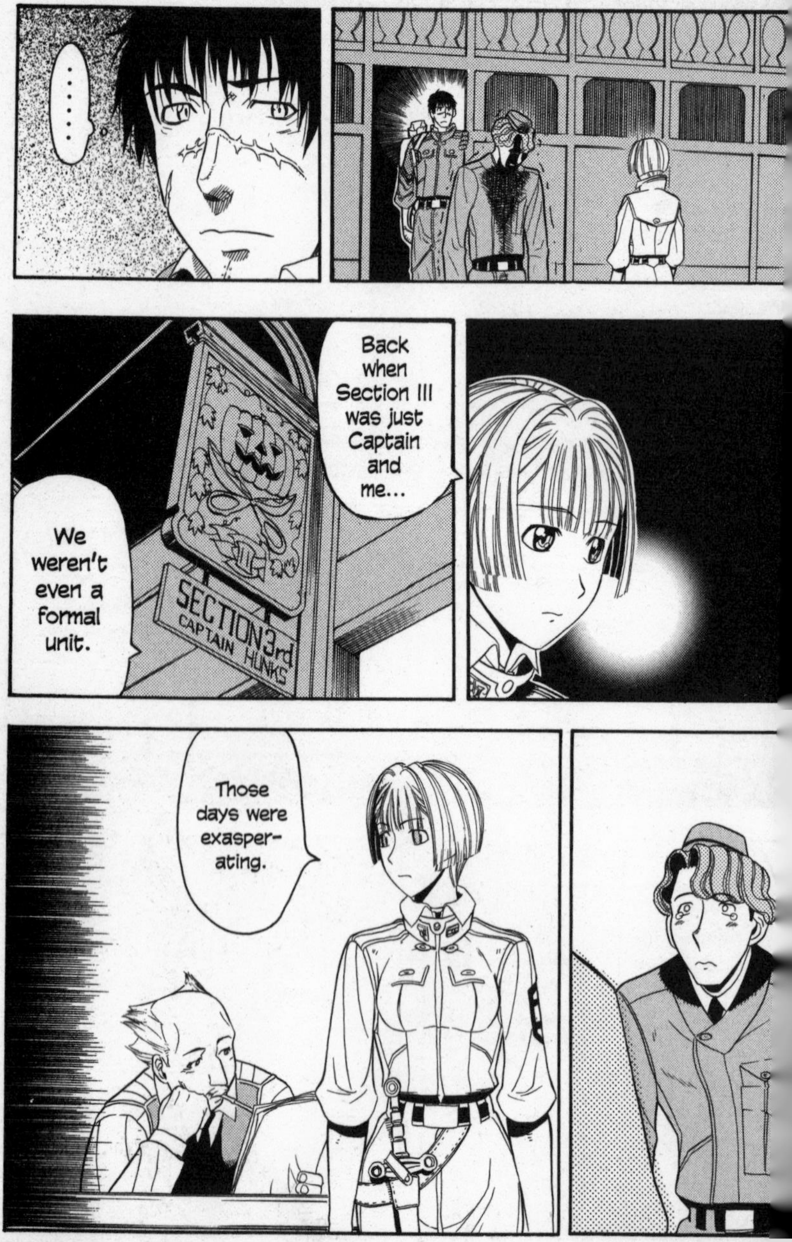
......
Back when Section III was just Captain and me...
SECTION 3rd
CAPTAIN HUNKS
We weren't even a formal unit.
Those days were exasper-ating.

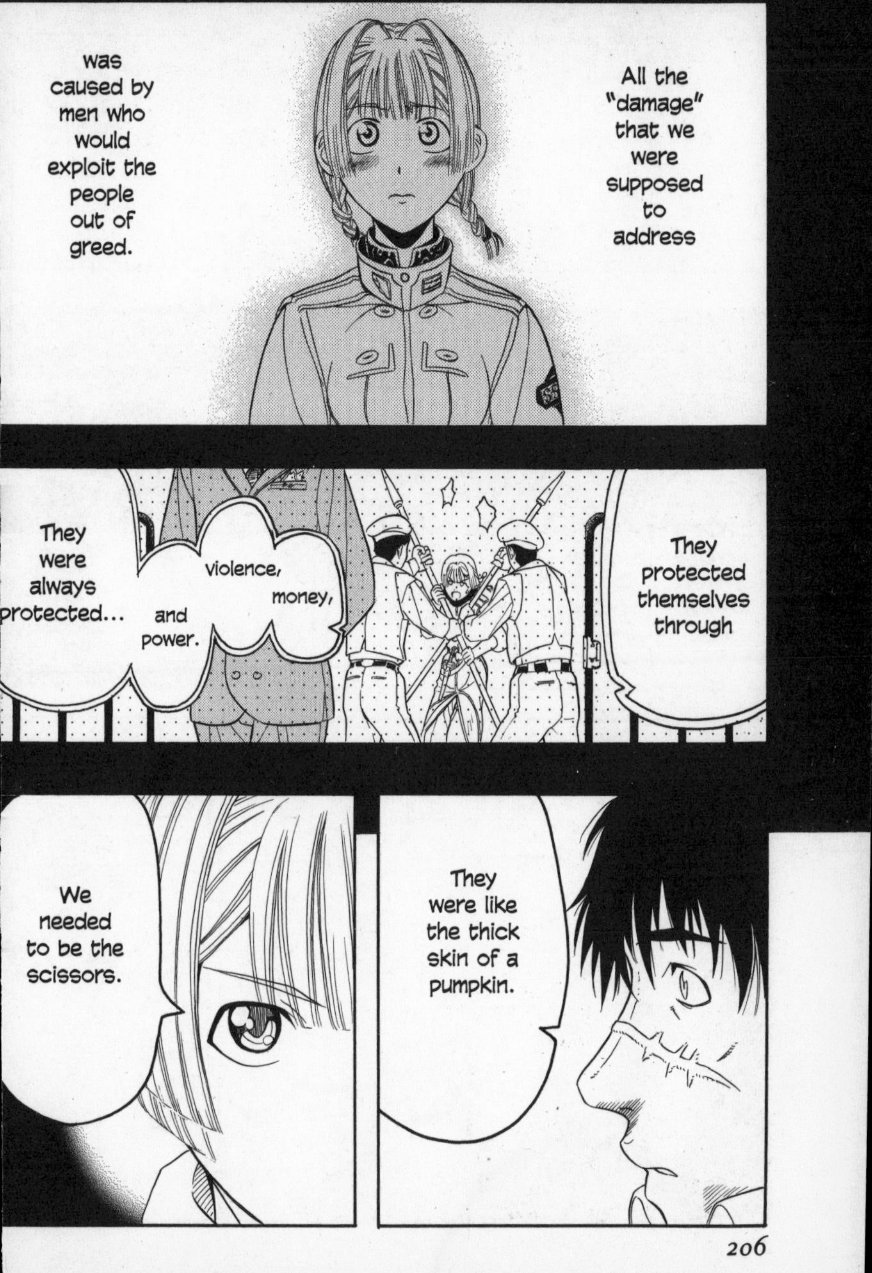
All the "damage" that we were supposed to address
was caused by men who would exploit the people out of greed.
They protected themselves through
violence, money, and power.
They were always protected...
They were like the thick skin of a pumpkin.
We needed to be the scissors.

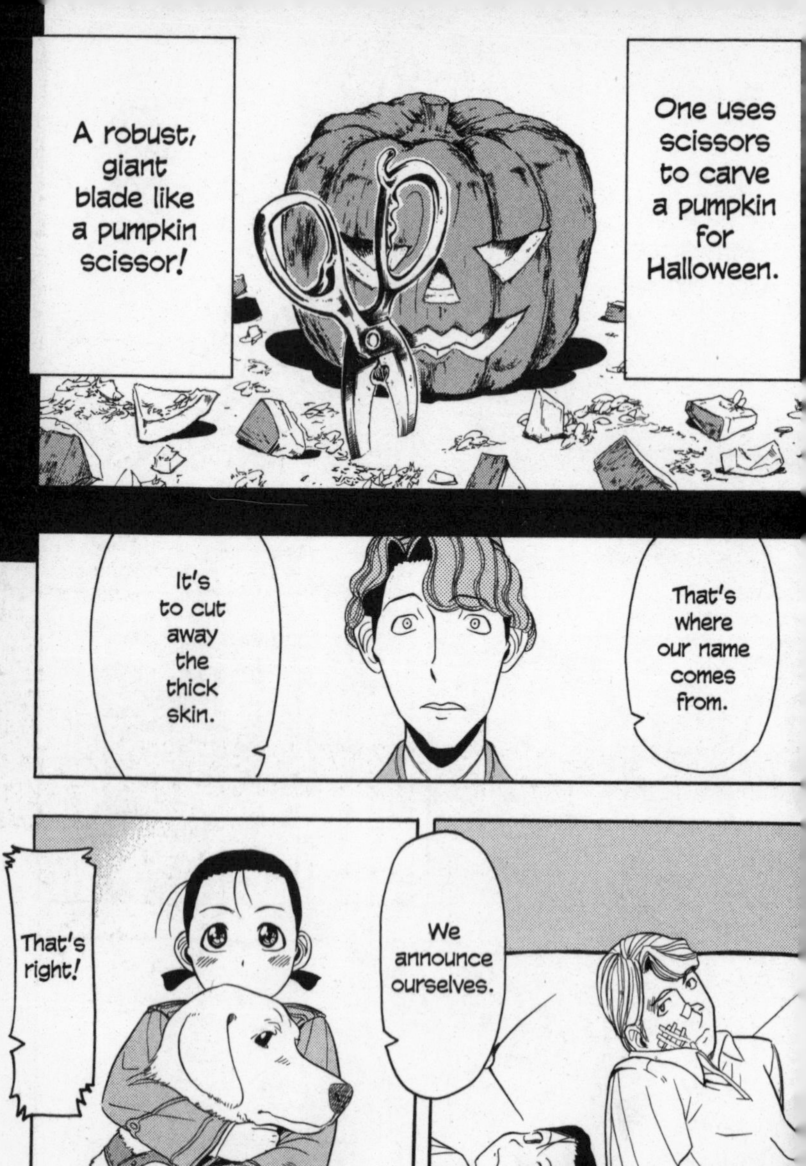
One uses scissors to carve a pumpkin for Halloween.
A robust, giant blade like a pumpkin scissor!
That's where our name comes from.
It's to cut away the thick skin.
We announce ourselves.
That's right!

We shout out the

name Pumpkin Scissors with pride!

SQUEEZE

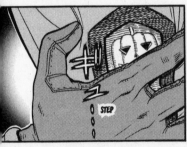

STEP

す

I'm the lieutenant. Let me just say

ポン TAP

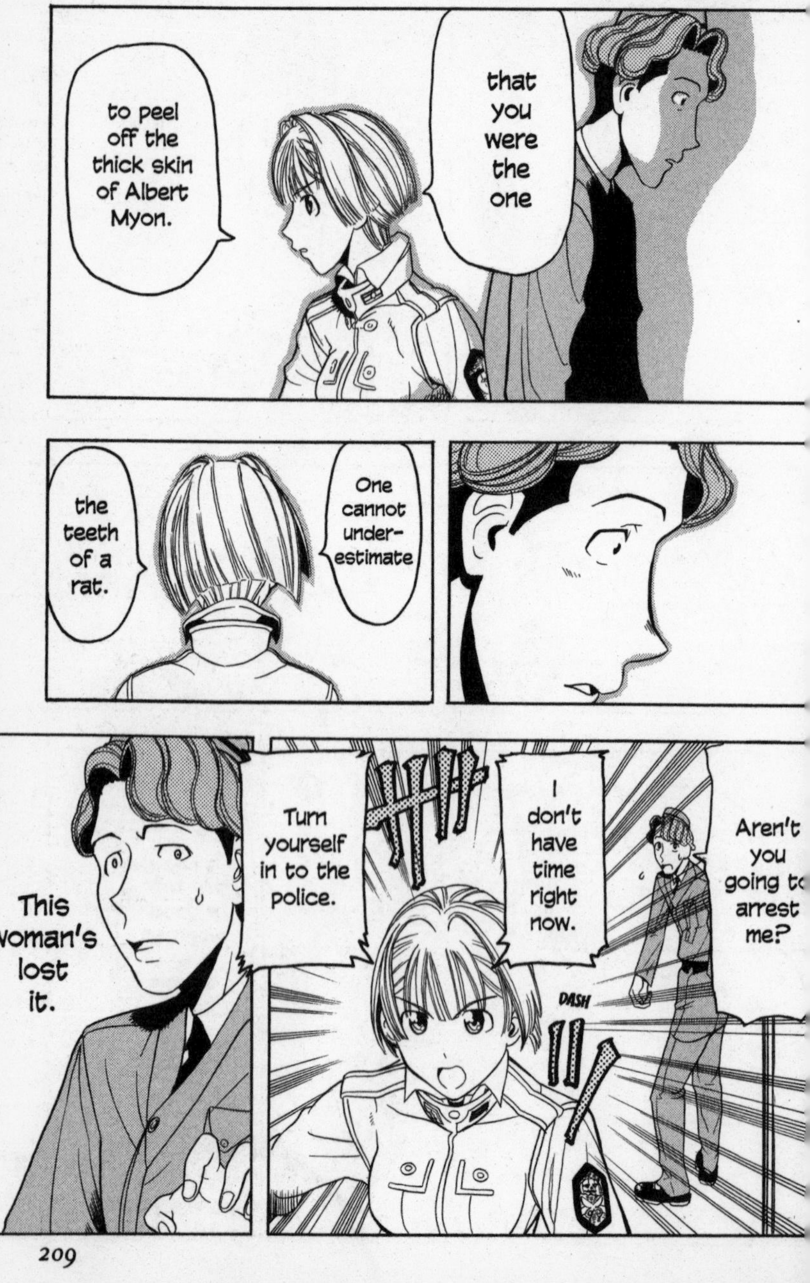
that you were the one
to peel off the thick skin of Albert Myon.
One cannot underestimate
the teeth of a rat.
Aren't you going t arrest me?
I don't have time right now.
DASH
Turn yourself in to the police.
This woman's lost it.

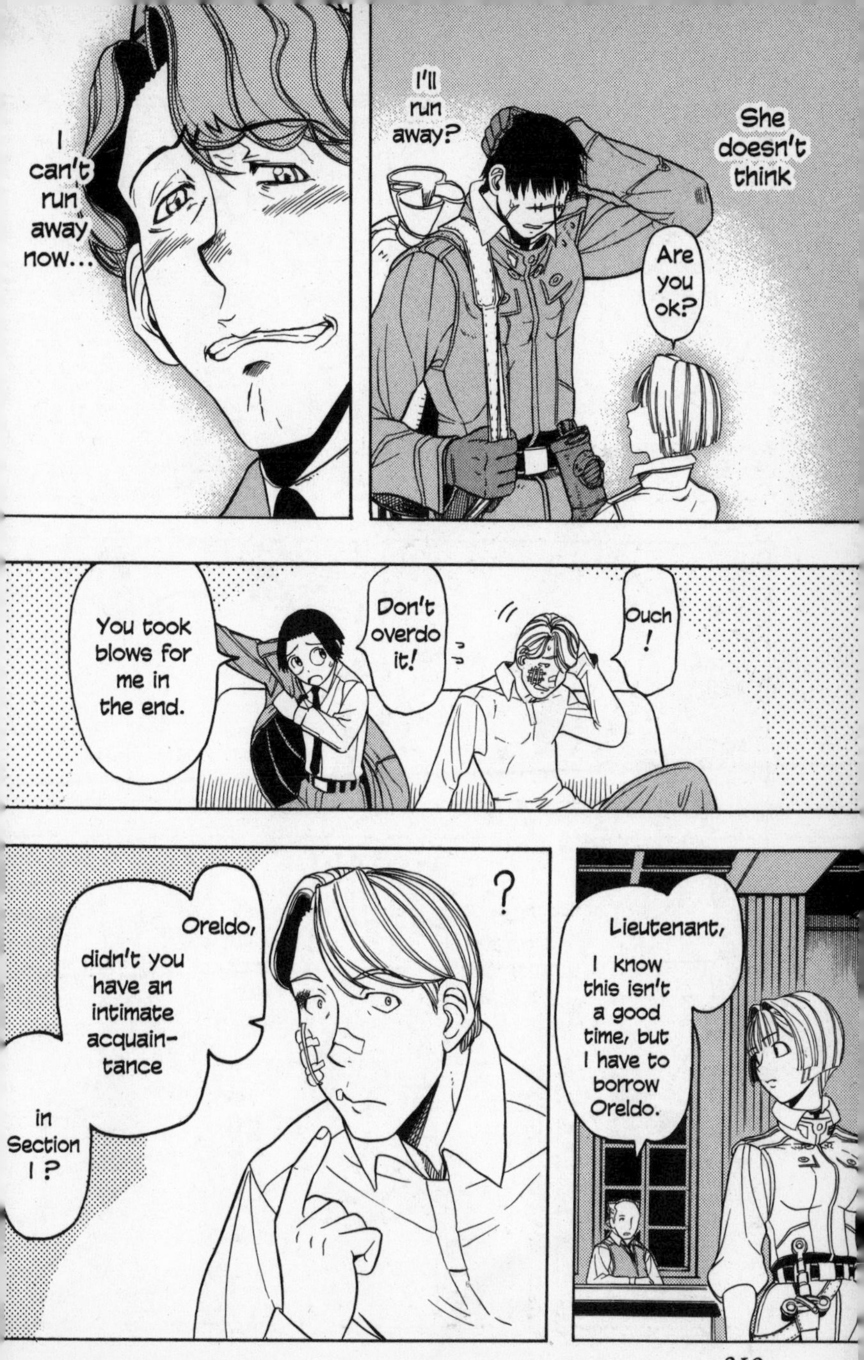
She doesn't think
I'll run away?
Are you ok?
I can't run away now...
Ouch!
Don't overdo it!
You took blows for me in the end.
Lieutenant, I know this isn't a good time, but I have to borrow Oreldo.
?
Oreldo, didn't you have an intimate acquaintance
in Section 1?

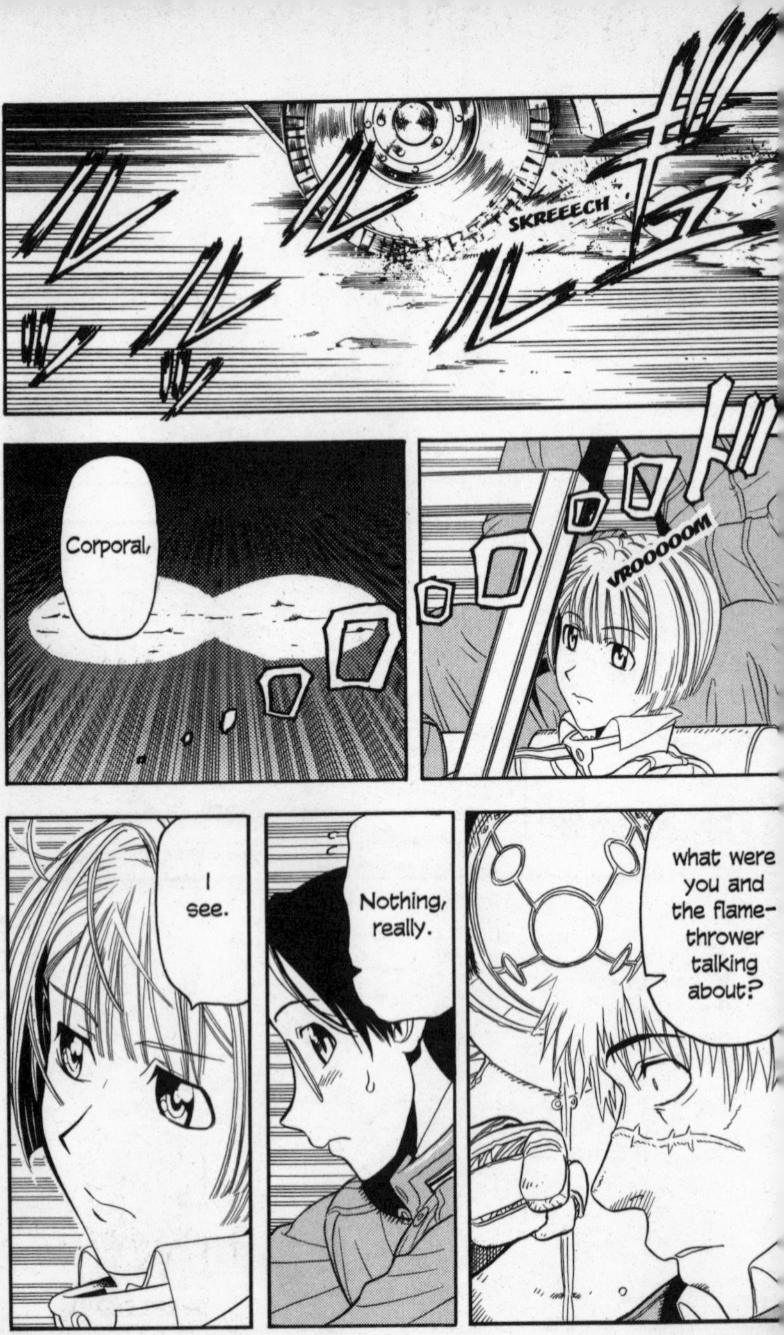
SKREEECH
VROOOOOM
Corporal,
what were you and the flame-thrower talking about?
Nothing, really.
I see.

Documents?

HEAVY

RUSTLE
RUSTLE

Hmmm, documents?

We were all given this book.

Welcome back!

Captain, something's going on!

KTZ
KTZ
KTZ
KTZ

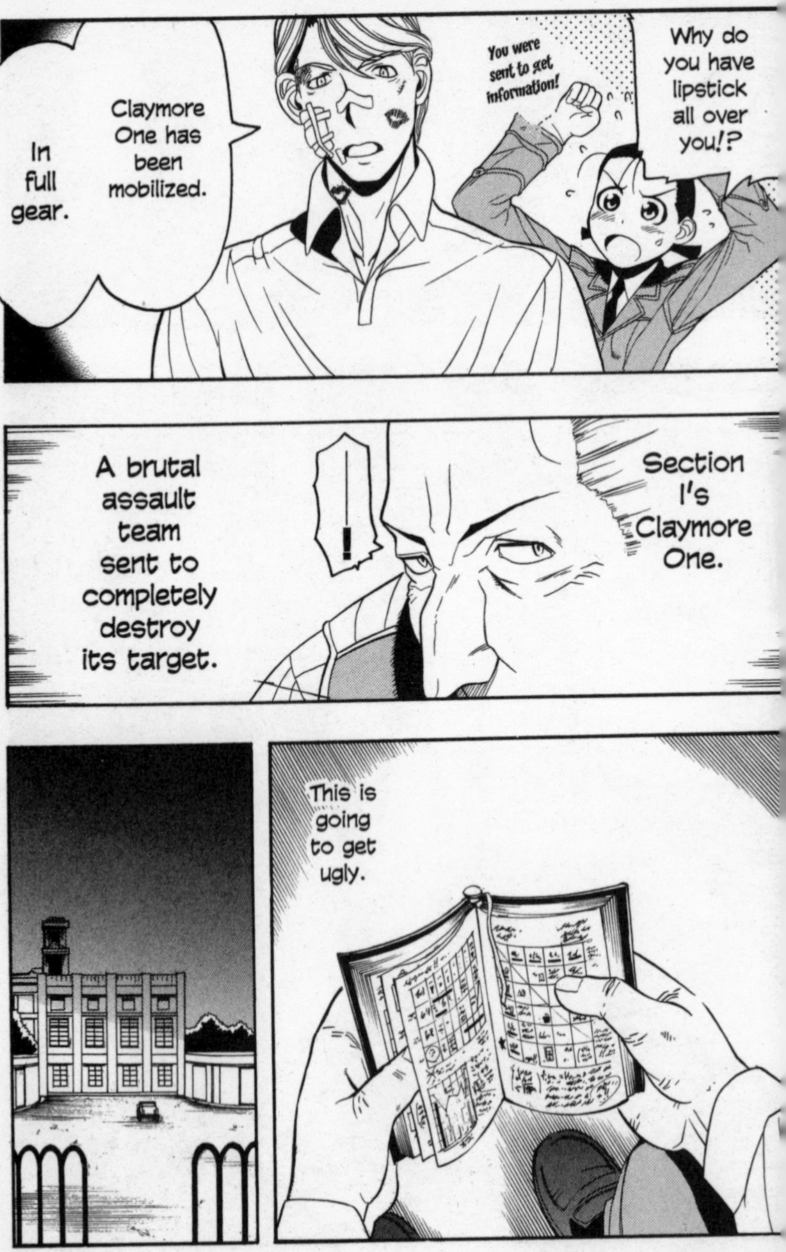
Why do you have lipstick all over you!?
You were sent to get information!
Claymore One has been mobilized.
In full gear.
Section I's Claymore One.
!
A brutal assault team sent to completely destroy its target.
This is going to get ugly.

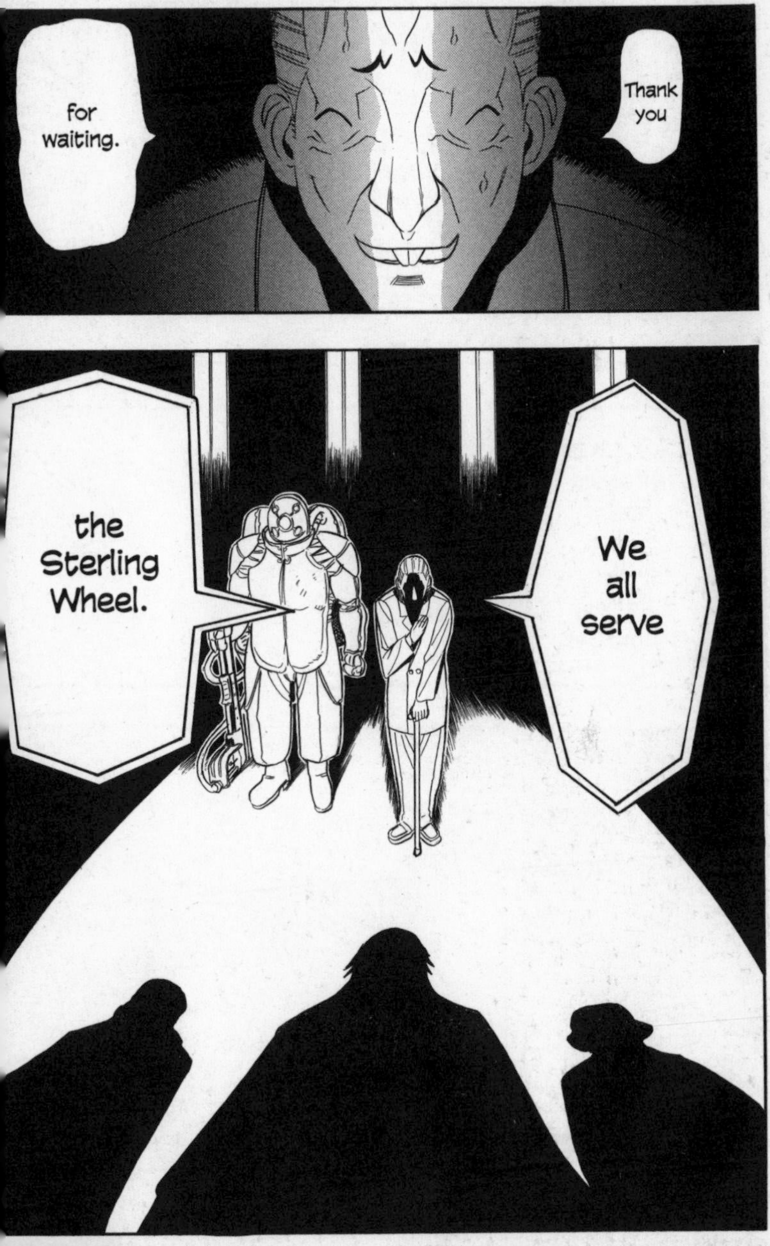
Thank you
for waiting.
We all serve
the Sterling Wheel.

#6/END

PumpkinScissors

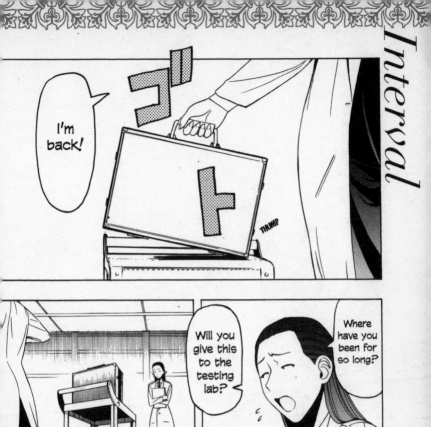

Interval

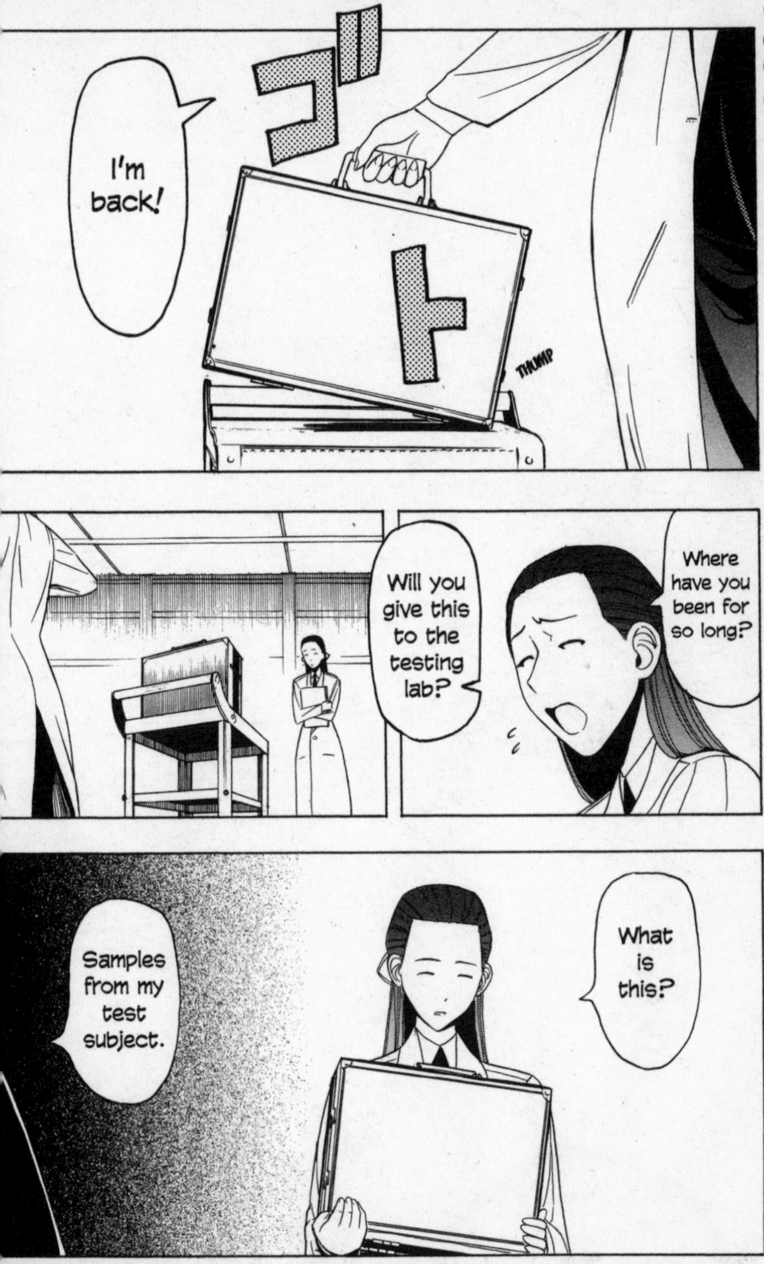
ゴト
I'm back!
THUMP
Where have you been for so long?
Will you give this to the testing lab?
What is this?
Samples from my test subject.

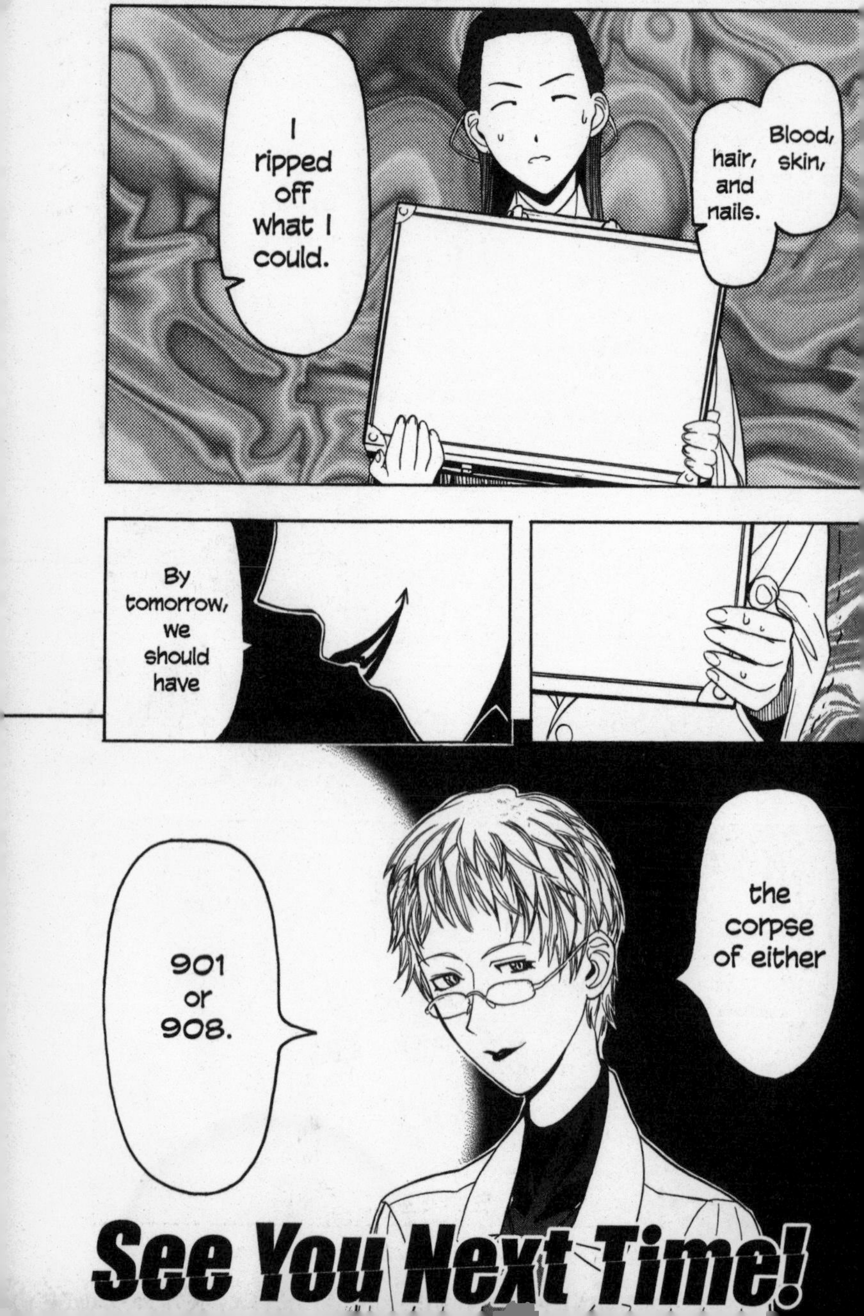
Blood, skin, hair, and nails.
I ripped off what I could.
By tomorrow, we should have
the corpse of either
901 or 908.
See You Next Time!

Translation Notes

Japanese is a tricky language for most Westerners, and translation is often more an art than a science. For your edification and reading pleasure, here are notes on some of the places where we could have gone in a different direction, or where a Japanese cultural reference is used.

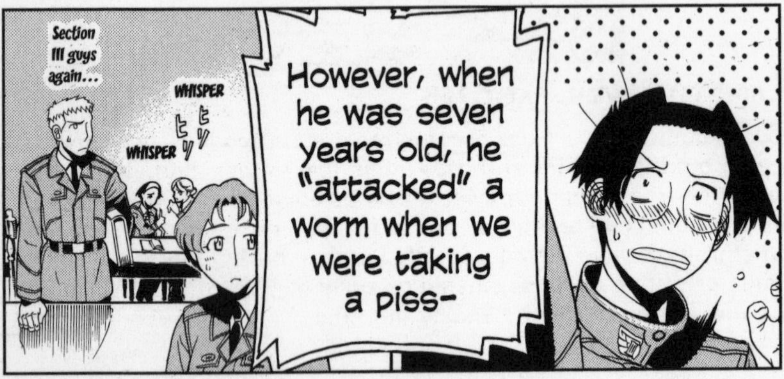
However, when he was seven years old, he "attacked" a worm when we were taking a piss-
Section III guys again...
WHISPER
WHISPER

URINATING ON A WORM, PAGE 69

In Japan, there's an old wives' tale that if you urniate on an earthworm, your penis will become inflamed. Earthworms were revered by farmers for their important role in soil aeration and fertility. The old wives' tale was probably a way for the farmers to prevent kids from disrespecting the earthworm that was so important to their survival.

a flame-thrower!

FLAMETHROWER, PAGE 165

Modern flamethrowers use pressurized gas (propane or natural gas) as fuel, but the military still uses liquid fuel in their flamethrowers. It seems that Hans's flamethrower also uses liquid fuel as Machs says "He was spreading fuel on the surface of the water!" on page 169. Modern flamethrowers were introduced into warfare during World War I, although primitive versions existed as early as Byzantine times in Europe and during the Song dynasty in China.

ORELDO AND MACHS, PAGE 192

I want to clarify that neither Oreldo nor Machs had any intention of raping Mariel. Oreldo was trying to show Mariel's father how he was ruining his daughter's life with his drug habit and incite the father into defending his daughter, so she could see that he still loved her very much.

Claymore, Page 213

Claymore is an English derivative of the Gaelic terms *claidheamh mòr* and *claidheamh da lamh,* both used to describe swords. A claymore is a type of broadsword, with the two-handed Highland claymore being the most famous type. They are very heavy, large swords with blades that can be four feet or longer and weigh about five pounds. Claymores are often associated with the Scottish culture, and as a result, you will see claymores in action in movies with a Scottish theme, such as *Highlander* and *Braveheart.*

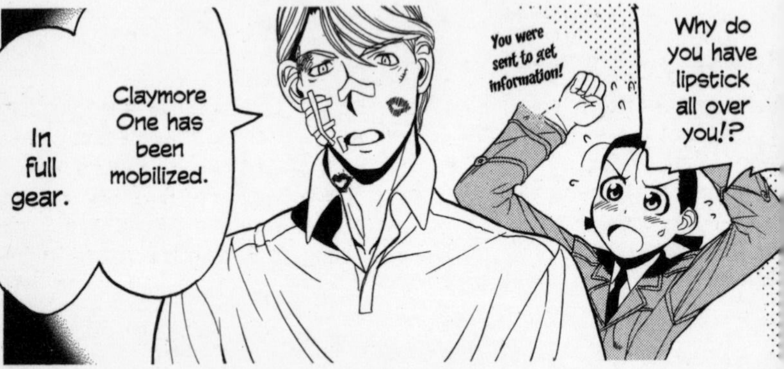
Why do you have lipstick all over you!?
You were sent to get information!
Claymore One has been mobilized.
In full gear.

Preview of Volume 3

We're pleased to present you with a preview of volume 3. Please check our website (www.delreymanga.com) to see when this volume will be available in English. For now you'll have to make do with Japanese!

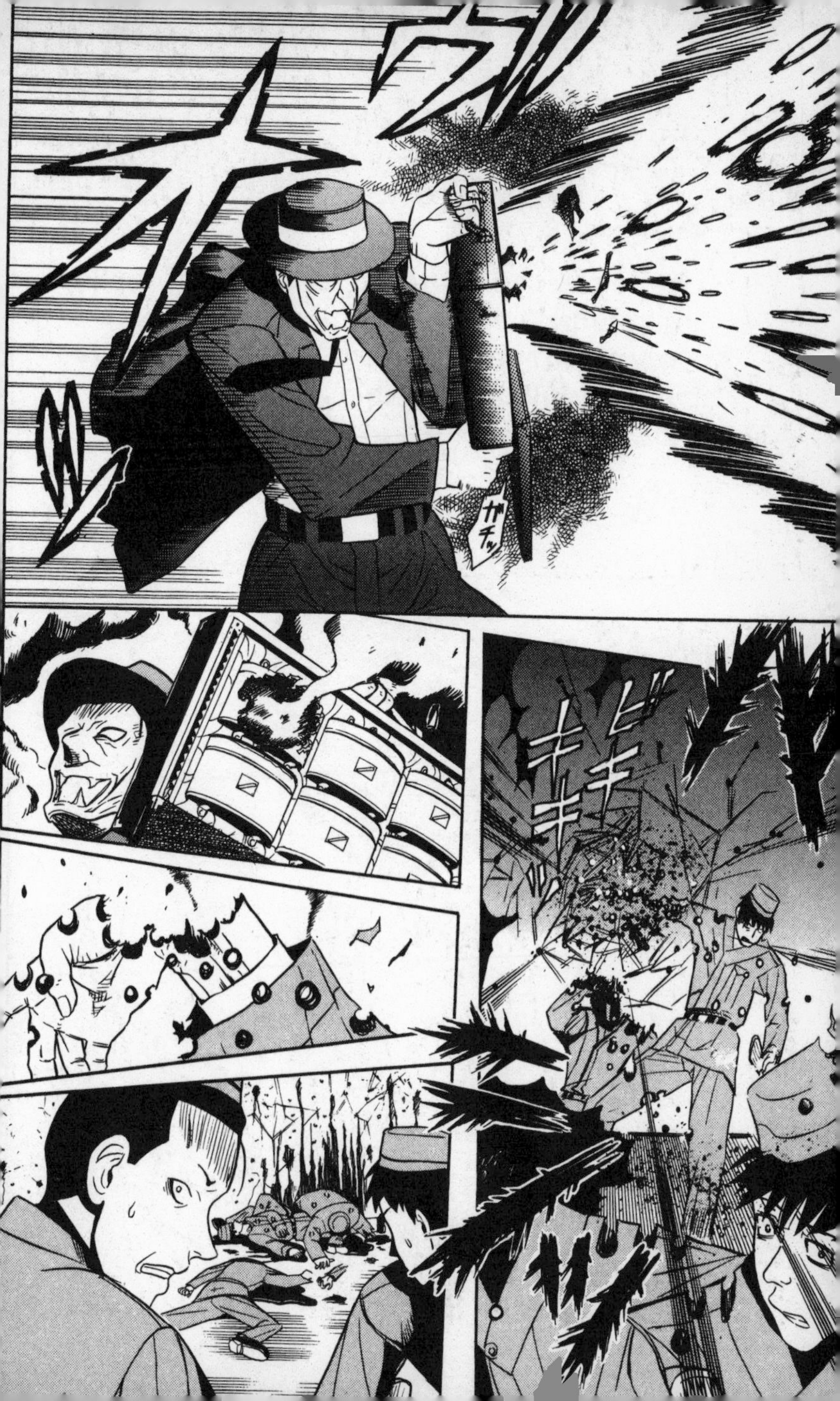
ズヴル
ガチッ
ビキキキ

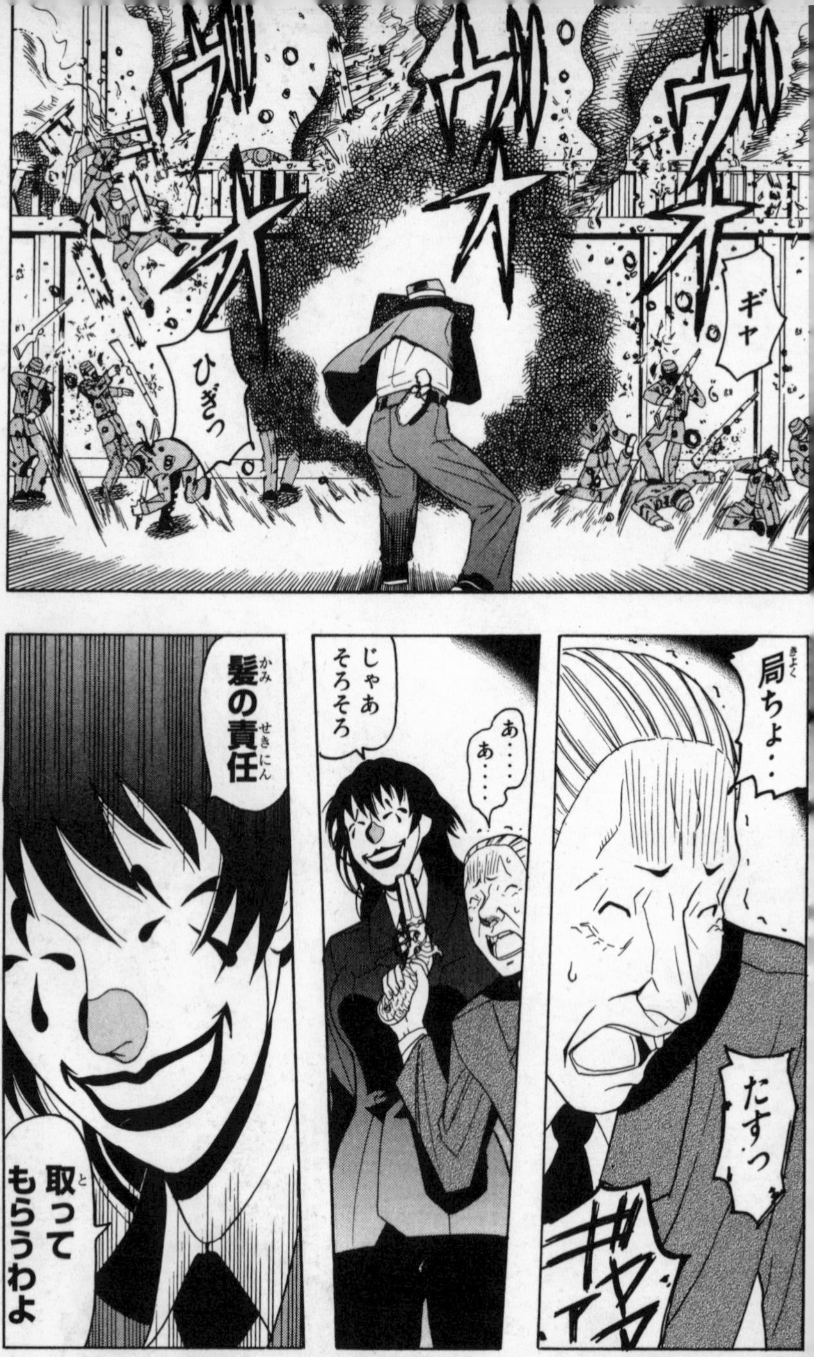
ヴ
ヴ
ヴ
ギャ
ひぎっ
局ちょ‥‥
たすっ
ギャア
あ‥‥
あ‥‥
じゃあ
そろそろ
髪の責任
取って
もらうわよ

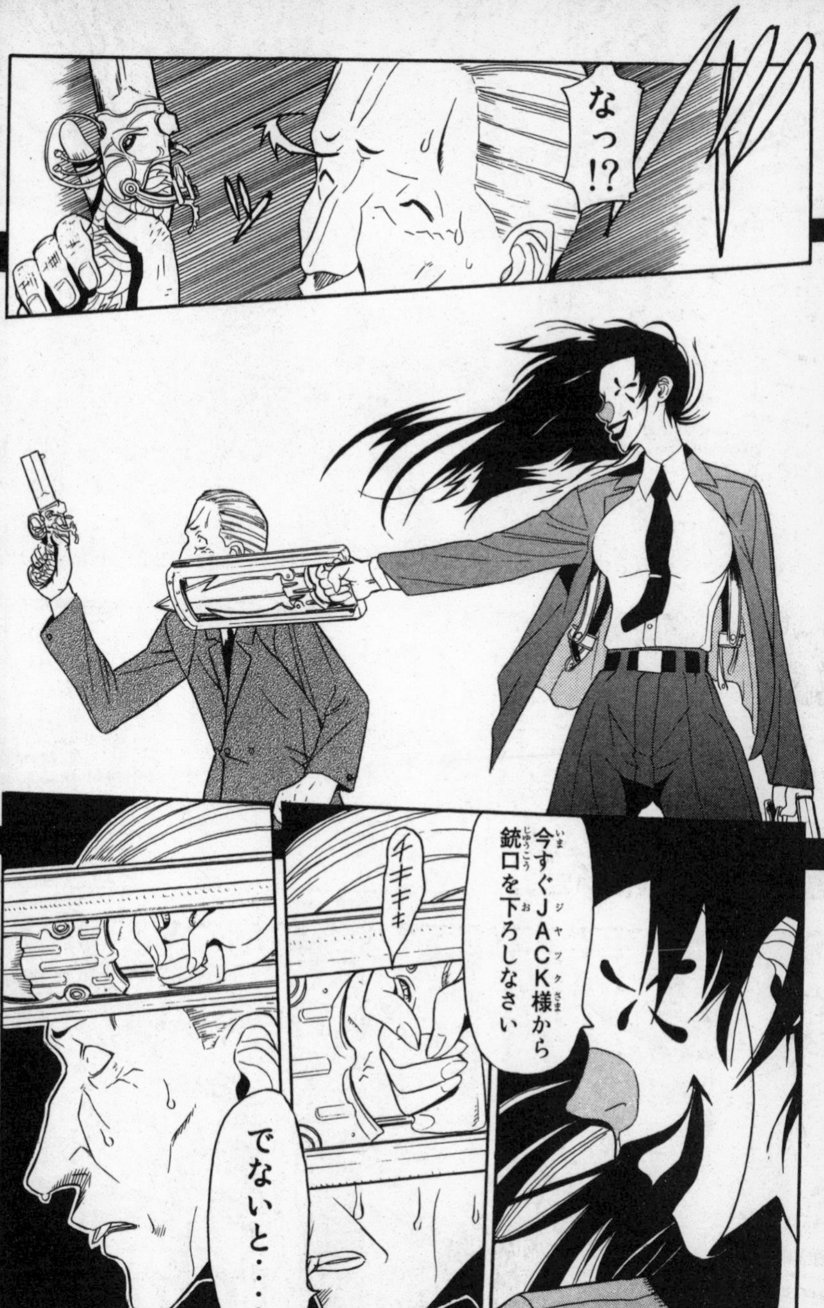
なっ!?
今すぐJACK様から
銃口を下ろしなさい
チキキキ
でないと・・・・

ナマス斬りにするわよ？

いや……その……なんだ……

ヌラ…

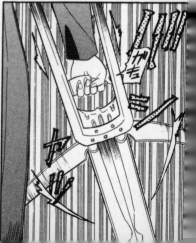

おおまえらッ

早く銃を捨てんかッ

ぴっ

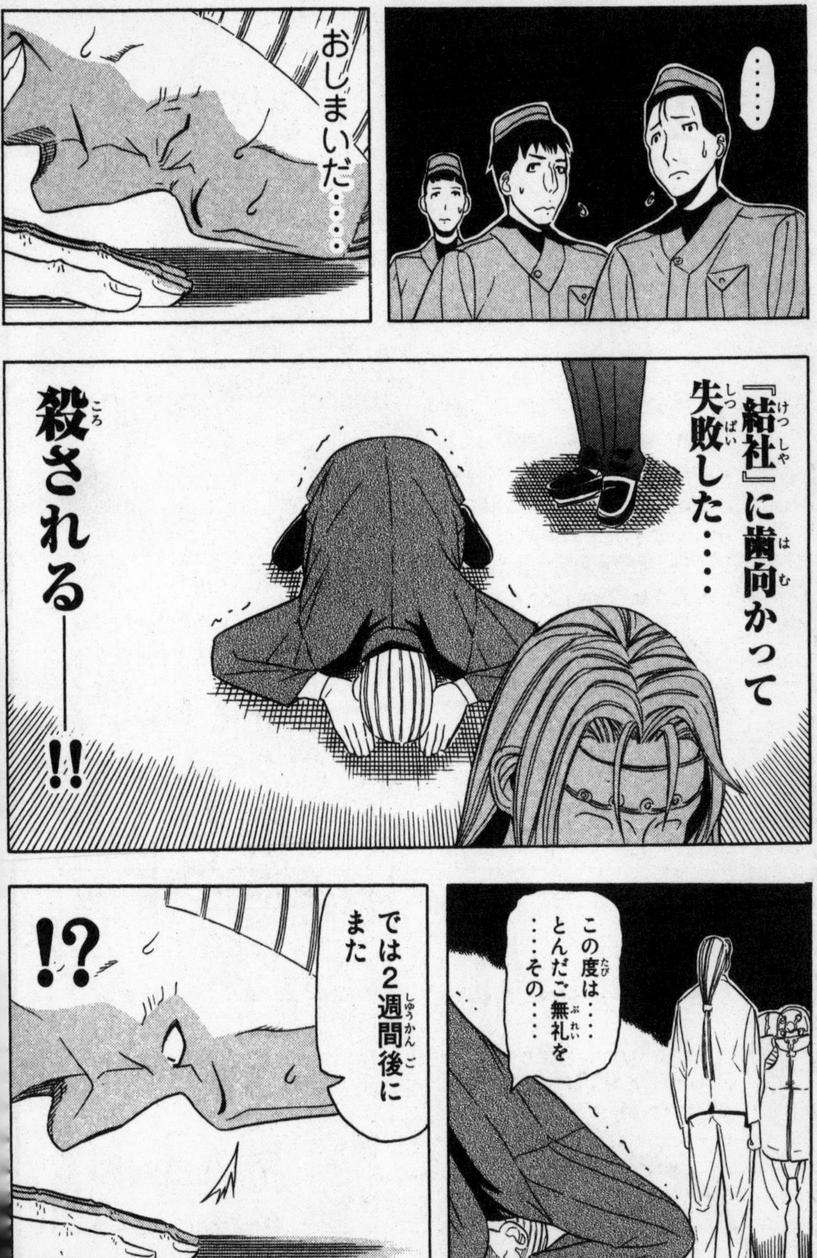
……
おしまいだ……
『結社』に歯向かって失敗した……
殺される――!!
この度は……とんだご無礼を……その……
では2週間後にまた
!?

Le Chevalier d'Eon

STORY BY TOU UBUKATA
MANGA BY KIRIKO YUMEJI

DARKNESS FALLS ON PARIS

A mysterious cult is sacrificing beautiful young women to a demonic force that threatens the entire country. Only one man can save Paris from chaos and terror, the king's top secret agent: The Chevalier d'Eon.

- Available on DVD from ADV Films.

Le Chevalier d'Eon I
Story by TOU UBUKATA
Manga by KIRIKO YUMEJI

Special extras in each volume! Read them all!

VISIT WWW.DELREYMANGA.COM TO:

- Read sample pages
- View release date calendars for upcoming volumes
- Sign up for Del Rey's free manga e-newsletter
- Find out the latest about new Del Rey Manga series

RATING OT AGES 16+

DEL REY MANGA
The Otaku's Choice™

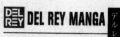

ALIVE

STORY BY TADASHI KAWASHIMA
ART BY TOKA ADACHI

SMART SCIENCE-FICTION SUSPENSE

Millions of people worldwide have taken their own lives, victims of a lethal alien pandemic visited upon the Earth.

But a group of Tokyo teens has somehow survived and now, facing a devastated world, must ask questions they never thought they'd have to ask:

Why did they abandon us?
Will we be next?
Why are we alive?

Special extras in each volume! Read them all!

Psycho Busters

MANGA BY AKINARI NAO
STORY BY YUYA AOKI

PSYCHIC TEENS ON THE RUN!

Out of the blue, a beautiful girl asks Kakeru to run away with her. This could be any boy's dream come true, but there's something strange afoot.

It turns out that this girl is on the run from a shadowy government organization intent on using her psychic abilities for its own nefarious ends. But why does she need Kakeru's help? Could it be that he has secret powers, too?

Psycho Busters
I
Manga by
Akinari Nao
Story by
Yuya Aoki,
the creator of
Get Backers

- Story by Yuya Aoki, creator of *Get Backers*

Special extras in each volume! Read them all!

VISIT WWW.DELREYMANGA.COM TO:
- Read sample pages
- View release date calendars for upcoming volumes
- Sign up for Del Rey's free manga e-newsletter
- Find out the latest about new Del Rey Manga series

RATING T AGES 13+

DEL REY MANGA デルレイ
The Otaku's Choice™

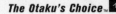

TOMARE!

[STOP!]

You're going the wrong way!

Manga is a completely different type of reading experience.

To start at the *beginning*, go to the *end*!

That's right! Authentic manga is read the traditional Japanese way—from right to left, exactly the *opposite* of how American books are read. It's easy to follow: Just go to the other end of the book, and read each page—and each panel—from right side to left side, starting at the top right. Now you're experiencing manga as it was meant to be!